STEVE JOBS
THE JOURNEY
IS THE REWARD

STEVE JOBS
THE JOURNEY
IS THE REWARD

JEFFREY S. YOUNG

Scott, Foresman and Company
Glenview, Illinois   London

IBSN 0-673-18864-7

Library of Congress Cataloging-in-Publication Data

Young, Jeffrey S., 1952–
  Steve Jobs.

  Bibliography: p.
  1. Jobs, Steven, 1955–   .   2. Microcomputers—
Biography.   3. Apple computer—History.   I. Title.
QA76.2J63Y68   1988   338.7′621391′6   [B]   87-28359

1 2 3 4 5 6 RRC 92 91 90 89 88 87

Excerpts from *The Little Kingdom* by Michael Moritz. Copyright © 1984 by
Michael Moritz. By permission of William Morrow & Company.

G. C. Lubenow and M. Rogers, "Jobs Talks About His Rise and Fall." From
Newsweek, September 30, 1985.

"Playboy Interview: Steven Jobs." Reproduced by Special Permission of PLAY-
BOY Magazine: From the PLAYBOY Interview: Steven Jobs, February 1985.
Copyright © 1984 by PLAYBOY.

Bob Dylan, "The Times They Are A-Changin'." © 1963 Warner Bros. Inc. All
Rights Reserved. Used by Permission.

Scott, Foresman Professional Publishing Group books are available for bulk
sales at quantity discounts. For information, please contact Marketing Manager,
Professional Publishing Group, Scott, Foresman and Company, 1900 East Lake
Avenue, Glenview, IL 60025.

TO JANEY,
FOR EVERYTHING.

Acknowledgments

Creating a book requires the help of dozens of people along the path. The beginnings of my involvement with Steve Jobs and the Macintosh computer, as well as the magazine *Macworld*, were rooted in the unshakeable belief of the late Andrew Fluegelman that there was a place for a nontechnical journalist in the world of personal computing. David Bunnell and Jackie Poitier created the business environment that allowed the magazine to flourish and created a home for me in the world of computer publishing. Daniel Farber provided irreplaceable counsel over the years as an editor of *Macworld* and a keen observer of the Macintosh community. Bill Gladstone put me, the idea, and the publisher together . . . and then ran interference on dozens of fronts. Phil Williams provided legal opinions. Jim Forbes opened his extensive Rolodex, Charlie Rubin offered professional advice and lent a sympathetic ear, and Denise Caruso shared a few secrets. Apple Computer's editorial product-loan group provided the computers on which the book was written, and the company's corporate librarians went out of their way to help ensure accuracy. The primary copy-editing was done by Evelyn Spire. The final manuscript was conformed, proofed, and line-edited by my wife Janey. Richard Swadley was my original editor, and the finished book was shepherded to completion by Amy Davis, his successor. Behind them both stood the head of the Professional Publishing Group at Scott, Foresman and Company, Roger Holloway, who always believed in me and the ultimate value of the project. And of course, there are the dozens of Apple employees and observers who've provided me with their time and memories. Without all of them I would have been lost.

Contents

Contents

"... I THOUGHT OF GATSBY'S WONDER WHEN HE FIRST PICKED OUT THE GREEN LIGHT AT THE END OF DAISY'S DOCK. HE HAD COME A LONG WAY TO THIS BLUE LAWN, AND HIS DREAM MUST HAVE SEEMED SO CLOSE THAT HE COULD HARDLY FAIL TO GRASP IT. HE DID NOT KNOW THAT IT WAS ALREADY BEHIND HIM, SOMEWHERE BACK IN THAT VAST OBSCURITY BEYOND THE CITY, WHERE THE DARK FIELDS OF THE REPUBLIC ROLLED ON UNDER THE NIGHT."

THE GREAT GATSBY
F. SCOTT FITZGERALD

Prologue

1
Landscapes

There's a magic in the canyons and arroyos of California's Santa Cruz Mountains. During late summer and fall, warm air from inland collides with cool, moist winds rising out of the ocean to create an infinite variety of sunlight and mist paintings above the mountains. Fingers of white fog creep over the ridge like tentacles, spilling down into the miles of protected forests, high reservoirs, and wilderness parklands that make up the spine dividing Silicon Valley from the ocean. As the sun sinks behind the hills, canyon after canyon up the eastern slope is picked out in a sequence of cascading relief, like a landscape of falling dominoes lit from behind. Dramatic, continuously changing, and breathtakingly beautiful is the view from the rolling lawns that stretch out for acres behind Steven Paul Jobs' Woodside home.

The two-story Spanish-style mansion of white stucco and red adobe roof tiles is set on a slight rise, with a sparse population of California oaks framing the rolling lawns. Cool and dark, it is decorated with an ascetic's restraint, or a Zen monk's minimalist style. The living rooms contain very little furniture. Very little of anything. A couple of chairs, enormous six-foot-high stereo speakers, a state-of-the-art stereo, and a laserdisc system. Rows of French doors and windows look out over the rolling lawns, trees, and canyons toward the west and the setting sun, toward one red navigational light set high on the ridge of mountains that burns constantly in the nighttime darkness.

On Tuesday evening, September 17, 1985, as the sun set with a particularly dramatic flourish, Steve Jobs, 30 years old, cofounder and resident visionary of Apple Computer, for almost a decade the primary worldwide evangelist for the coming of the personal computer age, and an all-around mythic American figure, turned in his letter of resignation to the company he had brought to life. The letter was composed on the Macintosh computer that he had muscled and cajoled into existence and was printed on the laser printer that he had at first opposed and then aggressively championed. He drove the three miles to fellow founder Armas Clifford (Mike) Markkula's nearby Woodside house to deliver the letter. It closed a remarkable chapter in American popular history.

Dear Mike,

This morning's papers carried suggestions that Apple is considering removing me as Chairman. I don't know the source of these reports, but they are both misleading to the public and unfair to me.

You will recall that at last Thursday's Board meeting I stated I had decided to start a new venture, and I tendered my resignation as Chairman.

The Board declined to accept my resignation and asked me to defer it for a week. I agreed to do so in light of the encouragement the Board offered with regard to the proposed new venture and the indications that Apple would invest in it. On Friday, after I told John Sculley who would be joining me, he confirmed Apple's willingness to discuss areas of possible collaboration between Apple and my new venture.

Subsequently, the Company appears to be adopting a hostile posture toward me and the new venture. Accordingly, I must insist upon the immediate acceptance of my resignation. I would hope that in any statement it feels it must issue, the Company will make it clear that the decision to resign as Chairman was mine.

I find myself both saddened and perplexed by the management's conduct in this matter, which seems to me contrary to Apple's best interests. Those interests remain a matter of deep concern to me, both because of my past association with Apple and the substantial investment I retain in it.

I continue to hope that calmer voices within the Company may yet be heard. Some Company representatives have said they fear I will use proprietary Apple technology in my new venture. There is no basis for any such concern. If that concern is the real source of Apple's hostility to the venture, I can allay it.

As you know, the company's recent reorganization left me with no work to do and no access even to regular management reports. I am but 30 and want still to contribute and achieve.

After what we have accomplished together, I would wish our parting to be both amicable and dignified.

Yours sincerely,

Steven P. Jobs[1]

Returning in his silver-blue Mercedes 500 coupe down the winding, overgrown lanes of the wealthy suburban cowboy's paradise that is Woodside, he hauled down the Apple flag that had been flying from his flagpole since he bought the house a year earlier. In its place he ran up a new red and black design to signify his next venture. It wasn't the tattered skull-and-crossbones that had flown over the Macintosh buildings a few years earlier, but the buccaneering spirit was definitely the same. Surrounded by five loyal former senior Apple employees who had resigned en masse the previous Friday, the young pirate king of American computing was setting sail. He was starting on the next leg in his journey.

This time his adventure was being played out in bold headlines and on the nightly news, and it was the power of free publicity that would catapult him to an even greater level of public notoriety. Over the years, he had learned how to work the press to maximum advantage. When he returned to his mansion that afternoon, a phalanx of reporters was waiting for him. He carefully read the letter of resignation into a forest of microphones and then started fielding questions. He looked weary. There were circles under his eyes, yet he was exceedingly gracious. It was difficult not to see him as the aggrieved party, the wronged founder cut adrift by an ungrateful corporation. His timing was impeccable. This press conference was staged to coordinate with the overnight deadlines of the big Eastern papers, and it superseded coverage of an enhanced Apple II product announcement scheduled for the same day. It was vintage Steve Jobs. He had hit the road running, and the world's media carried the story his way.

Could he do it again? And so soon? The stakes had changed drastically in the intervening ten years. The seas of personal computing were no longer uncharted, as they had been when Steve and his friend Stephen Wozniak first decided to sell a homemade circuit board called the Apple in 1976.

"Basically, Steve Wozniak and I invented the Apple because we wanted a personal computer. Not only couldn't we afford the computers that were on the market, those computers were impractical for us to use. We needed a Volkswagen.

"The Volkswagen isn't as fast or comfortable as other ways of traveling, but the VW owners can go where they want, when they want, and with whom they want. The VW owners have personal control of their car."[2]

Just as the original designers of the Volkswagen had envisioned an affordable car for the masses, Steve wanted to change the fabric of American life with his consumer-oriented computing machines. One person, one computer. It was Steve Jobs' religion.

An enormous industry had grown up around Steve, and while some aspects of it were definitely due to him, other developments had occurred in spite of him. The industry's meteoric growth was fueled partly by his personal charisma, partly by the neat meshing of a rapidly expanding technological capability with deep currents of America's psychic needs, and partly by a stroke of fortuitous timing and savvy packaging that catapulted the Apple II into the forefront of the personal computer age. His youth and good looks, his ability to say the quotable thing, his immense personal wealth after Apple's stock offering, and an American public looking for a hero to help it forget the disastrous seventies combined to make this one slender, intense young man a mythic figure amid the revitalized economy of post-Vietnam America. And like all myths, this one says more about our need for a person *like* the figure Steve Jobs has become than it does about the *reality* of who Steve Jobs is or ever could be.

Given his innate self-confidence, the explosion of the computer field, the public fascination with him that the press spawned and supported, and the power that he came to possess, it is not surprising that he began to believe in the idolatry directed at him. At 23 he was a millionaire. At 24 he was worth $10 million. By the age of 25 his net worth was over $100 million. He was the youngest person ever to make the *Forbes* list of the nation's richest people and one of only a handful to have done it without inherited wealth. Here was a young man who had provided more than 4,000 people with jobs and who wielded the power to fire people from those jobs at will. A man who could breezily name a major computer after his daughter, with millions of dollars in development and marketing behind it, and just as arbitrarily cancel the entire line when it took longer than projected to succeed and threatened to reflect poorly on his own pet project, the Macintosh. A man who could unilaterally decree that there would be no letter quality printer support for that Macintosh, even though the computer was ostensibly targeted at the business marketplace where those printers are standard, and even though excellent letter quality printers had been developed in his own labs and were ready to be shipped. How could he not believe that it was he, his unique set of skills and insights, that had almost singlehandedly made the personal computer industry what it was on September 17, 1985?

Steve Jobs was the charismatic leader who could galvanize the troops within Apple and charm the public. He was never the architect of Apple's success. Steve was neither the careful business and marketing planner, which was Mike Markkula's role, nor the brilliant creator of the company's machines. This latter role belonged first to Stephen Wozniak and then to a cadre of others of similar caliber whom the company could attract with its unique blend of business and high-tech utopia. Steve was the person who had the imagination and drive to translate dreams into profit, marshaling the company on to success while constantly reiterating and reformulating the dream. He was the bridge between bottom line profit and the top-of-the-mountain ideas of the computer visionaries that Apple always wanted to incorporate into their product line. And not least, he could always put into words—poetic, quotable, inspiring words—what engineers and programmers could only dream.

Was it blind luck that offered the opportunities he seized? Was his marketing of technology, the development of Apple's remarkably successful products, and the packaging of computing to the public a product of his particular personality? Was it merely serendipity that threw him into the headlines? Could anyone have sold computers as well, given the go-go years the industry went through from 1978 to 1985?

Although Steve was technically competent enough to direct an engineering design project, he was no Thomas Edison. He once called himself the Henry Ford of the computer industry, and perhaps there is some credence to that association. His gift was the ability to inspire engineers to superhuman feats. For what characterized Apple in the Jobs years was that its scientific staff always acted and performed like artists. In a field filled with dry personalities limited by the rational and binary worlds they inhabit, Apple's engineering teams had passion. In the beginning, working at Apple was never just a job; it was a crusade, a mission to bring better computer power to people. At its roots that attitude came from Steve. It was "Power to the People," the slogan of the sixties, remastered first for the seventies with the hobbyist's Apple II, then rewritten in an easy-to-use technology for the eighties and called the Macintosh.

From the start, Steve was the rejector, the critic, the person willing to demand that something be done over and over until it was perfect. Over the years, a phrase entered the Macintosh vernacular. It had to do with "having the chance to do something right"; if you didn't catch that spirit, you didn't last. Of course, as time went on and his power gelled, Steve had less doubt in his mind, and there was even less in the minds of those he surrounded himself with, that his point of view was the right one, the only way. Eventually, fewer people around him were willing to tell the emperor he had no clothes on. But when that did become apparent, it didn't take long to fell him, power and prestige notwithstanding. In the few months between April and September of 1985, Steve was first removed, by his board of directors, from a day-to-day role managing the fortunes of the empire he had created and then removed, by his own action, from its future.

On Monday of the Memorial Day weekend of 1985, four months before he would eventually resign, Steve hosted a small dinner at his hilltop mansion. The dinner consisted of whole-wheat pizzas, wine, and sparkling water. Present were a handful of his most trusted Macintosh lieutenants: marketing manager Mike Murray; manufacturing manager Debi Coleman; financial controller Susan Barnes; engineering head Bob Belleville; and Mike Markkula, cofounder of the company. The evening was a carefully orchestrated effort to sway Markkula—the only other board member present—to Steve's side in a battle of wills that was taking place in the executive board room of Apple.

Markkula wasn't comfortable. He knew hardly any of the young turks who worked for Steve. They were a generation apart from him.

By that Memorial Day weekend, Apple was indisputably an empire. In the early 1980s it had been the fastest growing company in the history of Wall Street. Its initial stock offering on December 12, 1980, was among the most eagerly anticipated events in the securities business. By 1985 the company had 5,000 employees and plants in California, Texas, Ireland, and Singapore. The company's success was largely founded on the Apple II, the best selling personal computer ever manufactured. More than 2 million had been sold by mid-1985, and even then, eight years after its introduction, the machine was still a hot item in the marketplace in its latest enhanced versions, the IIc and IIe. A couple of major failures had occurred along the way—the Apple III and the Lisa—but neither had permanently damaged the company.

In January of 1984, the Macintosh was announced with an enormous amount of fanfare and extraordinarily high hopes within the insulated enclave at Apple. It was Steve's baby, a new kind of machine that he hoped would become as common as the telephone. Because its champion was chairman of the board, the Macintosh seemed to receive all the attention and resources of the company while the bread-and-butter Apple II was conveniently forgotten.

But the Mac fizzled in the marketplace as the juggernaut that was IBM continued to capture business market share with its no-nonsense PC introduced in 1981. By early 1985, the promise of the Macintosh was unfulfilled, and some of the key players at the company were growing concerned. New products to enhance it were slow in reaching the market, and the Macintosh division, headed by Steve, was floundering. Engineering projects were months behind schedule; products were abruptly canceled, then reinstated; marketing strategies were being reformulated constantly in a frantic effort to find the formula that could savage IBM, a quest that had become Steve's holy grail. It wasn't enough to own a segment of the market. He believed his destiny was to win the battle of the personal computer in America's offices. By then, nothing less would do. Yet nothing was working.

John Sculley finally had to do something to salvage the company and solidify his position. The question was how to do it. Sculley had been hired by Apple in May of 1983 from PepsiCo, where he had shown his marketing skills by guiding number two Pepsi to challenge Coca-Cola in the ruthless cola wars. He was brought in to run Apple as a professional manager, the president to Steve's chairman of the board, when it became clear that Mike Markkula wanted to back out of day-to-day operations and that Steve Jobs was not ready to take the helm of the company.

For two years Sculley appeared blinded by the charismatic Jobs. Suddenly immersed in a new field, partnered with a powerful, intense younger man, Sculley did not have the force of personality to check the chairman's unbridled power. Apple teetered and tottered, moving this way and that, buffeted by the mercurial dictates of the brilliant but erratic cofounder. Chaos in the Macintosh division and the prospects of the first losing quarters in the company's history finally forced Sculley's hand in May of 1985. Egged on by powerful board member Arthur Rock, a legendary venture capitalist, along with his senior executives who finally got the message of urgency across, Sculley decided that he had to reorganize the company. His plan was to structure it not by individual products, which was how Apple's adversary internal product group relations had developed in the first place, but by overall business divisions: marketing, sales, manufacturing, product development, support. Furthermore, he realized that he would never be able to control a manager under him who was also chairman of the board. His reorganization plan removed Steve as the head of the Macintosh division and put him in charge of new product development. It was the same role the headstrong chairman had been given at Apple's inception nearly ten years before.

As soon as Sculley presented the ideas to the board of directors in mid-April, Steve rebelled. Realizing that he was being passed over, at least in terms of what he saw as his role at Apple, he tried to enlist support from the board and the executive staff for his own coup to take over the company and oust Sculley. The president caught wind of it and confronted Steve with his machinations the following morning at an executive staff meeting. That afternoon, in tears, Steve gathered his faithful and announced that he was leaving Apple. They physically restrained him and convinced him that he could do more good inside Apple than outside. He agreed to think it over.

That weekend he decided to try one last effort to convince Markkula to back him. The Monday dinner at his house was the last-ditch effort. It didn't work. Markkula had already decided to throw his support solidly to Sculley. As he saw it, it was for the good of Apple.

The next evening Sculley called Steve to tell him that he had the votes necessary to go ahead with the reorganization and that the founder would have no operating role within the new structure. Ten years after starting the company, Steve Jobs was a victim of the corporate monster he had created. Over those years, the friendly, cheery, amateurish world of computing had changed. In 1985 personal computing was the big leagues. The game was hardball.

Was it the end of the journey? Four months later, when he resigned and started a new company, his answer was clear. It was only the beginning. It was the journey that was the reward, not the destination.

Roots

2
Cauldron

Orphans have always been important to history, or at least to the retelling of it by novelists. Horatio Alger's tales are central to the American soul. Foundlings such as Tom Jones and David Copperfield have a special place in the hearts of readers. Those without a past, with no ties or history, tap some deep current in the subconscious of all of us. There is something both romantic and compellingly pitiful about a nameless baby given up for adoption. Abandoned by the mother and disavowed by the father, an orphaned infant is easily the most vulnerable of all, starting life with a disadvantage most of us cannot even imagine.

Along with that disadvantage comes a fundamental difference from the rest of society, a difference that might even be an advantage in certain cases: an internal emptiness that can translate into a drive, an obsession, a lifelong quest to fill the void at the core of an orphan's life. However, psychologically abandonment may create a pit that can never be filled. Orphans and adoptees comprise a disproportionately large percentage of prison populations. The determination to track down and be reunited with the natural parents can never replace a child's bewilderment and confusion, subconscious or psychological though they may be, at having been abandoned in the first place.

On February 24, 1955, a boy was born in San Francisco. The moon, the sun, and the rising star were all in Pisces, an astrological confluence known as "triple Pisces." County Recorder and Vital Records in the county of San Francisco are archaic and difficult to peruse because they've never been sorted or cataloged, so it is impossible to say for certain just how many births occurred on that date in San Francisco hospitals. The only available records are published notices of birth in the *San Francisco Examiner*, and they indicate about 40 live births that day. But would a child born out of wedlock, illegitimate and unwanted, be listed in the paper?

Birth and adoption proceedings are sealed in the State of California and only recently, with the advent of certain adoptive rights cases, have adoptees themselves been able to search into their pasts. Steve almost certainly knows who his natural parents are, but he has been resolute in not revealing the information publicly. The prevailing rumor, which comes from him, places his father as a visiting professor at a university in California who had an affair with another teacher.[1]

"I think it's a natural curiosity for adopted people to want to understand where certain traits come from," Steve explained in 1984. "But I'm mostly an environmentalist. I think the way you are raised, your values, and most of your world view come from the experiences you had growing up.

"But some things aren't accounted for that way. I think it's quite natural to have a curiosity about it. And I did."[2]

In the 1950s adoption of illegitimate children was much more prevalent than it is today. The stigma of single parenthood was intense, and abortion was a dangerous and illegal back-alley operation. An unmarried woman had only one legal option—adoption—and numerous private placement agencies brought childless couples together with women who were "in trouble." In this case, within weeks of the birth of her child, the mother of Baby John Doe signed over the legal custody of her infant son to an adoption agency. They in turn placed the infant with a couple living in San Francisco. Their names were Paul and Clara Jobs. They named their adopted son Steven Paul and brought him home to their 45th Avenue apartment in San Francisco.

Paul Jobs had been raised on a farm in Germantown, Wisconsin, and then moved with his family to West Bend, Indiana. Of midwestern Calvinist stock, with a no-nonsense approach to life and a tough self-educated way about him, Jobs had dropped out of high school early and spent several years in the late 1930s wandering around the midwest in search of work. He eventually enlisted in the Coast Guard— the "Hooligan Navy," as he called it[3]—working as a machinist in the engine rooms of various ships. He was a solid six-footer, wore tattoos on his arms from his days in the service, and kept his hair in a short crew cut. Always a little embarrassed by his lack of education, he had a hearty personality, a pitch-in-and-help style, no pretenses, and a broad sense of humor. Paul Jobs was a straightforward man and every inch the blue-collar American.

By the end of World War II, Jobs was ready to leave the Coast Guard, and when his ship steamed into San Francisco to be decommissioned, it seemed the perfect opportunity to start a new life. He made a bet with a shipmate that he would be able to find a bride onshore in San Francisco. He won the bet when he went on a blind date with a woman who had grown up in the city and promptly asked her to marry him. Clara had been raised in San Francisco's Mission district and was a cheery good-natured woman with a hearty laugh and a sunny disposition. She was never a brooder, took life straight on, and was a good match for Paul Jobs. In 1946 Paul and Clara Jobs were married, and they headed back to Indiana, where the machinist was hired by International Harvester.

Paul Jobs' real love was tinkering with cars. He reveled in buying a clunker and then spending his weekends underneath the hood, repairing and renovating it. When it was running again, he'd sell it, pocket the profit, and buy another. He was also a hard bargainer and a tough negotiator. After a few years, he left International Harvester and went to work selling used cars. However, the lure of San Francisco, her family, and her roots was too strong for his bride. In 1952 the couple returned to the "City by the Bay" and moved into an apartment in the Sunset, a foggy portion of the city close to the Pacific Ocean.

Jobs was hired as a kind of strong-arm man by a finance company with a large trade in auto loans. He collected on bad debts, checked the terms of auto dealers' loans, and was an early "repo man," picking the locks of cars and repossessing them. His no-nonsense, tough personality was well suited to the somewhat dangerous pursuit of overdue loan payments. A few months after the adoption was final, the family moved to a house in South San Francisco, a primarily industrial town with a number of inexpensive and newly built housing tracts.

Steve turned out to be quite a handful, bright and somewhat hyperkinetic. The parents found themselves dragging the boy to the hospital to have his stomach pumped after he and a playmate swallowed a bottle of ant poison, and again after he pushed a bobbie pin into an electric outlet and burned his hand badly. To keep him from waking them up at four in the morning, which was more often than not his arising hour, the Jobses bought him first a rocking horse and then a record player equipped with a collection of Little Richard records. Perhaps because of the battle they had waged to get him, and because they were adoptive parents, not natural ones, he was spoiled. Discipline was lax, and Steve found that he could often get his way by crying—it would be one of his personality traits for years afterward. Nonetheless, infant Steve's antics didn't dissuade them from adopting another child in 1957, a daughter Patty, two years younger than their son.

Steve's childhood was similar to that of millions of other baby boom children. The South San Francisco neighborhood was filled with small rented houses inhabited by young families. There were dozens of children and plenty to do. He attended kindergarten and the first few years of elementary school in that town and was simply another in the crowd. Perhaps he was a little more active, but like all the other kids at the time, he played parts in neighborhood super 8mm movies, roared up and down the local streets on his tricycle, and watched a lot of television.

While Steve Jobs was learning how to walk and talk, things were happening in the world that set the stage for much of what he would do later. In 1956 the Nobel Prize for Physics was awarded to three Americans, John Bardeen, Walter Brattain, and William Shockley, for the invention of the transistor. This device fundamentally changed the world of electronics, instantly making clunky, hot, vacuum tubes a thing of the past. At its core the invention turned on the property of certain substances—primary among them silicon—to conduct electric current in one direction only. Hence, as these minute devices grew more complex, they were dubbed "semiconductors." The use of transistor meant electronic design could be miniaturized as well as be made more sophisticated. The fallout from this invention was enormous. Pocket radios were among the first popular products to result from this technology, and their advent made possible the music industry as we know it today. Transistors changed life in America and in much of the world. As it happened, the world center for electronic research and semiconductor manufacturing would be located about 30 miles south of South San Francisco in Santa Clara County.

This area to the north of San Jose along the Peninsula came to be called Silicon Valley. Shockley, one of the Nobel laureates, set up his company, Shockley Semiconductor, in an industrial/academic park near the Stanford University campus in Palo Alto. In the 1950s the firm drew the best and the brightest electronics wizards in the world. Then, when the brightest engineers grew disgruntled working for someone else and began what would be a standard of Silicon Valley life—the spin-off, start-up firm—their companies would usually be located nearby. It became an incestuous world, and when the electronics business exploded during the late fifties and sixties, the region expanded right along with it.

Two other events occurred in 1957 that would thoroughly change the character of American life and deeply influence Steve . The first was local and created a milieu in the Bay area that would have impact for 20 years. In San Francisco's North Beach, the beatniks were gathering in the first coordinated rebellion against America's postwar conformity. It was a movement that developed around beat poets such as Allen Ginsberg and Lawrence Ferlinghetti and found its voice with the publication in 1957 of Jack Kerouac's *On the Road*. As they experimented with drugs and alternate lifestyles, the city's beatniks laid the ground-work for the hippie culture and the "Summer of Love," which would erupt in the Bay area ten years later.

The second event came in October of 1957 when the Russians launched their first unmanned satellite, *Sputnik I*. Suddenly, American pride in technology and progress was sorely wounded. Within a year, school curriculums changed to focus on science. Money from the federal government was available for science projects, and the focus of the country seemed, nearly overnight, to have turned from self-contented satisfaction to a driven competitiveness with the Russians. The nascent electronics industry of Silicon Valley was one of the first recipients of the largesse.

At the same time, America and its businesses were still smug and parochial. These were the Eisenhower years: The economy was growing, there was a chicken in every pot, and there was a car in every garage. Vietnam was only a distant echo, and the United States was rebuilding war-ravaged Europe and Asia with the Marshall Plan. The country was the trade leader of the world, especially when it came to manufacturing and engineering. The phrase heard throughout the world was "American know-how." In 1958 International Business Machines (IBM) was the undisputed leader in manufacturing and sales of both typewriters and mainframe computers. That year a group of scientists from Xerox, looking for a partner, revealed a new technique for copying documents to IBM. They were rebuffed. Complacency was endemic.

However, none of these events had much impact on the Jobs household. What was much more important in their South San Francisco home was Paul Jobs' transfer in 1960 from the San Francisco office of his finance company to Palo Alto. With the beginning of the Silicon Valley boom in the mid-fifties, there were more auto loans in the Valley, and where there were loans there were defaults. The idea of commuting to the Peninsula each day didn't appeal to Paul Jobs, so he gathered his family and down payment and in early 1961 bought a house in a modern tract section of Mountain View, just south of Palo Alto.

Mountain View was one of those towns that looked as if it had sprung up overnight. Just north of San Jose straddling the El Camino Real, it was a sprawling place of flat, stucco buildings, wide streets, motels, fast-food joints, and absolutely no character whatsoever. Mountain View was always used as the prime example of what was wrong with the meteoric growth of Silicon Valley.

The town provided cheap housing for the hordes of technicians and assemblers who showed up at Lockheed and NASA where, spurred by the *Sputnik* crisis, work shifts had started to go around the clock. By the early sixties, Mountain View's main claim to fame was that it was the location for the first covered mall in the San Francisco Bay area. What had once been a highly concentrated flower-growing region populated by Japanese-Americans had been all but trampled in the rush to tract home development.

The home that the Jobs family settled into was on Diablo Avenue, a block off the Central Expressway in a tract of curving cul-de-sacs and dead-end streets. The houses on Diablo had been built in 1956, and the Jobs family was the second owner of their corner unit. The place cost $22,000 in 1961 and was a modified, flattened A-frame design with a courtyard entryway.

The house was by no means opulent. The backyard was concrete and tiny, and over the back fence was a garden apartment complex. The area had a definite white, working-class population. There was an ever-changing collection of cars in the driveway, although Paul and Clara were both immaculate and kept the house freshly painted, the lawn neatly mowed, and the flowers carefully watered. Paul Jobs quickly became a regular at both the local Department of Motor Vehicles and the junkyards that fronted the highway in next-door Palo Alto. Jobs senior was a true car afficionado. He would concentrate on one model of car, buying, fixing, and selling car after car until another model caught his fancy. He kept a scrapbook of all his loving restorations and usually had a photo of the latest masterpiece framed in the living room.

Paul Jobs was meticulous and kept his garage spotless, his overalls pressed, and his toolbox perfectly organized. He loved working on cars and tried to instill that in his son. "I figured I could get him nailed down with a little mechanical ability," the elder Jobs recalled, "but he really wasn't interested in getting his hands dirty. He never really cared too much for mechanical things.

"Steve was always more interested in wondering about the people who had owned the cars."[4]

Paul was an exceptional bargainer who found pleasure in making deals, selling the cars he had fixed up for a profit, and buying a new one more cheaply. He honed his negotiating skills over the horse trading for cars and junked parts, usually taking his son with him. It was during these early years that Steve assimilated some of the negotiating skills that would become his trademark.

Steve didn't make friends easily. He didn't enjoy team sports and never played Little League baseball or Pop Warner football. Swimming became his sport, and its solitary nature fit the developing youth's personality. Swimming was in many ways the archetypal California sport, and the Jobses were convinced that their children should participate in it. Clara Jobs took up babysitting at nights to earn the extra money to send Steve and Patty to the Mountain View Dolphins Swim Club. Clara was a working mom from the time her kids went to school. For years she worked at the desk of a local Mountain View bowling alley and was considered a superb bowler. Steve started swimming when he was five and continued until he was good enough to be a member of the Dolphins team. Clara spent hours ferrying the kids to practices and meets and in the process became friends with another "swim mom," Margaret Wozniak.

Steve was an excellent swimmer, eventually reaching the "A" team in his age group at the highly competitive Mountain View club. Unfortunately, he was not much of a group member. He was a "loner, pretty much of a crybaby," recalls one of his fellow swim team members, Mark Wozniak. "He'd lose a race and go off by himself and cry. He didn't quite fit in with everyone else. He wasn't one of the guys."[5]

But in the dark and quiet of the family garage, Steve found solace for his lack of social skills. His real passion existed outside the classroom and the swim club. By the time he was ten, Steve was attracted by one thing: electronics. There was something compelling and open-ended about the potential of electronic gadgets.

The neighborhood was filled with engineers from companies such as Hewlett-Packard who spent their weekends with soldering irons and oscilloscopes. The myth of the "garage start-up" was alive in the Valley; after all, that was how H-P had started not so many years earlier. Countless engineers worked on their own in a driven fury of intensity, hunkered over workbenches in search of their own successful innovations and inventions. The garage doors open in the California heat were an invitation to a lonely and precocious child looking for something to keep himself, and more precisely his mind, busy.

One of their engineer neighbors, Larry Lange, brought home a rudimentary carbon microphone one day. Hooking it up to a battery and a speaker, he was able to produce sound. This fascinated Steve, who couldn't understand how a device without an amplifier could make sounds. He asked many questions and came to spend so much time at the engineer's home that Lange eventually gave Steve the microphone. Steve had an intensity, a single-mindedness that could blow away any roadblocks. He pursued electronics with an unyielding dedication. Night after night he would show up at Larry Lange's house to learn everything he could from the H-P engineer. Steve's wasn't a casual interest; he was a fixture in Lange's garage.

Hewlett-Packard, where Lange worked, would be an enduring influence on both the Silicon Valley and the boy. Bill Hewlett and David Packard had started out in a Palo Alto garage designing control devices for animation cameras. Walt Disney was one of their first clients. They graduated, on the basis of excellent engineering and a reputation for high quality, reliability, and scientific acumen, to creating small computer systems for engineering, medical, and scientific applications. By the time Steve was growing bored in elementary school, the firm had thousands of employees and was widely known for its progressive business practices.

H-P, as it was usually called, had a fundamental corporate engineering policy of "doing it right" regardless of the cost. The idea was that a piece of equipment should be designed and engineered correctly, not the cheapest possible way. Furthermore, the company had an attitude toward employees that allowed them to work flexible hours 20 years before that idea became popular. Company offices were spacious and located in beautifully landscaped environments that were conducive to creative work. Lifetime employment, in the mode of Japanese firms, was the order of the day at the Palo Alto company. H-P was a company capable of profit, but not at the expense of humanism. Those themes of the starting of a billion-dollar firm on dreams hatched at a garage workbench, a thorough-going dedication to quality, and an ongoing compassion for employees were widely influential throughout the Valley. The H-P story was popular in the press, and the H-P spirit was fostered in the informal garage instruction sessions of engineers like Larry Lange.

Lange was also instrumental in getting Steve enrolled in the Hewlett-Packard Explorer Club, a group for adolescent engineers that held Tuesday evening meetings in a company cafeteria. Various company engineers would show up and demonstrate the firm's latest products, including calculators, diodes, lasers, and holograms. At one meeting Steve cornered a scientist working with lasers and talked his way into a guided tour of the holographic lab. With his mix of total intensity and utter seriousness, Steve impressed the engineers enough that they let him have an old hologram etched on glass. It became one of his most prized possessions. At another session Steve saw his first computer.

"I was maybe 12 the first time," he has said. "I remember the night. They showed us one of their new desktop computers and let us play on it. I wanted one badly. I thought they were neat. I wanted to mess around with one."[6]

Instead of playing Little League baseball, Steve was off investigating the mysteries and magic of electronics in garages and the H-P labs. Engineers were only too happy to share their experiences with anyone who showed interest and enthusiasm, and the young Steve Jobs certainly fit the description of an avid listener. It was a part of the spirit of the electronics industry in those days to be open and share discoveries and the latest tinkerings. Competition, nondisclosure forms, paranoia, and security checkpoints had not yet taken over the industry the way they would 15 years later.

In turn, in his garage the bright youngster fascinated the local kids with his esoteric knowledge. "We couldn't understand what he was talking about half the time," recalls Jeff Eastwood, who grew up two doors down from the Jobses and broke a knuckle in a fight with Steve one day on his family's front lawn. "He'd show me things that I couldn't understand with all the electronic gear he'd taken apart, and I'd go home to my dad and say, 'He's lying again.'"

That same isolation carried over at both the elementary schools he attended. A class cut-up and a bright underachieving loner, he would not buckle under to the authority of teachers and refused to do anything that he felt was a waste of time. His mother had taught him to read before he went to school, and he "was pretty bored in school and turned into a little terror,"[7] according to him.

In the third grade—the year that John F. Kennedy was assassinated, Bob Dylan burst on the scene, and the build-up in Vietnam began—Steve was the ringleader in a group that exploded bombs and let snakes loose in the classroom. He was saved the following year when he came under the influence of his fourth grade teacher, Imogene "Teddy" Hill.

"She was one of the saints of my life," he says. "She taught an advanced fourth grade class, and it took her about a month to get hip to my situation. She bribed me into learning. She would say, 'I really want you to finish this workbook. I'll give you five bucks if you finish it.' That really kindled a passion in me for learning things."[8]

Steve learned more that year than in any other year in school. His teachers wanted him to skip the next two years in grade school and go straight to junior high to learn a foreign language, but his parents decided against it. Eventually, they agreed to let Steve skip one year, the fifth grade, and when he did so he also started in at a different school in Mountain View, Crittenden, a middle school. But the Mountain View school district made no provisions for the psychosocial adjustment of gifted kids. They were simply plunked down in an advanced class with older children, not grouped with others their own age who were similarly talented. Combined with the change of school, this situation made Steve very unhappy.

The years in Mountain View had not been terribly kind to Paul Jobs. A couple of years after moving the family to the Peninsula boom town, he changed jobs and decided to try his hand at selling real estate. A neighbor convinced him that the explosion of jobs in the burgeoning Silicon Valley would only make real estate continue to prosper. Mountain View, after all, was the site of Moffett Field, the major U. S. military airbase in the Bay area. As the sixties progressed, and NASA sent ever more elaborate space probes up into orbit, Moffett Field became increasingly busy. The blue-collar town with its unpretentious atmosphere and affordable prices was a favorite with the military personnel sent to work with NASA's chief engineers at the Ames facility on the edge of Moffett Field. The proximity of the major Lockheed missile and satellite manufacturing installation in Cupertino, and an advanced IBM data processing facility providing computer power to both programs, also served to keep the market lively.

The first year in real estate went well for the elder Jobs. He made enough money to stay at it for another year. The second year was a disaster. His drive, energy, and finance experience served him well for pursuing a deal and locking down all the details of the financing, but the personal finesse required to bring in new clients and become the listing agent of record for sale properties was not his forte. The family had to tighten their belts.

Surrounded by homes filled with the expanding consumer wealth of the American economy, Steve was filled with concern by the lack of all the latest gadgets in their house. Especially since the garages of their neighbors held a cornucopia of riches and magic: electronic magic.

In Steve's important fourth grade year, Imogene Hill once recalled asking her class, "What in the world don't you understand?" It was part of her approach to teaching that continually looked for areas to stimulate her charges. "Steve raised his hand and said, 'I don't understand why all of a sudden we're so broke!'"[9]

The following year, when he started going to the new school, his dad took a job with a machine shop in San Carlos. After 15 years away from the trade he returned to work as a machinist, the skill he had learned in the Coast Guard. He found that he had to start all over again from the bottom, but he was very good at it and quickly climbed the ladder. The family started to breathe a little easier financially, but at his new school Steve was still miserable.

Crittenden was a tough school. It served the poorest areas of Mountain View, the wrong side of the tracks, and was filled with toughs and hooligans whose exploits made Steve's pranks seem amateurish. Mountain View at that time was a real melting pot. A large Hispanic community lived in uneasy proximity to remnants of the town's Asian founders and the blue-collar but middle-class whites who were flocking to the tracts. The police were often called to the school to break up fights. The situation was basically out of control. For Steve, who was extremely bright but also a little wild, an environment where his wildness went unnoticed in all the commotion, as did his intelligence, was a prescription for unhappiness.

As the sixth grade ground on, he decided that he would not return the following year if it meant attending the same school. By the summer he had dug in his heels. He informed his father of the decision, and that was that. After weeks of discussion Paul and Clara realized that their son, who had been a discipline problem already, was on the verge of becoming a full-blown juvenile delinquent. The choice was either to stay and fight it out with him or to move.

Also contributing to their decision was the fact that Mountain View had the most notorious high school on the Peninsula. Their daughter Patty, whom neighbors recall as being secretive and a loner, was just about to enter Crittenden, and the stories Steve told were enough to help convince them to move.

"He said he just wouldn't go," recalled Paul Jobs. "So we moved."[10]

In 1967 the Jobs family bought a newer three-bedroom home in the flatlands of Los Altos, a few miles south of Mountain View. It was a low-slung, one-story white house with a big backyard—grass this time, not concrete—on a street with a row of identical houses. Located in an unincorporated pocket of Los Altos on Crist Street, the house was closer to the new job Paul had taken at Spectraphysics, where he was working on the mirrors for a supermarket laser-scanning device. The house was also within a half-mile of the new Interstate 280, in the flight paths of both San Jose Airport and Moffett Field, and just within the boundaries of the highly regarded Fremont-Cupertino school district.

Although cars continued to be the passion of Paul Jobs' life, he worked hard at keeping the lawn neatly manicured and the house perfectly in order. A bed of lantana flowers cascaded out of a brick planter near the front door, and there was never a drop of oil on the driveway that he didn't bleach out. The small but tidy three-bedroom house was just big enough for the family. Soon Clara went to work for the school district as an administrative secretary. And the kids, Steve and Patty, found themselves in the midst of an even greater concentration of electronic engineering families.

Cupertino, Los Altos, and Sunnyvale all shared the same school district, which was a quantum leap up from Mountain View's, but had the same overwhelming preoccupation with engineering. For years part of the ritual of school enrollment included filling out a card asking for parents' employer information to determine eligibility for additional federal funds depending on U.S. government project employment. Preprinted on the form was a place for "Lockheed Building Number." The long shadow of Lockheed hung over Cupertino and Los Altos as H-P's had in Mountain View and Palo Alto. There was always someone around to answer questions about electronics, and people had different specialties. Every garage had a box or two filled with spare parts or obsolete equipment that interested kids could take apart after school. Every garage was an Aladdin's cavern.

The area was booming. NASA's space programs were going ahead full steam, and Lockheed was at the center of them. A number of highly secret projects were underway: the Polaris missile, the spy satellite, space stations. There was precious little unemployment in the region, and the future looked very bright. Conservatism, patriotism, and Republicanism were the "ism's" of Cupertino.

In 1967, when the Jobs family moved from Mountain View to Los Altos, 475,000 American troops were in Vietnam and the first "Summer of Love" was held in San Francisco. Lyndon Johnson was president and both *The Graduate* and *Bonnie and Clyde* were released. Protests in Berkeley against the war began to attract attention around the nation, but in the Santa Clara Valley there never was heard a discouraging word. Silicon Valley was heavily dependent upon government defense contracts, and there was no future in biting the hand that fed. While less than 50 miles away, the hippies of San Francisco and the students of Berkeley were questioning the system, the engineers of Silicon Valley were digging deeper into their suburban comforts.

"If you grow up in a woodcarving community, with all the tools of professional woodworking around you, and everyone on the block talking about wood carving all the time, don't you think the kids will turn out to be good woodworkers?" asks Bill Fernandez, who befriended Jobs in junior high school. "We grew up in a town, on streets, in schools and garages where all we had were the tools of electronics. Isn't it natural that we ended up being pretty good at it, being involved with electronics, doing something in that field?"

In junior high school Steve continued to have problems making friends. Because he had skipped a grade, he was a year younger than the rest of the advanced placement group he was put into. This school district didn't believe in skipping grades, but it had a separate track for gifted kids. Steve joined. Fernandez, the son of a local attorney, was a year older than Steve when he met him at Cupertino Junior High. They were both in the same grade. "For some reason, the kids in the eighth grade didn't like him because they thought he was odd. I was one of his few friends."

They became close in the way that lonely outsiders do. Steve was younger than everyone else in his class and too bright to fit in. He was quiet and withdrawn and wasn't interested in team sports, the standard common denominator for adolescent friendships. Both Fernandez and Steve were skinny, scrawny, and uninterested in teams. (In fact, years later, in discussing the daily basketball games that the Macintosh team would have, one of the best software engineers and hoopsters described the two worst players as "Jobs and Fernandez. Neither one could so much as dribble the ball, let alone shoot it.")

Electronics was a perfect occupation for the socially inept. It was solitary and cerebral, and it took up all the hours that other kids used in playing sports or riding bicycles. They could pursue it in the dark silence of their parents' garages. It had an intellectual aura to it that allowed them to show their superiority to the jocks, and although it probably didn't attract the girls, there were a few other afficionados in the Valley who could share the passion.

The two became close friends, and since Fernandez's house was on the way home from school, and he had a well-stocked electronic workbench in his garage, they spent hours there together. One day Fernandez introduced Steve to the eldest son of the family who lived across the street from him, a family Steve had known through the Mountain View Dolphins Swim Club. Since Fernandez's parents had nothing to do with electronics, Jerry Wozniak had been his tutor in the subject. And Steve Wozniak, his eldest son, although five years Fernandez's senior, shared his own passion for electronics with anyone who was receptive, and Fernandez was. The two had built a number of science fair entries together over the years, and whenever Fernandez was stumped by some theoretical area of physics or mathematics that stalled his latest project, it was Steve Wozniak, known far and wide as "Woz," who could bail him out.

Steve had heard all about Woz from Fernandez and liked what he heard. Woz was a brilliant, intuitive designer of electronics who seemed to have the skill in his blood. He had won local electronics fairs with a simple but effective precursor to a computer. This was an impressive feat in the Silicon Valley, where the competition was a bit steeper than in most corners of the country. But while he certainly had the skill set of the "nerd," there was more to Woz than electronics. He was also a well-known prankster with enough smarts to launch highly sophisticated practical jokes and enough moxie and fearlessness to direct them against the authorities. This was a combination that immediately drew Steve to him. His most famous stunt had caused the Homestead High School's principal to go running out on the school's playing field with a gym bag, snatched from a student locker, that was filled with ominously ticking machinery. That little episode had earned the electronics club president a night in Juvenile Hall and a standing ovation from the school body upon his return the following day.

The first meeting between the two eventual founders of Apple was by no means auspicious. After all, Woz was a bona fide 18-year-old electronics whiz. Steve and Fernandez had just reached puberty, and neither knew much of anything about the magic world of electronics. Sure they liked to play with gadgets, but the two junior high schoolers were more interested in balancing mirrors on top of speakers, bouncing lasers off them, and then watching the reflected patterns on the wall, than doing anything more valuable. Woz had already read everything he could find about computers, was designing circuit boards for them on paper, and was regularly spending his weekends in the Stanford Linear Accelerator library poring over the most advanced electronics research materials. The two kids were eager technicians but no match for Woz. It wasn't until a couple of years later that they all grew close.

Steve continued to attend the H-P Explorer Club after the family's move to Los Altos and embarked on a project to build a frequency counter, a device that tracked the occurrences of a certain electrical frequency in a circuit. One day he found that he needed more parts. His next move displayed the chutzpah, guts, and brazenness that would become the hallmark of his character.

"I picked up the phone and called Bill Hewlett. He was listed in the Palo Alto phone book," explains Jobs. "He answered the phone and he was real nice. He chatted with me for 20 minutes.

"He didn't know me at all, but he ended up giving me some parts, and he got me a job that summer working at Hewlett-Packard on the line, assembling frequency counters. Assembling may be too strong. I was putting in screws. It didn't matter; I was in heaven."[11]

Steve never finished the frequency counter. He was capable of powerful enthusiasms and passions, but they were usually short term.

Another idea, a newer machine, another quest would present itself and his focus changed. The summer between junior high and high school, 1968, was very important for him. He was 13 years old and had a real job for the first time. He started to realize there might be more to life than electronics.

"I remember my first day on the assembly line at H-P," he recalls wistfully. "I was expressing my complete enthusiasm and bliss at being there for the summer to my supervisor, a guy named Chris, telling him that my favorite thing in the whole world was electronics. I asked him what his favorite thing was. He looked at me and said, 'To f - - -!'

"I learned a lot that summer."[12]

Sex was only one of the things he was about to discover at Homestead High.

3
Wireheads

"I have this vivid memory of Steve Jobs," recalls Bruce Courture, who attended both Cupertino Junior High and Homestead High—six years of school—with Steve. Courture was voted "Most Likely to Succeed" by the senior class and is now a partner at one of the most successful high-tech law firms in the Silicon Valley. "It's one moment that has always stuck in my mind. It was a very foggy day. All the boys in our freshman class were running a couple of laps around the track.

"All of a sudden, Steve, who was ahead of me, glanced back across the field at the PE coach, who was hidden by the fog, and saw that he couldn't possibly see the far side of the field. So he sat down. I thought that was a pretty good idea, so I joined him. The two of us just sat and watched everyone else run by. When they came back around for the second lap, we stood up and joined them.

"We had to take some ribbing, but he had figured out how he could get away with half the work and still get credit for the whole thing. I was really impressed, especially that he had the guts to try it, even though he was just a freshman. I would never have thought to do that on my own."

That individualism and spirit of nonconformity characterized Steve Jobs throughout high school. It was an attitude that was also encouraged by the liberal teachers at Homestead High. Isolated by both his youth, and the special attention he was given as an accelerated student, he marched to his own tune. In an America that was changing from the conformity of the sixties to the individuality of the seventies, he was quick to grasp the values of the counterculture that interested him—individuality, the questioning of authority, mind-expanding drugs—without ever wholly embracing the hippie ethic.

He was always outspoken. Courture recalls him "never backing down in a Situational Ethics class we had. No matter how unpopular his view might be—and I recall that he had pretty unconventional views on a lot of issues—he would never change his mind. He was very smart, a brain, but no joiner."

Steve entered Homestead High in 1968. The makeup of that year's class was homogeneous American middle-class. Looking through the yearbook, one can search in vain for a black or Hispanic face. There was a sizable community of Asians, but page after page, row after row of photos for all four classes show nothing but smiling, clean-cut white kids, the suburban troops who within a couple of years would be wearing flowers in their long hair and flocking the 50 miles to the Haight-Ashbury. These were the last days of the halcyon America of the fifties, the last year before the rebellion that was bubbling in hip outposts around the world would come home to roost in America's middle-class suburbs. Five years earlier, an individual, a nonconformist, someone with unorthodox ideas was suspect, a freak. By the time Steve graduated, being a freak would be a badge of honor. And if not a freak, the alternative was ersatz-proletariat: Work boots and work shirts were all the rage in the Cupertino high school.

Homestead is a low, squat school thrown up in the postwar boom that hit the Valley. It sits hard by two freeways and is the kind of campus-like school that California specializes in. Classrooms are located in building modules that were added as needed. Student lockers are outside, under covered walkways, since the weather is usually mild. The parking lots are huge, and so are the playing fields.

That previous summer, Steve and Bill Fernandez had built a silicon rectifier, a device that allows alternating current to be controlled, and had entered it in a local science fair. Although they were not the winners, the collection of homemade devices filled them with enthusiasm. Both Fernandez and Steve felt at a distinct disadvantage because they didn't come from heavily scientific households. When Woz told them about an electronics class that they should take at the high school, the pair of freshmen formed a pact to enroll in it together.

They became "wireheads"; the slang name Silicon Valley high school kids gave to electronics club members had a hip connotation.

The name combined the drug orientation of the time with electronics, avoiding the bumbling image of "nerds." In Silicon Valley it could be "cool" to be into electronics.

For students interested in electronics one class was absolutely required: John McCollum's Electronics 1. Up to that point, Steve had been fiddling with electrical components without any understanding of the theoretical underpinnings of electronics. His untutored approach exemplified the differences between a technician's understanding and an engineer's. McCollum mixed theoretical underpinnings with a strong practical, product-oriented approach that over the years turned out a lot of engineers who could actually make something. He was also a stickler for detail and obedience.

Woz thrived under the authoritarian and practical regimen. Four years before, he had become the prize student in the electronics classroom, president of the math and electronics clubs, winner of science fair awards, and the designer of endless electronic schematics. For Steve, the hip wirehead and questioner of authority, the subject never quite caught fire, and as he went through high school he lost his interest in electronics as McCollum taught it. He became more interested in other subjects as well as his own extracurricular efforts in the electronics realm.

Perhaps it was partly an issue of personality. McCollum was an ex-Navy fighter pilot with a disciplinarian attitude that permitted no questioning of his authority. Woz had no problem with this position. When he began school, he was always a well-behaved student ready to listen to authority. He was, in his mother's words, "a square."[1] Woz retained the provincial certainty and straightness of an isolated electronics genius throughout high school. The world was very simplistic—black and white, good and bad—and moral values could be equated to the binary values of the electronic schematics he drew with abandon. He had little time for girls, an abhorrence for drugs, and a respect for his elders. Nonetheless he grew to challenge McCollum publicly, but for the glory of it. As a senior, Woz was right often enough to get away with challenging the teacher, but basically the two were cut from similar conservative cloth.

Such was not the case with Steve. By 1969, when he came to McCollum's class, he was not about to kowtow to anybody, and the cultural changes in the world were altering the way that students and younger teachers interacted. McCollum was set in his ways, and the new generation of kids were not his cup of tea. After years of teaching well-behaved proto-engineers like Woz, a Steve Jobs was not the kind of student John McCollum could understand. Steve had another trait that impaired their interaction. An arrogance was starting to appear, perhaps to disguise his shyness, that showed itself in a "know-it-all" attitude, especially when it came to electronics. This attitude did very little to endear him to the teacher.

"I only vaguely remember Jobs," recalls McCollum. "He kind of faded into the background. He was usually off in a corner doing something on his own and really didn't want to have much of anything to do with either me or the rest of the class.

"But I do remember that one day he was building something and needed some parts I didn't have that were only supplied by Burroughs. I suggested that he call the local number for the company, talk to the public affairs people, and see if they wouldn't let him have one or two of the components for his school project.

"The next day he came in as pleased as could be and told me that Burroughs was sending him the parts, and they should arrive very shortly. When I asked how he had managed that, he said he had called the main office collect and told them he was working on a new electronic design. He was trying various components and was considering using theirs.

"I was furious. That was not the way I wanted my students to behave. And sure enough, in a day or so the parts arrived by air freight. I didn't like the way he had done it, but I had to respect his results."

By the end of his sophomore year, Steve had about given up on McCollum's class. He was 14 years old and was starting to move in other directions. He was watching girls, but from a distance. Lanky and introverted, he wasn't a lothario. A girl in high school then describes his manner as "awkward. He really was an oaf. There were a lot of other guys around who were more comfortable in different settings. He'd get kind of weird."

Swim team practices at the Mountain View Dolphins Swim Club were taking up too much time, so he switched to water polo. But that was another short-lived interest. He found that he didn't have the physical or mental discipline that it took to be a jock. He took up the trumpet and joined the Homestead marching band, one of the best precision units in Northern California. He was looking for something new to get involved with in which he could excel.

Though he was tiring of the design aspect of electronics, with its scientific mumbo-jumbo and McCollum's requirement for allegiance, he was fascinated by the world of components and parts. His attention was turning from the uses of the components to using the components to make money.

One shop in Mountain View, Haltek, was the electronics equivalent of the automobile junkyards that Paul Jobs frequented. It was a block-long warehouse stuffed full of abandoned, rejected, obsolete, and unsorted electronic components. Steve talked his way into a weekend job at Haltek during his sophomore year in high school and loved it. It was an electronic scavenger's paradise.

In the Silicon Valley, components could be rejected for any number of reasons: a flaw in the paint, too high an incidence of failure in a particular batch, a newer design that obsoleted an entire warehouse filled with perfectly good parts. More often than not, these orphaned parts showed up at Haltek, as did all the garage designers and high-school wireheads working on their homebrewed electronic constructions.

Steve began to develop a sense for electronic components and their prices that would stay with him for years. While Fernandez and Woz liked the supply house for what they could buy there, Steve made studying the prices of components his specialty. This was no mean feat in a business where there were thousands of varieties of logic gates, capacitors, resistors, and the like. Furthermore, quality was usually not immediately obvious to the eye. The purchaser had to know about serial numbers, parts runs, good and bad assembly lines, and all the esoterica of the business of components.

Rummaging through aisles of steel shelving, sorting through dozens of unmarked boxes, looking for one component in thousands was not everyone's favorite pastime. However, Steve's interest in the prices, and his willingness to bargain and debate quality and price with them, impressed the fellows who ran Haltek. He became an expert in the prices of electronic components. Steve worked at Haltek on and off over the years, and he rarely missed an opportunity to use his knowledge to make a little extra pocket money. At the San Jose Swap meet he would regularly buy parts, bargaining the price as low as possible, and then sell them to Haltek for a profit. His father's skills in haggling and dealing had worn off on him.

Woz often came into Haltek to get surplus parts. In the late summer of 1969, Bill Fernandez assisted his neighbor in constructing his first computer. It was the summer after Woz had spent his first year in college at the University of Colorado. He had been rejected by his father's alma mater, Cal Tech,[2] so in rebound he went to McCollum's school in Boulder.

It was not a great success. Woz played too many all-night bridge games. His grades were poor. The summer after his freshman year he returned to his parents' house and knew that he would not go back to school. As an interim measure, he enrolled, with his high school wirehead buddy Allan Baum, in a course on programming at the local community college. Although he did well, college was not right for him yet. Eventually, he landed a part-time job programming a mainframe computer system tied into the Department of Motor Vehicles. With time on his hands, he started designing his first computer.

At the same time that thousands of Americans were gathering at a farm in upstate New York for the Woodstock Festival, Woz and Baum filled a folder with schematics and the specification sheets for the parts they needed for their computer. Then, when Baum left to attend MIT in the fall of 1969, Woz decided that he would build the computer, scavenging parts from surplus stores or directly from sympathetic companies. He convinced the methodical Fernandez, who had a neat and carefully designed workbench in his garage, to help him.

The computer was designed by Woz and built by Fernandez after school. With painstaking care, they created a working computer. Instead of wrapping long lengths of wire to make connections for convenience's sake, they meticulously cut every wire to length so the machine looked neater and more finished. It consisted of a row of eight mechanical binary switches, an enter button, and eight red lights. Programs were entered by setting a combination of switches; all eight could either be up or down, thus either 0 or 1 in the binary logic of electronics. This value was then sent to the computer's 256-byte memory registers with the enter button, and another number could be created. Sequences were built up out of numerous sets of switch combinations in order, and the machine allowed two four-digit binary numbers—each entered with four of the switches—to be added, subtracted, multiplied, or divided. The answer was then displayed in the row of eight lights.

"That was the 'Flair pen' or 'cream soda' computer," says Fernandez. "Woz was always drawing schematic designs with them. He said you could tell a real engineer by the Flair pens in his shirt pocket. Purple was the color of choice that year. And all we drank was cream soda in bottles. We were so broke that we'd save up the bottles and walk over to Safeway to get the deposits back so we could buy another."

One day at school, as it neared completion, Fernandez invited Steve over to see the computer that the two neighbors had been building for nearly six months. Although Woz and Steve had met before briefly, this was a much more important encounter. Both were quiet and withdrawn: Woz, carried away by the technology and engineering behind his first computer creation, had trouble speaking in comprehensible terms; Steve was silenced by his respect for the raw ability that this feat demonstrated.

Steve had been toying with electronics through the projects that he and Fernandez launched as well as at the Tuesday night Explorer Club meetings at H-P that he still attended on and off. His fantasies were chastened by the encounter with Woz's computer. "He was the first person I met who knew more electronics than I did."[3] They shared some similarities, although their differences would become more important in the long run. Neither had many friends, and both were superior and isolated. They were not joiners or jocks. Both were extremely bright but for the most part were misunderstood by their peers and left alone. If anything, Woz was the more outgoing of the two. With a glint in his eye, he was a true practical jokester. Steve was quieter, more intense, less accessible.

Their age difference of five years was less important than the passions they shared. Woz had the kind of zeal for electronics that made his sentences run into one another and his thoughts jumble when he tried to explain a particularly beguiling new concept. Steve's enthusiasm about his latest interest would translate itself into similar language. He had a way of getting very close to the person he was speaking with, invading his or her space, and then intently explaining his newest discovery. You couldn't avoid Steve once he made up his mind to buttonhole you.

Whereas Woz was completely immersed in computers and technology, Steve was immersed in himself. Woz participated in pranks because they were fun; Steve took part because he saw himself as an outsider. Being a prankster was an essential part of the counterculture that was beginning to have an influence on the precocious Steve Jobs. His interest in the trumpet soon waned; instead he took up the guitar and harmonica. He became a disciple of Bob Dylan, and the goings-on in San Francisco's Haight-Ashbury intrigued him. He also started to ask the "big questions" about life.

Steve had a deep-seated need to understand the world and was weighted down throughout high school with questions that he shared with Bill Fernandez. What was at the root of his questioning of the meaning of life was never clear to his closest friends.

"We used to walk for hours in the evenings," remembers Fernandez. "We were both interested in the spiritual side of things, the big questions: Who are we? What is it all about? What does it mean? We strolled along through the curving tracts and past the schools, talking about everything and resolving nothing. Mostly it was Steve who would do the talking. I was a very good listener. We always talked about philosophy or the issues of the day, religion mostly, but also Vietnam, drugs, music, girls. He would have a grand passion of the day, or something that was on his mind, and he would bend my ear for hours as we walked.

"But Steve never shared a lot of personal things with me. When I look back on that time, I realize that. We avoided those sorts of things. It wasn't until more than ten years later that I found out he was adopted. He never told me, and I just assumed that his family was his own."

Steve must have known by then that he was adopted. His sister Patty was dark, Hispanic in appearance, and to even the most casual observer, little physical similarity existed between the two. Finding out that in a world of conformity and suburban middle-class values he was adopted would certainly make a highly intelligent adolescent ask some questions. It also made him fundamentally unsettled and fueled his quest for something that would give his life meaning. As it turned out, the machine that Woz and Fernandez were completing would fit the bill.

The early computer that Steve saw that day in Fernandez's garage was by no means the kind of device to build a business around. It barely worked. The only functions it performed were of interest solely to hobbyists, fanatics, and wireheads. Steve was all of 15 years old—not quite ready to become an entrepreneur—but the occasion allowed him to get to know Woz, and through him Allan Baum, and started him thinking about electronic products.

As the year passed, Steve spent more time at Fernandez's garage. While Fernandez was a superb technician, he was also cautious and not given to impulse. Woz found in Steve a perfect partner for practical jokes. Woz could design them, and Steve, with his chip-on-the-shoulder cavalier attitude, disdain for school and authority, and willingness to be an outlaw, was ready to carry them out.

In mid-1970, at the end of his sophomore year in high school, when he finished McCollum's electronics class, Steve was also finished with formal training in electronics. That summer he worked at Haltek and became close friends with both Woz and Baum, who were working as systems programmers on a nearby mainframe computer. Much of his advanced training in electronics would come at Woz's elbow, and the two older boys, who were both deeply involved in improving the design of the Flair pen computer of the previous year, allowed Steve to tag along as they conducted research deep into the stacks at the Stanford library and pored over the product literature and specifications that arrived daily at Woz's house.

When he reached 15½ in August, just before starting his junior year, his father helped him buy a red Fiat 850 coupe. Paid for largely with his earnings from Haltek, it was an undependable sports car that nonetheless fulfilled one major need: It provided freedom. After Woz enrolled early in 1971 in Berkeley, about 40 miles away, Steve made the journey two or three times a week. The ambience of protest and coffeeshops was to his liking, and soon he also discovered the Stanford coffee house in Palo Alto, where he liked to study. Steve started to miss school and headed for more interesting places. He was always most comfortable around older people—like Woz.

Steve was more adventurous than his classmates, and throughout his junior year he ranged all over the Bay area, investigating and delving into various facets of life that were rare in Silicon Valley. The year marked a major change for him. He discovered marijuana and literature. "I got stoned; I discovered Shakespeare, Dylan Thomas, and all that classic stuff. I read *Moby Dick* and went back as a junior taking creative writing classes."[4]

He was sure that he knew more electronics than his classmates after spending the summer apprenticing with Woz and working at Haltek, and he made no bones about letting his fellow students know it.

He refused to join the electronics club that year at Homestead and instead, with his best friend Steve Echstein, began to put on light shows for avant-garde jazz concerts. Homestead had a very active extracurricular music program, and some renegades from the marching band formed a jazz band. Led by student Mark Izu, an experimental composer who has since recorded a number of albums, they experimented with new forms of music, while Steve and Echstein played with lights. It was a perfect occupation for a wirehead.

"Steve was kind of a brain and kind of a hippie," recalls Terri Anzur, editor of the school newspaper and now a television anchorwoman with the NBC affiliate in Houston, "but he never fit into either group. He was smart enough to be a nerd, but wasn't nerdy, and he was too intellectual for the hippies, who just wanted to get wasted all the time.

"He was kind of an outsider. In high school everything revolved around what group you were in. If you weren't in a carefully defined group, you weren't anybody. He was an individual in a world where individuality was still a little suspect."

That junior year he did join a club, a school-sanctioned practical joker's band. Called the Buck Fry Club (with a little transliteration the name represented a scatological suggestion), it specialized in adolescent pranks that every teenager dreams of but few ever carry out. They set up a breakfast table on the roof of the cafeteria, gummed up the locks on all the school's doors, and breached the security of the school's fire alarm system, setting it to constant buzzing.

But this wasn't enough for Steve, who was growing ever bolder. Aided by Woz and Baum, Steve had serious practical jokester firepower behind him. And in an America where Abbie Hoffman and Jerry Rubin were leading hordes of yippies in absurdist, dadaist protests, pranks seemed of great importance. The group winched a Volkswagen up onto the roof of the cafeteria and cemented a gold-painted toilet seat to a planter box. In their crowning achievement for graduation, they unfurled a building-sized sheet with a painted hand showing a single digit raised in an obscene symbol. As if that wasn't enough, the three added their signature "SWABJOB" to the bottom of the sheet. Since the other two were long gone from Homestead and only Steve's name was obvious, he was quickly apprehended.

Other things had started to capture Steve's imagination, and he found it difficult to be fenced in by high school. He became captivated with literature and the arts. Shakespeare and old movies intrigued him for a while. He idolized one English teacher and decided that this was what he would study, not science. The Vietnam War was winding down, and the protests that had occurred even at Homestead seemed less important now. The counterculture was changing. Hippies were leaving the Haight and heading for the forests of Northern California. Ecological issues replaced foreign policy as the touchstone for protest.

By the beginning of his senior year in high school, Steve was contributing his light show skills to a multimedia event to raise money to feed the hungry. His senior class elected an easygoing, bike-riding ecological activist as president. "We thought it was so cool to be environmentally hip, " laughs Anzur, a former pom-pom girl, "that for our school spirit day, after all the other classes had painted traditional posters and things, we cleaned up the entire campus, piled up the garbage bins, and added a single poster that said 'Spirit Comes From Within.'"

Sixteen-year-old Steve was in his senior year at Homestead, his hair was straight and down to his shoulders, and by then he was spending less and less time at the school. His world revolved around Stanford, where he was taking freshman English classes, and his girlfriend, Colleen Sampson, who was his age but in the class behind him.

Colleen was the kind of high school student Steve could relate to, and they had moved in similar artistic, bohemian circles for a while. When he met her, she was in the midst of illustrating an animated movie at Homestead that used music composed by Izu. To avoid supervision, they did much of the work at night, from 1 A.M. to dawn on the weekends. And since the band would jam at the same time, working on the film turned into a kind of free-form party with Steve running the light show.

"He walked around with the most torn blue jeans—more rips than pants actually," recalls Colleen. "He shuffled around and looked half-mad. That's why I liked him. He had a lot of angst. It was like a big darkness around him."

Colleen was caught in the cross fire of a home life that was coming apart as her parents approached divorce. "Then Steve came along. There was all the darkness, but another side to him as well, nothing but softness about him."

It was first love.

One afternoon in October of 1971, the phone rang at the Jobs house in Cupertino. It was Woz. He had reenrolled in college at the

University of California at Berkeley, was living in a dorm, and had grown his hair long. Steve was a frequent visitor. Woz's mother had given him an article in that month's *Esquire*. When Steve came to the phone Woz proceeded to read him long passages from "Secrets of the Little Blue Box."

The article, published in the October 1971 issue of *Esquire*, introduced the shadowy world of "phone phreaks" to the general public. With the hyperbole common to journalism, the writer painted a picture of emotionally crippled, lonely souls scattered around the country, communicating solely through the telephone. The phreaks were to phones what hackers were to computers, although they had an edge of the outlaw to them that made their preoccupation both more glamorous and dangerous. They were a band of technologically savvy hippies, counterculturally influenced scientists who had abandoned convention to pursue their knowledge of electronics in illegal channels. They had discovered that by playing certain frequencies of tones into telephone receivers they could fool AT&T's long-distance switching equipment into placing calls for free.

The game turned on the tones that the telecommunications giant used internally to place and route calls. By knowing these codes and understanding the elements of phone system hardware and software— the bridges, tandems, switching trunks, routing indicators, supervisory signals, and traffic position stations—an astute player could make calls anywhere in the world without paying for them. Phone phreaking was easy to justify in the climate of the early seventies. After all, placing calls for free wasn't really stealing or hurting anyone. The only one losing was the phone company, which was inextricably linked to the establishment. In the youthful view, pulling the wool over Big Brother's eyes was an admirable pursuit. After all, 1971 was the year that Lt. William Calley was convicted of the My Lai massacre, the year of the publication of the "Pentagon Papers," and the year when the power of youth to influence events was at its greatest—America was pulling out of Vietnam after all. If you were smarter than the phone company and could get away with it, all power to you. It was Power to the People at the phone booth level.

While the idea of circumventing Ma Bell's billing cycle may have been interesting as a footnote to the history of the counterculture, what really made phone phreaking intriguing was the cast of characters that the *Esquire* article introduced. They had names like Captain Crunch, Dr. No, Peter Perpendicular, and The Snark. Suddenly engineering types, those who could manipulate machinery and build scientific devices, were colorful. They were unique and dimensional, not gray and boring like the engineers in the Silicon Valley. For a pair of young wireheads who loved pranks for the fun of them, who were immersed in the culture of electronics, and who had a taste for outsmarting authority, phone phreaks sounded like true brothers in arms.

They headed for the Stanford library to do some research. Woz understood the idea behind an oscillator, an electronic device that generates tones, and armed with the technical information in the *Esquire* article and a book of tables he located at Stanford, he built one from a rudimentary design in an old engineering article. Steve had built a frequency counter several years earlier and at H-P had worked on assembly lines putting them together. These were close enough to oscillators that he was able to test the devices that Woz produced.

At first they went nowhere fast. Analog oscillators, machines that work in the traditional electronic world of tubes and wires to produce tones, are notoriously finicky. Weather, dust, jolts, and stray jiggles can set them off calibration. After a month or so, Woz decided to build an entirely digital blue box. After all, he had built a computer, why not a ten-key box that could emit tones? As usual, he dove into the project, neglecting his coursework and using Berkeley's computers to help design the logic of the box.[5] Steve spent all his free time in Woz's dorm room, helping test and debug the circuitry as they built prototypes.

Finally, after the first of the year, Woz came up with a schematic that he was sure would work. Part of the challenge of building the box was to do so in as small a packet as possible. It was no good to design a clunky blue box—the idea was to design a better blue box than any other phreaks were using. That made the quest worthwhile, that was the thrill of electronics. To reduce the number of parts and the complexity of the device, Woz added a feature that foreshadowed some of his later innovations: He removed the on-off switch and made the box work automatically whenever one of the keys was pressed. A small modification, but it was that kind of personal attention to detail that would always characterize a Woz design. With the design completed, they built the box and it worked like a charm. Woz chose the name Berkeley Blue and Steve, always the more adventurous, selected the moniker Oaf Toebar for his phreak alias.

Just as hanging the sheet with the obscene finger design was only worthwhile if everyone knew who was behind it, the two cohorts were determined to show off their newest invention. They knew that Captain Crunch—whose name came from the fact he had discovered a whistle in a box of Cap'n Crunch cereal that emitted the tone needed to breach AT&T equipment—lived in Northern California. Steve set off to track him down. After calling the writer of the *Esquire* story and being rebuffed, Steve found that Crunch was well known in the San Jose area FM radio world, which in the early seventies was a weak competitor to the all-powerful AM radio. Crunch was an amateur radio operator and broadcast a pirate FM signal, San Jose Free Radio, from the back of his van on weekends. Eventually, through a fellow Berkeley phreak, they identified him as John Draper and left a message for him at a local FM station. Within moments Draper called them back.

They arranged a meeting in Woz's dorm room several nights later. At the appointed hour, with Steve and Woz on tenterhooks, Draper showed up. He was filthy from living in his van and had missing teeth, wild unkempt hair, and a gleam in his eyes that matched his moniker and appearance.

"Are you Captain Crunch?" Woz asked incredulously.

"I am he," replied the famous phone phreak, and with no further ado he walked to the telephone and started to send calls across the world.[6] For hours he led the two fledgling phreaks through the world of telephony, using Woz's blue box throughout. He taught them everything they needed to know about outsmarting the phone company. "It was the most astounding meeting we had ever had," recalls Woz.[7]

That night they were so excited that Woz drove back to Los Altos with Steve. On the way, the temperamental Fiat broke down and the pair decided to use the blue box to call for help. When the operator asked one question too many, the two hung up and were dialing a legal call when a police car stopped to take a closer look at the two stringy-haired boys. Certain that they had been discovered, Steve was about to toss the box into the bushes when he thought better of it and palmed it to Woz. It was swiftly uncovered when the cops frisked the two long-haired youths for drugs.

"What's this?"

"A music synthesizer," said Woz, thinking fast.

"What's this orange button for?"

"Oh, that's for calibration," Steve explained helpfully.

"It's a computer-controlled synthesizer," added Woz.

"Well, then where's the computer?" asked the still-suspicious cop.

"That plugs inside," replied Steve.

"Too bad, but I think a guy named Moog beat you to it."

"That's okay. He sent us the schematics," concluded the younger phreak.[8]

They got away that night and decided they had to be extremely careful about using the boxes, but the close shave did nothing to dampen their enthusiasm. The fact that using the blue box was illegal only made it more fun. Because Draper had been impressed — "it never drifted or needed tuning, like most of the ones around" the notorious phreak explained[9]—they knew they were onto something. As soon as they started to show the two prototypes to friends, it became obvious that there was a lot of interest in them.

Everyone wanted one, and Steve delighted in doing demonstrations, especially at Homestead High, where the school's two pay phone booths were about ten feet apart. Starting from one phone, he could ring the other, speak into one receiver, and then hear his own voice on the other as the signal went through numerous circuits and telecommunications satellites around the world. Steve had another demonstration that made sure the rest of the school knew what he was up to as well.

"He liked to call Dial-a-Tune in London from one of the pay phones," recalls Carl Ho, a high school classmate. "He'd attach a card saying 'Listen, but don't hang up' and then leave the phone off the hook. On the other one he would call the number for 'time' in Nepal and leave it off the hook. All day long the lines would be open."

Woz plunged into the world of phreaking, subscribing to newsletters and clipping every article he could find, becoming an absolute expert on the subject. Just as he had done when he became obsessed with computers in high school and college, he systematically scoured the literature. He became a tireless researcher and through Draper became acquainted with various cells of phone phreaks in the Bay area. He refined his design and was eventually able to fit the blue box into a case the size of an H-P calculator, then the sine qua non of engineering calculators. It was an elegant device, Woz's first working digital design, and it did what it was supposed to do.

Steve convinced Woz to sell them. Woz would have been perfectly content to play with the toy on his own, but Steve was a scrappy kid with a nose for money, and he wanted to buy a new car for the upcoming school year. He took care of procuring the parts while Woz did the assembly. At first it took four hours to assemble the boxes with $40 worth of parts. They then sold the boxes for $150. Later, as the orders continued, Steve arranged to have a printed circuit board made up, which cut the assembly time to less than one hour. In addition to fitting the whole package into a small blue box, they added a card, handwritten with a purple Flair pen, saying "He's got the whole world in his hand." It represented an informal guarantee: Any box returned with a card inside would be repaired by Woz. They also raised the prices, depending on who was buying: They charged students $150; they charged people with real money as much as $300.

They began their sales effort in the dormitories at Berkeley. Because the two phreaks couldn't exactly advertise, they decided to knock on doors. The idea was to ask for a fictitious person and in doing so mention phone phreaking, making long distance calls for free. If the person who answered was interested, he or she would be invited to a demonstration; if not, the two apologized and tried another door. It was not a high-volume approach, but there were more than enough interested students to fill Woz's room once a week for demonstrations. As they sold more boxes, word of mouth expanded their business.

The demonstrations were a point of honor for Woz, who thoroughly enjoyed being in the spotlight. He would begin by explaining the principles behind the phone company switching equipment and then proceed to make a series of international calls. One evening Woz called the Vatican. He told them he was Henry Kissinger, and they sent someone "to wake the pope in the middle of the night before they figured out it wasn't Kissinger," recalls Steve.[10]

As Steve's senior year in high school continued and the business of selling the blue boxes netted him more money, he grew less interested in spending time at Homestead. He was known throughout the senior class as the guy selling blue boxes, and his girlfriend was the girl making the crazy movie. The two spent many idyllic afternoons that year taking long walks in the Santa Cruz Mountains or along the Pacific Ocean beaches. He introduced her to Bob Dylan, Beethoven, and the music of the Big Bands, which he had developed an interest in. They drank wine, smoked pot, and Steve dropped LSD for the first time in a wheat field.

"It was great. I had been listening to a lot of Bach. All of a sudden the wheat field was playing Bach. It was the most wonderful experience of my life up to that point. I felt like the conductor of this symphony with Bach coming through the wheat field," remembers Steve.[11]

It was not just the idyllic life of a teenager; there was also something in the California air. "This was California. You could get LSD fresh made at Stanford. You could sleep on the beach at night with your girlfriend. California has a sense of experimentation, an openness to new possibilities."[12]

Woz didn't quite understand all this. He harbored suspicions about the movie Colleen and Steve were making at Homestead and never warmed to her. She wasn't a wirehead and only seemed to get in the way of their friendship.

Woz never had time for drugs and couldn't understand his younger friend's interest in them. Woz's idea of a good time was to talk about esoteric points of electronics, a line of conversation that Steve could follow but wasn't interested in. Steve was interested in making money, and the blue boxes were selling. They also shared a passion for Bob Dylan that kept them together. All three spent hours at a Santa Cruz store that specialized in Dylan memorabilia, and Steve prided himself on having all the bootleg and basement tapes he could find. Steve fumbled with the guitar, played his harmonicas, and they all pored over Dylan's lyrics looking for meaning.

Selling the blue boxes had been fun for a while, but by the summer before he left for college Steve was growing bored with it. First, there was the illegal factor. Draper was arrested in 1972, fined $1,000, and placed on five years' probation for wire fraud.[13] Rumors were rife throughout the phreaking world that the mafia was about to enter the lucrative business of free calls, and many of the phone companies were hiring security guards and paying informants to squeal on manufacturers of boxes. The whole business was losing its prankster edge and was being replaced by something more sinister.

There was also raw danger. One summer evening in Sunnyvale, as Steve escorted a customer to the parking lot of a pizza parlor to turn over a blue box, he found a gun in his stomach. "There were 1800 things I could do, but every one had some probability that he would shoot me in the stomach. I handed over the box."[14]

Steve had broader vistas and was searching for the answers to something that was smoldering inside him. It wasn't something that he could discover with a blue box. The summer after high school, he and

Colleen rented a cabin deep in a canyon up Skyline Drive, which runs on the ridge of the Santa Cruz Mountains. Steve had the money from the blue boxes, and the two of them envisioned a summer of love. Steve's father was a little less enthusiastic.

"I just said, 'I'm going to live with [. . . Colleen],'" remembered Steve.

"My father said, 'What?'

"'Yeah. We rented this cabin. We're going to live together.'

"He said, 'No, you're not.'

"I said, 'Yes, I am.'

"He said, 'No, you're not.'

"I said, 'Well, bye.'"[15]

Steve supported them by selling the boxes. He had saved some money, but the supply of new income was not very dependable. A month later, when the red Fiat caught on fire, Steve had to come up with the money to fix it. His father helped him tow it, but he wasn't about to lend him money while he was living with his high school sweetheart in a shack in the woods. With that Steve, Colleen, and Woz went looking for a job.

The Westgate Mall in San Jose is one of those covered concrete shopping centers with piped-in Muzak and artificial lighting. Enormous and air conditioned, it is the kind of place where parents can let their children run free to play in the building's specially supervised indoor playground. Not far from Homestead High School in the sprawling flatlands of San Jose, it was also popular as an after-school meeting place for the region's teenagers. There were a couple of fast-food outlets and plenty of tables at which to sit and while away the hours.

In the summer of 1972, parents and children who arrived at the mall were treated to special entertainment. In an effort to increase traffic, the mall decided to hire Steve, Colleen, and Woz to perform a kind of ersatz skit for the kids. The pay was $3 an hour, which translated to $12 each day for the part-time performers.

Daily, three characters from *Alice in Wonderland* danced and pranced their way around the mall's playground for four hours in the afternoons. Dressed in heavy papier maché costumes, the boys were able to hide their long, stringy hair. Portraying the Mad Hatter and White Rabbit, they chased a demurely attired Alice, whose long blonde hair was covered by a thick wig, down the slides and around the climbing gyms of the playground. Every once in a while Steve would break out his guitar and sing a few songs. The toddlers didn't find the musical entertainment inspiring.

As the summer wore on, the costumes were bashed and broken, and the enthusiasm of the trio wore thin. Woz thoroughly enjoyed playing the roles and had a great time. Steve, who traded roles with him, found it tedious and exhausting. Although he needed the money and enjoyed spending time with Colleen, he couldn't wait for September, when he would leave for college.

Headstrong, forthright, and determined, Steve Jobs was ready to set out on his own. He couldn't wait for the future that college promised.

4

Academia, Acid, and Atari

For many emotionally immature kids, trekking off to college means getting away from home—freedom from parents. Steve was no exception. He didn't want to go to Berkeley or Stanford because they were too close. The college that Steve decided upon, early in his senior year of high school, was Reed College in Portland, Oregon. Reed was, and is, the Pacific Northwest's premier liberal arts college. Private and expensive, it was founded in the late nineteenth century by an eccentric millionaire and has always had the reputation for attracting brilliant individuals.

His parents were horrified. Not only was it expensive, but it was a long way from home. "Steve said that Reed was the only college he wanted to go to," recalls Clara Jobs, "and if he couldn't go there, he didn't want to go anywhere."[1] Once again the spoiled, young, headstrong boy prevailed over his parents. They bit the bullet, saved their money, and sent him off to Reed.

The parting on campus a few days before school started in 1972 was anything but warm and teary. "It wasn't real cordial. I sort of said,

'Well, thanks, bye.' I didn't even want the buildings to see that my parents were there. I didn't want parents at that time. I just wanted to be like an orphan from Kentucky who had bummed around the country hopping freight trains for years. I wanted to find out what life was all about."[2] There was no role in that quest for adopted parents.

The Reed campus is physically gorgeous, with ivy-covered red brick buildings, steep gabled slate roofs, verdigris-coated copper gutters, and lots of bay windows looking out over endless gardens. The academic program is rigorous and is designed to nurture the individual talents of the student. The reading lists for freshmen are long and difficult, not the kind of easy laissez-faire courses Steve had taken at Homestead High. Although liberal politics were important at Reed, the school had none of the political fire and brimstone for which Berkeley was famous. Especially in the waning days of the Vietnam War, the privileged student body at Reed was more interested in personal pursuits than political activism. That suited Steve perfectly.

In the fall of 1972, Richard Nixon was on the verge of winning reelection to the presidency by a landslide over George McGovern. The damage of the Watergate break-in looked as if it had been contained. The age of the "Me Generation" was about to dawn. Steve's was the first college class in a decade that hadn't had to face the draft. In the wake of the pull-out from Vietnam, the powerful political currents of the preceding years were giving way to an inwardly directed search for answers, and middle-class American youth was about to abandon political activism. Without that conflict to galvanize them, the inner voyages of discovery that the counterculture's fascination with drugs, alternative religions and lifestyles had produced suddenly veered from a political statement to a tool for self-fulfillment.

Psychedelic drugs opened an entirely new inner realm, but they were also dangerous. Spaced-out kids took walks off rooftops sure that they could fly. Others snapped in the midst of soaring experiences and never returned to reality. If one were going to try to stay in the state of enlightened consciousness that LSD, or acid, could produce, it would be necessary to find a safer way to get there than through chemicals. Eastern, meditative religions seemed the logical path to safely reaching the state of higher awareness. Like many of his peers, Steve was searching for a way to comprehend his universe, to find out who he was. The tools for the journey were mind-expanding drugs and Eastern mysticism.

Throughout the year, Steve went barefoot, except in the deepest snow, when he would wear his Birkenstock sandals. He tried dance and Western history courses, but he wasn't interested in the rigorous academic study required at Reed. Sitting cross-legged in a crawl space above a dorm room, fasting, meditating, and dropping acid were much more suited to his quest for understanding.

"I was interested in Eastern mysticism, which hit the shores about then. At Reed there was a constant flow of people stopping by, such as LSD guru Timothy Leary, Harvard lecturer and mystic Richard Alpert, a.k.a. Baba Ram Dass, and poet Gary Snyder. That was the time when every college student in the country read *Be Here Now* and *Diet for a Small Planet*."[3]

Pursuing his own journey of internal discovery did little to endear Steve to his teachers. By the end of the first semester, his grades were poor, and in the wake of pressure from his parents to shape up and make something out of the thousands of dollars they were spending on his education, he did just the opposite. With typical Steve Jobs contrariness, he dropped out of school. He didn't leave the campus but stayed on living in dorm rooms vacated by other students who had left to pursue other interests. It would be a year before he actually left the campus.

Reed, being a good liberal school, didn't mind Steve's vagrancy. Steve made friends with Jack Dudman, the school's dean of students. The two engaged in endless discussions. "Steve had a very inquiring mind that was enormously attractive," Dudman reports. "You wouldn't get away with bland statements. He refused to accept automatically received truths. He wanted to examine everything himself."[4]

Steve's decision to drop out but live off the school's good fortune made him something of a celebrity. His hair was long, lank, and stringy. He dressed in torn trousers and shirts and smelled bad. But he was seen as someone on a quest, and that gave him a certain right to be eccentric.

"I met him at a party in my dorm early in our freshman year," recalls Elizabeth Holmes, a striking six-foot-tall blonde with clear blue eyes who was also a member of the freshman class. "He made a real impression on me because of what a jerk he was. I instantly disliked him and didn't talk with him for months."

Lively, cheerful, and wholesomely perfect, Holmes has the kind of California good looks that the state exported to the rest of the world.

She also possesses a quick, analytic mind; later she would off-handedly join MENSA, the "genius" club with a notoriously difficult entrance exam, to qualify for a scholarship they offered. Furthermore, she understood the milieu that Steve came from. Holmes grew up in Saratoga, California, about four miles from Homestead High, in a household ruled by a father who managed major engineering projects at IBM's enormous Silicon Valley installation.

"I skipped my senior year in high school because I just had to get away from home. As soon as I got out of the house, I could turn into the flower child I really wanted to be." She was two weeks older than Steve, and the two were the youngest kids in that year's freshman class.

"I was standing by myself at a party one weekend, and I noticed him talking to a guy I knew from the dorm—it was a coed dorm. Next thing I knew he came over and asked me this question: 'Would you sleep with that man,' indicating the guy he had been talking to, 'for $20?'

"I looked at him and said, 'What?!'

"'How about for $50?'

"I was very righteous in those days, so I started to get upset.

"'How about $100?'

"I was really steaming now, so I said, 'What do you think I am?'

"To which he replied, 'We know what you are, we're simply trying to determine your price.'"

The two did not become fast friends.

Steve did find one kindred spirit who shared many of the same interests on the spiritual path. Dan Kottke was a wild-haired freak in his own right, with a cascade of frizzy, tangled hair that surrounded his head like a kind of mane. Soft-spoken, diffident, gentle, and very bright, Kottke was a musician with a guitarist cousin, Leo Kottke, who was known in certain hip music circles. He had grown up in a suburb of New York and was a National Merit Scholar and a superb pianist.

"He was incredibly dashing," recalls Holmes, almost wistfully now. "I know it is hard to imagine a long-haired hippie as dashing, but for me, coming from such a strait-laced family, he was what I dreamed of."

Kottke was as interested in raising his spiritual consciousness as Steve and was already dabbling with psychedelics and pot. The two of them fell into a close relationship almost at once. "I don't think he had any other friends," says Kottke, "so I thought, 'here is someone I can relate to.'"

During the second semester of their freshman year, when Steve was sleeping wherever he could find space, their relationship intensified. Above Kottke's room was a crawl space where the two of them experimented with sleep deprivation, drugs, and diets. They were searching for a way to extend the high of LSD to life itself. Steve took to spending most of his days in the campus library reading about Eastern mysticism and traded books with Kottke. With Suzuki's *Zen Mind, Beginner's Mind*, the two discovered Zen Buddhism.

"It placed value on experience versus intellectual understanding," says Steve. "I saw a lot of people contemplating things that didn't seem to lead too many places. I got very interested in people who had discovered something more significant than an intellectual, abstract understanding. I started to see intuition, spontaneity, as a higher form of consciousness. It was closely tied to the fundamental elements of Zen and I thought that was a pretty interesting idea."[5]

By this time, the group included Elizabeth Holmes, who had became Kottke's girlfriend. According to Holmes, who didn't use drugs, the two went through weekly adventures with chemical substances to unlock the doors of perception.

"I remember one night," she says, "we were sitting by a big fire and there was a raging storm outside. The two of them were playing a game called *kriegspiel*, which is German for 'war game.' It's a version of chess, with two separate boards and sets of pieces, and neither player is allowed to see the other player's moves. A moderator, who was me this particular time, tells you if the next move you want to make is possible. It was very popular with the IBMers and my father had taught it to me.

"They sat there with their backs to each other and moved blind. The added wrinkle was that the two of them were tripping. I remember feeling that I could barely keep up, and I was completely sober. It was really wild."

On a small campus like Reed, two guys dropping acid every week or so were visible. They soon came to the attention of one of the campus' other most formidable personalities, Robert Friedland. Friedland was elected student body president during their freshman year and was one of the most notorious characters on campus, where he was perpetually dressed in Indian robes. He had been arrested a year before at San Francisco International airport for possession of LSD. Sentenced to several years in jail for 30,000 tabs of acid he had in his raincoat when arrested, he reenrolled at Reed after he was released and ran for student body president to prove that he was really a good person. He won the election easily.

Steve met him when he was trying to sell his electric IBM typewriter, a high school graduation gift from his parents. He came to see Friedland, who had expressed an interest in it. The student body president was in the midst of making love with his girlfriend, and instead of telling Steve to return later, invited him to come in and watch. "He wasn't intimidated at all," says Steve. "I thought, 'This is kind of far out. My mother and father would never do anything like this.'"[6]

Soon Kottke and Steve became friends with the student body president. Friedland, another seeker on the road to enlightenment, was from a wealthy family and had a farm nearby. He named it the All-One Farm.

"Robert was the first person I met who was firmly convinced that the phenomenon of enlightenment existed," recalled Steve. "I was very impressed by that and very curious."[7]

Friedland, for his part, found Steve's personality compelling. "He was always walking around barefoot. He was one of the freaks of the campus. The thing that struck me was his intensity. Whatever he was interested in he would generally carry to an irrational extreme. He wasn't a rapper. One of his numbers was to stare at the person he was talking to. He would stare into their eyeballs, ask some question, and want a response without the other person averting their eyes."[8]

According to Kottke, Steve learned an enormous amount from Friedland, much of it having to do with personality and charisma. "Robert was very much an outgoing, charismatic guy, a real salesman. But he's also a con man, and when I first met Steve he was shy and self-effacing, a very private guy. He had long hair down to his shoulders. I remember myself being a lot more extroverted, with lots of friends.

"I think Robert taught him a lot about selling, about coming out of his shell, of opening up and taking charge of a situation. Robert was one of those guys who was always the center of attention. He'd walk into a room and you would instantly notice him. Steve was the absolute opposite when he came to Reed. After he spent time with Robert, some of it started to rub off."

Nonetheless, Steve was always extremely private. Kottke considered Steve his best friend at Reed, but in all the time they were together, Kottke never knew that his friend was involved in blue boxing. And it's all the more unusual because Kottke was always interested in electronics.

"We were good friends, but it's just the kind of guy he is. It's like there are separate compartments in his head, and certain people get to find out one thing or another. No one gets to know all the pieces but Steve."

At the end of the freshman year, with the dorms empty for the summer, Steve had no choice but to move out. He rented an unheated room over a nearby garage for $25 a month. Friedland headed for India to study with Ram Dass' guru, Neem Kairolie Baba. Steve was in desperate need of money and took a job in the school's psychology department repairing laboratory equipment. Ron Fial, an assistant professor of psychology, worked with him. "He was very good. He often didn't want to just fix something. He would bring in something that had been completely redesigned."[9] The experiences with frequency counters and blue boxes stood him in good stead.

When the next school year started, he stayed on at Reed. He very shrewdly perceived that he could get just as good an education without the credit. He audited classes, lived in his tiny room, and experimented with various sleep and dietary deprivation schemes. Fasting was a part of this regime. Steve was so poor that he was on a continual fast anyway. For a long time all he ate was Roman Meal cereal.

"After a few days you start to feel great," Steve says about fasting. "After a week you start to feel fantastic. You get a ton of vitality from not having to digest all this food. I was in great shape. I felt I could get up and walk to San Francisco anytime I wanted."[10]

His friends Kottke and Holmes kept an eye on him and fed him. Holmes was living in a specialty dorm devoted to German language students and had finagled a special dietary clearance to cook her own meals.

Holmes recalls Steve coming to dinner frequently, and that he and Kottke tripped often. Indeed, much of their relationship was based on the close rapport that they had while tripping. They would get into a state and start free associating. Holmes would always feel left out, but they needed someone to keep it together, "to be the dorm mommy," as she puts it.

Sundays were the night of the Hare Krishna feasts at the Portland temple. The group, including Friedland, would head for the temple, sit through a lecture, and then take part in ecstatic dancing and chanting that was a fundamental element of the religion. Finally, they would eat heaping quantities of food and take plates home. It was the only full meal they would have for the week.

By the fall of 1973, the major influence on the band of friends was Neem Kairolie Baba, guru to Richard Alpert/Baba Ram Dass. The guru had rescued Alpert when, after taking hundreds of acid trips and voyaging to India in search of the truth, he was in despair of ever finding the right teacher. The result was the book *Be Here Now*, which was a partly drawn, partly written document about the spiritual journey that Alpert took as a consequence of meeting Neem Kairolie. The book was a favorite among acid trippers because Alpert whole-heartedly supports taking psychedelics throughout the book. Neem Kairolie was Friedland's guru also, and the charismatic student body president had spent the summer of 1973 in India sitting at the great man's feet.

"Robert Friedland very much got the real transmission of what Neem Kairolie was all about, and it was obvious in his life when he returned," explains Kottke. "He was a very enlightened guy, and Steve and I saw that light in his eyes that fall. We determined to go the following summer and follow in his footsteps."

Soon the group took to spending weekends on the 200 acres of wheat fields, pine forests, and apple orchards at the All-One Farm. To scare the deer away from the wheat, they blew conch shells. This contrasted with their neighbors, who fired shotguns. They worked on their consciousness and pursued self-sufficiency and living off the land. The spread was listed in the hippie directories of the day as a stopping place on the spiritual journey, a country commune where anyone who wished could practice their agrarian, pacifistic ideals.

A stream of people stopped in and stayed throughout the early seventies. Colleen, Steve's high school sweetheart, showed up to stay on the farm after she graduated from high school and became involved with another character on the periphery of the group. She and Steve had drifted apart during his first year in college; he had wanted her to drop out of school and come with him but she hadn't.

Steve had few girlfriends during that period, according to Holmes. The focus of the All-One Farm was never on sexual freedom or heavy drug use. Although Kottke and Steve experimented with psychedelics, the farm was a spiritual mecca of sorts, and among the forests and buildings a variety of meditation retreats and encounters were the order of the day.

"While Steve was always very interested in the spiritual ideas behind it, and he was very sincere," says Holmes, "he also had a much more practical bent than the rest of us. He was involved with that esoteric electronic stuff in California."

By the beginning of 1974, Steve was back in California living at his parents' house. Although the spiritual side of things was important, the practical issues of finances and making ends meet provided an anchor. The days of bumming around on campus were nearly over for him. Steve traveled up to the Farm often to visit. He took over an apple orchard that had been neglected and brought it back to life, and wired a barn for electricity so that they could sell wood stoves from the *Whole Earth Catalogue*. But he was growing a little tired of being a pauper and was still as much an outsider, even in his group of close friends. Something else was driving him.

"I think it's clear that Steve always had a kind of chip on his shoulder," says Kottke. "He always had to prove himself. Steve was the kind of person just waiting to find the right cause. He needed a banner to carry. He was waiting for the right crusade."

In the spring of 1974, he was living at his parents' house idly looking through the *San Jose Mercury News*, when he saw an ad from Atari, a company that was a little outrageous even in wild and woolly Silicon Valley. In the aftermath of the remarkable success of the company's video game *Pong*—within days after installing the first game at a tavern in Sunnyvale there was a line of players stretching down the block—Atari was looking for electronics technicians. A famous ad in the world of high-tech, their recruitment ads promised, "Have fun and make money." Steve applied.

To his shock he was hired.

The terrific success of *Pong* fueled the video game world, and since this new industry was headquartered at Atari, the company was growing rapidly in 1974. The games were in bars and taverns. The arcades had yet to become the craze that they would in a couple of years, but that too was beginning. Al Alcorn was the chief engineer at Atari and had helped design and build *Pong*. He worked with Nolan Bushnell, who started the company.

"Atari was the biggest name in video games," says Alcorn. "We were used to folks showing up and saying something like, 'I like your location, I like what you're doing, so I'm going to work here.' It was part of the brashness of the Valley. When I heard what their skills were, more often than not I'd say, 'That's it, you're great, you've got a job.'"

"One day the personnel director came by and said, 'We've got this weird guy here. He says he won't leave until we hire him. We either call the cops or take him.' So I said bring him in.

"Steve appeared dressed in his usual scruffy outfit, an 18-year-old, long-haired drop-out of Reed College. I don't know why I hired him," remembers Alcorn, "except that he was determined to have the job, and there was some spark, some inner energy, an attitude that he was going to get it done."

Alcorn gave him to Don Lang, who said, "What are you giving me this guy for? He has b.o. and he's different, a goddamn hippie." Alcorn wound up cutting a deal with Lang: Steve could come in at night and wouldn't bother anybody. Alcorn and Lang then sent him off with Ron Wayne, a technician, who had previously worked in Las Vegas fixing and designing slot machines.

Wayne and Steve got along. With 15 years separating them, they were both social outcasts of a certain kind. Steve had aggressively adopted the unkempt, unwashed appearance of a 1970s version of Bob Dylan. Wayne was a kind of artist, or so he fancied himself. His art was in spray painting murals on slot machines and video games, an esoteric skill most closely related to van painting. Although these two were the prime eccentrics, Atari's engineering department wasn't quite sane anyway. For example, Alcorn had hired a backup engineering chief, Rod Holt, because of the hobby that the team shared: off-road motorcycling. Every Monday would be high anxiety for Alcorn as he waited to find out who would come back with broken legs, hands, or faces.

In the wild world of Atari, a long-haired hippie, Steve Jobs, a kid who worked through the nights, fit in. He was given a number of minor tasks during that spring of 1974, as befit his role as a technician. He wasn't unhappy with his employment at Atari, but he had an insatiable urge to make the pilgrimage to India, to find spiritual enlightenment, and to do so he needed the money they were paying plus more. He was prepared to make the journey as a mendicant, a spiritual beggar dependent upon the kindness of strangers, but to get there was still expensive. In typical fashion, Steve strolled into Alcorn's office one day and asked for the money to go to India. "To see his guru," recalls the former head of engineering, who laughed in his face.

"Steve was determined to go," Kottke says, talking of India. "I didn't have any money, and he had this great job at Atari. He had saved thousands of dollars and offered to pay my airfare, which was very generous. Had he not offered it, the trip probably wouldn't have happened because he wanted someone to travel with."

Kottke called up his parents and told them he was going to India with his friend, who was going to pay for his ticket. Kottke's parents, worried that their son would never come back, gave him a round-trip ticket and plenty of money.

Alcorn, who was amused by Steve's weirdness, came up with a way to give him the time off. It so happened that he had a problem with the Germans who were selling Atari games in that country. Atari was selling overseas versions with circuit boards that made the games work in different countries, each of which had a different mix of power supplies, voltages and wattages. But the local distributors had to assemble the boards and put the games into place. The Germans couldn't figure out how to do the grounding properly.

"The problem was with the power. The Germans were at 50 cycles per second, as opposed to the U.S. at 60. When you plug a TV set meant for 60 cycles into it, if the chassis wiring isn't absolutely right and perfectly grounded, you see bands of color moving through the picture—humm bars. It's all very irritating."

Alcorn finally decided, "Hey, Jobs is going to India. I'll cut a deal with him and send him to Germany one-way to do the rewiring work." As it turned out, it was more expensive to do the journey this way, but Steve had money in the bank. He'd been living at home with his parents while being paid $4 an hour to be a technician, and he was always good at saving money.

When he arrived in Germany, he caused a sensation. The Germans weren't expecting a wild-eyed, hippie technician. He solved their problem in two hours, thanks to a two-hour course in ground loops that Alcorn had given him.

When he headed for the airport in Frankfurt, he was prepared to give up all his worldly possessions and desires as soon as he landed in New Delhi. He was completely wrapped up in his own spiritual agenda. When he arrived in India he discovered what having nothing really meant.

5
Enlightenment

In the summer of 1974, America watched its government come unglued. The Senate Watergate committee hearings were televised, and the country was riveted to the proceedings. The unraveling skein of political misdeeds and criminal obstruction was reaching closer and closer to the Oval Office. Liberal and conservative, hippie and flag-waving patriot were all joined in this national paroxysm of guilt and distaste.

However, there was a difference for those who had grown up just after the height of the Vietnam protests. For the younger brothers and sisters, the ones who had missed the passion of protest and the personal involvement in politics of the sixties, the Watergate hearings were of less interest. The new generation, the junior versions of the hippies and countercultural bombers, were concerned with other, more personal matters.

The hippie movement was fizzling out. Self-fulfillment was of less concern than self-satisfaction. While the lure of India was waning for many, Steve Jobs and Dan Kottke were still pursuing the dream. Steve had a hole in his heart to fill, and he thought that India might hold the answer. Dan was looking for new experiences.

Steve headed to Switzerland after completing his duties in Germany. Then he flew to New Delhi, three weeks earlier than Kottke, and proceeded to see true poverty.

In 1974 the Bangladesh disaster was in its aftermath. War between Moslem factions in Pakistan during the early seventies had created a famine, exacerbated by heavy monsoons and flooding that threatened millions. To quell riots, troops from the conservative West were called in to quash the Bangladesh separatist movement. Atrocities were rampant, and more than one million were killed in the civil war. Then war broke out between India and Pakistan, and millions of refugees were caught in the middle. India's already heavy concentrations of beggars were swollen by an estimated ten million refugees who fled the internecine warfare. The resulting uneasy truce came apart at the seams early in 1974 when the Soviet-backed leader was assassinated and the country again plunged into civil war.

Into this swirling maelstrom of humanity, Steve appeared. He was barefoot and dressed in nothing more than jeans and a T-shirt. But these were his choices. He was confronted with people who had no choices.

Since the idea behind the trip was to make the journey as a mendicant, he immediately traded his Western clothes for a lunghi, a loin cloth that is the standard clothing for mendicant travelers, and gave away everything else he had. He headed north from Delhi, which sits on a high plain, toward the Himalayas, the center for spirituality in India.

The well-worn route for seekers of the truth involved following the Ganges, the great river of the Indian subcontinent, up to its source high in the Himalayas, and that was exactly the path he took. The Ganges is the heart of Indian civilization. All along the brown and muddy river, festivals and religious events combine with the daily ritual of clothes washing and the passing of hordes of disciples and seekers to create an astonishing transient ritual. The Hindu religion puts great store on the ecstatic and visual, on the celebration of Krishna's vitality, and those celebrations generally occur along the Ganges.

As he walked up the river, Steve saw sights that were as foreign to him as they had been to thousands of Westerners for hundreds of years. Brightly decorated funeral rafts were set afire and then set adrift. Holy men sat cross-legged on rock ledges carved out high in the faces of sheer river walls. Festivals sported hundreds of banners and brightly colored floats borne on the backs of hundreds of followers. The aromas of incense and saffron, herbs and tea, lotus flowers and patchouli mingled with the odors of human excrement and disease. Hand-in-hand with being a spiritual center of India, the Ganges is also the last stop for most of the country's starving beggars. It is the place to die, and every day hundreds do so along its banks. Steve Jobs saw death close up.

As he waited for Kottke to join him, before the two took off for Neem Kairolie's ashram, Steve attended the Kumbhmela, a large religious festival held once every 12 years. He slept in deserted, abandoned ashrams. He pretended to be as poor as the people surrounding him.

"I was walking around in the Himalayas," Steve relates "and I stumbled onto this thing that turned out to be a religious festival. There was this baba, the holy man of this particular festival, with his large group of followers. I could smell good food. I hadn't been fortunate enough to smell good food for a long time, so I wandered up to pay my respects and eat some lunch.

"For some reason, this baba, upon seeing me sitting there eating, immediately walked over to me, sat down, and burst out laughing. He didn't speak much English, and I spoke only a little Hindi, but he tried to carry on a conversation, and he was rolling on the ground with laughter. Then he grabbed my arm and took me up this mountain trail. It was a little funny, because here were hundreds of Indians who had traveled for thousands of miles to hang out with this guy for ten seconds, and I stumble in for something to eat and he's dragging me up this mountain.

"We get to the top of the mountain half an hour later and there's this little well and pond at the top. He dunks my head in the water, pulls out a razor from his pocket, and starts to shave my head. I'm completely stunned. I'm 19 years old, in a foreign country, up in the Himalayas, and here is this bizarre Indian baba who has just dragged me away from the rest of the crowd, shaving my head atop this mountain peak."[1]

By the time Kottke showed up, three weeks later, Steve was already deeply imbued with the spirit of his quest. His hair was shorn, he was barefoot, and he was dressed in light cotton. He was also very quiet and contemplative. Kottke was impressed that he had shaved his head—it was several years before he found out that it hadn't exactly been Steve's idea. The two of them set off immediately to the ashram that Friedland had been to the year before, located in a place called Kainchi.

"The trip was like a kind of ascetic pilgrimage, except that we didn't know where we were going," according to Kottke. Their chief objective was to follow the path of Friedland and his guru who had lived in Kainchi. "We went there, and there was nothing going on," says Kottke. "Neem Kairolie had died during the year, everyone else had scattered, and there was basically nothing there. But we had a good trip anyway."

They found the town overrun by the commercialization of religion—plastic trinkets and remembrances of the great guru himself. They decided to make the place their base for a period of meditation. However, even in the midst of the haze of selflessness and personal quest, there were still tensions and hidden facets to their relationship. Secretive and silent, Jobs could keep his closest friend and traveling companion off-guard.

While the two were at Kainchi they found out that Lama Govinda, author of *Way of the White Clouds*, lived just up the road in Almoora. Govinda was a Dutch aristocrat who had come to India in the 1930s and had stayed to become a holy man himself.

Steve decided that he wanted to see him, and Kottke simply wasn't invited. "It was clear to me that he wanted to go off by himself," says Kottke. "I can understand that, I guess. I'm not that way, but I don't think it means that he's a bad person. It's like it was his vision quest and there was just no room for me in it."

They rented a room from some farmers near a field of marijuana, which they dried and smoked. Steve bargained hard. He checked prices on everything, found out the real price, and haggled. He didn't want to be ripped off. His aggressiveness with a woman who sold them watered buffalo milk nearly caused them to be run out of town.[2]

Steve was discovering his own truths. "We weren't going to find a place where we could go for a month to be enlightened. It was one of the first times that I started to realize that maybe Thomas Edison did a lot more to improve the world than Karl Marx and Neem Kairolie Baba put together."[3]

After a month in Kainchi, the two traveling mendicants took off again. It was the height of the summer. India was hot and dusty, and the two were growing weary of the constant hassles and poverty. However, they'd heard about a guru called Baba Ji, a well-known mystical yogi who keeps reincarnating and is supposedly hundreds of years old.

Presently he was incarnated as Harikan Baba, and they decided to visit the holy man. The journey turned into a real quest. It was a ten-mile hike up a dry riverbed, over boulders and along a trail that was almost impossible to follow. Their feet were rubbed raw from the flip-flop sandals, and all they had on were the lunghi, not much protection from the merciless sun. Finally they found a cliff with a stairway that led up to the ashram.

"We'd been going so long and put so much effort into it that we weren't about to go away. Even though when we got there we both thought the guy was a bit of a bozo," remembers Kottke. After a couple of days they had had enough. "I'm sure he was a very far-out guy but he was really into his wardrobe, changing his clothes all the time. He was very flowery with his language, too. All this 'The essence of existence is so and so,' which did not impress us one little bit."

They left in the afternoon, even though they knew it was a long journey. That night, as they were sleeping in the dry riverbed, a thunderstorm blew in, like nothing they'd ever experienced before. The two of them, wearing only flip-flops and thin cotton shawls, were paralyzed by the torrential rain beating on them, accompanied by roaring thunder and lightning breaking across the sky. Surrounded as they were by 20-foot-tall boulders, far from home, in a strange and fearsomely different country, the two young seekers were about to come face to face with their own bogeymen. Kottke recalls the scene:

"Let's run," screamed Steve.

"Where?" shouted Kottke. "There's nowhere to hide!"

The rain grew, if anything, more intense. It beat on their shoulders; it blinded them. They scrambled one way and then another, but the only illumination came from the lightning flickering all around them, and within minutes they were totally disoriented. The thunder sounded as if it were directly overhead.

Steve started to sob. They had come all the way to India and had not found enlightenment. The gurus didn't have the answers he sought, he had tried everything, and now before he reached satori he was going to be wiped out in some freak storm far up in an abandoned riverbed.

The storm became so bad that they tried to dig a hole in the sand to crawl into to defend themselves from the pelting rain. Finally, in absolute, total helplessness, at the mercy of the elements, they did the only thing they could think of.

"We prayed," Kottke says. "Out there in the dry creek bed, in the middle of India, completely disoriented, all our rhythms and beliefs shattered, sobbing, where we were sure a flash flood would come through at any moment, the two of us prayed to any god that could hear us.

"'Dear God, if I ever get through this, I'll be a good person. I promise.'"

Although the experience didn't totally dampen their spirits, it marked the turning point in the journey. They wanted to see Tibet, so they headed up the mountains. After the lice, fleas, and filth drove him to it, Kottke cut off all his hair. Both contracted scabies in the town of Menali, site of a famous spa, to go along with the dysentery they'd had for a while. Kottke also had his traveler's checks stolen. It was the end of the journey. When he went to the bank in New Delhi, they refused to refund his stolen checks. Steve, who was leaving in few days, gave Kottke all the money he had left: $300.

When they returned from India, the two seekers of truth were distant. Aloof. The whole experience had been intense and disturbing. Steve had experienced a life far different from anything he had known in booming Silicon Valley, but it had not been the answer. The inner fire wasn't satisfied. Steve came back determined to work to the root of things in a different way.

"The day Steve came back, Ron Wayne came to my office," says Alcorn. "He said, 'Steve's back! You gotta see him man.' This time he was wearing saffron robes, had a shaved head, and was walking about a foot off the floor. Baba Ram Dass, the whole bit. But hey, this was Atari and we didn't mind. He asked if he could have his old job back. I said sure. So he started working again."

But not before he took another trip to Oregon. Kottke had returned to Portland to live with Elizabeth Holmes, even though both had dropped out of Reed at the end of the sophomore year. Steve visited them and they took him to the Primal Therapy Center in Eugene. During the previous year he had become fascinated with primal therapy, a radical theory of psychotherapy.

The center was the brainchild of Arthur Janov, a psychiatrist with a best-seller the two college friends had discovered the previous year: *The Primal Revolution*. Basically, Janov was a Freudian with a unique method of working through the neuroses of early childhood, which he believed were the primary shaping events of the personality. After realizing that the way of the yogis was not going to provide him with the solutions to his inner yearnings, Steve decided to enroll in a 12-week intensive course in primal therapy. The therapy consisted of individual guidance and exercises to facilitate cracking the self and confronting the formative childhood experiences that forged the personality.

"Steve was really into it," recalls Kottke. "He felt some kind of unresolved pain over being adopted. During the same period Steve even hired a private investigator to try and track down his mother. He was obsessed with finding his origins."

The key feature of Janov's primal therapy was the use of sensory deprivation boxes to recreate the experience of being in the womb. The boxes were lined with carpet, were sound and light proof, and were designed to withstand the loudest screams. The idea was that students would meditate for a while until, in the absolute stillness and darkness, they reached a disorientation point. Then they would start to scream — hence the *primal scream*. During that time, they would try to recreate and break down the pains and tears of childhood in an environment where no one could watch.

Like other interests that captured his attention momentarily and then faded away, the primal therapy experiment didn't last long. He came away from the experience disillusioned. "Janov offered a ready-made, button-down answer which turned out to be far too oversimplistic. It became obvious that it wasn't going to yield any great insight," he says.[4]

However, some of his friends did notice a difference in him. Elizabeth Holmes felt that Steve had settled some deep issues with the primal therapy. "He was a lot easier to be with after that. He started to think a little more about how things he said might affect other people. He'd never given that much thought before."

With that experience over, he returned to Silicon Valley, rented a room in Los Gatos, and went back to work at the wild and woolly Atari. Part of his heart was still pursuing the quest that he had embarked upon at Reed, and he moved freely between the Bay area and Portland, often driving the 1,000-mile journey in his Ford Ranchero and later in a beat-up Volkswagen bus. He was torn between the search for truth that he and Kottke had embarked on and the new veracities of electronic game playing and engineering, the wirehead roots that he shared with Woz and Fernandez, which were pulling him back to the Valley.

Atari was presided over by Nolan Bushnell, an eccentric idea man who could conjure up visions and change directions in the blinking of an eyelid. His business and managerial skills were equally mercurial.

Although the company took in more than $13 million during its first three years in operation, by the fall of 1974 Atari was often on the verge of bankruptcy. His unique style colored everything that happened at the booming company.

Upon his return, Steve convinced Alcorn, on the strength of his performance in Germany, to elevate him to engineer status. In the hierarchy of Silicon Valley, the difference between a technician and an engineer was vast but the dividing line fluid. It could take years to become an engineer—or months. The difference was both financial and egotistical. A technician was assumed to know nothing and needed to be guided every inch of the way. An engineer was presumed to know how to do it.

Steve felt he knew how to do engineering better than anyone else at the company—"the only reason I shone was that everyone else was so bad."[5] That attitude, combined with his thoroughly unconventional appearance, did little to endear him to his fellow engineers. He had a scraggly, skimpy beard that looked more like he was trying to grow a beard. And he had one pair of jeans with the knees completely ripped out that he wore day in and day out.

Steve wanted to be different, and he projected disdain for his colleagues by looking different, acting different, and pointing out to them that he had done something none of them had by voyaging to India. Steve's disdain also surfaced in other ways at Atari. "Some of their engineers were not very good, and I was better than most of them. I wasn't really an engineer at all."[6]

He continually experimented with diets. After returning from India Steve had developed an obsession with the dietary regimen of Arnold Ehret, a nineteenth century German philosopher. Ehret believed that diet was the root of physical, mental, and spiritual well-being, and in a series of arcane books explained that the elimination of mucus was the key to a healthy life. Ehret's philosophy, called the *Mucusless Diet Healing System*, became an obsession for Steve. When he saw Kottke merrily munching on a bag of bagels, Steve read him the riot act about all the mucus he was ingesting.

"When he started crusading, Steve could be overbearing," recalls Holmes.

The way to eliminate mucus was to go beyond being a strict vegetarian, which Steve promptly did. "I still believe that man is a fruitarian," he said recently. "Of course, back then I got into it in my typically nutso way."[7] Steve thought that his fruitarian diet meant that he did not have to take showers. He was celibate for a time after India, trying to emulate the Hindu sadhus. Then for a while, all he ate was raw carrots—after a few weeks, he looked orange.

Once he returned to work at Atari in the fall of 1974, Steve got back in touch with Woz, who was by then working for Hewlett-Packard as an engineer in their hand-held calculator division. Woz had watched his friend's journeys through mysticism and drugs with bewilderment, never quite trusting the innocence of the All-One Farm that Steve had described. Woz was a realist. He believed in the concrete. Sure he was a prankster, but no one ever accused him of having his head in the clouds. Steve was definitely a dreamer, and although the two could share certain things, Steve again compartmentalized his friends. Woz was good when he needed engineering work done, and Kottke was his partner in spiritual discovery.

Steve was working his Atari night shift and often let Woz in to play *Gran Track*, the first driving game with a steering wheel. Woz was a *Gran Track* addict. When Steve came upon a stumbling block on a project, he would get Woz to take a break from his road rally for ten minutes to come and help him.

The partnership worked. Woz had no thought of glory; all he wanted was to do something neat like design a computer or play the games that he craved. Steve was the hustler, the manipulator with the work, the income, and the unique job that he had created. Bushnell eventually hired him as a consultant.

"He was causing so much trouble with the other engineers that I had to step in and do something," says Bushnell. It was the forestalling of a would-be firing. "I said, 'If you guys don't want him, I do.'

"When he wanted to do something, he would give me a schedule of days and weeks, not months and years. I liked that."[8]

As 1975 began, Steve was still very unsettled. He moved back into his parents' Crist Avenue home. Kottke had quit his job as a night janitor in Portland and ended up staying in the Jobs' house in Los Altos, sleeping on the floor of Steve's room. Atari wouldn't hire him, and Kottke spent his days wandering around Silicon Valley with Steve, playing the video games in the Atari factory at night. But even so, even though he was living at the Jobs household and spending evenings at Atari, he never met Woz, the other best friend.

Steve and Kottke were still searching for a religious answer to their quest, and that year Steve found it. Or, better, rediscovered it. While he was working at Atari, after the primal therapy interlude, Steve started to attend meditation retreats at the nearby Los Altos Zen Center. Zen had attracted him earlier, during his spiritual reading period at Reed, with its emphasis on experience, intuition, and self-fulfillment through inner consciousness, not an exterior religious structure. This time, as he was reeling from the unsatisfactory and incomplete answers he was finding about his heritage, and still searching for spiritual truth, Zen Buddhism provided some answers.

Zen Buddhism offered a self-oriented approach to religion that was important to a terribly self-important young man. He had no need to depend upon anyone else for guidance. Zen fought rational, analytic thinking by elevating intuition and spontaneity. For a young man who had essentially no formal education in anything, this was important. And Zen was mystical and concerned with the big issues. Zen koans such as "The journey is the reward" or "What is the sound of one hand clapping" appealed to Steve's sense of truth as well as his love of song lyric poetry like Dylan's.

His former high school girlfriend Colleen ran into him one day at the zendo, where she too was studying with Kobun Chino, the Center's teacher, and although she had other boyfriends, the two became friends again. Early in 1975 she headed for a year in India herself, and Steve gave her some advice. Steve and Kottke often visited the Zen master, mostly at his house near the Zen Center, where they would have tea, sit, and talk.

"Kobun was a very far-out guy," Kottke remembers, "but he had just arrived from Japan, and his English was atrocious. He would speak in a kind of haiku, with poetic, suggestive phrases. We would sit and listen to him and half the time we had no idea what he was going on about. I thought it was sort of fun, and took the whole thing as a kind of light-hearted interlude, but Steve was really serious about it all. He became really serious and self-important, and just generally unbearable.

"I remember one time we were sitting there and all of a sudden Steve says to Kobun, 'What do you think of speed? You know, doing things fast?' He was really into this idea that the quicker you could do something the better person you were. Kobun just looked at him and started to laugh, which is what he did whenever he thought something was irrelevant. I thought it was pretty irrelevant, too."

Nonetheless, Steve studied with Chino for several years and considers him one of the most important influences in his life. (Years later Chino would become the official "roshi" of Steve's second company, NeXT, and some consider him Steve's closest friend.) The Zen master's way of answering a question with whatever was on his mind would become a lifelong habit for Steve. The development of his management style might be said to start here, since his study with Chino began the year before he founded Apple.

With Zen, Steve had found a path, though narrow, that could hold his attention. It was time to move on. It was half a decade since the wild rebellions of the sixties, and the mood of the country was swinging in new directions. Steve recognized the trend.

"As it was clear that the sixties were over," says Steve, "it was also clear that a lot of the people who had gone through the sixties ended up not really accomplishing what they had set out to accomplish, and because they had thrown their discipline to the wind, they didn't have much to fall back on.

"Many of my friends have ended up ingrained with the idealism of that period but also, with a certain practicality, a cautiousness about ending up working in a natural food store when they are 45, which is what they saw happen to their older friends.

"It's not that that is bad in and of itself, but it's bad if that's not what you really wanted to do."[9]

He wouldn't have to worry about that, as it turned out, because the January 1975 issue of *Popular Electronics* had the first hobbyist computer kit featured on its cover, and the world of Silicon Valley wireheads was about to blow apart at the seams.

Hackers

6
Apple I

In 1975, Steve was 20 years old, living at his parents' house, and making good money at Atari between trips to the All-One Farm and the Zen Center. The memories of his journey to India were receding. Gerald Ford, caretaker President of the United States, was about to be superseded by Jimmy Carter. Watergate was still fully on the minds of Americans. The Vietnam War came to its undignified conclusion with an airlift of Americans out of the heart of Saigon.

Computers were far from the mainstream of American thought. The promise of computing in those days was the specter of a dehumanized, faceless Orwellian "1984"—computers were behemoths with spinning tape banks and batches of cards that had to be fed into the machines in a precise sequence to execute a program. No-nonsense and built to stay that way, they were of interest only to the subculture that had discovered that their programmability offered a kind of gigantic mental chess game. But it was a chess game of value almost exclusively to big corporations.

But the times were changing. Steve was working at the one place in the world where electronic devices were indeed fascinating and easy to use. Arcade games, which were Atari's bread and butter, have almost no instructions. Kids who play video games are not about to try to decipher complex directions. The Atari arcade game *Star Trek* explained: "1. Insert Quarter. 2. Avoid Klingons." The games that succeeded with adults, such as *Pong*, did so because they were so idiotically simple that anyone, even an inebriated customer, could have some fun.

Up to then the most public attention computers had received in the 1960s came as the result of bombings at the University of Wisconsin during the height of the country's antiwar demonstrations. Work on computers was being done at the Pentagon, MIT, the University of California's Lawrence Livermore Labs, along Route 128 in Boston, on either side of the El Camino Real running through Silicon Valley, and in the data processing centers of Fortune 500 firms. It took years to understand the assembly and machine languages required to speak with these gargantuan machines, and most of the engineers who had invested the time had little interest in simplifying the process for those following them on the path. In any case, computers were just that: They computed. Unless you wanted to solve equations or manipulate large databases, you had no need for a computer.

Then, the cover of the January 1975 issue of *Popular Electronics* featured the first computer kit. Called the Altair, it was sold by MITS, a former mail-order calculator company operating from a hole-in-the-wall storefront next door to a laundromat in a Phoenix, Arizona, shopping center. This hobbyist machine was a $495 bucket of parts that had to be soldered, fine-tuned, tweaked, and cajoled into operation by someone with a hobbyist's passion, an excellent grasp of electronics, and the enthusiasm to persevere when the undocumented computer didn't work or was missing parts, both of which were regular occurrences.

None of these problems mattered, however, to the thousands of enthusiastic engineers who worked with computers from 9 to 5 and were salivating at the thought of having one they could play with at home. It didn't matter that they could do almost nothing except watch a few lights dance around on the display. The Altair was in many ways similar to the Flair pen computer that Woz and Fernandez had produced several years earlier. The difference was that this computer you could actually send for in the mail. People tripped over themselves to order one.

In California at that same time, a small group of people were developing a set of computer-related ideas that eventually sowed the seeds for a new industry. The roots of the personal computer industry that Steve Jobs would ride to fame and fortune were firmly anchored in the fertile cultural landscape of Northern California, which had produced Silicon Valley. In a tiny storefront office across from the train station in Menlo Park—a commuter stop just north of Stanford University and about 30 miles south of San Francisco—a group called the People's Computer Company (PCC) was founded in the late sixties. An underfunded, ad hoc group, their ideas came from a cross-pollination of the counterculture flower power of San Francisco's Haight-Ashbury and the close-knit scientific community centered on Stanford that was already beginning to be known as Silicon Valley.

Nurtured under the protective wing of the Portola Institute, a progressive nonprofit foundation run by Richard Raymond, the PCC had foreseen computers as powerful tools that could give more power to individuals, more "power to the people"—not less. The group was passionate about using computers and included some of the first hackers on the West Coast. The term *hacker* derived from a word coined at MIT in the mid-sixties to describe an inelegant but effective wiring hack. It came from the college's model railroad club, whose exceedingly complex track and wiring layouts were the precursors of personal computer circuitry. These computerists discovered a certain high while sitting in front of a computer. It was a heretical idea in the days of mainframes and timesharing, before personal computers had even been imagined.

Nonetheless, the PCC group, along with their share-the-wealth ideas, found a small but dedicated audience among the research scientists at the nearby Stanford Research Institute (SRI), one of the country's leading think tanks, and at Xerox's Palo Alto Research Center (PARC), that company's most advanced electronics research lab. The ideas floating in the air then would form the basis of the personal computer industry and, more particularly, Apple's contribution to it.

Steve's interest in the computer was purely intellectual at first. Making a computer work required intelligence. You had to organize your thoughts, display them in a logical stream, and then run them through the microprocessor. If you did it right, something would happen. If you failed, you knew instantly and could start again. It was a natural extension of the wirehead ethos that had kept him going through high school. A computer kit offered a perfect way to while away hours in a Valley garage, but he had given that up a few years back.

By the time the first computer kits appeared, Steve's only interest in using them was to create games, less sophisticated versions of those he was working on at Atari. Many thought that if they could write an intriguing enough software game, perhaps they could sell it. Or perhaps they could build their own computer and sell it like the illegal blue boxes that went like hotcakes. However, none of this was clear by the summer of 1975, as the infant industry arose. And since the first machines didn't have monitors, only a row of lights along the front, when Woz excitedly showed him the *Popular Electronics* article, Steve was less than enthused. He was used to video games, with which you could actually do something. These computer kits looked like intellectual electronics toys. He couldn't see what value they could possibly have.

The Portola Institute and PCC's goal was to harness technology and make it accessible to the masses, regardless of the origins of that technology. So when a sometime SRI researcher by the name of Stewart Brand asked for space to open a mail-order *Whole Earth Catalogue* business, Raymond was happy to oblige. The spirit was of openness, trust, and sharing the wealth. The movement that grew from the Whole Earth beginnings was about making use of tools, and the computer was the latest tool.

Steve dove into the Whole Earth movement wholeheartedly. It combined his two passions at that time: electronics and counterculture politics. On his trips north to the All-One Farm, he brought the latest *Catalogue* and the friends pored over it meticulously. He dropped in to the storefront Menlo Park offices a couple of times, noticed the PCC literature and their single cranky teletype terminal, but had too many other things going on to become a regular. By 1975, the Bay area's alternative culture was in full flower. There was a circuit of health food stores, spirituality centers, and relaxed bookstores and tea rooms. Steve considered himself a traveler on the path and very much a part of this movement toward self-awareness. He didn't know where it would take him in the end, but his direction then seemed far from his teenage electronics apprenticeship.

The band of folks who migrated to the Menlo Park PCC/Whole Earth offices were very eclectic and had little formal engineering training: Bob Albrecht was a maverick educator involved in the "alternative school" movement, Jim Warren had taught at a Catholic women's college, Fred Moore was a peace activist and an organic vegetable distributor, Gordon French built custom slot car engines, and Keith Britton was a demolition expert and the company's treasurer. The idea was to offer a storefront environment where anyone interested in computers could learn and share experiences. Prior formal training in computers was by no means a prerequisite for admission. All you needed was enthusiasm and a willingness to learn. The group published a hand-drawn and lettered newsletter and was dedicated to using the power of computing in education.

In those days, the only computers available were terminals tied to mainframes, and it was difficult to preach the promise of humanitarian computing while navigating through the arcane commands and procedures required to accomplish anything from a remote terminal in a shabby storefront. Nonetheless, a few adherents from the nearby high schools were attracted and became entranced with the binary electronic bug that had bitten Woz and Steve earlier. But the PCC gradually receded into the background, overwhelmed by the success of Brand's *Whole Earth Catalogue.*

With the publication of the *Popular Electronics* article in January of 1975 announcing the Altair, the era of personal computing was at hand. Headed by ex-Marine Ed Roberts, MITS just avoided bankruptcy by getting his machine on the cover of the magazine. You couldn't do much with the Altair except watch rows of lights dance in response to chains of binary commands entered by meticulously flipping a series of eight switches along the front. But that was enough, mainly because you could do so at home—not in an office with a mainframe. The Altair came in a metal box and required hours of precise soldering. A perfect enthusiast's product, it was not likely to offer much threat to the home stereo and calculator businesses, which were hot in the consumer electronics fields of the mid-seventies. But it thrilled the PCC crowd.

Within a month, the tottering mail-order company received a staggering 4,000 orders. During the following year, MITS had sales of $13 million, and by the end of 1975 there were a number of other hobbyist kits around. Kentucky Fried Computer, Golemics, the Itty Bitty Machine Company, and The Sphere were some of the early competitors, and their names reflected the countercultural roots of the business, at least on the West Coast. Anyone with garage space and a soldering iron could enter the market, and many did. *BYTE*, the first computer magazine, was started, and a number of other magazines and newsletters dedicated to the new computer field quickly followed.

Soon the first working version of the programming language BASIC was created to work on the MITS Altair by college drop-outs Bill Gates and Paul Allen, who would later found Microsoft. Another company, Processor Technology, went into business selling add-on memory and processor boards to improve the performance of the various machines on the market.

Following the publication of the *Popular Electronics* article, Albrecht and his cohorts decided that it was time to issue a call to the troops to form a computer hobbyist's group to share tips and information. They called it the Homebrew Computer Club. Since computer kits were still quite expensive, the democratic idea behind the club was to allow those who had the machines to share them with those who were not so fortunate. About 30 hobbyists attended the club's first meeting, which featured, among other things, a report on the Altair by a member who had just returned from the MITS offices in Albuquerque. Within months membership swelled to more than 100, and the meetings had to be moved out of a garage into the Stanford Linear Accelerator Center auditorium.

It was a heady time. Designers swapped stories and revealed their new prototypes, asking for criticism and feedback. The chairperson at the meetings was Lee Felsenstein, a former editor of the *Berkeley Barb*, an alternative newspaper. He was involved in an abortive attempt to link the Bay area's telephone "hot lines" via computer terminals, which was called the Community Memory Project. Each meeting saw businesses formed, alliances begun, and a lively trade in parts carried out. At first salesmen worked out of the trunks of their cars, but eventually anyone with something to sell set up folding tables outside the auditorium. There was something magical about the camaraderie and spirit of the group.

Homebrew was a place of sharing and giving, an open forum for all the wild-eyed engineers who didn't fit in the button-down roles of traditional engineers. Because members had to build their own machines, write their own programming languages, and voyage into uncharted territory, the club attracted the very brightest of these blithe spirits, the renegade geniuses of the Bay area. A few months after the first meeting, 75 percent of the members were designing their own computers. But the passion, the creative drive that fueled the development, was not profit. It was not power. It was not sex, drugs, or rock 'n' roll. It was bragging rights, pure and simple.

The Homebrew spirit was healthy engineering competition—to design a better machine, do a more elegant schematic, sell more computer kits. It was also the innocent, good-natured sharing of skills, knowledge, tools, and experience that had always characterized the dream behind the counterculture and San Francisco's Summer of Love. The combination fueled the engines of these enthusiast's minds, and most of the second generation of commercially available computers and peripherals were produced by members of this single club in Silicon Valley.

Woz attended the first meeting and most subsequent ones as well, and at a few he was accompanied by Steve. Woz was a computer designer; he was content to create ever more elegant designs that would never go beyond paper schematics and enjoyed endless debates about the fine points of circuit design. Steve had no such skills or interests. He was bored at the Homebrew meetings, but he was a sharp kid with an eye for business and electronics in his blood. He was too young and inexperienced to know what he couldn't achieve. He had the impetuousness of youth and the ambition to run through brick walls. He had no caution lights or a sense of the impossible. He could be carried away in the passion of an idea, and instead of looking for the ways it might not succeed, he simply went ahead and did it. But Steve wasn't a real political radical, and the angst of the poet never caught hold either. He was living at home after all, letting his father keep his cars running and his mother fix his strange meals. Although he had the money to move out, he didn't. He was 20 years old and going nowhere. But he was doing it in a hurry. He had ambition, drive, and energy, but no clear idea of what direction he should pursue.

As more commercial kits started to appear at Homebrew, Steve started to think about how he and Woz could profit from this new field. Ever since they had been able to turn the blue boxes into profits, he had realized that there was money to be made in electronic devices. Steve's strange part-time job left him free during the days to pursue his own projects, and electronics was nearly the only thing he knew. He had to find an angle if he were to get involved in the fledgling industry.

Most of the garage-based Homebrew hackers didn't think about products in 1975. Woz and his colleagues' idea was to give schematics out and let anybody who wanted build a computer for themselves. The fundamental idea that ran through the Homebrew meetings was that the computer was only as good as the designing and building of it. Who would want one that came preassembled?

No one was sure what people could do with the machines or what their ultimate power might be, but Steve began to see that there had to be a market in selling them. But the market was only other hobbyists. Who else would be interested?

At the same time he decided to audit an advanced physics course at Stanford taught by Mel Schwartz. Whenever he went, he made sure to stay after class to ask questions.

"Very few people turn up who say they want to learn something," recalls Schwartz. "I was impressed by Steve's enthusiasm. He was really interested and curious."[1]

As the months passed, Steve took to dropping by Woz's apartment and offering him suggestions about the design of the machine that was being continually updated on his kitchen table. Woz lived in a kind of programmer's madness. He allowed white mice to run freely through his apartment. He had the Bay area's Dial-a-Joke operation running from a bank of phones in his flat. Every day he would read a new joke onto the machines, usually selecting them from a book of Polish jokes that he owned. He had met his first girlfriend, Alice Robertson, when she called the joke line and he answered as his nom de plume, Stanley Zeber Zenskanitsky. They were married not long after that, but only after Woz spent hours flipping three dimes until they all came up heads.

A pile of videotape players, in their boxes, was stacked up in a corner. A band of fellow engineers at H-P had bought them at a ridiculous price but then couldn't sell them. Woz agreed to see what he could do with them and took a couple completely apart. The pieces were strewn around his apartment. Two high school kids, Randy Wigginton and Chris Espinosa, usually hung around as well. The two were ten years younger than Woz but were fascinated by the electronics wiz. He would answer their questions with his rapid-fire delivery for as long as the two could ask.

Wigginton had met Woz at a local timesharing computer company, where he was allowed to indulge his passion: writing program code. Wigginton, a blonde cherubic kid, found in Woz an endless source of information. There was nothing the burly designer liked more than explaining esoteric points of electronic design, and Wigginton was an avid listener.

Espinosa was a bright student in John McCollum's class at Homestead High who looked about five years younger than his 14 years. He had met Woz at the Homebrew meetings and immediately idolized him, and since he lived a few doors away, Woz drove him to meetings. Together with Wigginton—they were both too young to drive—they all went to Homebrew meetings, sometimes joined by Steve, where they would sit in the back of the auditorium, along with John Draper, making fun of the straighter engineers in the crowd. They all made it a ritual to stop at a Denny's restaurant after the meetings to talk computers until late into the night.

Woz and his teenage disciples were completely wrapped up in the machines, while Steve spent most of his time involved in other pursuits. Atari was still paying him, and through the summer of 1975 he had Dan Kottke as a house guest at his parents' home. There weren't many girls around, and with his long hair, dark intensity, strange diets, and conviction that he needn't shower because of his fruitarianism, he was not a compelling catch. The courses at Stanford and his studies in Zen were still not consuming him—he was looking for new challenges. That fall Kottke headed east to attend college again and get a degree. Steve started working for Alex Kamradt, another enterprising business type who showed up at the Homebrew meetings.

Kamradt, a Lockheed engineer, had taken all the money he had made from selling a house in 1974 and bought a minicomputer. Then he formed a business, Call Computer, which rented time on this computer to small accounts all over the Bay area. He was effectively selling timesharing services to smaller businesses and programmers, who could link up with his machine by telephone. Wigginton had been working at Call Computer since Kamradt loaned him a terminal to teach a computer class at his high school, and Captain Crunch was a nightly fixture there as well.

When the Altair computer kit appeared, Kamradt thought he could improve his business by providing not only the big computer, but also a terminal that a customer could rent or buy to hook up to his computer. It was the first inkling of a consumer product. Until then you had to be a dedicated engineer to have a terminal and a modem capable of linking with a timesharing system such as Call Computer's. This limited the market, but Kamradt saw the possibility of providing a ready-made terminal device that would expand his market from enthusiasts to mainstream consumers. He started attending Homebrew meetings looking for someone to hire to design this "smart terminal" for him.

"I asked who was the best electronics designer around," Kamradt recalls, "and the name that kept being mentioned was Wozniak. He had shoulder length hair, talked a mile a minute, and was sort of weird. But I didn't care. Hey I had John Draper working for me then, and Woz looked a lot more normal than he did."

Kamradt wanted to sell an attractive-looking computer terminal for about $200. He found a ready-made beige plastic case to fit the keyboard. The user could hook the terminal up to a phone modem by putting the handset into a cradle on top of the device, attach an output to a television set, and then call up the minicomputer. The entrepreneur saw this as a serious business venture and offered to divvy up the company with Woz in return for designing what they finally called the Computer Conversor.

When it came time to negotiate a deal with Kamradt, Woz brought Steve along. Woz had always wanted to design his own computer system, and this sounded like a good chance. But Woz, who was to get 40 percent according to the original plan, wanted 20 percent of the company for himself and demanded that his friend, the inexperienced Steve Jobs, also get 20 percent. Steve was to run the business and manufacture the devices that Woz designed, while Kamradt bankrolled the operation. Kamradt agreed, only because he needed the machine designed and built and he still had his ongoing business to attend to.

"Jobs didn't know anything, even though he thought he did. But I figured he could learn," Kamradt remembers.

Kamradt put up the money and made space at Call Computer to do the work. He figured that they would build the terminal first and then move on to microcomputers. The Mountain View offices of Call Computer and Computer Conversor were a beehive of programming activity in 1975. Almost anyone could work on the computer after prime hours if they were interested in programming. Woz would get his expenses paid, while Steve was on salary at $8 an hour. Kamradt was sure that Woz could design the machine, but he wasn't as sure of Steve.

"Steve was a very young man," recalls Kamradt. "He had a tremendous amount of confidence, or conceit. He thought he could do it, so I thought I'd see if he could. He tended to put everybody else down, and this turned a lot of people off. It was hard to deal with him because he would speak without thinking of the consequences. He would call people stupid when they made mistakes."

Kamradt had a vision of a consumer product, but he made the fatal error of building his terminal around a design without a microprocessor. They were too expensive, he reasoned, in mid-1975, and he didn't expect prices to plummet significantly even if demand rose. Kamradt believed in the promise of computing and was the first person besides the wireheads and engineers that Steve had met who could become animated talking about the promise of machines. That sense of wonder and awe in the power of the machinery, coupled with an ongoing, apparently successful business and a generous attitude influenced Steve deeply. He would come away from the experience determined that there was a place for a consumer product in the computer business.

Kamradt let the 20-year-old Jobs draw up the bill of materials for the Computer Conversor and shop for the parts, providing a formal apprenticeship in the fundamentals of high-technology manufacturing that the young man desperately needed. Up to then the only product he had been involved with was the blue box, which Wozniak had assembled from parts procured by Steve.

Because this was to be a serious product, Kamradt sent him to Robert Way, a printed circuit board designer, to come up with the final layout for the machine's motherboard. It was there that Steve's perfectionism and intensity really showed itself.

"Nothing was ever good enough for him," explained Way. "He was the rejector. Every check I ever received was signed by Kamradt. But the responsibility for seeing that the design got done was Jobs'."[2]

The problems on the project were getting Woz to document his engineering work and finish it. Wozniak steadily worked on schematics for his own computer even as he worked for Kamradt designing the Conversor. He was not an amateur, but a professional hardware guy working on calculators for H-P. He delivered a prototype machine to Kamradt within a couple of months. But once he produced the prototype, he wanted to move on to something else, and the Computer Conversor project became a lead weight around his neck. Kamradt never could get him to complete it.

Steve learned several key things from his experience with the owner of Call Computer and the ill-fated attempt to bring the Computer Conversor to market. Foremost was an appreciation for just how excellent Woz's design skills were. Kamradt, although furious with the engineer for not completing and debugging the terminal, recognized great design when he saw it and impressed upon Steve how good his friend was at designing electronics. Over the months, Kamradt begged Woz to finish his machine, but Woz ignored him. As Steve watched Kamradt try in vain to rejuvenate Woz's interest in the project, he resolved to use other methods to bring his friend into partnership with him, not the least of which was to use a microprocessor chip.

During the heady time that Woz was working on the Computer Conversor design, as well as the first of his legitimate personal computers, he and Steve also created a video game for Atari. Bushnell had come up with an idea for a game called *Breakout*, in which the player tries to break out of a brick wall.

"The way things would get done at Atari was that Nolan Bushnell would come up with ideas a mile a minute," explains Alcorn, "so our job really was to kind of slow it down, take one idea when it came off, and say, 'Great, do it,' and just keep it going for six months or whatever it took to get it done.

"Nolan did not have the patience. So one day he grabbed Jobs and made a deal on the side. On his blackboard, Nolan defined the game. He said that for every IC (integrated circuit) under 50 he would give him a bonus to his salary."

Breakout was designed in one 48-hour stretch. But instead of Steve doing the work, as the company thought, Woz did most of the electronic design.

"Steve's role was to buy the candy and cokes, while Woz did all the design work," according to Alcorn, who didn't have much of an opinion of Steve's engineering: "Jobs never did a lick of engineering in his life. He had me snowed. It took years before I figured out that he was getting Woz to come in the back door and do all the work while he got the credit."

This wouldn't be the last time Woz provided the genius to fuel Steve's glory. Part of Woz's talent was his ability to minimize a design. One of the true rewards of electronic design comes from using the fewest components to make something work. The elegance is in simplicity. A complex minimization succeeds only when the designer has every single piece of the design in his head. Woz's head was alive with complex integrated circuits; he dreamed of them and had been dreaming for ten years. He completed *Breakout* with a ridiculously small number of ICs—36 in all. And it worked . . . somewhat. Just as for the Computer Conversor, Woz's design was one that only he could comprehend.

"Ironically, the design was so minimized that normal mere mortals couldn't figure it out," says Alcorn. "To go to production, we had to have technicians testing the things so they could make sense of it. If any one part failed, the whole thing would come to its knees. And since Jobs didn't really understand it and didn't want us to know that he hadn't done it, we ended up having to redesign it before it could be shipped."

Bushnell ended up paying Steve his bonus in cash. Steve split $1,400 with Woz. They had another feather in their caps. Once more they had been able to squeeze money from electronics by combining Steve's hustle and Woz's design. It was becoming a habit.

But the *Breakout* experience was harrowing. Within weeks the two contracted mononucleosis. While Woz suffered at home in Silicon Valley, Steve took the cash he'd made and headed for Oregon to recuperate on the All-One Farm. He also wanted to help with that autumn's apple harvest.

Steve spent the fall of 1975 at the Farm, but the counterculture didn't hold the same lure that it had previously. The atmosphere was changing at the farm, and neither Steve nor Kottke was particularly enthralled by it anymore. "Friedland was calling himself Sita Ram Dass," recalls Kottke, "but we called him Robert."

"Robert walks a very fine line between being a charismatic leader and a con man," recalled Steve. "It started to get very materialistic. Everybody got the idea that they were working very hard for Robert's farm, and one by one they started to leave. I got pretty sick of it and left."[3]

When he returned from the autumn apple harvest at All-One Farm late in 1975, Steve found that Kamradt had hired someone else to run the Conversor project during his absence. Steve had neglected to inform Kamradt that he would be gone for a few months. Nonetheless, he was furious that Kamradt had replaced him and stormed out of the office. He visited Woz and saw his latest computer, a working and enhanced version of the schematic Woz had handed out earlier. Attached to a standard television set and with a keyboard to enter BASIC and then programs, it looked like a machine that somebody could actually do something with. Perhaps the computer that Woz had fine-tuned was the project that could take up all Steve's energy and give him the crusade he was so desperately searching to find.

As 1976 rolled around, he began to turn his attention to the personal computer industry. By early in 1976, he started bending Woz's ear about having some printed circuit boards drawn up to sell the computer to others. He had already worked with Robert Way on the board for the Computer Conversor and was eager to translate his experience into something that he and Woz could sell. With the success of the Altair, another company had already started selling a kit and several other Bay area designers were readying their machines.

At this point, the only possibility was to have a printed circuit board made up that the purchaser could then load with components. Woz would not have to leave H-P, and Steve could continue at Atari. It would be a sideline, Steve patiently explained to the conservative Woz, who didn't want a repeat of the Kamradt experience. Steve understood that his friend wanted nothing to do with serious business, so he devised a strategy whereby Woz could have total freedom. Steve would handle making and selling the boards during his free days, and Woz could continue to work on his new designs at night, keep his daytime job, and share any profits.

It was an ideal situation for Woz, and since he trusted Steve more than Kamradt, he agreed to the partnership. Now they needed to come up with a name for the new partnership. In the end, with a self-imposed deadline for delivering the partnership papers to the local newspaper for publication, they went with the gentle, nonthreatening, hardly serious name *Apple Computer*. It derived partly from the Beatles' record label name, because Steve was an avid fan of popular lyrics, especially those of Bob Dylan and John Lennon. It also came from Steve's fruitarian diet and from his having spent months harvesting the Gravenstein apple crop in Oregon that previous fall. Other factors were wanting a name that would come before Atari in the phone book, and Steve concluded that almost everyone in the world liked apples.

In the following weeks, Steve decided they could really make some money if they went full time in producing Woz's computer. Woz was skeptical. He didn't want to have to give up his job at H-P. His family was none too supportive of Steve, either. Jerry Wozniak couldn't understand why his son should go 50–50 with a kid who hadn't done any of the design work on the computer. Woz's wife Alice was fed up with having parts strewn all over in the apartment, and Woz himself wasn't so sure that he wouldn't decide to throw in with Alex Kamradt, who was still pressuring him to go full out on the Computer Conversor that was about to come to market. Woz was in demand as an electronics designer in an exploding field. Why should he get tied up with either of these guys? Why not hold out for a company with more substance? Woz was noncommittal and cautious.

Steve was sure that they needed another partner and kept pushing for a business agreement. He brought in his friend Ron Wayne from

Atari. Wayne was a chief field service engineer who dabbled in artwork. His artistic specialty was a "Dungeons and Dragons" type of art that was suited to airbrushing. He would be in charge of testing, help design ads, write the manual, and draw schematics for the documentation.

Woz had a hard time with the concept. He couldn't see how to equate his invention, the electronic design issues that he had solved, with the cash and hard work the other two were putting into the partnership. And if H-P asked him to work on something for which he could use the same electronic tricks, would Apple own the rights?

"It was almost as if Wozniak would condescend to allow Apple to use these principles," recalls Wayne, "but he wanted to reserve the rights to sell them to other people as well."[4]

They were moving into an uncharted realm of electronics law. Steve pushed and pushed. He explained that they had to have a company or their work wouldn't be taken seriously and they would never really do it. Finally, Steve prevailed. On April Fool's Day, 1976, with the teenage Randy Wigginton as witness, they signed a ten-page document dividing the company among three partners. Ten percent went to Ron Wayne who agreed to come aboard, and the remainder was split evenly between Steve and Woz.

Their plans were circumspect and small time. They weren't dreaming of taking over the world, but they were sure they could handle a tiny piece of the new business of personal computers. It was a part-time venture, after all. They were thinking they could make the boards for $25, sell 50 at $50 apiece, and let the customers stuff the boards with components. That would cover the money they had to put in for the circuit board layout—about $1,500—and make a nice profit of $1,000 that they could split while going on with their other work.

Raising the capital was another matter. Although Steve had some cash in the bank from the *Breakout* deal, he couldn't let Woz know. He sold his VW bus for $1,300. Unfortunately, a couple of weeks later the engine gave out and the buyer came back for his money. Steve ended up paying for the repairs, which reduced his investment to less than $1,000. Wozniak was making $24,000 a year at H-P but was saving nothing. He sold his H-P 65 electronic calculator for $500, but the guy only paid half. Altogether they had around $1,300 as a bankroll.

Undaunted, Steve took the money and approached Howard Cantin, a printed circuit board artist who did work for Atari, and convinced him to produce one for the new Apple computer at a little less than his standard rate. They called their computer the Apple I and planned to have at least one more. Woz was already hard at work on the next one anyway. Cantin did the job as a favor to Steve, and with that Steve was off and running. He negotiated for parts and oversaw the layout of the board and the first batch of tests. Woz attached all the components to the board, and together they appeared at the Homebrew meeting one Thursday in April, held up the printed circuit board, and described its capabilities. Woz talked about its technical features: 8 kilobytes of memory, a version of BASIC that he would give away with the computer, and a microprocessor at its heart.

The 21-year-old Steve stood up and asked a single rhetorical question in his high-pitched voice, reflecting his role in the partnership. "How much would you pay for a computer with all the features of the Altair loaded on a single board?"

There was not much response. He was trying to gauge the price for the circuit board alone, without any parts. Could they charge $50 apiece and sell the 50 required to break even? He sat down. Although the reaction of the group was not particularly favorable, they had already invested in the printed board and the first ten, so they had to keep on. In the computer world of 1976, the success of the Apple I looked pretty unlikely.

Their computer was limited to black-and-white displays and used a microprocessor that required entirely new versions of programs and equipment that currently ran on the Altair. They had chosen a new inexpensive, knock-off chip from Motorola, the MOS-TECH 6502. Powerful though the new Motorolas were, they were incompatible with the already standard Intel 8008 that was at the heart of the Altair and most of its early competitors. The cofounders were painting themselves into a corner, but the decision fit Steve's determination to be different at all costs and Woz's passion for electronic one-upmanship—Apple was first to make use of this new chip. Besides, they weren't thinking of the endeavor as big business; it was a fun little sideline.

That lack of seriousness was obvious to the more staid older engineers who attended Homebrew by early 1976 with plans to make a real business out of computers. Already, the Dazzler add-on board from Cromemco—two professors from Stanford ran the firm—offered a color upgrade for the Altair, and lots of other advanced computer kits were right around the corner. After the Apple I was shown at Homebrew meetings in schematic form for six months, the attendees became jaded. The partnership didn't look that promising. Steve was an aggressive know-nothing in the world of electronics and business, and everybody who counted knew that Woz had already designed a better computer. Why buy last year's design?

Then something happened that set the stage for the explosion that was about to follow.

"The guy who started one of the first computer stores told us he could sell them [Apple I's] as fully stocked boards if we could make them up and deliver them," says Steve. "That had not dawned on us until then."[5]

Paul Terrell was the first retailer of the computer revolution with the Byte Shop, opened in Mountain View in late 1975. But he had grander ideas than a single computer store. His vision was of a chain of consumer computer electronics shops along the lines of Radio Shack. He attended Homebrew meetings to keep up on all the latest gossip, machines, peripherals, designers, and everybody at the folding tables outside the door. But he was also trying to build a nationwide network of retail outlets, and he needed product to fill the stores and fuel his dream of franchising.

A former parts salesman, Terrell quickly sewed up the Northern California distributorship from Altair after seeing one early in 1975. When he saw the Apple I at the Homebrew meeting, he thought it looked promising and suggested that Steve keep in touch. The very next day Steve came waltzing barefoot into the Byte Shop with, "I'm keeping in touch."

Terrell had seen him before at Homebrew meetings but had always avoided him. "You can always tell the guys who are going to give you a hard time," says Terrell. "I was always cautious of him."

Terrell needed product, however, and couldn't afford to be choosy. He told Steve that he couldn't sell naked circuit boards but that he was prepared to buy fully assembled Apple computers for around $500 each—and he would buy 50, cash on delivery. Steve saw nothing but dollar signs. He ran to a pay phone and called Woz at work. Afterward, stunned, Woz told his buddies in the lab. Nobody believed him.

Instead of being responsible for 50 circuit boards that cost them about $25 each, a total investment of around $1,000, they would now be paid $25,000 by Terrell, but they would also have to put in all the components and parts themselves. That meant the two of them would have to buy all the components first, then deliver the completed boards to Terrell, collect $500 a board, and finally pay off the suppliers. It was a business!

"That was the biggest single episode in the company's history," says Woz. "Nothing in subsequent years was so great and so unexpected. It was not what we had intended to do."[6]

It completely changed the rules. They now needed money, or credit, and the best parts Steve could find at the cheapest prices. He drew up a bill of materials and set about finding someone who would supply them.

Then there was the question of where to assemble the boards. Woz's cramped apartment was too small. Steve was still living at home, but his sister had just married and moved out. He commandeered her bedroom and turned it into the office, storeroom, assembly area, and test site for Apple Computer Company.

With the parts order in his back pocket, Steve traveled tirelessly over the Valley looking for credit. Banks turned him down. Al Alcorn at Atari agreed to buy some parts for him, but only if he paid cash on delivery. Alcorn didn't have much faith in the hobbyist computer market, in either Steve or Terrell paying their bills, and he wasn't about to get stuck with the tab.

Steve then went to Hal Elzig, the owner of Haltek who had hired him once as a counter clerk, but he was turned down again. Finally Mel Schwartz, the Stanford physics professor, agreed to buy a few parts on his account with a big supply house, Kierulff Electronics in Palo Alto.

That opening provided Steve with the opportunity he needed. He approached the manager of Kierulff, Bob Newton, directly.

"Steve was an aggressive little kid who didn't present himself very professionally," remembers Newton.[7] But Newton agreed to check with Terrell to see if there was indeed an order. Steve refused to leave until he did so. Newton tracked Terrell down at an electronics convention and summoned him to the phone, whereby he proceeded to confirm that the long-haired boy in sandals had a contract worth $25,000. Newton advanced Apple Computer credit to the tune of $20,000 on 30 days net.

"We didn't know what 'net 30 days' was," explained Steve.[8] He soon realized that it meant he had to pay no interest on the price for 30 days, which started another elemental characteristic of Apple Computer:

Always use the maximum amount of time in the grace period and then pay bills on time, just at the 30-day limit.

With Kierulff's line of credit and a steady source of parts, they were ready to build computers. Still insulated by the world of electronics enthusiasts and the engineering life of the Valley, their concept of a computer was relatively limited. After all, they knew how to hook up the two power supply transformers necessary: one for the main circuit board, and the other for the memory. They knew how to hook a television set up to the machine through the Atari radio frequency modulator. And they knew how to attach the keyboard to the innards of the circuit board. They were willing to put up with laboriously typing in all the lines of Woz's BASIC each time they started up the computer. So they pressed on, making computer circuit boards, fully loaded with components, that still required serious engineering help to get them up and running.

"The Apple was consuming all his time," said Woz's wife Alice, an early computer widow. "I saw very little of him. He'd go off to H-P and eat something at McDonald's on the way to Jobs' house. He wouldn't get home until after midnight, then he'd work some more on his stuff and leave all the parts on the kitchen table with big notes saying that nothing should be touched. I was going nuts."⁹

Steve hired his sister Patty, who was pregnant with her first child, to sit on the living room floor and, while watching television, push the components onto the circuit board. He paid her $1 per assembled board, and she was eventually able to produce four boards an hour. After the first 50 were built, Steve hired Bill Fernandez, his teenage cohort who had recently been laid off at H-P. He also recalled his friend Dan Kottke from college on the East Coast to spend the summer sleeping on the family sofa and helping out. Parts were lined up in plastic bags along the walls of the spare bedroom, and as long as they worked, the assemblers stuffed them into the circuit boards. There was no quality control or systematic testing of components.

The total cost of the parts that made up an Apple computer was about $250. It consisted of a printed circuit board, the microprocessor, a memory array of 8 kilobytes, and a number of off-the-shelf integrated circuits. Woz thought they should sell the machines for that price, or at best a little more than the cost of the parts. Steve disagreed. He thought they should double the cost of the parts and add a markup for the dealers. If they charged about $500 to dealers, Apple would make a profit. But what should the retail price be?

Terrell had told him that he wanted to be able to add a 33 percent markup when he sold the machines in his stores. That could bring the price to $666. It sounded good to Steve. The book *Be Here Now* by Baba Ram Dass sold for $7.77, and the number had a nice ring to it. $666.66 seemed as if it had the same ring, and since Woz wouldn't allow them to set the price as high as $777.77, which Steve had wanted, they decided that would be the retail price. It would cause them grief, however, when the movie *The Omen* was released the same year and revealed that the number 666 was the numerological personification of evil. A group of Sikhs running one of the first computer stores in the Los Angeles area boycotted the computer, and Steve, whose telephone number was listed in the phone book, grew accustomed to explaining to callers that there was absolutely no evil significance in the $666.66 price.

While Steve had been lining up the parts supply and supervising the circuit board layout, he and Ron Wayne were also involved in designing the first Apple Computer manual as well as the company's logo. The manual was a four-page document produced on an IBM typewriter with a separate page of schematics. Steve demanded that they use shading for various parts of the book to improve its appearance, but when it was printed, this artistic flair obliterated essential information. Sparse and difficult to follow, the manual was a true hobbyist's document.

The logo was even worse. With his commercial art skills honed on the painting of slot machines and video games, Wayne came up with a black-and-white pen-and-ink drawing of Sir Isaac Newton lost in thought under an apple tree. In the branches of the tree was one haloed apple, and around the perimeter of the drawing was a scroll-work sleight of hand that contained a pretentious line from Wordsworth. It was a line that nonetheless might well have been the two isolated founders' motto: "Newton, a mind forever voyaging through strange seas of thought, alone."

It was the kind of artwork that had been popular in the underground press of the late 1960s. It was simple to produce on offset presses and reflected both the nature of the computer vision quest that the two had in mind for their product as well as the hobbyist, amateurish origins of the business in those days. That it was accepted at all reflected the company founders' lack of sophistication.

When the first dozen units were finished, Steve staggered into the Byte Shop in Mountain View carrying a box filled with computers. Terrell kept his bargain and handed over a check for $6,000. He was not impressed, however: The unit lacked a case, a power supply, a monitor, and a keyboard. Steve had promised computers when the retailer told him he needed complete machines, not just circuit boards. A loaded circuit board was a computer as far as Steve was concerned, but for Terrell it was only half a machine. A lot more work was required to turn it into a salable product. But he paid up, and over the next few weeks Steve delivered the rest of the computers to the other three Byte Shops that had opened up along the El Camino corridor. He also helped them order the peripheral parts required to turn the assembled circuit boards into computers.

On that first day, Steve walked out of the door with a profit for Apple Computer of about $3,000 that he plowed back into the company. He hired an answering service and set up a mail drop in Palo Alto to make the company appear more substantial. He bought advertisements in the only two magazines that existed then for hobbyists: *Interface Age* and *Dr. Dobb's Journal of Computing*. Terrell started pressing Steve to design a case for the naked circuit boards and to provide an interface card so that at the very least customers could load in BASIC from a cassette without having to type it into the computer's memory each time they wanted to program.

The case Steve came up with was a polished koa wood box constructed by a local cabinetmaker. It was solid but heavy and did not dissipate heat easily. They weren't very popular and were extremely expensive, costing nearly as much as the Apple I's themselves.

The cassette interface was a more complex matter. Woz, who was feeling the pressure of a full-time job and an expanding sideline business, didn't have time to design the interface, so they farmed the work out to another H-P engineer. His design didn't work, however, and Steve decided to buy the guy out for $1,000 instead of paying royalties when they had to build a new interface anyway.

"We weren't going to go ahead with our own design and then pay him for each one we sold," he explained.[10]

Then Woz created the very simplest interface card he could imagine, and it worked. Less than two inches high, it sold for $75, and to really hook buyers included a cassette tape with Woz's BASIC, a programming language that was undergoing continuous upgrade. Steve decided that he didn't want to try to assemble this card—they were having enough trouble with an overflowing garage taking over his parents' house—so he approached Dick Olson, one of the first "board stuffers" in the Valley. These firms provide the labor to assemble the parts and printed circuit boards for companies too small to have their own assembly operations. Steve walked in one day, barefoot and wearing his usual torn jeans, and gave the "I won't leave until you agree" pitch to Olson.

"I still don't know why I did it," recalls Olson, "but I gave him credit. He had already figured out that if I gave him 30 days credit, he would be able to get paid by his customers and pay me before I charged any interest. I figured that if he stiffed me, I'd be out only a few hundred dollars. And if he did well, I would have gained a good customer. I didn't think I had much to lose.

"I had learned one thing about the electronics business by then: You can't judge anybody by how young they are or how they look. The best engineers don't fit into any mold. Steve Jobs was definitely somebody who didn't fit."

The cassette interface only exacerbated the chaotic development environment at Woz's nighttime apartment software works. Now that there was a way to provide a standard version of BASIC to every user, they couldn't quit until it was even more amazing than the day before. They were driven by the love of computing, and it was their duty to keep adding to the cassette version. Every day after school Wigginton and Espinosa would head for Woz's garden apartment, where they drove his wife crazy. When Woz appeared after work, the three worked until late in the night, with frequent trips to the nearby Jobs garage on Crist, where Steve, Dan Kottke, and Bill Fernandez were almost always burning the midnight oil, too. BASIC was in a constant state of development. Every day Woz or Wigginton would come up with a new feature that they felt they had to add, so they would.

A few days later Steve would cruise along the El Camino Real in one of his father's cars, usually accompanied by the similarly barefoot Kottke. At each Byte Shop carrying the Apple computer he handed over a new set of cassettes and collected the old ones for recycling. That was their update policy. Finally, late in the summer Steve put his foot down and told all of them, "Enough. No more features. I'm sick of all this driving."

Even though Terrell was dismayed by Apple Computer's lack of amenities, the orders were coming in, albeit slowly. As the summer wore on, Apple's answering service called daily with orders. In 1976, Terrell opened 74 Byte Shops around the country, and even if only half of the stores ordered one computer to have on display, that was most of the original order. Computers were shipped via UPS, and by the end of the year the company had sold about 150 machines. Multiplied by $500, that represented an amazing $95,000 passing through the hands of a hardware hacker and his salesman partner. About half was profit. It was obvious that they were onto something worth pursuing.

"I was getting a chance to do some things the way I thought they should be done," Steve explains. "I felt I had nothing to lose by leaving Atari because I could always go back."[11]

But it was more than that. Steve had discovered that a product, a machine, a computer occupied his unfulfilled, unsettled spirit. Selling and making them could take every ounce of his spirit, drive, and Zen-trained concentration. It was what he had been searching for all these years, and since he was still living at home, with no responsibilities, it was not hard to make the choice. At heart he was a wirehead after all, and this was his chance to make it pay.

His two partners were not so cavalier and certainly not so emotionally needy. Although Woz made almost as much from Apple sales as he did from H-P that first year—$22,000 against the $24,000 he made at H-P—he had no intention of giving up his security. Shortly after they had filled the Terrell order, Ron Wayne came down with a case of cold feet and backed out of the partnership. He wrote a formal letter of resignation and renounced his 10 percent interest in the company. As Steve's dreams grew, the company planned to go deeper into debt with parts suppliers and board stuffers to finance another order of 50 computers and cassette interface cards. Wayne could only see his responsibility for 10 percent of any loss the company would have.

"I had already learned what gave me indigestion," Wayne says, "and I was beginning to feel the months running by. If Apple had failed, I would have had bruises on top of bruises. Steve Jobs was an absolute whirlwind, and I had lost the energy needed to ride whirlwinds."[12]

With Wayne out of the picture, Steve and Woz, emboldened by the success of their order to Terrell, approached Woz's old friend Allan Baum and his dad Elmer for a loan. Steve was ready to throw caution to the wind and build a new batch of 50 machines, this time on speculation, without a firm order. Although Terrell wasn't having much luck selling the Apple I and by the end of the summer was considering dropping it, this had no effect on Steve. The Altair and the IMSAI, an Altair-compatible machine manufactured by another garage consortium along the Peninsula, were the machines that sold, and the Apple I's 6502 processor looked more and more suspect.

Steve was working 24 hours a day to get the best deals for the company, and the Baums, who had helped Woz out with money before, agreed to loan the fledgling Apple Computer Company $5,000 at a hefty rate of interest.

"I had no doubt that the loan would be repaid," said Alan Baum. "Steve Jobs had this silver tongue that could talk anyone into anything. And he was working his tail off. He told me about the prices he was getting for parts, and they were more favorable than the prices H-P was paying."[13]

With the new infusion of money, they invested in more machines and the interface card. The orders trickled in. They attended the Homebrew meetings and kept up to date on the latest developments in the inchoate business. Steve Jobs knew that his friend already had just the right computer for the next wave of the business sitting in prototype on his kitchen table. From his adoptive father he had learned all the right skills to negotiate and sell them, combined with healthy doses of confidence, charisma, and the posturing of an individualistic smart ass that allowed him to ignore self-doubt. He was an excellent, fearless salesman. That, combined with an absolute, bottom-line need for the product to be a success for his own emotional well-being, created a high-tech evangelist with a single-minded drive that simply could not be stopped.

By mid-1976, Apple had their first product for sale as well as another improved one in the pipeline, and a true believer whose intensity and passion could sway the uncommitted. The thing the two diamond-in-the-rough Valley boys lacked was the muscle to take that product and build a company out of it all. That would come later. But not much later.

Steve Jobs as a freshman at Homestead High School in 1969.

The Electronics Club at Homestead High School in 1969. Advisor John McCollum is at the left; a grinning fourteen-year-old Steve Jobs is at the right.

Steve Jobs as a senior at Homestead High School in 1972.

Nolan Bushnell, founder of Atari, for whom Steve Jobs worked on and off from 1974 to 1976.

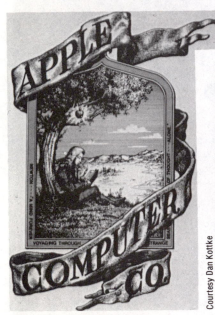

The original Apple Computer logo, designed by Ron Wayne and Steve Jobs.

Stephen Wozniak, Steve Jobs, and Dan Kottke with an Apple I at the first Personal Computer Festival, Atlantic City, late summer of 1976.

"31,000 student hours later, we still love Apple Computer."

When the Minnesota Educational Computing Consortium recommended Apple Computer to the state's school districts—well, it started something big.

Today there are hundreds of Apple Computers in use in 35% of Minnesota's elementary and secondary schools, and nearly all of the colleges and universities in the state. Most communicate with the Consortium's CYBER 73 mainframe in a state-wide educational computer network.

The educational computer

Dr. Kenneth Brumbaugh, Manager of User Services, heads the team responsible for supporting instructional computing.

"MECC evaluated personal computers and chose Apple because it was the one that met our rather rigid specifications.

"And, we employ a conventional timesharing system, with remote terminals. But that means high phone costs. And limited user access. Apple solves that. It gives schools a stand-alone computer for about the price of a terminal. Also, Apple interfaces directly to our CYBER, so we can download programs to any Apple in the state. That also means we can serve as the communication link for the wealth of new programs students and teachers are writing themselves. For us, Apple is an excellent educational computer.

The kids—and the teachers—love Apple

"One big reason we chose Apple is that it is so easy to program. Now, with Pascal, Apple can provide even more programming flexibility.

"For example, MECC has written a note-recognition program to help teach music that takes advantage of Apple's unique built-in speaker. And Apple's color graphics make programs far more interesting than conventional black and white terminals can.

"To date, we've logged over 31,000 student hours on Apple Computers. We even have schools trying out computers for home study. The kids love the Apple. And so do the teachers."

Is Apple for you?

For the name and address of your local Apple dealer and your free copy of Apple's *new* Curriculum Materials Kit, call **800-538-9696**. In California, **800-662-9238**. Or write us at 10260 Bandley Drive, Cupertino, CA 95014.

apple computer

A 1979 Apple Computer ad that ran in Scientific American.

Steve Jobs and Stephen Wozniak in Apple's middle years.

© Liane Enkelis

Steve Jobs on the cover of Time Magazine, *February 1982.*

John Couch and Steve Jobs in the hills of Los Gatos at the time of the introduction of the Lisa Computer.

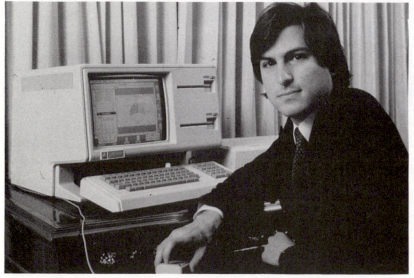

Steve Jobs demonstrating the Lisa during the 1983 product introduction tour.

Steve Jobs with cofounder of Apple, Mike Markkula, in front of a Lisa computer assembly line.

Public relations advisor Regis McKenna with Steve Jobs at an informal press briefing and barbecue in McKenna's backyard.

Steve Jobs standing on an Apple sign outside the Cupertino headquarters in late 1982.

7
Apple II

In the midst of producing the boards for Terrell in the summer of 1976, Steve found time to visit the Los Altos Zen Center, where he frequently ran into California's Governor, Jerry Brown, another Zen disciple. Steve was still studying with Kobun Chino at the Los Altos zendo and was as dedicated as ever to the life of meditation and contemplation. His room in his parents' Los Altos home, which was also the assembly factory for Apple Computer, was devoid of any furniture other than a mat and a single meditation cushion. He was deeply involved with his fruitarian diet and spent his day either barefoot or wearing Birkenstock sandals. He had no time for the trivial concerns of baths and cleanliness. He was on a crusade to get the computers out the door. Higher realities were at hand.

Steve was constantly hunting for parts at better prices, negotiating with the burgeoning number of computer store owners, checking up on the progress of the new cassette interface card for the computer, and riding up and down the Peninsula delivering new versions of BASIC on cassette tapes as quickly as Woz and Randy Wigginton could generate them.

Steve was seeing Colleen again, although he was still living at home. It had been four years since high school, yet both were following the same paths: Zen Buddhism with Chino and even the journey to India. In 1975, Colleen had spent a year in India searching for her own truths. She had traveled with a different boyfriend since she and Steve

109

had severed their relationship after his return from India in late 1974. The year changed her, the way India changes most Westerners, and when she returned in mid-1976, one of the first persons she called was Steve.

In some ways their relationship was more by default than anything else. Steve had trouble finding others who would put up with him, and Colleen found him and his intensity magnetically alluring.

"Colleen was always chasing Steve," says Kottke. "It was never the other way around. The problem was that although Steve was consumed by computers, she had nothing like that in her life. She was consumed by Steve." But she was still unwelcome in the Jobs house. Paul Jobs still disapproved of her for the summer she and Steve had spent in a cabin together. Upon her return from India in 1976, she moved in with her father, who didn't mind her relationship with the scruffy boy in torn jeans. The lovers meditated together, studied with Kobun Chino, and used her family house for their time together.

As orders streamed in for the Apple I, the operation moved from the spare bedroom into the Jobs' garage. Steve's dad built a "burn-in box" to test the newly assembled circuit boards and load the memory codes into the special ROM chips. It took up one wall. The garage was a hot and dark place, with rows of neatly labeled drawers for his father's auto parts. One wall had a large schematic of the computer itself. Tacked above the long metal engineering table across the back was a picture of Mr. Spock from *Star Trek* next to a blowup of the company's first ad. Steve bought the workbench from the same firm that supplied H-P. For Steve and his cohorts, H-P was the company to emulate. The established company had also started in a garage, was considered benevolent and progressive, and produced superb electronic equipment. But that emphasis on excellence never came cheaply.

Steve always wanted to make high-quality products and have the best equipment, to do every little thing right. The legacy from his father, the art of buying and selling and the meticulous attention to detail, came in handy during those times. In fact, his father was often around in the garage giving the guys advice. It wasn't much different from when Steve was younger. When Steve needed help doing something, his father helped him. They might have yelled at each other, but his father never rejected him, no matter how strange Steve's beliefs and enthusiasms became.

Steve tried to come off as antiestablishment, but he was not a destructive radical. He was more a poking-holes-in-the-argument type of radical, or a satirizing-the-establishment type. He combined Zen, chutzpah, and a well-developed sense of deal-making to become a kind of countercultural businessman. But as much as he wouldn't have wanted to admit it, he was as addicted to the comfortable middle-class life as anyone. He was 21 years old and was still living in his parents' house—the same house on the same block in which he had spent his teenage years. If he were truly an outlaw, a misfit, a malcontent, he would have been long gone. His appearance and abrupt, abrasive, disconcerting personality were all part of a posture. Steve was just a Silicon Valley boy.

After Kottke went back to Columbia for his senior year in the fall of 1976, Bill Fernandez was the only employee at the Apple Computer garage. He made sure that the company's founders wrote a formal employment contract. Orders were coming in and money was to be made. They needed help. Apple couldn't afford to advertise in a newspaper, so they hired friends.

Elizabeth Holmes became the company's accountant. She was living in San Francisco, was working as a diamond cutter, and was starting to dive into the Da Free John religious movement. Once a week on her way to visit her parents in Saratoga, she would stop by the garage, take Steve's checkbook, and put all the expenses and income into a bookkeeping ledger.

"I knew nothing about accounting," she explains, "but Steve sat me down at his kitchen table and said, 'Here's a ledger sheet, here's what you need, do it.'"

Steve's sister Patty had her baby and spent much of the time at the family house as well. In a suburban world of tracts and working fathers, the Jobs household, with its comings and goings and motley crew of workers, was the talk of the neighborhood. The neighbors knew that something was going on in the garage, where the door was open much of the time during the summer heat.

With all the extra activity, Steve's dad had a family room built on behind the house to accommodate some of the overflow and serve as a kind of ad-hoc office for the business. Steve then didn't have to hog the family dining area with his paperwork, and his employees weren't always tramping through the small three-bedroom, one-bath house.

When it became apparent that the garage wasn't going to be his again any time in the near future, Paul also added a second garage, behind the first, to house his automobiles. This was a family that humored their son. Steve was oblivious to everything except his work.

All that year Woz had been building a better, advanced version of the Apple computer. A couple of design considerations were clear, and both Woz and Steve agreed on them: The new computer had to include a keyboard, a case, and a power supply. The Sol, an Altair-compatible machine about to be released by Processor Technology in Berkeley, had these things, so, of course, Woz had to do at least that much. Beyond that, Woz was determined to include a few other features to impress his fellow hobbyists. By making the computer use a standard television for display, they ensured the broadest possible market and made the machine both more affordable and less intimidating to a new user.

They were also determined to introduce a number of refinements with the next effort, the Apple II. Color was at the top of the list. Woz wanted to be able to bring up his own version of *Breakout*, the game that he and Steve had produced for Atari, and color was a prerequisite. He came up with a neat way to send color signals to the television screen. Woz discovered that a television or computer monitor screen is "painted" by successive beams of electrons about two-thirds of the time, and for the other third the gun pitching the electron beam is resetting. Why not have the microprocessor do its work while the screen is inactive, and then let the display take over for the time it needs? In the world of digital electronics, that kind of timing was possible, and it meant that the computer's memory array could do double-duty, serving both the screen and the microprocessor. It was a typical Woz feat of minimization, creating on-screen color with only half the circuitry.

Another of Woz's decisions held hidden benefits that would become apparent only much later. It concerned expansion slots. Minicomputers, those behemoths of computing that Woz and Baum had drooled over in high school, introduced the idea of slots to the computing world. The idea was that peripheral, or add-on, circuit cards could be pushed into slots purposefully designed into the hardware architecture, thus enhancing the range of functions that the machine could perform. You bought a basic machine and then customized it as needed. The Altair introduced expansion slots to the personal computer universe, and Woz was determined to go that computer one better. Steve disagreed violently with Woz on the slot issue.

"I was used to computers with 20 slots that were always filled up with boards," says Woz. "All Steve saw was a computer that could do a couple of things: write BASIC programs and play games. He thought you might add a printer and maybe a modem, but that you would never need more than two slots. I refused to let it go with two slots."[1]

What made the addition of expansion slots so important is that it provided an open door for other companies to build products to enhance the computer that Apple would sell. This was an overwhelmingly intelligent choice. Not only did Woz add eight slots, but he designed the slots in such a way that it was very easy and inexpensive to build circuit boards for them—his scheme allowed peripherals to share the power of the Apple II's microprocessor without having to go to the expense of adding another one.

Over the years, numerous companies grew rich designing add-on circuit boards to expand the capabilities of the computer Woz created.

Although Woz was fascinated with the hardware, he had much less interest in the interminable lines of programming code that made the computer do anything other than sit on a desk. That was left to the two local high school kids, Wigginton and Espinosa. Nonetheless, he made a design decision for the new computer that had a significant impact on the machine's eventual army of programmers.

After their experience with BASIC on the Apple I, Woz and Steve were determined to take an entirely different tack with their new machine and provide a language free to the user. The version of BASIC on the Altair cost $500. This went against the populist aspirations of the Homebrew-influenced Bay area hobbyists, and the language quickly became widely pirated. Woz decided to design a chip that would permanently hold the programming language BASIC and place it directly onto the circuit board. This unalterable ROM chip would hold a complete version of BASIC so Apple would never again have to deal with the hassles of cassette interface cards—or the expense of building them.

By having the programming language built into the computer, the machine could be configured to start up with a program instead of forcing the user to go through loading the language first, only then to run a program. This meant you could do something with the computer from the moment you turned it on, with no additional expense, and it would also make the Apple II more accessible to the nontechnical public later on when sales started to soar.

By the fall of 1976, Woz and Wigginton had built a mock-up prototype of the new Apple II in a cardboard box. Bolstered by the success of their first computer as well as the cash the business had already generated, Woz and Steve were ready to show their improved machine to the world. That Labor Day weekend the two founders flew to Atlantic City for the Personal Computer Festival, the first trade show for the fledgling industry. They had a working mock-up of the Apple II and a folding table from which to sell their entire Apple product line: the Apple I computer and the cassette interface card. However, the world's first personal computer festival proved to be a very humbling experience.

The trip to Atlantic City started on a red-eye flight to Philadelphia. In addition to Steve and Woz, a number of other West Coast computer-niks were on the flight. Most significant was the team from Processor Technology, who had with them a working version of the Sol. Enclosed in a sleek metal-stamped case with a keyboard built in, the Sol was the first of the new generation of personal computers. It was self-contained and came completely assembled and ready to plug into both the wall and a monitor. It used the same microprocessor as the Altair, so it was compatible with programs written for that predecessor. By comparison, the crude mock-up of the Apple II was positively amateurish.

During the flight, Lee Felsenstein leaned over the back of his seat and talked to Steve and Woz. Felsenstein, who had been a design consultant to the folks at Processor Technology, as well as the emcee at Homebrew, took one look at the crude circuit board with its drastically minimized number of ICs and chips, and decided: "It was thoroughly unimpressive. All they had was a cigar box. I thought Woz might be riding for a big fall. And I wasn't about to get in his way."[2]

The buzz on the floor of the convention, held in a decaying Atlantic City in the days before casinos revitalized that seaside resort, was about what was going to happen to Ed Roberts and MITS. He was casting about for buyers, and rumors were swirling. Worried by the competition that was suddenly erupting all over the country, Roberts wanted out, but he was shrewd enough to know that he could probably sell for substantial cash. Some of the biggest names in the retail electronics business were looking at the personal computer market. Notable among them were Tandy, with its chain of Radio Shack stores, and Commodore, a cut-throat Canadian firm known for its aggressive marketing of calculators during the early 1970s.

While Roberts looked around in search of cash, dozens of hobbyists and engineers were looking to take over the number two position in the business. The Altair was still unquestionably the premier personal computer, but the explosion of retail stores and computer kit sales made it clear by the fall of 1976 that there was a real market for computers. The scramble was on for dominance. At that show numerous new computers were on display: the IMSAI 8080; the Polymorphic Systems Poly-88; MOS Technology, the builders of the 6502 micro-processor, had a machine called the KIM-1; Cromemco was previewing the Dazzler, which sported color; and two other prototypes, The Sphere and Southwest Technical Products' 6800, were both based on another processor, the Motorola 6800. It was impossible to know who would succeed.

Walking around the convention floor, Steve realized that to be competitive the new Apple had to be a complete, self-contained device. The early enthusiasts had been willing to put up with some soldering, but the new wave of computer buyers wasn't, and the retail stores didn't want to handle the old-style computer kits. Although Terrell of the Byte Shops had been telling Steve this, faced with the advent of a second generation of machines that reflected this wisdom, Steve finally realized the truth. Several new machines included a keyboard, and it was clear that to be competitive the new Apple had to have one, too.

Apple's booth was fronted by a card table and framed from behind by a row of yellow curtains. Two other shoestring operations were set up on either side. A laminated copy of an article about the Apple computer from a hobbyist magazine and a single printed name card were the only sources of information about the company. The Apple set-up was far from impressive compared to the enormous booths of MITS and IMSAI, which included all the flash, dazzle, and sizzle of trade show hype: mini-skirted girls, hourly demonstrations, three-piece-suited marketing sharpies, and button-down engineers. While Apple was back in the side rows where only the dedicated enthusiasts dared to go, the other leading companies were out in the high-visibility center of the floor. With the open-necked shirts, long hair, and scraggly beards and moustaches that Steve, Woz, and Kottke—who had come down from college to lend moral support—sported, Apple Computer was not the firm to inspire confidence or competitive fear. None of the power brokers came to see them.

Building a complete circuit board like the original Apple I, which had components but no case, power supply, monitor, or keyboard, cost around $250 per unit. That was difficult enough for Apple to raise. With ambitions of adding all the elements that the market seemed to require, Steve knew that he would have to find investors and professional help to turn the tiny company into one that could compete with others in the marketplace. By the time he left the show, Steve understood that to succeed with the new computer that Woz had designed meant a new orientation to the business of computing.

When they returned from that first show in the fall of 1976, the two partners were energized. It was time to get serious and look for the help they needed. Steve signed up for a large space in the first West Coast Computer Faire, planned for the following spring in San Francisco, even though he had no idea where he would get the money to pay for it. By the time he needed to put down the cash, he was sure they would either have the money or be broke.

Woz went to his bosses at H-P. They promptly told him that his extracurricular design work was very interesting but that H-P didn't want to get into that kind of market. Nonetheless, the benevolent grandfather of garage-based computer companies did sign a release allowing the young engineer to continue to build his own machine. At this time, the semiconductor companies in the Valley were investigating the phenomenon of hobbyist computing and were forming the same opinion as the managers at H-P—the market for small assembled computers had little future.

Woz was having second thoughts about throwing in his lot with Steve. Since the days of the original agreement forming Apple, just six months earlier, Woz had been leery about pairing his inventions with his friend's energy, drive, ambition, hustle, and hard work. His parents, especially his father, didn't trust Steve. "We wondered about Steve Jobs," said Jerry Wozniak later. "We thought he was the kind of person who felt he should start right up at the top and didn't care to work his way up." [3]

Part of the Wozniaks' distrust resulted from the generation gap: Steve was a hippie and a freak who seemed like nothing but a bad influence on their eldest son. The senior Wozniak was a straight-arrow, golf-playing, Lockheed engineer who saw the value of an electronics design in the board, not in selling or packaging it. Everything came to a head that October when two men made an appointment to see Steve at his garage. They were Chuck Peddle and Andre Sousan.

Peddle had headed the design project that resulted in the MOS 6502 microprocessor. Then, to take advantage of the chip, he built a limited computer, the KIM-1, which was based on it. Just after the first Personal Computer Festival in Atlantic City, he sold his company to Commodore, where Andre Sousan was vice-president of engineering. The idea was to use the 6502 microprocessor as the basis for a newly designed and inexpensive home computer. The only other machine using that processor was the Apple, and because they had heard rumors of a new Apple computer in the wings, it seemed to make good business sense to find out what they were up to or even buy them out, giving Commodore a head start in bringing out the new computer.

When the pair showed up at his modified garage, Steve was willing to talk buy-out. But he had his price and wouldn't budge: $100,000, Commodore stock, and salaries of $36,000 for both Woz and himself. Peddle thought it was a good idea, but Jack Tramiel, the tough president of the company, thought that it was ridiculous to spend $100,000 on two guys in a garage. For Steve's part, the more he investigated Tramiel the less he liked him and the less he wanted to make a deal with Commodore.

The offer also raised tensions between the two partners another notch, when Woz, buttressed by his father, became convinced that Steve deserved less than 50 percent of the proceeds of the sale, should it go through, for his share of the work so far. Steve spent night after night at the Woz house, trying—sometimes in tears—to sway his partner's parents. Back and forth the argument raged, until finally the deal fell through anyway, much to Steve's pleasure.

During that period, Steve had several insights that would deeply affect the future Apple II. As he contemplated the walls of his room, pursuing his Zen influenced meditations, his mind drifted to various elements of the computer that they were building. One had to do with the case.

"I got a bug up my rear that I wanted the computer to be in a plastic case," he explained later.[4] He went to local department stores to look at the appliance and stereo products they carried. Steve was convinced that if a consumer market existed for the computers they were building, making the computer look right—in a molded plastic box with smooth edges and sleek lines—was essential to its success.

To create the box he wanted, Steve approached Ron Wayne, their former partner. Wayne, who was the only artist Steve had met who had any experience with electronic product design, agreed to try his hand at the Apple II case. Steve turned his attention to other matters.

He became utterly convinced that the Apple II should be silent— without a fan. This conviction grew from his meditation interests, because the noisy fans that all the other computers included were intrusive and distracted from the pure elegance of the machine. He also had an intuition that consumers would be more enticed to buy a noiseless computer.

Eliminating the fan required a special low-heat power supply. Since they were intending to sell the new Apple II with a power supply anyway, Steve headed for the only source of engineers that he knew: Atari. He asked Al Alcorn to recommend somebody who could help design the unit. Alcorn suggested Rod Holt, one of the motorcycle-racing contingent in the Atari engineering department who had recently sustained nerve damage to his hands and couldn't race anymore. He was a unique individual who believed he knew more about anything than anyone else . . . and usually did. In his forties, with a daughter older than Steve, he told Steve that he was expensive—$200 per day.

"We can afford you," replied Steve. "Absolutely no problem."[5] Of course, at that point he had almost no money and was trying to bring the Apple II to life with nothing more than moxie and youthful exuberance. He was going to will it into existence.

"He just conned me into working," remembers Holt,[6] who worked on a new design for the power supply at night, during weekends, and whenever he formerly would have been racing motorcycles. Instead of using a conventional linear power supply, which was heavy, hot, and based upon technology more than 50 years old, Holt struck out in a new direction. Having been a long-time professional analog engineer, he had designed a switching power supply ten years earlier for an oscilloscope and had no fears of doing the unconventional. He created one for the Apple II. A switching supply is much lighter, smaller, and cooler than traditional ones but also more complex. For hobbyists, who were working as amateurs, the design was far too complex, and none of the computers designed by late 1976 had such an exotic unit. The power supply later became one of the patents in the Apple II, substantially reduced the size required for the computer's case, and made a fan unnecessary.

Holt also offered Apple a much-needed, important quality: He was a finisher, unlike Woz, who was always in a hurry to get on with the next challenge once he solved the fundamental problem presented by his current project.

"I was the everything else guy," Holt says.[7] He took care of all the details of the design that had to be solved, even though they might not be glamorously digital or visible to buyers. He arranged wires, made internal connections, and soldered parts together. He marshaled the prototype machine from a working model that Woz had designed to a finished, integral whole that Steve could sell.

Holt also tried to solve the frequency modulator issue. In the mid-1970s the Federal Communications Commission had rigid rules concerning the amount of radio interference a new electronic device could give off. Unfortunately, as Holt tested the circuit boards, he found that the amount of radio interference the Apple II emitted was far too great to comply with FCC guidelines. No matter how he arranged components or adjusted the internal layout of the power supply, circuit board, memory, and slots, he could not bring the radio interference within acceptable levels. Eventually, he told Woz and Steve that they would have to redesign the entire circuitry of the Apple II to pass FCC testing.

Steve was not about to do that. In meditating on the problem, he came up with a remarkable solution rooted in both his pragmatic approach to business and the Homebrew spirit. Because the problem only occurred once a radio frequency modulator was attached to the computer, and it was the radio frequency modulator which in turn attached to a home television set that the FCC tested, why not remove the modulator from the computer? If the consumer bought a modulator and then attached it to the Apple computer, it was the consumer's problem if the device did not meet FCC standards, not Apple's. To date, all computers had been sold with their own modulators, but there was no rule saying they had to be so equipped. By having the purchaser buy a modulator from a different company, the purchaser—not Apple—was liable to the FCC for the interference generated.

With that, Steve called Marty Spergel, known as "Junk Man" at the Homebrew meetings. Spergel showed up at meetings with boxes of discarded parts and gave them away, figuring some of the enthusiasts would return as legitimate customers some day. Steve offered him a business proposition. Apple would provide Spergel with the specifications for the modulator, which Spergel could build and ship under his firm's label, M&R Electronics. Dealers could sell a modulator whenever they sold an Apple computer.

"My part was keeping the FCC away from Apple Computer," says Spergel. "I shipped modulators out of my door while Apple shipped Apples out of theirs. When both items got to the dealers, the dealers would sell a modulator to the end user, and when the end user went home he could plug in the modulator. Consequently, it was not the computer maker's responsibility to prevent interference.

"Steve told me that the volume would be enormous for the Sup'r Mod, as we decided to call it. He thought I could plan on about 50 units a month at $30 each. As it turned out, after a couple of years I had sold over 400,000."[8]

If there is one exceptional skill that Steve demonstrated in the rush-and-hectic turmoil of the months late in 1976, it was an awareness of his own limitations and an almost uncanny ability to locate and cajole exceptional people into providing the skills he lacked. He had a salesman's belief in the product that he was producing, an evangelist's bible-thumping passion, the zealot's singularity of purpose, and the poor kid's determination to make his business a success. He also had an ability to juggle the numerous demands of making and selling the existing Apple circuit boards to an exploding world of retail computer stores, while building a new and much improved machine that was a quantum leap forward in both capability and cost. His studies with Kobun Chino, his daily meditation sessions investigating the character of zen, and his rigorously minimalist diet all contributed to a kind of power of concentration that was fundamental to keeping up with the growing new industry that personal computers were becoming.

By late 1976, the rush was on, and because no one had ever sold personal computers before, the entire field was filled with risk and opportunity. Did consumers really want a keyboard? Did they need uppercase and lowercase letters? At Apple they decided that since the only times they themselves used the computers were for games and programming color displays, uppercase letters alone were sufficient. Although that decision was a mistake, what characterized Apple during that period was that they made fewer mistakes than their competitors. No one had any idea how computers would be used, let alone what the market would respond to.

In they all rushed—all the would-be, shoestring, and garage

manufacturers—and soon they tripped. Most companies had no financing, they angered retailers with demands for exclusivity, they shipped products with unfixed bugs and shoddy documentation, or they kept delivering revised hardware versions of their machines so that customers quickly lost track of the bewildering array of options available to them. Companies appeared and disappeared with startling frequency.

Sooner than most, Steve began to understand that it took more than money to sell a new kind of product in the diverse, fractured marketplace. You had to be able to grab the attention of the media and bring your product to the public's notice. Success was partially a great product, but another part of the mix was savvy advertising combined with a new field that had only made its appearance after World War II—public relations.

Steve looked for the best advertising and public relations person regardless of cost. While the others were trying to keep their heads above the water, Steve was after bigger things. He had seen the kinds of promotions that MITS and IMSAI had laid on in Atlantic City, and he was determined to take Apple along a similar, but even better, road.

That fall, the semiconductor company Intel was running an intriguing advertising campaign that used symbols—poker chips, hamburgers, race cars, and cleavers—to depict the strengths of Intel's business, without once referring to the schematics or engineering details of the chips the firm sold. The campaign was unique in the electronics industry and caught Steve's eye. With his characteristically forthright approach, Steve called the marketing department at the company and asked who had been responsible for the advertising campaign. He was told it was the work of the Regis McKenna agency, so he immediately called Regis McKenna.

Instead of reaching McKenna, he talked with Frank Burge, who handled new business for the agency. After he found out a little about what Apple had, Burge did his best to discourage the young entrepreneur, but Steve would have none of it. Daily, for more than a week, he called the account executive and badgered him to come over and see their new product—the new computer he claimed would set the world on fire. Finally, as much to get rid of the persistent kid as out of any interest in actually handling their business, Burge made an appointment for a demonstration.

"As I was driving over to the garage, I was thinking, 'Holy Christ, this guy is going to be something else. What's the least amount of time I can spend with this clown without being rude and then get back to something more profitable?'

"When he came out of the kitchen, I forgot all about being rude. For about two minutes, I was just thinking of escaping. Then in about three minutes, two other things hit me. First, he was an incredibly smart young man. Second, I didn't understand a fiftieth of what he was talking about."[9]

Burge and McKenna hadn't made a success of their business by taking on only the sure things. They specialized in start-up companies and understood that looks don't mean much when it comes to inventions. McKenna, who speaks in slogans and aphorisms, was especially fond of "Inventions come from individuals, not from companies." Steve was certainly an individual in his Birkenstock sandals, "Ho Chi Minh beard," as McKenna described it, and torn jeans. Furthermore, because the agency was already handling the explosive growth of Paul Terrell's Byte Shops, they had some understanding of the personal computer phenomenon. Indeed, perhaps the only raw information at that time about the personal consumer computer business was researched by the focus group and marketing studies that Regis McKenna's firm was conducting for Byte Shops nationwide.

Nonetheless, Burge wanted a second opinion and sent an underling back to the garage a week later. In a memo that would later become well-known throughout the agency, the staff analyst wrote about Steve and the original Apple computer. In part it said, "Though he moved a quantity into retail distribution, there is as yet no evidence that the retailers are successful in finding customers. Steve is young and inexperienced, but Bushnell was young when he started Atari. And he claims to be worth $10 million now."[10]

Notwithstanding the semirecommendation of the memo, the agency turned him down. Burge explained that they might be interested in taking a percentage of Apple's retail sales volume in exchange for marketing and advertising aid, but only once the computer had been completed and was shown to be a viable commercial product. Part of the reason was that McKenna had already signed up another client, Video Brain, another in the stream of personal computer companies that came and went throughout the early days of the industry. Video Brain looked like a better bet. It was founded by two guys from Intel's marketing department who had been rebuffed by the semiconductor firm's management when they made a business case presentation about personal computers, so they went off on their own. McKenna planned to use his clout with the Byte Shop chain to make sure they succeeded.

By then Steve was determined to have McKenna as his agency. He started calling the smooth agency head three or four times a day, until he finally got him on the phone. His persistence was impressive to the PR man. McKenna was a specialist at cultivating relationships with the press and making small companies look much larger than they were. He had a particular knack for public relations, working with journalists instead of taking an adversarial approach to them. At Intel, his first major client, he had worked hard to make the company executives a quotable source for the primary business journals of the country—*Fortune*, *Business Week*, *Forbes*—and later it would pay off with clients such as the Byte Shop.

That Steve could persist and finally convince McKenna, no naive businessman, to handle Apple is a testament to his powers of persuasion and perseverance. After he finally wheedled a meeting with the dapper McKenna and then showed up in his standard smelly garb dragging a very reluctant Woz along with him, it took all his eloquence to complete the deal. The idea was to impress McKenna with enthusiasm and brilliance. This strategy very nearly backfired right out of the gate.

Woz was opposed to the idea of bringing in a slick advertising and marketing guy. He had inherited his father's belief in pure engineering—not hype—as the root of success. He believed their new computer had a market but that at the most they might sell 1,000 or so to other hobbyists. He had no faith in Steve's vision of a consumer revolution. For him the market would always consist of other hackers. With the pressure he was getting from both his wife and his family, who all felt that he should be concentrating on his job at H-P, not the whimsically named and highly unlikely Apple Computer, he was having serious doubts.

In McKenna's office, Steve mentioned an article that Woz had been working on for the hobbyist magazine *Dr. Dobb's Journal of Computing*. McKenna asked to take a look at the draft article, adding that he thought it was important not to make it too technical. Woz, bristling, blurted out "I don't want any PR man touching my copy!"[11] To which McKenna retorted that in that case they had both better get out. Steve calmed the ruffled feathers and convinced McKenna that they were indeed a viable company with a superb product, and that he should take them on. McKenna still demurred. In typical fashion, Steve refused to leave the office with no as an answer. McKenna finally relented.

Once he agreed to take on the company, McKenna was determined to change the logo. He set one of his best art directors, Rob Janov, to work on it. Janov came up with the multicolored apple, built of stripes of rainbow colors and a bite taken out of the side that has endured as the company's emblem to this day.

"Steve Jobs always wanted a very high-quality look," explains Janov. "He wanted something that looked expensive and didn't look like some chunky model airplane.

"I wanted to simplify the shape of an apple, and by taking a bite—a byte, right?—out of the side, it prevented the apple from looking like a cherry tomato."[12]

Steve was a demanding client. He was determined that the bands of color should be right next to each other, even though for production purposes adding a thin band between them would have substantially reduced printing costs. With the logo designed, the next step was to create some bona fide advertising.

McKenna was convinced that the only way the computer could break out of the hobbyist market was to advertise in a visible publication where no electronics company had ever dared to roam. Part of this strategy was to build a personality for the company from day one—a personality that was unafraid to take risks, unafraid to set off into uncharted territory, and unafraid to be different from all the other start-up computer companies. But there was more to it than that. McKenna was looking to get national attention, to make the media sit up and take notice of the little company with the garage-built computer. He thought the best place to advertise was in a market that had a high male readership (all his studies showed that computers were bought by men) and that would never be thought of as a forum for computers. He chose *Playboy*.

Running ads in magazines like *Playboy* was expensive. By now Steve had the circuit board that Woz had designed, the rudiments of a power supply from Rod Holt, some preliminary designs for a case from Ron Wayne, a logo, and an agency ready to help catapult them into the big leagues. There was only one thing missing: money. As it turned out, it wouldn't take him long to find that.

8

Cash, the Faire, and Disk Drives

Money means something different in Silicon Valley. It simply does. Mike Markkula made millions by being at Intel when that company went public during the early seventies. A lower echelon marketing executive, Markkula bought options for stock from other employees who needed the cash and couldn't wait. When the company went public, his shares made him a wealthy man. Markkula would supply the final component that could catapult Apple Computer to fame and massive fortune.

Markkula didn't come knocking at Steve's garage door, however. The quest for money to fuel Steve's dreams of promoting the new Apple Computer began with the only electronics business he'd known: Atari.

"Steve wanted to sell the Apple II to Atari," says Alcorn. "I thought it was a neat machine. It's really clever, innovative, and wonderful, but I didn't see the market for it. Steve would never take no for an answer, and he wanted to have a chance to pitch it to the company president, Joe Keenan. Nolan was different. He was the chairman, and he was really out there thinking, but Joe was the president. He had a normal office with a desk and was a stand-up kind of guy."

Steve walked into Keenan's office with his brash "You ought to buy our product" rap. He then sat down and put his dirty bare foot up on Keenan's desk. According to Alcorn, Keenan said, "Get your feet off my desk, get out of here, you stink, and we're not going to buy your product." And that was the end of Atari's involvement with the Apple II. A couple of years later Atari brought out its own computer because the Apple II was so successful.

Steve called Alcorn to ask what he should do next. Alcorn told him to look for some venture capital first, someone who would invest in the company. He suggested that Steve ask Bushnell for advice.

The venture capital (VC) community was not large at that time, but they all knew one another, drank in the same bars, and played golf in cozy foursomes. Bushnell, who knew more about the give, and especially the take, of the VC world, told Steve how it really was. In exchange for money, he said, the VC boys would take the shirt off your back by owning controlling interest in the company—shares—in exchange for their money. "The longer you can go without them, the better," was his counsel.

Steve needed something else besides the money that venture capital could provide. Apple was having major credibility problems in the Valley. It didn't help that he and his partner looked as unlikely for success as they did. They had trouble even getting in to see the sales managers of some of the larger parts manufacturers. Apple may have built 100 circuit boards by late 1976, but they were still thinking like a small company. Their vision was that if they were lucky, they might sell a few thousand new computers. This was not the kind of thinking that impressed aggressive, go-go semiconductor companies during the mid-seventies. These companies routinely sold batches of tens of thousands of components, and an order for a few hundred from a long-haired 21-year-old kid wasn't going to spin a salesman's wheels.

Nonetheless, Steve was determined that they should not have to pay the higher distributor prices for the several thousand parts they might eventually order from one component maker or another. He was particularly determined to see the guys at Symantec, who made the processors and high-speed ROM that were essential to the new Apple II circuit board that Woz had designed.

Again Alcorn helped out. He called the sales manager at Symantec and suggested that even though he would think they looked really silly, the pair were smart guys, with a good product, and he ought to at least meet them. His pitch worked. Alcorn tells the story of the meeting:

"Steve arrived with Woz at Symantec. He was trying to negotiate a better price on the ROM chips with the sales manager but had no leverage whatsoever since they had never bought from the company before and were talking about a maximum of a few thousand chips. The sales manager was debating whether to give them credit, let alone a better price. Angry that he wasn't being taken seriously, Steve threatened to pull his business from the firm, which wasn't doing any business with them anyway.

"The conversation wasn't going anywhere, and Woz, who didn't have the faintest sense of how to turn a deal, interrupted Steve saying, 'But these are the only guys who can make the parts that will work.' Steve, the master negotiator, tried to get Woz to shut up by kicking him under the table, and then proceeded to slip off his chair and disappear under the table.

"The Symantec sales manager was so tickled that when Steve crawled back into his seat, he refused to cut the price but offered Apple a $40,000 line of credit for 30 days. The sales manager called me up the next day and thanked me for sending him the funniest pair of guys he'd ever met."

Steve's comical persistence had paid off. Brash, aggressive, and sometimes outrageous, but ultimately successful—that was Steve's style.

Working capital was a little more difficult to land. Steve finally reached Don Valentine, a burly VC player on the board at both Atari and Regis McKenna who had been recommended by both Bushnell and Alcorn. Steve convinced him to come over to take a look at their garage operation. Valentine was a self-made man, the son of a truck driver, who had been successful heading the marketing departments of both Fairchild and subsequently National Semiconductor. In the early seventies, he quit working for others and started a venture capital group. In the closed world of Silicon Valley, he was perceived as a no-nonsense guy who knew the electronics world and wasn't about to be taken in by any hype.

Valentine was also neat, well-heeled, and well-tailored. He wore Brooks Brothers suits in a business filled with open-necked polyestershirted engineers, and he drove an immaculate Mercedes Benz sedan. When he showed up at Steve's parents' house, the scruffy entrepreneurs he encountered were not his idea of a good business bet. After looking at their newest product and listening to their plans for selling a few thousand computers a year, he told them that "neither one knew anything about marketing, neither had any sense of the size of the potential market, and they weren't thinking big enough."[1] He would only be willing to talk about investing if they brought in someone who had marketing expertise. Steve, with characteristic directness, asked him to recommend someone. Valentine demurred. But after a week of three or four phone calls a day from Steve, the venture capitalist finally cracked open his Rolodex. Valentine suggested three names, one of which was Mike Markkula.

When Steve called him, Markkula was living the life of leisure. He was casually looking around for new ventures, but with his nest egg from Intel he was in no hurry. He had two small children, houses in Cupertino and Lake Tahoe, and enough money to keep him going indefinitely. Markkula, a short, slender, lithe man who had been a gymnast in high school, was quiet, reserved, and precise. His manner was cautious. With wire-frame glasses and a diffident manner, Markkula looked more like an accountant than a shrewd investor. But his appearance was deceiving. He played the guitar, wore an expensive gold watch, and drove an ostentatious gold Corvette. He was another individualist to add to the team at Apple, but one who had the couth, the polish needed to balance the brash Steve Jobs and the socially inept Steve Wozniak, two Valley kids with little in the way of social graces.

Markkula also understood the impact that the microprocessor might have on the world from his days at Intel, where the device had been first perfected. He figured that it was only a matter of time before someone came up with the right computer, one that made use of the microprocessor and did something more thrilling than display the time or add lines of numbers. When Steve showed him their new machine and ran through a few displays, Markkula forgot about how Steve looked. He forgot about where the company was headquartered. He forgot about all the reasons he shouldn't get involved and offered to help them draw up a business plan to get the venture off the ground. Steve knew that he needed help to make Apple into the kind of successful business that he had imagined at the recent Personal Computing Festival. Woz was leery about bringing someone new into the venture, but Steve convinced him. When he saw the glow in the new potential investor's eyes after he pitched the dream of a personal computer revolution to him, Steve knew that he was an ally. Markkula was the kind of businessman he needed, an unassuming financier whom Steve believed he could overpower.

Markkula was bitten by the seductive bug of personal computing. He started dropping by the garage regularly. He was an engineer by training and soon became intrigued by writing software. He quickly developed into a full-fledged amateur hacker. He talked things over with Steve, Woz, and Rod Holt, and pretty soon he was convinced that they could put Apple onto the Fortune 500 in less than five years. It had never been done so rapidly before. None of his friends or business associates believed him. But Markkula was right.

Markkula started out giving business advice but ended up investing $91,000 in cash in Apple, with a personal guarantee to a bank for a line of credit of $250,000. All this in return for equal one-third ownership with Woz and Steve, and 10 percent going to Rod Holt. The deadline for the venture was April 16, 1977, the date of the West Coast Computer Faire. They had to have the new Apple II ready to be unveiled there.

On January 3, 1977, they gathered at Markkula's poolside cabaña. On that day, Jimmy Carter was about to take the oath of office in Washington, D.C. The weather was crisp and sunny. Mike Markkula, Steve Jobs, Rod Holt, and Steve Wozniak spent the day hashing out the fine details and eventually formally signing the papers that turned Apple Computer Company into a corporation.

Markkula had made it a condition of the deal that Woz and the others work full time at Apple. Convincing Woz to agree had been a major soap opera. Quitting H-P was a step that Woz and his parents and family weren't sure he should make.

"It was different from the year we spent throwing the Apple I together in the garage," remembers Woz. "This was a real company. I designed a computer because I like to design, to show it off at the club. My motivation was not to have a company and make money. Mike was giving me three days to say yes or no: Was I going to leave H-P? I liked H-P. They were a good company, I was secure, and there was a lot of good work. I didn't want to leave, and I said no."[2]

Woz was torn. He wasn't convinced that the Apple venture would succeed, and he was obviously a highly talented engineer. Why should he join and limit his value in the marketplace? As far as Woz was concerned, the Apple was only one of a series of computers that he could design. His wife was upset with all the work he was doing for Apple, and she liked the idea of security, a regular check coming in. Surely H-P would do its own personal computer, and he could have a hand in it. However, his H-P division was moving to Oregon. If he took the riskier choice, he could stay near home, with his friends, in the milieu he knew. At least they had an investor, but that only made the decision tougher.

Steve went on a campaign. Gross manipulation was the method, as Wigginton describes it. Steve called all their friends and begged them to talk to Woz. At one point, he broke into tears while trying to convince Jerry and Margaret Wozniak that Woz should sign up. There was no love lost between them, and there was not much indication that Apple Computer was going to create the dominant machine in the computer marketplace. Why should their son throw in with this shaky venture? Besides, Jerry had been involved in a partnership that went belly up when he was about the same age as his son.

Steve begged Woz to change his mind, but Woz kept saying no.

As the story goes, he finally acquiesced. It had to do with stepping over an imaginary boundary. "You go to a company when you want to turn an idea into money. Once I decided I was doing it to make money, it made the rest of the decisions easy," Woz says.[3]

Markkula was the one who made Woz understand the financial end of it. Steve was working on the emotional level. Two months later they officially bought out the original partnership for $5,308.96 and as part of this they sent a check for $1,700 to Ron Wayne. Now that Apple was serious, with money that he had invested, Markkula also wanted someone around who could keep the money straight. Two erratic founders, a band of teenagers, and an ornery misfit engineer weren't the big-time investor's idea of a viable company.

Markkula brought Mike Scott around to meet the team. Scott was another engineer-turned-manager who had the same birthdate as Markkula, although Scott was a year younger, and had started work in an adjoining office on the same day in September of 1967 at Fairchild Semiconductor. Raised in Florida and educated at Cal Tech in Pasadena, the West Coast's equivalent of MIT, Scott was an aggressive and argumentative character who would rarely back down. Where Markkula was mild-mannered and always working with the soft side of his tongue, Scott had the rough edges of the common man and wore them for all to see.

Markkula might have been mild-mannered, but he was shrewd, and he fully understood his deficiencies, his inability to go head to head with Steve. Scott, a working man's manager who had no time for the intricacies of Eastern thought, wasn't afraid of clashing with the vice-chairman of the board. A brilliant intellectual, Scott was blessed with a nearly photographic memory. He delighted in quoting co-workers' previous comments verbatim to destroy their arguments in meetings. But he, too, loved computers, personal computers, and quickly became another closet hacker. He could spend hours working out some esoteric nuance of programming.

From the outset, Steve didn't like Scott. Holt spent endless hours at Silicon Valley coffeeshops, places like Bob's Big Boy and Denny's, trying to counsel the cofounder over the decision.

"Steve didn't know whether he wanted to run the show or not," remembers Holt. "He didn't have much confidence that Woz had any business sense or acumen, or that he would help, if push came to shove, keep the company on the right course."[4]

For his part, Scott was not at all certain that he wanted to throw in with this band of motley characters. "I wondered whether I could get anything done or whether we would argue all the time," he says. "My biggest concern was whether Jobs and I could get along. He was concerned that I wasn't doing consumer stuff. I was concerned that he didn't know what he was doing."[5]

Eventually Markkula played the diplomat and swayed Steve to accept Scott. The issue, Markkula said, was management—not power—but it was the first of what would become a continuing saga of power struggles at Apple. The seesaw battles between Steve and Scott colored the company's first years. As Steve gained experience, he learned how to find his way through the corridors of power, until eventually he was able to remove Scott and consolidate his power. But as Apple started, there was little doubt in anyone's mind that Steve should have nothing to do with running the company.

Scott was hired at $20,001 with the title of president. His salary represented $1 more than any of the three major shareholders, but the power resided in Woz, Steve, and Markkula, and Scott knew it. Scott joined Bill Fernandez, Randy Wigginton, Chris Espinosa, and Rod Holt in the trenches, and since there was already a Mike, he took the nickname Scotty.

The newly incorporated company rented offices in a recently built office complex along Stevens Creek Boulevard. It was a low-slung stucco building constructed around a central atrium. From the start, Scotty's idea was to maintain a streamlined operation. All circuit board manufacture and board stuffing, as well as power supply assembly, was farmed out to two board-stuffing companies in the Valley. Scotty wanted to keep Apple focused on engineering, software, and marketing. Everything else could be done by others.

Dick Olson was given the task of stuffing the main circuit boards; Hildy Licht assembled the power supplies. Licht, who was married to one of the best-known parts salesmen in the Valley, provided Apple with its first delivery vehicle, a 1967 Plymouth surfer wagon that had belonged to her brother. Acquired for the princely sum of $600 and known as the Whale because it sported a "Save the Whales" bumper sticker, it also had a great, gashing hole in the front fender. The inside was covered in red paint, not because the company was called Apple, but because tested and untested circuit boards were differentiated by whether they were in a red box, and the paint rubbed off.

While Scotty worked on the assembly and business arrangements, Steve worked on the advertisements and a case for the Apple II. Woz and Holt were trying to complete the machine, and Markkula was trying to formulate a compelling business plan. The first design for the Apple II case submitted by Ron Wayne had been far too intricate and amateurish; it included a rolling "tambour" top and wooden sides. Just after the papers were signed in early January formally creating Apple Computer, Steve phoned industrial designer Jerry Mannock, who had been recommended by some of Woz's former co-workers at H-P. They met at a Homebrew meeting soon thereafter.

Mannock had never designed a computer case before, but he agreed to do mechanical drawings for $1,500. Steve told him that he had rented space at the first West Coast Computer Faire and needed to have the case designs in three weeks so he could get the tooling done in time to produce a finished computer by the April show. However, since the fellow at the folding card table didn't look too successful, Mannock told him that he needed cash up front. Steve took the designer aside and convinced him that Apple's credit was good. He could check with the Bank of America if he wanted.

The design Mannock created was essentially the Apple II case as it is today. A thin wedge of plastic holds the keyboard in the front. This is molded with a box about four inches deep and a foot square behind it that holds the workings of the machine. The top is removable to facilitate access to the expansion slots, circuit board, and memory connectors. It is correctly proportioned and relatively simple to mass produce. Steve loved it, and so did the rest of the company. It was almost sleek in appearance, and it was certainly nothing like the competition. With only a couple of minor changes, primarily eliminating the finger grip holes on the sides since the computer was thin enough to be grasped easily, the design was accepted from the first drawings.

The next trick was to produce the machine. Steve approached Howard Cantin, who had done the circuit board layout of the Apple I, and asked if he would do the II. Cantin agreed, but this time Steve was not as affable as with his first order. This being his third completed circuit board in a row, he knew what he wanted. Steve was developing a style of circuit board layout that reflected his artistic, emotional heart. If he couldn't design the schematics, he could at least make sure that the board looked beautiful. This was previously unheard of—engineers cared only that it worked, not how it looked. Apple was after something different, though.

Steve rejected Cantin's first design and demanded that every line of solder connecting chips and components be perfectly straight and, worse, that the whole design look nice when the lid was raised. This was partly the influence of Woz and Fernandez, who had been building beautiful wire-wrapped prototypes for years. They loved cutting and snipping every piece of wire on a prototype to perfect length, so that there was no rat's nest of jumbled wiring which most engineers settled for. More than that, however, the machine was meant to be opened and investigated—it had to look right. These computers weren't only products; they were a work of art, a labor of love for Steve and Woz, and no detail was too tiny.

Steve's demands drove Cantin up the wall: "He irritated me so badly that I swore I'd never work for him again."[6] He then took Cantin's work and had it digitized and fine-tuned by computer—the ultimate insult to a board designer.

All the attention to detail paid off. The board used at the heart of the machine was extraordinarily produceable. Steve approached Dick

Olson of General Technologies to stuff the main circuit boards. "From day one we had remarkably high acceptance results with that design," Olson recalls. "Usually, if 70 percent of stuffed boards work when you go to test, you're doing well. But the Apple II board always yielded in the 90s right from the start."

Not everything that Steve did was appreciated by Scotty. The first big difference of opinion came with the logo itself. The multicolored Apple with a bite out of it, designed by the McKenna agency, might have been all right for a special ad, but for day-to-day letterhead it was prohibitively expensive. Scotty was dead set against it; Steve was for it, Wigginton recalls. "Of course Jobs won. He was always battling Scotty. There were two ways to do everything: Jobs' way, and then there was the right way, which was usually Scotty's."

They fought over awarding employee numbers. Steve was upset that he was number two to Woz's number one. In tears, he demanded that he be given zero. He lost that one, but eventually, when Scotty was fired, Steve got it. One day some bean bags that Steve had approved for the offices were being filled, and the tiny plastic beads escaped to coat the interior of the suite. Scotty and Steve went at it again, and Scotty won: Bean bags were no longer acceptable office furniture at Apple. They fought over signing purchase orders, office layouts, and even the color of the workbenches, typewriters, and telephones. The battles were known as the "Scotty Wars" around the company, and they were a daily occurrence.

Steve was in the midst of the most intense time of his life. Thousands of details had to be attended to, issues resolved, and decisions made. All the experience that he felt he had at 22 in designing and building computers and electronic products was being tested to the limit. He was furious when the wrong color equipment was installed. He worked harder and harder at whittling the price of components from supply houses to the bone. He tried to meddle in every decision, making certain that his opinion was heard. After all, he loved the product so much that every little detail mattered; nothing was too small to escape his attention.

Steve was also toying with the idea of the "Zen Crazy." As he dug deeper into the Zen Buddhist religion, he became more enamored of this kind of monk. There were always a few monks who smelled bad, were rude, made no attempt at social grace, and said whatever came into their minds without thinking of the consequences. In the small family that was Apple, filled with idealists, it was easy for Steve to see himself in the role of the Zen Crazy. He would be the one to make the others question accepted truths. He would make the off-the-wall comments and keep everyone on his toes. He was the unwashed, barefoot, unconventional innocent in their midst.

It was a role that fit his personality, since he liked to react with an immediacy born of intuition. It annoyed some but energized others. In the free-for-all of Apple during the early days, anyone could call anyone else a fool. It was only later, as Steve's power grew, that he became unbearable and disruptive.

In a garage, with three or four friends doing all the work, surrounded by the warm security of family, Steve could control everything. In a brand-new office complex, with an investor and a serious line of credit, ten employees, and the pressure of a fast-approaching deadline for the West Coast Computer Faire, he could not. Steve had always had an impatience with others as well as an absolute drive for perfection and a compulsion for speediness. With Apple's collection of people, he couldn't understand why things took longer than he thought necessary.

Software was a mystery to him. He was a practical, tangible salesman of machines. He could get a handle on a circuit board held in his hands, but the interminable lines of code that make a machine do something were beyond his interest or attention span. Steve wanted everything done instantly, and software requires weeks of testing and debugging to perfect. The only two programmers the company had— Wigginton and, sporadically, Espinosa—were even younger than he. They were the objects of his disdain, and as the software continued to have problems in debugging, they were increasingly the objects of his wrath.

"I was just this kid to him," says Wigginton, who graduated from high school in 1977. "I was working for $2.50 an hour. I'd get up at 3:30 in the morning and work from then until I went to school, then come back after school and work until 7 or 7:30 at night. I was doing little demonstration programs in BASIC and adding features to the pro-gramming language as Woz thought of something new we should add.

"Steve would come in, take a quick look at what I'd done, and tell me it was 'shit' without having any idea what it was or why I had done it."

Woz lost interest in projects rapidly and was an untouchable. Wigginton, who grew close to Scotty, was the one Steve could push and badger into finishing the things that Woz had started and subsequently dropped. Steve was in a constant state of flux and fury—too many details to attend to, too much pressure, and for the first time he could not control everything.

Steve decided that the keyboard for the new machine should be brown and the case a nice warm beige plastic. His parents liked those colors. Since he set himself up as the protector of the common user, his edicts were hard to ignore for the fellow crusaders at Apple who were trying to bring computing power to the masses. He felt very strongly that they should have a polished manual for the computer and wanted to hire a local documentation group to create it. As the introduction date of the Apple II approached and the software was still unfinished, Scotty—the pragmatist and the only one who could really stand up to him—took it upon himself to copy data sheets and include them in binders.

At one point, Scotty took Steve out into the parking lot for a walk, which was where most of the company's important decisions were made. Steve thought it was about the manual, which they had been fighting about for days. But as they circled the building, the company president told the founder that they were going to have to do something about his body odor—no one in the office could stand to work near him.

The work at Apple in those days was overwhelming, but Steve was also spending as much time as possible with Kobun Chino. He was seriously wondering whether he might not prefer to head for a Zen monastery in Japan rather than run Apple. "I didn't want to be a businessman because all the businessmen I knew I didn't want to be like," says Steve. "I saw Mike Scott, and I saw Mike Markkula, and I didn't want to be like either one, yet there were parts of them that I admired. I thought that living in a monastery had to be different from being a businessman.

"I had a sense that Apple would be consuming. It was a real hard decision not to go to Japan. Part of me was a little concerned because I was afraid that if I went I would never come back."[7]

In 1976, Lockheed had been convicted of bribing officials of numerous countries to gain business. With the appearance of Jimmy Carter, the antibusiness flow of Steve's thoughts appeared to find the mainstream. Less than a month after he was inaugurated, President Carter pardoned all the draft resistors of the Vietnam War era. In early 1977, the values of the counterculture seemed to have come into more equal footing with the values of the older generation. For Steve, the personifications of those traditional values were his new partner Markkula and Markkula's hand-picked henchman Scott. They were the straights. He was the outlaw.

But Steve's personality was more complex than that. He was not just some hippie refugee stranded in the business world. No one had ever tamed his individualistic, self-confident spirit. He was basically a stubborn know-it-all clothed in the easy-come, easy-go clothes of the counterculture. If Zen is supposed to dissolve the ego, he was a miserable failure. If he had gone to a monastery, as he seriously contemplated during this period, it would have been to be lord over the other monks, not to sweep the floors or tend a rock garden in perpetuity.

"Markkula absolutely could not stand to work with Steve," says Wigginton. "He pawned most of it off on Scotty. Markkula was in charge of marketing, Woz and Holt were in charge of engineering, and Scotty was supposed to find Steve something to do.

"Steve was in charge of purchasing and interior decorating. The weirdest odd jobs. Anything, just to get him out of Markkula's hair. There wasn't a day that went by without a shouting match between Scotty and Steve. But it was really Scotty doing the dirty work for Markkula."

Steve saw himself as a whirlwind, driven to complete the machine, cajoling and annoying everyone enough to keep them at it and to produce results. Scotty viewed Steve as a pain in the ass, an annoying and largely unnecessary fly in the ointment. "Jobs cannot run anything," said Mike Scott once. "He doesn't know how to manage people. After you get something started, he causes lots of waves. He likes to fly around like a hummingbird at 90 miles per hour. He needs to be sat on."[8]

Nonetheless, Steve was respected as a superb and persistent negotiator for prices. Apple's costs for components were consistently lower than those of any other hobbyist computer company. He was always on the phone, and his favorite phrase was, "You'll have to sharpen your pencil." He was one tough poker player with "brass balls," as Wigginton described him.

Amid the chaos, Markkula was trying to draw up the documents he needed to raise additional venture capital. He spent the months between January and April of 1977 trying to come to grips with the marketplace that the company was about to enter. He hired a business acquaintance, the financial controller of a local pharmaceutical firm, to help him write the business plan. After endless meetings and speculation, they decided to aim for three market segments: the computer hobbyists who were already committed to buying computers; professionals such as doctors and dentists, who had the spare cash to buy gadgets and the intellectual skills to appreciate computers; and the home security/control market, where a computer could conceivably run sprinklers, burglar alarms, lights, and garage door openers.

Markkula's business plan was a document that demonstrated one of the fundamental elements of the computer world in those days—no one had any idea what the market would be. Apple was successful in spite of its players, not because of any magic they possessed. No one knew what the future of personal computing held, but everyone at Apple felt that they were on the verge of an enormous breakthrough: personal computers as a mystical experience. It was a crusade to turn the world on to Woz's magical machine, and everyone who worked in the offices in Cupertino thought so. At least the younger kids did, and Steve was the keeper of the flame.

One thing that Markkula, Scotty, and Steve agreed upon was the importance of their presence at the first West Coast Computer Faire. Since Steve had been one of the first Homebrew hobbyists to sign up for space with organizer Jim Warren, Apple procured a prime location: directly opposite the entrance doors. Markkula spent $5,000 designing their booth, which shocked Woz but delighted Steve. It had an elegantly smoked and back-lit Plexiglas sign sporting the name Apple Computer and its logo. The booth itself would be wrapped in black velvet draperies, and the two tables would hold three computers. One large-screen television monitor would display the antics of the games and demonstration programs that Wigginton, Woz, and Espinosa had created.

The contrast of Apple's booth against the aisles of folding tables and other companies' handwritten signs was dramatic. A ragtag company only six months earlier in Atlantic City, Apple now looked serious and professional, a true competitor for the Altair, IMSAI, and Commodore, even though the three Apple machines on display would be the only three working Apple IIs then in the world.

Two days before the show, the first plastic cases arrived from the fabricator. Steve and Jerry Mannock had chosen the reaction-injection method of forming the case as opposed to structural foam. Steve knew absolutely nothing about plastic fabrication, but then neither did anyone else in the company, and since he was the most adamant about the look of the case, he took over the project. Although this method produced a less finished product—bubbles tended to appear on the surface of the case—it required less expensive tools on the assembly line than the other methods. The downside was that the tools, or forms, were good for only about 7,000 impressions, but the cost difference was substantial enough to warrant this choice. Besides, in their wildest fantasies, several thousand Apple IIs were as many as they would allow themselves to dream about selling.

Unfortunately, the first cases looked terrible and Steve was furious, roundly cursing the "plumbers" who had molded them. Since it was only a few days before the West Coast Computer Faire, the team of Apple hopefuls spent the next 48 hours sanding, scraping, and spray-painting the plastic boxes in an attempt to produce something decent enough to display in their expensive booth. Furthermore, Wigginton and Woz were still staying up nights trying to complete the version of BASIC to be included in the machine. They finally finished the software at 1 A.M. in their hotel room at the elegant St. Francis Hotel in San Francisco. The machines were finally completed. They ordered burgers and milkshakes from room service to celebrate.

The next morning, when the doors opened at 10 A.M., Apple Computer was ready with the sleekest, most attractive computer that the world had yet seen. There was no metal case, no screws, or ugly sharp corners, just a beige plastic box that looked more like a fancy typewriter than an engineer's toy. When the hood was lifted, the engine that drove the machine was easily the most advanced little motherboard in the world of personal computing. Woz had been able to shrink all the workings of a personal computer into 62 chips and ICs. It was an unparalleled achievement. People didn't believe that the tiny machine in front of them could produce the spectacular kaleidoscope of color that kept swirling across the giant display screen. Time after time Steve, dressed in his first suit, or one of the other demonstrators had to whip away the draperies below the table to prove that there wasn't a big computer lurking underneath.

The West Coast Computer Faire astonished everyone by its popularity. It was the Renaissance Faire gone twentieth century. By midway through its first day, lines of enthusiasts snaked around the building. Most hobbyists had thought they shared a secret passion with only a few fellow crazies, but by the end of the two-day event, more than 13,000 people had paid for admission. It was far beyond the organizers' wildest hopes, and it heralded the beginning of the personal computer age.

While Woz, Espinosa, and Wigginton manned the booth for the most part and proudly ran the Apple IIs through their paces, Markkula, Scotty, and Steve stalked the floor separately. Markkula and Scotty worked on the dealers, meeting with them endlessly, cosseting them, and getting them to agree to handle their product. Steve, who wanted to know every intimate detail about his competition, spent hours quizzing the Cromemco, Commodore, IMSAI, and MITS folks. The show was awash in paper—product literature, specification sheets, and flyers—but amid all this detritus one advertisement caught Steve's eye. It was a flyer for a new computer from the Altair crowd called the Zaltair. He blanched.

The Zaltair promised even more than the Apple II:

> Imagine a dream machine. Imagine the computer surprise of the century here today. Imagine Z-80 performance plus. Imagine BAZIC in ROM, the most complete and powerful language ever developed. Imagine raw video, plenty of it. Imagine autoscroll text, a full 16 lines of 64 characters. Imagine eye-dazzling color graphics. Imagine a blitz-fast 1200 baud cassette port. Imagine an unparalleled I/O system with full Altair-100 and Zaltair-150 bus compatibility. Imagine an exquisitely designed cabinet that will add to the decor of any living room. Imagine the fun you'll have. Imagine Zaltair, available now from MITS, the company where microcomputer technology was born.[9]

The ad went on to describe the other features of this machine in equally glowing hyperbole. Steve ran through the crowd to find Woz. At the booth he read it breathlessly to the Apple crew and didn't notice the smirks on the faces of his partner and teenage crew members as he buried his nose deep in the purple prose. Finally, he came to a performance chart which showed that the Apple II ranked third to two Altair machines, and he was somewhat appeased.

According to Wigginton, he finally looked up and said "Hey, we didn't do too bad." When he looked around though, Woz had disappeared. He went to the Altair booth to try and find out more about the machine and discovered that the whole thing was a prank, and the company had stamped thousands of the brochures "Fraud." It wasn't until months later that he found out it was Woz who had written up the ad, printed it in Los Angeles to avoid detection, and then, with his accomplices Wigginton and Espinosa, scattered them around the Faire. The only serious competition to the Apple II turned out to have been created by the creator of the Apple II.

"After the Faire we had a sense of exhilaration," explains Espinosa, "for having pulled off something so well, not just for Apple, but for the whole computer movement."

Even though the report on the Faire in *BYTE* magazine several months later didn't mention Apple, it was clear from the response at the show that the boys from Cupertino had been a hit. By the end of April, Steve was ecstatic. The company had received 300 orders for Apple IIs, which was double the number of Apple Is sold. Owners of the original Apples could upgrade, and the business was taking off. Upgrades were the kind of issue that Apple understood intuitively by having its heart on the line. By allowing previous buyers the chance to upgrade, they created loyal customers and expanded their base with each new hardware release. It was a corporate policy that Steve fought for, and it became an integral part of Apple's product development strategy through the 1970s. For all his personal complexities, Steve always had the heart of a liberal and worked by the ethic of "what was right," even when it cost extra money.

Every day orders appeared in the mail, and computers were shipped by UPS. As the days went by and the orders increased instead of dropping, changes at Apple started to occur. First, they hired more people: a real accountant, a sales manager, another engineer, and a secretary. Then Scotty, who was fed up with the laissez-faire attitude of the kids—not to mention John Draper, Captain Crunch, whom Woz had given engineering space to create a phone card—decreed that there should be confidentiality and at least a semblance of professionalism to the engineering department.

Draper had to go, and the assorted friends who dropped in were no longer welcome. It was the transition to a real company, and Steve was willing to go along with it. He thought that Draper's phone card—which allowed an Apple II to endlessly dial telephone numbers—was a throwback to the old days of phone phreaking for which the new Apple had no need. Woz, whose motivation was often pranks and fun rather than business and changing the world, was upset by the change and it contributed to his withdrawal from the company. While Steve's fascination for business made him ascendant as Apple sold computers that had already been designed, Woz was neglected. The friendship between Woz and Steve began to dissolve in that period.

According to a woman who had grown up with him, Steve's personality had changed by then. He had become self-consumed. He was no longer fun to be around—he was driven. The soft side of him, the charming and gentle side that had counterpointed his dark allure, was no longer visible. He was arrogant from the success of Apple's computers, and he started to treat people like servants.

"He expected them to do things for him instead of asking," she opined. "He was as rude as could be. He had no manners. Common courtesy went out the window."

Woz, too, noticed the change. He found all the hubbub about the machines he had designed interesting, but all he really wanted to do was have a good time and create more computers. He wasn't an ambitious man. As he watched the changes in Steve—the petulance, arrogance, crying spells, and tantrums—he started diving deeper into his cubicle and withdrew from the day-to-day operations. This might be what business was like, but he didn't have to join in.

In the summer of 1977, Dan Kottke returned from the East Coast to work at Apple. Moving out of his parents' house to get his own place, Steve rented a house in Cupertino with Kottke that they called Rancho Suburbio. It was the same kind of low-slung stucco tract that Steve had grown up in—with a big difference. While the garden went to ruin, Kottke filled one room with styrofoam packing chips for his meditation and acid trips. Steve was too busy for frivolities anymore. Moving in with them was Colleen, who was working at Apple assembling the computers. She and Steve tried to make a go of it, but the relationship was doomed. Steve was consumed by Apple, as was Kottke. Colleen was low on their list of priorities, especially when late that summer she became pregnant. Steve refused to have anything to do with her anymore, claiming that he was not the father. Colleen threw plates and glasses, scribbled on the walls with a charcoal briquette that took dozens of coats of white to obliterate, and broke doors and windows.

Steve made it clear to her that he wanted nothing to do with the child and would not support it. He didn't care what decision she made about the unborn child—it was her decision, not his. The relationship broke down completely, and for months she agonized about whether to put the child up for adoption.

Steve's adoptive mother Clara, who had at least been civil in the past, withdrew her support. Colleen was made to feel unwelcome by her co-workers at Apple, and she eventually quit. Then she found herself rejected by the one place she and Steve had shared, the one place she needed for strength, the community of Zen students and teacher Kobun Chino. According to a student at the time, the Los Altos zendo, which had always been a warm and supportive place, deliberately turned against her, making her a pariah. Chino reportedly at first offered to take the child while she completed her studies in art, or to help her support it with modest financial aid. But then, as she grew more visibly pregnant by the day, and Steve grew more and more convinced that she was trying to drag him down and destroy his life, the teacher suddenly stopped offering support. The community chose Steve. She stopped attending classes. Pregnant, without money or her spiritual community to fall back on, Colleen felt abandoned. She moved out of the house and back in with her father, where she had a miserable confinement.

Meanwhile, the success of the Apple II and the swirl of continuing orders exacerbated the battles between Steve and Scotty. Scotty was outraged that Apple was even considering a one-year warranty since the standard for electronics apparatus was 90 days. Steve became upset and in the midst of a heated argument started to cry—it was his standard response to most furious arguments in the early days. Steve never had learned how to handle not getting his way without letting his emotions get tangled up. The spoiled child was still a crybaby into his twenties.

Steve was convinced that the only way Apple would be successful was to be different from the competition. He felt that offering a long-term warranty was a symbol of a humanistic approach to business that he was determined to push—a humanistic approach that he hardly understood but had decided was right for Apple. After a cool-down walk around the parking lot, Steve prevailed.

Steve and Scotty weren't always at odds. Steve's interference sometimes was beneficial. When the accountants found an overlooked $27,000, he negotiated favorable enough terms that Apple could buy an ad in *Scientific American*, which Markkula wanted, and a new mold for the case, which Scotty wanted. Steve also convinced Markkula that having the full-color Apple logo on the cassettes they sold containing various software programs was not frivolous.

He was always willing to fight for what he believed in. The problem was that oftentimes the fights were over trivial matters, his passions changed with the phases of the moon, and his persistence wore everyone down in the long run. Having that fearless attitude, that strong and unbridled counterbalance for the less sympathetic, more traditional business attitudes of Scotty and Markkula was important in the constellation that would become Apple. Steve Jobs was the guy who kept the Apple polished and got things done in spite of himself. And he could be tough as nails when he needed to be.

One day Wigginton, who was working feverishly on a new cassette-based version of BASIC that would enhance the ROM-based version contained inside the Apple II, found that his last six months of work had been erased from the Call Computer's timesharing system. In late 1977, Apple was still too unsteady to have its own mainframes. Most serious software development was done with an account on Alex Kamradt's timesharing system from one of the few working Computer Conversor terminals in the world. Devastated, Wigginton tried everything he could think of to resurrect his work, to no avail. Somehow thousands of lines of codes had been destroyed during a routine backup at the computer center. The only existing version was on the previous magnetic reel, but, although a much earlier version, it was better than nothing.

Wigginton asked to have the previous reel mounted so he could at least work with something. Kamradt refused. Not only was he angry with the success of Apple and the way he had been treated by the two Steves, but Apple was in a financial crunch and hadn't paid its bill at Call Computer for several months.

At this point, Steve got on the line and very coolly calmed Kamradt down. He agreed to give the owner a check if he would come over right then. Kamradt, who couldn't believe what he was hearing, agreed. But then, just as they were hanging up, Steve asked if he would just put the older data reel on the machine before he left so they could get to work on it right away. The unsuspecting Kamradt did so.

When he appeared half an hour later, he was met by Steve, who told him to go to hell—he wasn't going to give him a check. He didn't like him and wasn't about to pay him since his computers had wiped out two months of Apple's work. In the interim, Wigginton had quickly downloaded the previous version of the file, signed off the system, and, along with the rest of the staff who didn't want to see what looked to be a fight, left the office.

Kamradt was an ex-boxer with cauliflower ears and a mashed nose. He could get angry fast. Steve, a skinny vegetarian with few athletic skills, stood chin to chin with him in the battle of wills. Eventually Kamradt backed down and stalked out. Steve didn't fear anyone when his products were at stake. He was willing to take on any company, any person, and go for broke. At that point, Apple had very little to lose, but the attitude came from Steve. He was a tenacious negotiator who could obtain favorable terms with any supplier, go toe-to-toe with any competitor, break anyone who got in his way. For Steve, his latest computer, his latest product, was always a "jihad," a holy war: Winning was a holy quest, a crusade, and anything was justified and could be forgiven, if the victory went to the forces of Apple.

In September the machine tooling for the Apple II case finally broke. The company was doubling production every few months, but at that point a steady stream of product was crucial and there was no back supply. With customers demanding machines, suppliers demanding payment, and completed, stuffed circuit boards sitting in cartons, the company came within a few days of bankruptcy. Scotty was riding the thin edge of financing by taking in parts and keyboards on 45 or 60 days credit and then billing customers at 30 days. As long as they could collect, they could stay afloat. No cases meant no computers, and that meant no income.

Steve flew to Portland to visit the head of one of the West Coast's foremost plastic tooling makers, Tempress. This time Apple was going to use the structural foam method and needed proper metal tooling.

"I thought to myself, 'Does he know what the heck he's doing?'" said Bob Reutimann, an executive with the firm. "I was a little afraid of going ahead with the project. I thought 'Here comes another guy with big ideas.'"[10]

With characteristic drive and determination, Steve offered a bonus of $1,000 a week for every week ahead of schedule the company delivered. Even though Apple was still small compared to the firm's other customers, his exuberance and aggressiveness paid off. The tooling arrived ahead of schedule; Apple's financial crisis was temporarily solved. However, the financial crisis was such that Markkula had to go to the well to find venture capital earlier than he had intended simply to tide the firm over. Nonetheless, it was already obvious that Apple Computer was a viable business and that the personal computer market was exploding.

At that point, Steve was worth almost a million dollars on paper, although that was more ephemeral than real, and his appearance was starting to change. At the West Coast Computer Faire he wore his first suit, and now, with his hair still long but carefully styled, he was enjoying the role of boy wonder and working very hard at learning the intricacies of big business from Markkula. When Apple made its presentation in Manhattan to the Venrock investment group, an arm of the Rockefeller family, Steve accompanied Markkula and Scotty. Woz had no interest in the business end of Apple and, according to Kottke, had given Steve all the proxies for his shares so that the younger partner could vote them however he saw fit in company board meetings. This gave the 21-year-old control over more than 50 percent of the company's outstanding shares—no wonder Markkula treated him deferentially.

Although the Apple II had been a major step forward as a consumer-looking product, and even though nearly 4,000 were sold in 1977, the hottest machines on the market were not Apples. That distinction went to the Altairs and the Altair-compatible IMSAI. Late in 1977 there was no reason to believe that the Apple II would take over the market. It was an attractive computer, with a dedicated band of enthusiasts pushing it, but since it was based on a distinctive microprocessor, its future seemed to be in the home market, not the business market, and that was a much less lucrative arena.

At a major meeting of the Apple staff in December, a plan was hatched that would revolutionize the computer business and put Apple far ahead of its competitors. Data storage and retrieval was a troublesome problem for all early machines, especially since memory chips were very expensive. Operating a computer required thousands of instructions, in sequence. Those instructions either had to be typed in by hand—which was what Woz did with the first Apple computer to make it do anything—or stored in some machine-readable medium. Mainframe computers used magnetic tape spools and floppy disks, but in 1977 they were prohibitively expensive solutions not cost-effective for the inexpensive personal computers. By 1977 cassette tapes had replaced the paper punch tapes of the first Altair programs, but they were still slow and unreliable. Until a more efficient way to store or retrieve data was devised, the machines weren't going to make an impact on the general market.

Markkula urged Woz to build a floppy disk drive in time for the Consumer Electronics Show, which would be held in Las Vegas in the second week of January—only one month away. It was an almost impossible challenge for anyone but Woz.

IBM had been selling floppy disks for several years. A year before, Woz had drawn a schematic for a disk drive circuit as a mental exercise. He studied the North Star/Kentucky Fried Computer Company machine, the only personal computer that had a disk drive. He saw that he could do in very few chips all the things that the North Star machine did. He also attacked IBM and that giant's disk drive system with the kind of engineering brilliance that was his hallmark. IBM used complex circuitry to synchronize and time the disks and data on their drives, but Woz came up with an entirely different method that eliminated the need for all that circuitry. He based his design around a distinctive electronic "format" for every disk. To make his system work, however, he needed a formatting program that would wipe each disk clean and set it up in a standard way so that the simplified disk drive would work. He enlisted Randy Wigginton's help, and together they worked day and night throughout the month of December.

"On Christmas Eve of 1977, Woz and I finally got the disk drive to write and read something," says Wigginton. "Something simple, like some nibbles off the disk. To celebrate we went out for a milkshake.

"I remember the night before CES. We got to Las Vegas and it still wasn't finished. The hardware was working but the software wasn't. Woz and I would work for an hour and then go out and gamble for an hour. I was 17 at the time, and we were out there throwing craps.

"At about seven in the morning I finally got it working. Woz said, 'You better back it up.' I backed it up the wrong way and destroyed what we had done during the last hour. We had to do it over again.

"We were there for three days, and between the show and the gambling, I don't think we slept."

The design was an enormous step forward. Not only was the

simplicity of the disk controller card astonishingly elegant, but the idea of sidestepping the issue of synchronization was a brilliant move that made the competition stand up and take notice.

"I nearly dropped my pants," remembers Lee Felsenstein, the Homebrew emcee and a design consultant to Processor Technology on the Sol, referring to his first sight of the disk drive. "It was so clever. I thought, 'We better keep out of the way of these guys.'"

Camelot

9
Growing Pains

The Apple II disk drive enabled software programmers, would-be programmers, and amateur hackers to produce workable software for the Apple II that operated at reasonable speeds, could be transferred easily from machine to machine, and was reliable. It had enormous impact. In 1978, programs began appearing in the mail at the company's new offices in an industrial park in Cupertino, around the corner from the original location. The majority were games cobbled together by enthusiasts who had bought Apple IIs and found that they actually could produce something with them. There was almost no money in software at that point. The idea was to share programs, offer them to fellow enthusiasts at local versions of the Homebrew Club that had sprung up around the country, and use them to demonstrate one's own unique talents as a programmer.

By January of 1978 Apple was valued at $3 million, and Markkula had convinced Venrock to sink money into the company—$288,000. They were joined by Don Valentine, who happened to see the Venrock representative dining with Steve and Markkula and changed his mind about investing, putting in $150,000. The third member of the group was the legendary venture capitalist Arthur Rock, who had been involved with both Xerox and Intel and was considered one of the shrewdest technology investors in the world. His stake was $57,600. They were all elected to the Board of Directors, and Apple was finally, one year after the founders had huddled in Markkula's pool house, a properly capitalized business.

By mid-1978, the marketplace reaction was overwhelming. The drives were finally ready to be shipped in quantity, and the Apple II could not be kept in stock. At one point there was a 26-month backlog. Woz's final drive design added a few other touches to the circuit board that he had discovered while laying out the printed board. It was widely hailed as the most remarkable single design breakthrough in the young personal computer world. Working on a similar design, Commodore had endless problems and finally ended up shipping their drive at the end of 1978, nine months later than Apple's, but by then the damage had been done. Apple took the market by storm and never looked back.

Steve had no idea who was buying the computers that Apple was selling. Sales were pouring in so fast that they had no time to analyze the marketplace and fine-tune their sales pitch. People seemed to love the computer because it was a great machine. Computers were just good in the scheme of things, who needed to know more?

Regis McKenna did. Starting as early as 1978, the public relations and marketing guru for Apple began to wonder about the home market. The problem was, as McKenna saw it, that by calling the Apple II a home computer they were implying that the machine was not serious— that it was a toy and thus they were missing the much more lucrative business market. Furthermore, by implying that the machine was a home computer but not delivering anything that would support the claim, he was afraid of annoying consumers so much that they would never get back in the fold if the computer did eventually become a home computer. Starting in 1978, the ads the agency created sounded a new call, moving away from the early images of friendly personal computers in kitchens. The new ads took pains to show Apple II computers in friendly settings, but doing serious jobs. McKenna reasoned that since there was no reason to buy one for a home, they had better start going after the business market.

In the wild days of orders that wouldn't end, McKenna seemed to be the only one thinking about the developing market. Apple suffered from an extraordinary dearth of consumer marketing skills.

"People who knew Markkula and Apple wondered whether they would make it," says Frank Burge, Apple's account executive at the McKenna Agency. "We kept saying, 'These guys are flakes. They're never going to make it.' Jobs and Wozniak looked as if they were on something. It was counter to everything we believed in."[1]

Markkula's marketing ideas were based on a trio of concepts that he expressed in a kind of fuzzy-headed memo that every new marketing employee received for many years. The memo, shown here in part, described the company as follows:

Empathy: If we have empathy for our customers and dealers, we will truly understand their needs better than any other company. We will know how they feel about our products and about Apple.

Focus: To do a good job of those things that we decide to do, we must eliminate all the unimportant opportunities, select from the remainder only those that we have the resources to do well, and concentrate our efforts on them.

Impute: People DO judge a book by its cover, a company by its representatives, a product's quality by the quality of its collateral materials. We created the impression that the Apple II was a high-quality product by producing high-quality ads, brochures, manuals, and other collateral materials.[2]

These were the three tenets of Apple's remarkable success? Hardly. Apple succeeded in spite of its founders. The market was soaring, and through serendipity, having an excellent product, and making fewer mistakes than its competitors, Apple enjoyed astonishing growth.

The company entered the education market in 1978 because Markkula's daughter was learning grade school math. Apple's chairman thought that there should be a program that offered math problems, then displayed a smiling or frowning face depending on your answer. Markkula's efforts led to the Apple Education Foundation. The idea was to provide computers at cost to schoolteachers who wanted to develop educational software. It was a great success and linked the company with the educational marketplace. This was years before any of their competitors even noticed that the K-12 market segment was extraordinarily influential, even though it might not have the full profit margins of the retail channel.

Steve saw to it that Apple supported user groups from day one. It was part of his "share the wealth" roots. Apple was always willing to help these groups of users who banded together to share software and expertise. That attitude developed loyal owners who sold the Apple concept of computing far and wide. The groups also provided a source of employees for the company.

"I bought an Apple II early in 1978," explains Bruce Tognazzini, an early employee and another free spirit, "and I immediately signed up to become a dealer. I was selling TVs and Apple computers in San Francisco, but there was absolutely no documentation—maybe 12 sheets of Xeroxed paper. A friend and I started the San Francisco Apple user group because we couldn't figure out how to use the computer.

"Eventually, I wrote a few programs in BASIC. Most were silly. One day I called Steve to come down and show them to him. He thought they were great, so he called all the other guys who were around that day into the demo room and then took me to lunch. He was kind of wild-eyed and crazy. But no crazier than I was. He eventually paid me $50 for one of the programs, which was pretty good, since it had only two lines of code."

For Tognazzini, walking into the Apple building was like coming home. "I was one of the original organizers of the Peace and Freedom Party, so I was favorably impressed by Apple." He signed up as a dealer after changing the name of his store from Village Discount to Village Computers at the insistence of Gene Carter, Apple's head of retail relations. A few months later, he was hired by the company to write business software. He was part of the first team of software programmers that the company hired and, this being Apple, they were an eclectic group. The crew was headed by renaissance man and computer scientist Jef Raskin, a former professor at the University of California at San Diego. But no matter who joined the Apple Corps, the force was always with the mercurial cofounder, who blew hot and very cold.

Tognazzini was an inveterate prankster of a programmer. One day someone showed up at Apple with a silly program called Mock-BASIC, which parodied the programming language. Soon most of the company's employees were huddled around the machine on which it was running. Then Jobs walked in.

"He went into an absolute tirade," recalls Tognazzini, "about our wasting the company's time and being frivolous. He had this squealing voice when he got mad, and he could seethe with coldness. So he finally told us to erase the program and get back to work.

"We all looked at each other and of course, as soon as he left, I went right back to playing with the program. We all knew he was a jerk. In those days, you just ignored him."

In early 1978, the first serious retail operation, Computerland, was born, and Apple was a key supporter and midwife. Apple had always been very liberal with its dealers. Again the attitude was tempered by the belief that enthusiasm and the intuitive feel that Steve and others had about someone was more important than any other consideration. The business was changing, however, and Apple was trying to increase the professionalism of the dealer channel. Many of the oddball dealers who jumped on the bandwagon early were being squeezed out by better capitalized, more serious retail operations.

"One dealer was operating out of his home in a Florida suburb," says Trip Hawkins, a marketing MBA who was hired by Mike Markkula fresh out of Stanford during the summer of 1978. "Another dealer was on the second floor of a walk-up in Manhattan with incense burning on the floor, Buddhist publications everywhere, and a couple of computers in the corner."

The company's cozy dealer relationships frightened other computer manufacturers, especially when Apple started co-op advertising programs. Co-op is a standard in the retail marketplace. A large manufacturer pays a portion of the cost of advertising when a retailer places an ad mentioning that manufacturer's product. No computer company had ever tried it before, but it was an instant success with the financially strapped retailers, who were trying to sell the dream of personal computers a few years before the idea was truly accepted by the mass market.

As Apple ascended during the spring months of 1978, another event occurred which would ensure that Steve's feet stayed firmly on the ground. In response to an old friend's entreaty, he traveled 1,000 miles north of Cupertino to Robert Friedland's farmhouse in Oregon. A few weeks prior to that, Friedland had taken pity on Colleen. A short time before her due date he had driven to Silicon Valley to get her. On May 17, 1978, a girl was born on his farm with the help of a midwife. Steve appeared a couple of days later and helped Colleen name her.

The farm was still a spiritual enclave of sorts, a kind of ashram with the self-styled guru Friedland at its head. In keeping with the times, children were being given names like Omar, Gobin, Govindas, Ashberry, Silver Moon. Although Steve believed in Eastern religions, he was adamant that since the child had been born in the West, she should be given a Western name. Against the counsel of the communards, Colleen agreed, and a few days later they chose the refined Western name Lisa Nichole.

Then Steve left. Colleen couldn't handle the disapproval of the commune that she sensed—Steve's persuasive ways had again made her look the villain. She bounced from place to place, living in Los Angeles and Lake Tahoe, and ended up on welfare in the Bay area. Over the months that followed Steve paid voluntary child support when Colleen's father threatened a lawsuit, but then always stopped again. He refused to admit that he was the father. Colleen was leery of pushing him too hard but finally asked for a $20,000 settlement. Markkula, a family man, reportedly thought that the amount was too little and suggested that Steve up the ante to $80,000.[3] He refused.

It is hard to understand the virulence of his rejection. He was an orphan and was doing his best to create another; it was almost like a self-fulfilling legacy. But his anger may have come from a deeper river of the subconscious. Perhaps it was the first time in his life that he had not been able to control the agenda. He had dictated to his parents, manipulated his friends, and started a hugely successful business. But he was faced with a woman who refused to get rid of a child, a child he had not wanted her to have, who refused to fit in his program. It was a bitter lesson for Steve. Colleen was also a link to the past, to his days as just another Valley kid at Homestead High. He could never escape that legacy.

It was time to find someone else, to distance himself from Colleen. Steve was never much of a womanizer. He found the social process, the dating scene, unappealing. He solved the problem in a simple way. As the months went on, he fell in love with Belinda Kreski, a strikingly beautiful account executive of mixed Polynesian and Polish descent who worked for the Regis McKenna agency. He was still paying rent on the Cupertino house that he shared with Kottke, but by the second half of 1978 he was hardly ever there. They had a long string of roommates, including a stripper who stalked through the house naked and a guy who made a practice of shooting his Colt 45 pistols into the air. Kottke continued to take psychedelic drugs. Although Steve had given up hallucinogens, he still considered them an essential element in gaining perspective and an important test of a person's mental acuity.

"For the first couple of years that I was at Apple, before I left for college in the fall of 1978, I remember Steve asking me two questions over and over again," remembers Chris Espinosa. A moderately capable programmer, but not in Wigginton's class, Espinosa had gravitated to the customer service function at the company. In 1978, he spent his afternoons after high school fielding questions from Apple's customers. "I had very little direct contact with Steve. He was off doing other things while I was working the phones for $3 an hour.

"But every time I saw him, for years, he asked me if I had a girlfriend yet or if I had dropped acid. That was all he cared about. It got so that I would be embarrassed before he even opened his mouth because I knew what he was going to ask. Since I had done neither, I dreaded his questions."

Steve's battles with Scotty continued unabated. One enormous conflict erupted over signing some purchase orders. Jobs reached them first and claimed that he would sign them, but Scotty tried to grab them away from him. They almost came to blows. Scotty appealed to Markkula and threatened to resign if he weren't given the authority to approve spending. Steve finally backed down. At the company's first Christmas party, in late 1977, Steve was furious when Scotty refused to have vegetarian food catered. On his 23rd birthday, in early 1978, he walked into his office to find a wreath of white roses propped against his desk. The message, which was unsigned, read "R.I.P.—thinking of you." Only later, when the white rose became Scotty's emblem, did Steve realize who had been behind it. When Scotty found out that Steve liked to immerse his feet in a toilet bowl and flush it to relieve the tensions of a tough day, Steve became the butt of the company's jokes.

In a small company, Steve could wield his influence even though Scotty tried to minimize his participation in day-to-day operations. Apple was never a comfortable place to work if you were near the front lines, where Steve liked to spend his time. Steve had two faces: a charming evangelical side and a hard-edged, impulsive, tongue-stinging side. He was the seeker of wisdom, the Zen voyager, but he was also the tough, hard-ass, Silicon Valley version of surly Bob Dylan. Unrelenting and overbearing, alternately charming and abrupt, he goaded brilliant engineers and bright people to both the heights of genius and the depths of despair. Steve's way of testing the mettle of his employees was to make unreasonable, and basically impossible, de-mands. His style produced one of two reactions: The recipient either quit, refusing to do the impossible, or did it, proving that he or she could do the impossible. If your personality were disposed to the former, you left the company. It was the latter personality type who stayed.

Although the Apple II was still being expanded with ROM cards, new programs, and more memory, the computer was basically finished. The challenge then was to support it and build incrementally on its success. By 1978 the company was doing extremely well, but it was time to think about new products to replace what would soon certainly be an obsolete computer. Steve, along with Markkula and the other managers the company had hired—the employee count was around 60 in summer 1978—were convinced that the Apple II had nearly reached saturation. In the semiconductor industry—in the American business market in general, for that matter—product cycles last a couple of years. The words "new and improved" were America's standard advertising slogan, and in a country where a new model of every car was expected annually, it seemed self-evident that the same would be required of computers.

The first step was to plan for the Apple II Plus, an enhanced version of the original machine with a better version of BASIC, an easier start-up routine, and much more memory. As personal computers started to take off, the cost of memory chips had dropped while the sizes available expanded. The new enhanced machine would be available with up to 48 kilobytes of main memory, compared to 24K in the original Apple II. This was 48,000 bytes. Only three years earlier Woz had been working with 256 bytes total on his precursors to the Apple I.

Although the Plus was an interim step, the time had come to supersede the Apple II with a new machine. Feedback from dealers and customers had made it clear that there were a few key items that should be corrected in a new release: The computer needed to display both uppercase and lowercase letters to a width of 80 characters, not 40, and it should be able to address more memory so that more sophisticated programs could be written for the newly envisioned business market that McKenna was predicting. At the same time, it was deemed essential to make the new machine fully compatible with Apple II software and "bundle" it with all the software that one could possibly want so that upon purchase it would be a complete package. The machine was code-named Sara, after chief engineer Wendell Sanders' daughter, and was to be released as the Apple III.

The project was launched in late 1978, and throughout 1979 Sanders worked on it, assisted by Dan Kottke. Steve had a hand in it as well. He wasn't much of a caretaker but thrived in the environment of creation.

"Steve Jobs got involved in the Apple III in a way that was really disruptive," says Trip Hawkins. "The Apple II is a consequence of Woz's dreams. He is a really integrated thinker. He was able to consider all the things that had to be considered and integrate all those thoughts into the design of the product.

"But with the Apple III, Steve decided to design the external package, and he had it underway long before they decided what the CPU [central processing unit] was going to do. So as time went by, they kept putting more and more onto the PC board, and then when the time came they couldn't fit it all in the box that he had approved. But he wouldn't change it."

As they worked their way through the digital design, Steve wouldn't let them adjust the physical design of the computer. After the success of the Apple II look, which he was widely credited for, he had come to believe that he had a magic touch with industrial design. In consequence, the Apple III engineers had to come up with a piggyback circuit board to accommodate all the circuitry. Then, to save manufacturing money, they did not make the connectors between the two boards out of gold, which does not corrode. Eventually, when they shipped the computers in autumn of 1980, the connectors corroded, the electronic impulses were corrupted, and the Apple IIIs never worked correctly. By then Steve had long since washed his hands of the project, and the blame fell on the engineers.

"Apple was the company that could do no wrong," according to Hawkins. "It was the Camelot of business. Basically, market demand propelled the growth of the company, and it covered up a lot of mistakes. So you could have incompetent people running around spending a lot of money, and it wouldn't be noticed because the demand for the Apple II was so strong.

"Every now and then somebody would stand up and say 'Okay, that's it! I won't take it anymore. We've got to make this change.' And then a lot of other people would react by saying, 'What! You mean I have to wake up from this dream?' Things would go on just the way they had been."

Demand for the Apple II never relaxed. In 1977 the company sold 2,500 computers, in 1978 that figure was 8,000, and in 1979 the sales quadrupled to 35,000. "In 1979, we did $47 million," says Steve, "and that's when we all really sensed that this was going through the rafters."[4]

As sales went through the roof, they tried to hire the right people to help manage it. But the prospective employees had to fit the Apple mold; they had to have enthusiasm and humanistic values; and they had to be believers. Steve's evangelism and belief in the goodness of the dream, the truth of computers, took hold and spread throughout the employee base. People came to Apple who had found the religion, and they in turn pushed the religion further. It was evangelical fervor, a sect that grew from Cupertino and blazed across the country. If you didn't catch the religion, or tried to buck the system, you were excommunicated. Steve made sure of that.

A manufacturing man was hired from strait-laced National Semiconductor. He ordered sweeping changes in the way the computers were assembled. No longer was the assembly area open for anyone to come through. Bare feet were outlawed. Hidden microphones and security guards were installed to monitor employee work habits. He didn't last long.

Apple *was* personal computers by 1979. The company had all but destroyed the competition, and as computers started infiltrating American society, reaching people whose interests and skills were further away from the original hackers, they convinced others even less interested in the programming and hardware to buy them. It was no longer just the logo and design of the case that made Apple the consumer product of choice.

One of Steve's demands was that the company produce manuals that were consumer oriented. Steve understood that the machine had to look inviting and that the documentation had to be appealing and complete enough to reassure potential buyers that they could use the machine.

Jef Raskin managed both the software development and the documentation. He wrote the first true manual for the Apple II, and by early in 1979 the company was shipping the wire-bound book that accompanies it, effectively, to this day. This was a manual that a nontechnical person could read and understand. It was typeset with clear, comprehensible text and illustrations, all of which were light years ahead of the competition. (Of course, it was still Apple—the typesetting was done by an Apple employee and UC Berkeley student at night on the university's equipment.)

Another part of their success in the consumer arena was rooted in Regis McKenna's clever manipulation of the press—the "opinion makers" as he liked to call them. Ben Rosen was one. The editor of an influential newsletter about the electronics industry, Rosen was also an early Apple owner. He numbered much of Manhattan's journalistic corps in his circle of friends, and he became a tireless promoter of the personal computer, but especially Apple's. As the press started to take notice of the phenomenon of personal computers in 1979, Rosen was there to lend credibility to the anarchic company in Cupertino.

Although word of the personal computer revolution started to seep into the news media, the press tours that McKenna organized for Markkula and Steve had little impact. There was still no overwhelming business reason to buy a personal computer, even though a word processing program did finally appear in early 1979. Called *AppleWriter*, it was created by a former company employee who, after losing a girl to another Apple programmer, headed for a wood cabin in the Oregon mountains to work in misogynous isolation. The program worked hand in hand with the company's first printer, the Silentype, and heralded the beginning of a loosely comprehensive set of products. At that point Apple was publishing software that was written in house under the Apple Software label. *AppleWriter* was one of the key programs. The *Dow Jones News/Retrieval* package had just been finished, as had an unwieldy checkbook-balancing effort, partly written by Markkula.

The company also hoped to market software from sources outside Apple, but outside software varied in quality and more often than not was riddled with bugs. Apple started to work with so-called third-party developers during this period, trying to upgrade and standardize the software they produced. In these early days of software, it was unclear whether anyone could actually make money writing and packaging a program to the public. In 1978, the best bet for a programmer was to make a sale to Apple and let the company worry about distribution and support.

The explosion of the Apple II's popularity came from a market that the original business plan had overlooked: the educational world. With BASIC included inside the computer, the Apple II was ideal for learning programming. Schools could see the handwriting on the wall, and by the late seventies most high schools in the country were teaching BASIC programming literacy as a standard part of the curriculum. The best available machine to use was the Apple II. Furthermore, the machine had color and, important for the teenage market, a number of games had been written for it. The Apple II quickly became the computer most requested by high schoolers bent on convincing mom and dad to buy them a computer for Christmas. In 1979, the education market sustained Apple, since very little useful work could be done on the computer other than programming in BASIC.

Nonetheless, the company was a success, and in the summer of 1979, Apple sold $7,273,801 worth of stock. There had been a smaller sale one year earlier, and in between, several of the key players had cashed in a few shares to private individuals. But this time the shares were valued at $10.50 each, and among the 16 buyers were some of the largest venture capital and merchant banking companies in the world. Steve sold just over $1 million of his own holdings and at the age of 24 became a legitimate millionaire.

He bought a house, which he shared with Belinda in the hillside town of Los Gatos, nestled under the Santa Cruz mountains. He also bought his first of a series of Mercedes coupes. He added a BMW motorcycle, with orange pom-poms on the handlebars, on which he and Kottke took endless spins through the mountains and backroads behind Stanford, skinny-dipping in a reservoir that was hidden by a slight rise from the streaming cars along Interstate 280. He bought art, such as a painting by Maxfield Parrish, but little else. His house was a paean to asceticism, although he claimed that he was just too busy to decorate it and would eventually get around to it. For years there was no furniture in the place other than cushions, a single dresser, and a mattress on the floor of his bedroom. With some of his wealth, he financed a charitable organization concerned with blindness in Nepal and India and bought land in the Pacific Northwest with his old college friend Robert Friedland.

During this time, Steve made a conscious decision to become a businessman. He was determined to learn what he could about running a business by running Apple. He continued to meditate, but his weekends of zazen and retreats at the Los Gatos Zen Center were over. There was simply no time. He was wearing his hair neat and wore suits when he needed to. He tried not to buck the system. Apple had developed into a bureaucracy, albeit a benevolent one with quasi-humanistic values, where topics like the official company culture could be endlessly debated. The unorganized, chaotic structure of the early days was gone. Apple had to pump out existing products and prepare for the future by creating new ones. That took rigorous planning and, as the people now surrounding him explained, decisions by consensus.

Steve worked hard to curb his impulsiveness. He stayed out of Scotty's way. As the success of Apple started to sink in, he changed in some ways, but other parts of his personality didn't alter. He always took himself a little too seriously, inflating an image of his own importance that Scotty loved to puncture. Scotty was fond of dressing in outrageous cowboy hats or Napoleon outfits and busing dozens of employees to private screenings of movies. Steve had no such deft touch. At what would become an annual Apple extravaganza—the company Halloween party—he appeared the first year in a toga as Jesus Christ. He thought it was funny. Most of the rest of the company did, too, but not for the same reasons.

As if all this success weren't enough, in late 1979 a piece of software appeared that broke the back of the competition. By then Apple programmer Bill Atkinson had succeeded in bringing a high-level programming language, UCSD Pascal, over to the Apple II. Atkinson, probably the company's leading software programmer, had an enthusiasm and a quest for perfection that matched Steve's. A computer science student of Raskin's before he did work on a Ph.D. in neurobiochemistry at the University of Washington, Atkinson was hired by Apple in mid-1978 to write a few programs. His first effort was the *Dow Jones News/Retrieval* program, which allowed stock information to be downloaded to an Apple II. A wild-eyed computer enthusiast whose interest in neurobiochemistry had grown from his experiences with LSD, Atkinson was a brilliant man with the madness of a hacker. He would get an idea and stay up nights, days, and weeks on end until he had it working well enough to show to others. He didn't spend time worrying about how to do something, he just went ahead and did it. His was a can-do attitude, to which Steve responded.

Neither Scotty nor Steve really understood the potential of software. The company's reputation had been built on Woz's hardware, and up until then, software had to take the back seat to the company's wireheads in the engineering department. Atkinson had fought hard for bringing the higher level language Pascal over to the Apple II. He stood up to Steve and convinced him that he could indeed do it, in an incredibly short time, and that it was good for Apple.

Atkinson says that Steve told him "Our users only want to code in BASIC or assembly, but I'll give you three months to prove me wrong." When Atkinson delivered early, he cemented his relationship with

Steve. Fundamentally, what made the appearance of Apple Pascal so important was that it provided a much better programming environment than BASIC for creating sophisticated business applications. Soon Apple was attracting a better breed of programmer.

It wasn't long before the investment paid off. *VisiCalc* was the first spreadsheet for personal computers. A year earlier, Steve had sold an Apple II at cost to Dan Fylstra, a Boston-based, would-be software entrepreneur. In January of 1979, Fylstra returned with a prototype program two of his colleagues had produced that allowed columns of numbers to be manipulated instantly, and more important, if one number changed the entire row recalculated. It was a remarkable achievement. It was something that could not have been done before computers existed, and it offered an absolutely new and potentially valuable use to business users. It was the first spreadsheet for a computer.

Markkula and Steve were not that impressed by the program, but Trip Hawkins claims he was. "I wanted to buy the company the moment I saw it," he recalls. "I wanted to make sure that it was exclusively an Apple product. I had just come out of business school, and I knew how much calculating you had to do. And I could see that this made the process of doing forecasts and what-ifs a breeze."

However, no one at Apple wanted to pay the $1 million that Fylstra wanted.

As it turned out, it didn't matter. When the program shipped in the fall of 1979, it ran only on the Apple II and wasn't transferred to any other computer for another year. The one-two punch of the disk drive and *VisiCalc* destroyed the competition. Apple took over the personal computer market for good. The advent of the spreadsheet made the computer a useful business tool for the first time. A business could justify buying computers, Apple computers. This was the absolute stamp of approval. The next year, sales doubled again, and until IBM entered the market two years later, Apple had no competition to speak of.

The Apple II, far from being at the end of its useful life, was going stronger than ever. But the Apple II was Woz's machine, and the Apple III, while still under development, was never meant to be more than an interim computer. Steve was 24 years old in 1979, and he was looking for something radically new to form the basis of an absolutely new family of Apple machines. They would be conceived and engineered by him. This would be his chance to design and build a computer, to show that Steve Wozniak wasn't the only genius at Apple. His would be a new generation of computers far beyond anything imagined at that time. This would be his baby.

To identify the project, he gave it a name that he had already used for a child. He decided to call the computer Lisa.

10
The Lisa Project

Building another computer based on the same microprocessor as the Apple II held about as much fascination for Steve as taking a vacation. He was determined that Apple would change the world with computers, but it couldn't be done with the Apple II. The company had to pioneer the next generation of personal computing. The Apple III was not it and was never meant to be. It was a serious project for the serious engineering types, but Steve was not welcome in their meetings. Of course, as the company cofounder he could say whatever he liked, and often did, but no one paid him much mind. He had to find a new technology to supersede the Apple II and III. Part of that motivation was his desire to build the most incredible machine ever made as well as his love for the cresting edge of new technology, the latest in "whizzy" gear. He also wanted to prove that he was a responsible and serious person who could run a complicated project.

"Markkula never let Jobs have any power," says Tognazzini, an early member of Apple's software team. "No one in the early days thought Steve was running anything. He was always looking for something to get involved in, and no one wanted him."

Steve would show up every once in a while at meetings and go on a tirade, as he did during a demonstration from a group that had designed a touch-sensitive monitor for the Apple II.

According to Tognazzini, "He appeared in the middle of the meeting, hung around, and listened nervously for a few minutes. Then he said, 'Well, thank you very much.' The visitors looked at Steve and at us in the assembled group. Steve repeated his thank you and the visitors asked, 'Would you like us to leave?' Steve replied, 'Yes, thank you.' When they left, Steve went off the deep end, berating the Apple employees about how we were wasting time and the company's money and should be ashamed of ourselves.

"It was like something out of a bad movie," says Tognazzini. "The reason we stayed at all was that none of us were working for him. We were working for Markkula, or Scotty, or John Couch, or Tom Whitney, but not for Steve. If we had been, most of us would have left."

Wendell Sanders' group was working to get the Apple III out the door, and the Apple II group, writing documentation and performing after-market support, was handled by Jef Raskin. Steve was on the loose, searching for the way to make a totally new kind of computer. The best example he knew was that of his garage predecessors, Bill Hewlett and David Packard.

"A lot of Steve's product design instincts came from working on H-P products," says Hawkins, "and looking at them. The two of us went to the H-P offices one day and practically got kicked out because he was so obnoxious and started climbing around looking underneath their latest model, the H-P 150. It was pretty obvious we weren't there for a sales call."

Steve hired two seasoned engineering managers from Hewlett-Packard, John Couch and Ken Rothmueller, to design a brand new computer. He named the project Lisa. In addition to being the name of Colleen's daughter, the choice grew out of Apple's tendency to use female names for projects: Sara, Annie, and Twiggy, for example. Lisa was never intended as anything but an interim internal code name, but it stuck. They launched the Lisa design project in earnest early in 1979.

That same summer he submitted to a paternity test at UCLA when Colleen's father threatened another lawsuit over nonpayment of support. Apparently it revealed a 94.97 percent chance that he was the father of Lisa Nichole.[1] Still, he refused to pay child support with any regularity. Colleen and the baby were on welfare in San Mateo County, living in a tiny house, while he and Apple made millions. He refused to visit them.

In 1979, as he was launching the Lisa project, he was also deeply involved with Belinda. It was a relationship that gave him his first taste of the sexual perks of fame and allowed him to dictate terms. "She was genetically perfect. I've never seen any woman who looked so lovely," recalls Bana Whitt, an early employee who later married Bruce Tognazzini. "She was always reserved, and a little curt, so she never endeared herself to us. Steve always liked his women to be 'good girls,' and Belinda was. It was like a masochistic relationship; she did whatever he wanted and was very demure."

He might act like a wild, off-the-wall character around the guys, but he wanted his women to take care of him and look gorgeous. Belinda fit the bill, and he eventually gave her a job at Apple. He was the leather-jacketed tech prince bestowing favors on his mistress. But there were always contradictions. "We were at a trade show that year, and at dinner one night somebody told a dirty joke," says Whitt. "Steve got freaked out, because he didn't want anybody to be nasty in front of Belinda. Well, we all thought, 'Belinda, Steve's little princess.' He could be really conservative that way. For all his unorthodox ways, he was a real male chauvinist at heart."

But Steve's all-consuming passion was always the new product, the next generation of machines. "I wrote the original Lisa plan with Steve," says Trip Hawkins. "It called for a $2,000 system that would be based around a 16-bit architecture, rather than the 8-bit Apple II architecture—exactly what the Macintosh turned out to be. We were real excited about it. We were convinced we could change the world."

The basic machine was supposed to have two floppy drives and be targeted at the office market. Ken Rothmueller was to be head of engineering. John Couch was to head up the software divisions. From the second half of 1979 through 1980, a design war was on. Couch stayed out of the Lisa project at first because he had never been a big fan of Rothmueller. It was part of Steve's thinking that if the two guys heading the project were at loggerheads, they would compete better and bring a further drive for excellence. It quickly developed "that to a lot of us, with the exception of Rothmueller, we weren't happy with the direction in which it was going," says Hawkins.

By late 1979, Rothmueller had designed a bit-mapped, green phosphor monitor machine with a built-in keyboard. It was not very attractive or inspiring and looked like the kind of machine that H-P would have built, not the innovative kind of design that Steve specialized in. This early Lisa was large and clunky but was based around an expensive and powerful new microprocessor from Motorola, the 68000. The microprocessor, so new it wasn't available yet, was the hottest thing in the business and Steve characteristically loved it already. Rothmueller didn't seem to be able to do anything very stimulating with all its power. The prototype was slow in both processing speed and screen refresh. Steve started to grow antsy.

The Lisa software group was doing some interesting tricks with screen graphics, however. Atkinson was experimenting with various-sized letters and proportional spacing by controlling every dot on the screen. The rudiments of on-screen computer painting—bit-mapped graphics—in higher resolution than the Apple II or III could support were also possible, and it seemed that if only the 68000 could be pushed to near its limits, they might have a machine that would really excite the public.

As 1979 drew to a close, the vice-president of research and development and vice-chairman of the board, Steve Jobs, wanted a few more things in the works. He wanted something more compelling to a consumer than the box Rothmueller was designing. Steve wanted something sexy, as sexy as the latest in home stereos. He started with a detachable keyboard. Steve believed that a movable keyboard would offer users a much more comfortable relationship with the computer. It was not a brand new idea—IBM had used them in the 1960s with some mainframes—but it was fresh to the brave new world of personal computing.

Beyond that, he was having a hard time conceptualizing or articulating what he wanted for the look of the on-screen environment that the user would employ to operate the machine. All he knew was that it had to be new and radically different from anything yet seen. Steve needed something to stimulate him; he wasn't an original thinker. He was great at taking the ideas of others and massaging them, spinning them into something better and more accessible. He needed inspiration, and he needed it soon. He was obsessed by speed and had convinced everyone on the Lisa project that they had to have the machine ready to ship in 1981.

Rothmueller didn't see it the same way as Steve, and more important, he never had the same sense of urgency about the project. He "was a real linear thinker," says Hawkins. "He didn't have a really great feel for the average idiot in an office trying to use a machine, and he had a real H-P design mentality: Build them for an engineer, and everybody else will follow. He wasn't a particularly creative designer, and he didn't have a consumer products mindset."

The Lisa, like the Apple III, was aimed at the nebulous office market. The Apple heads of state convinced themselves that the Lisa would be an office solution, while the Apple III would be aimed at small businesses. The Apple II would keep its focus on homes, kids, and schools. This was how they segmented the market for personal computers.

To develop the right product for the office market, Steve became convinced that Apple should consider a strategic alliance with one of the giants who already had a firm foothold in that territory. He was smart enough to realize then that he knew nothing about offices and those kinds of businesses. So he hired people from H-P, who he was convinced did know that market, but as he saw what Rothmueller and his colleagues were coming up with, he also knew enough not to put all of Apple's eggs in their basket.

Steve went in search of a partner. There were only two choices, and one, IBM, was anathema to all the countercultural blithe spirits and make-the-world-a-better-place types who populated Apple. IBM was the enemy; Apple couldn't get into bed with them. The other choice was Xerox, whose name was synonymous with office automation and copying systems, and whose reputation was unbesmirched by the long shadows of mainframes.

In the company's second private investment placement, a mezzanine financing concluded that summer of 1979, among the Arthur Rocks, venture capital firms, and investors was Xerox. Early in the year, Steve had approached the Xerox Development Corporation, the venture capital arm of the office copier-based empire, and told them, "I will let you invest a million dollars in Apple if you will sort of open the kimono at Xerox PARC." The Xerox Palo Alto Research Center was rumored to be a Land of Oz of computer knowledge and advanced research and was whispered to be on the verge of an enormous adventure in personal computers. With his remarkable salesmanship, he succeeded in getting exactly what he wanted. Xerox signed an agreement never to purchase more than 5 percent of Apple's shares and invested $1 million by buying 100,000 shares at $10. Steve got the chance to see what a real revolution in computing could be.

Steve had been encouraged to pursue Xerox by a collection of Apple's characters, with Jef Raskin and Bill Atkinson at the forefront. By that time Raskin, concerned that the company's new machines were ever more expensive, was heading a small R&D project of his own at Apple to build an inexpensive home computer, one that would cost less than $1,000. This machine would come as a self-contained unit, software included. He had three engineers working on it, and they were casually focusing on this proposed "desktop appliance." But Raskin had worked with the fellows at PARC a few years earlier through some work he did at the Stanford Artificial Intelligence Lab, and he knew that Apple should find out what they were up to.

Atkinson's interest lay in the world of graphics—how to make a computer draw rectangles, spheres, or half-moons smoothly, quickly, and simply. As soon as the Lisa project was launched in early 1979, he joined up and began to work on a series of programming routines that would define the way every Apple computer after the Apple III looked and worked. His procedures, which he first called LisaGraf primitives, would give the Lisa complete control over the screen display.

The Apple II had been a bit-map machine—all the dots on-screen were controllable with programming—but it was crude. What the Lisa team and Atkinson had in mind was something more sophisticated. There would be many more dots, or "pixels" (the word came from the combination of *picture* and *element*) on-screen, resulting in much more detailed graphics. They would actually control each pixel individually. What they gave up with all this manipulation was color—adding color to every dot was prohibitive in cost—but they gained elegant graphics and an appealing visual look. By late 1979, Atkinson had a sketchy collection of his LisaGraf primitives running, but he was faced with a few problems. While the Lisa team members were providing new graphics capabilities for their inchoate system, they still didn't have any idea about what their on-screen environment should look like.

At Xerox PARC, Larry Tessler was working with the Smalltalk programming environment that his group had created for the Alto computer, an office computer systems project. Xerox was having trouble figuring out how to manufacture computers cheaply enough and was looking at Apple to possibly build cheap versions of Xerox machines, which is why they had invested. In many ways, the Alto was what the Lisa was aiming for. It reflected a number of the ideas of seminal computer thinker Alan Kay. Kay was a firm believer in simplicity, smaller is better, and the mouse, but he also had a classic academician's problem: He was working toward a holy grail of computing that was still at least a dozen years away in 1979.

"Up to then I had believed in the Alan Kay vision," says Tessler, "that computers would not really happen until they had the power of a VAX [a type of minicomputer], could be held in your hand, and cost $1,000 or less apiece. He called that computer the Dynabook."

Kay's vision was part of the ivory tower research atmosphere that pervaded the PARC campus. The goal was not to produce workable, salable products—the driving force was to expand the possibilities of computing for the good of mankind. The group was hooked on making computers easy for humans to use, but they never welded that to bringing computers to market and getting their hands dirty selling computers in the bazaar. That was where Apple and its chief barker, Steve Jobs, excelled.

Tessler was the designated Xerox personal computer expert. He was the only person in the Smalltalk group who believed that personal computers—the ones on the market, not the ones Xerox was developing—were serious. He had purchased several computers by the time Apple came around to look at what Xerox was doing in December of 1979. Tessler had dealt with Commodore over a personal computer at his daughter's school and was not impressed. When the group from Apple came by, he figured, "These were a bunch of hackers and they didn't really understand computer science. They wouldn't really understand what we were doing and just see pretty dancing things on the screen." It was part of the superiority of formally trained computer scientists, an attitude that was just beginning to infiltrate the original corps of self-taught hackers at Apple as more and more "trained" people, especially H-P engineers and MBA marketers, were hired.

Unveiling the working Xerox system at PARC had been preceded by several meetings where the ground rules were laid out. Finally Steve, Couch, Scott, Rothmueller, Hawkins, Atkinson, Richard Page (a Lisa systems software architect), and Tom Whitney (Apple's head of engineering and another H-P alumnus) were taken into a demo room. Then Tessler unveiled the machine and operating environment Xerox had developed. It was instant pandemonium.

What they witnessed was like nothing they had ever seen on a computer before. The revolutionary element of the Xerox Smalltalk environment was that the user could interact easily with the computer through icons, windows, and menus without ever typing a single letter or command. Xerox's concept was of a computer-style "desktop." The environment of the screen was graphically based with icons instead of typed names to represent files and programs, used a mouse for pointing and moving things on the screen, had individual windows open containing different documents, and demonstrated rudimentary, on-screen pull-down menus. It was thoroughly intuitive and clearly the right way to interact with a computer.

The keyboard was nearly superfluous. Up until then, all computer operations—such as those on both the Apple II and III—had been invoked by typing at least one, and usually several, lines of programming code or instructions. You might eventually get to a game that used a joystick or a spreadsheet that employed cursor keys, but lines of characters were always essential to start off.

The mouse, a three-button, plastic, deck-of-cards-shaped box that fit into the palm and rolled across a desk or table, moved the on-screen cursor or insertion point, which could be centered over an icon or menu title. Clicking one of the three buttons performed different operations on the file or program represented by that icon. Furthermore, across the top of the screen were also a series of menu titles, each of which could hold a number of choices such as Save, Close, and Quit. These were also reached by using the mouse and buttons. It was an absolute revelation to the visitors from Apple.

"Atkinson was peering very closely at the screen, with his nose about two inches away from it, looking at everything very carefully," remembers Tessler. "And Jobs was pacing around the room acting up the whole time. He was very excited. Then, when he began seeing the things I could do on-screen, he watched for about a minute and started jumping around the room, shouting, 'Why aren't you doing anything with this?? This is the greatest thing! This is revolutionary!'"

The Xerox machine demonstrated the fundamental idea behind the bit-mapped screen concept, and though they had grasped it intellectually, the Apple contingent had never before seen it in operation on such a sophisticated level. It was all done with layers of dots. You could look at a drawing and then zoom in to look deeper and find more dots. For Steve and the other Apple acid-heads, the PARC experience was like dropping acid for the first time and getting the big insight—satori. This was the tao of high technology, the right way to build a computer.

With LSD they had seen the layers peel away, felt the very essence of the beingness of a flower or dived into a piece of wood. LSD works on the visual nerves, cracks the retina and the color generators in the back of the eyeball, to create a different view of the world. The high-resolution, bit-mapped screen, with all the dots arrayed before their eyes, allowed them to voyage inside the digital world and swim around among the pixels. Like opening the doors of perception, this was crossing the boundary. It was the electronic acid test. If you got the idea, you were on the bus. If you didn't, you were left on the curb.

Atkinson and the others were asking Tessler questions, one after the other. "What impressed me was that their questions were better than any I had heard in the seven years I had been at Xerox—from anybody: Xerox employee, visitor, university professor, or student. Their questions showed that they understood all the implications and the subtleties. They understood that it was important that things looked good, that the font was attractive, that the icons were cute. That everything worked together smoothly."

By the end of the demo, Tessler was convinced that he was going to leave Xerox and go to Apple, which he did a few months later. These guys understood what personal computing could be, and they could make a mass market product. They had the right stuff as far as Tessler was concerned.

What the Xerox group had shown them was a revolution, but it wasn't an earth-shaking revelation, according to Atkinson. "I was aware of most of what they were doing from the trade press. But here it was working. It looked nearly complete. They had actually done it, and that reinforced our direction, which was along the same path.

"If they could do it, we could do it. It energized us. It gave us something to strive for."

Steve immediately wanted to create a computer like the one at Xerox but much better. On the drive back to Cupertino, he turned to Atkinson, who was equally inspired, and asked how long he thought it would take to get a system like that up and running on a 68000 machine like his Lisa. Atkinson, a gifted programmer who had little experience writing operating system languages and interfaces, said "About six months." That was all Steve needed. He was off and running.

At Apple, the most advanced programming to date had been done with the new Apple III operating system utilities, where menu commands could be stepped through from the keyboard. But this system, called SOS (for System Operating Software), was still a command-oriented environment, with none of the finesse and ease of use of the mouse and icon world they had just seen at Xerox. For Steve, it was obvious: Throw the old-fashioned work on the Lisa out the window and start over again on a new operating environment. Rothmueller clung to his early SOS-like world and had a conviction that the answer was not the mouse but "softkeys," a variation on function keys developed at H-P. According to Steve, the mouse was obviously a superior way to operate a computer, and when the cofounder and resident evangelist went on a crusade, he usually won.

Steve wanted Rothmueller to redesign the Lisa to make it work with a mouse and support a new graphics-oriented interface with icons and windows. The former H-P engineer didn't want to and resented having to make the whole machine over again. It started a seesaw battle through the corridors of engineering at Cupertino. Steve and his band of cohorts, including Atkinson, Page, Hawkins, and Couch, started proselytizing and building demonstration programs. Rothmueller, with Raskin, fought them. Steve ordered Rothmueller to do it. He refused.

"Steve has a power of vision that is almost frightening," says Hawkins, who is a believer in that vision. "When Steve believes in something, the power of that vision can literally sweep aside any objections or problems. They just cease to exist."

Less than a month before the presentation at Xerox, 90 people, including 63 Americans, were seized at the U.S. Embassy in Tehran. It began more than a year of frustration and anguish throughout the world. The Russians had invaded Afghanistan and the United States was powerless, its attention focused on a walled compound held by militant followers of the Ayatollah. With videotapes seen nightly, the country watched in horror as images of an inept rescue operation screamed from every television.

Then the United States pulled out of the Moscow Olympics that summer. Good news was necessary; everyone in the country was looking for it. The Apple story was a natural. The Apple II could do no wrong. It was pouring cash into the company's coffers. The first general press coverage started to come during the summer of 1980. It was a great American success story: Two kids bet the farm and made it. For Regis McKenna, it was a PR dream and a chance to take the Silicon Valley story national. He pulled out all the stops.

Scientific American wanted Steve in one of their ads. He bought another suit. The ads pictured him with a child in front of a TV set, skiing in the mountains, sitting cross-legged under a tree, riding his motorcycle. He was capturing people's imagination, but more important, he was capturing the imagination of editors. Ben Rosen was also working hard selling Apple's credibility in the press. He was another apostle for the gospel of personal computers, especially once *VisiCalc* made it to the market. He believed in personal computers and at every chance told the world of big league journalists in Manhattan how great Apple was. Everything was coming up roses.

Inside the company, it was "get the software out," recalls Phil Roybal, who was in the Apple II support and marketing group. "The thing that united us all was that we loved to write software. Since we didn't have any idea what the public wanted, we did anything anyone could think of." Scotty was in charge of the internal office computing and electronic mail system developed at Apple. He was the system operator and controlled it with his own unique touch—his code name was Baal. He could shut the entire system down if he wished, and he did when he was piqued about something. He could lock individual users out or sit over their shoulders and suddenly pop up on their screens. It was still Apple.

Optimism in the form of unrealistic schedules was the order of the day. Mostly it came from Steve. He was so seductive that others got carried away in his fantasy. He had an extraordinary ability to sway a room full of people. He wielded the psychological tools he had developed over the years, offering visionary pronouncements while he goaded and ridiculed the same people who bought into his wildest fantasies. He kept everyone off-guard and thrived on argument. Because he always wanted to do it right—as opposed to the rest of the computer business and, eventually, the rest of Apple itself, who didn't in his view—the best and the brightest, the noblest computer-smitten engineers and marketing people stayed with him, even as he destroyed their egos and raked them over the coals.

Steve, Hawkins, Atkinson, and Couch began to map out a new vision of an office computer. Steve and Hawkins wrote up a new specification for the machine in the wake of the Xerox visit. At one point they typed "THINK DOTS" in the middle of a section about what the screen should be based on. They showed it to the head of engineering, Whitney, along with a few demonstration tricks that Atkinson and Page had put together.

"There were no mice for computers in those days," recalls Hawkins, "so to prove how great the mouse was, we found the only guy who made them, in Berkeley, by hand, out of a single block of wood. We gave one to Atkinson, and he wrote some kind of driver for it so we could show a simple little drawing program that he called MouseSketch.

"We called it the 'clandestine mouse' and when we started to demonstrate it around the engineering labs, we won about half the crew over to it."

It was by no means an instant sale. The mouse was an entirely heretical way of interacting with a computer for those who had been formally trained on mainframes. For the self-taught Steve Jobs and his corps of supporters who had no tie to the past, the guys who saw computing as an exciting quest based in giving as much power as possible to the user, for people who were not comfortable typing letters and commands like the BASIC commands that a programmer had to work with daily, it made perfect sense.

It was all going Steve's way. He possessed confidence that grew daily. He made hundreds of decisions daily, hourly, that affected numerous lives. He was in the midst of a stable relationship with a stunningly beautiful woman, the kind of woman who made men's heads snap around. He had it all.

Although he was deep at work on a computer project named after his daughter, he still refused to see her. Colleen and Lisa were living in a tiny house behind another in nearby Menlo Park, a house that a neighbor described as squalid. She was on welfare and in the summer of 1980 the county of San Mateo finally sued Steve for child support. Colleen could never bring herself to do it on her own. Whenever she asked him for money, he refused and she left it at that, sure that he could grind her down with all the lawyers and paperwork he might produce with his financial muscle. She was having enough trouble just making it through each day.

When the county sued him, he and his attorney intended to fight it out. Then he thought better of it. At the end of the year, he signed a document agreeing that he was indeed Lisa's father, reimbursing the state for the money it had paid to her and agreeing to provide health insurance and make ongoing payments of $386 per month. These were pegged to the welfare level in 1980 for a single mother and child. He was also given visitation rights, but for a long time he didn't use them.

In 1981, the Apple II had reached critical mass in the marketplace. Enough Apple IIs were out in the world that it made some business sense to write a program for them—you could make money doing it. This was a watershed. By late 1979, Apple had sold about 50,000 computers. With the success of *VisiCalc* the next year, that number more than doubled to 125,000.

Apple was also changing direction in its software development for the Lisa. The decision had been made to offer a complete set of application programs that would be created within the company. The idea was to move away from the haphazard, uncontrollable way that software appeared on the Apple II. For the Lisa, it was all going to be Apple Software. This was partly to control the profits and partly to ensure that there were quality programs in the key software areas. There was no guidebook on how to write programs for personal computers, with their extremely limited memories and erratic operating environments, and there were few people competent enough to write them. Instead of depending on the Apple II hackers, who had proved their worth, Steve believed his advisors from H-P, who told him that the Lisa needed classically trained programmers with experience. It was the best of choices—but also the worst of choices.

The company had previously employed teenagers and self-taught hackers—Wigginton, Espinosa, Don Bruener, Kottke, Tognazzini, Scott, Atkinson, and Markkula—all of whom loved to cut code. Their attitude toward traditional programming values was typified by something Wigginton once said about someone's program. "You've got too many comments," he complained. When the programmer explained that you had to have comments to tell other people what you were doing, the teenager replied, "Comments are for sissies."

For the original Apple hackers, the brilliant overall design and haphazard writing of a program counted much more than methodical planning. They were the maestros of software. Child prodigies and idiot savants, passionate plodders and inspired amateurs, they pursued programming the way Mozart wrote symphonies: They never outlined and never looked back—it was all intuition.

A macho developed among the early hackers that had to do with how fast you could get something up and running. A program riddled with bugs that took a day was worth much more than a clean, neat program that took a month. After only one day a decision could be made about whether to continue with it by actually seeing the working model, not by discussing theoretical issues ad infinitum. As the company grew, these differing viewpoints became a bone of increasingly cantankerous contention between the classically trained engineers of Lisaland and the self-taught hackers from the company's founding.

As the Lisa project gelled and more programmers and engineers with formal degrees were hired to work on it, the software-by-trial-and-error teenagers were left out. The new pedigreed programmers built programs after long discussions, carefully debugging on paper before ever beginning a prototype. This was programming as a profession. Steve and the hackers saw themselves as artists, and artists lived by the seats of their pants, not some cast-in-bronze rules. The dichotomy created dissent and tension at the heart of the team building Apple's new computer.

Steve was at the center of this controversy. He knew little about designing computers in the professional world on which the Lisa group was focusing, but he desperately wanted to know more. He wanted to learn how to build a real computer system, and he believed the software team models that the H-P guys were telling him about were the way to proceed. When Couch jumped onto the bandwagon with him and told him that designing software took dozens of meetings, he believed it. He also believed that it would take only a few months. He abandoned the teenagers and adopted the "professional model" with the same gusto he brought to all his enthusiasms.

By 1980, serious frictions were developing among various factions of the company. The first and oldest faction, the Apple II camp, was populated by "the straights," the plodding thinkers and organized folks who handled the day-to-day details of running a mature product line. These people were working at noncreative functions, as Steve saw it. They had an exploding bureaucracy of software and hardware managers, tech support, and engineering support folks who were far removed from the creative flow of building new machines. These people had come in after the fun part was finished.

Then there was the team of incremental thinkers who were deep into creating the interim step, the marginally improved Apple III. They were primarily advanced hobbyists, hackers who had learned enough to try to follow Woz. The group was peopled with the early joiners, the first engineers and technicians the company had hired. It was a true group effort. All the key people in the company were part of the planning stages.

Everyone had certain features that they were sure would make the machine a success in the business market. It quickly became a kind of catch-all computer. It was the company's first effort to build a computer as a company, as opposed to by an individual, so the specifications kept growing . . . and growing . . . and growing. Soon there were too many features, and to do all of them meant doing many of those things only moderately well. Especially since the charter for the machine required that it be completed in a year. The plan was to announce the Apple III in the summer of 1980, but the project was started late in 1978. This was Apple, the little "company that could," after all.

Finally, there was the Lisa group, which was searching for the breakthrough computer product to take Apple into the eighties. The Lisa was meant to be a professional computer, not a hobbyists' hacked up machine. To do it right, the company had to bring in serious professional engineers. A large part of this was Steve's doing. He was determined that if the company was going to strike out in a bold new direction and finally leave the legacy of Woz behind to create a machine with his indelible stamp on it, they had to start fresh with new people who weren't tied to the ghosts of the past.

He was tired of seeing the Apple II referred to as Woz's machine. The relationship between the two cofounders was definitely languishing. As the company grew, Woz showed less and less inclination to work, while Steve grew more and more driven. His older cofounder was in the midst of a bitter and protracted separation, and eventual divorce, from his wife Alice. And he was seriously considering returning to college, at his parents' suggestion, to complete his degree.

Privately, Steve complained about Woz's lack of dedication. But no matter how he really felt about Woz, since he knew very little about the mysteries of digital design Steve continued to invoke his name whenever he wanted to punctuate a conversation. "I guess I'll have to get Woz. He could do it cheaper, faster, and better."[2] The words he filled in at the end of the sentence depended on what he was trying to achieve. While he could use Woz to stimulate the hackers who were all in awe of the legendary designer and wanted to emulate him, he was also increasingly determined to exorcise Woz's overwhelming spirit throughout the company. He wanted to have a machine that was his alone, and he knew that the Lisa, with its mouse and icons, was his answer to the Apple II. By late summer 1980, they had a crude working prototype of the hardware and were predicting, in all their naiveté, product shipment in 1981.

By late summer 1980 the Apple III was falling into disrepute internally. It still didn't work well, and no software was available for it; but since they had preannounced it, they would have to ship no matter what or lose market credibility. Like Pontius Pilate, Steve washed his hands of the entire project. He would stay out of their rat's nest, not help them solve their problems, and they were going to stay out of his baby, the Lisa. He and Couch devised a management theory that isolated and separated the new team from the rest of Apple. The Lisa group had an elitism that was quickly apparent to the rest of the company. You couldn't even enter their quarters, a new building along Bandley Drive, unless you were wearing a special orange badge. For an avowedly democratic, humanistic company, it was a startling contradiction in terms. They weren't going to do it like the hackers of the Apple II world, and they weren't going to make the mistakes of the Apple III. Lisa would do it right.

Steve had seen Apple go from nothing more than a few dreams and a computer designed by Woz to a serious business enterprise that was making him a rich man. The acid-dropping, India-tripping, Zen Buddhist meditator had, in the space of three years, surrounded himself with layers of management and bureaucracy that could stifle anyone. Success bred management, and while he knew that the cash cow of the Apple II had to run smoothly to ensure the company's future growth, he also knew that he wanted to work on a more spontaneous level. There had to be a way to mix corporate structure with humanistic values. Steve was determined to find it, and somehow he thought that the Zen monk's off-the-wall craziness might be the ticket. He became all the more impossible.

When the company was small and Steve could be reined in by Scotty, Markkula, or Woz, it was good to have a house loony whose reactions were sure to be crazed and emotional. Calmer voices could intercede. In the early days, there was a "no-gloves" attitude at the company, a give-and-take that allowed anyone to make a comment on any other aspect of the company. An engineer could call a marketing campaign "crap" as long as he could justify his reasons. That atmosphere, which Steve fostered and supported both consciously and subconsciously, grew less prevalent as the company burgeoned to 200, then 600, then more than 1,000 employees in 1980. Apple started as the employees' company, with everyone holding a stake in the quality of products as well as the prevailing attitude. By 1980, Apple had become a place that looked good on a resumé. Working there was no longer powered by passion; it was powered by the career ladder.

As the company grew, corporate culture changed. Apple actively worked at having an enlightened management style. This was partly a result of Steve's espousal of the currents and winds of the time and partly a matter of prevailing Valley culture. H-P had built a company on a foundation of enlightened management, and in Steve's mind, Apple was going to emulate and surpass H-P. Furthermore, the Valley, with the explosion of consumer electronics and computers, had dozens of start-up companies and an almost unwritten rule that they had to provide the most advanced working environments in the world.

Creating a clan of Esalen types was not compatible with the bang-'em-up abrasive management style of Steve Jobs. He hated long meetings, with their interminable discussions of petty details. He wanted to be able to look at an approach to some problem, make an instinctive decision, and then move on to another without looking back. Snap judgments were his style. If you could be passionate about your opposing point of view, about the reasons he was wrong, you could push Steve back onto the right track. But you had to use aggression and force to counterattack him.

But because Steve's off-the-wall attacks could come at any time, Apple's people learned to marshal all their arguments, to think through every angle, and be prepared to defend a point of view with eloquence. It created an environment of excellence, so that even when he did not question your decision, when he surprised you by agreeing without argument, you had already done the requisite thinking.

By threatening irrational, emotional responses, the company cofounder produced remarkably well-informed employees. Fuzzy, un-clear decision-making was unacceptable. So was democracy when Steve was involved. The constant exchange of ideas, the building to a consensus as it had developed in Apple's no-confrontation, modern management style never worked for him. He might have been from the counterculture, he might have been deeply influenced by aspects of the self-realization movement, but he was not of that world. Steve never had any trouble saying exactly what was on his mind and letting the chips fall where they might.

What happened, as the company went through its paces and tried to deal with its explosive growth, was that the only person who continued to operate under the aggressive, say-what-you-will, tell-the-truth-if-it-hurts attitude was Steve. He became even more combative, abrupt and, yes, obnoxious.

Steve had his enlightened visions, and they were part of what drove Apple to be the kind of company that it was. "Super-site" was one of his main fixations. He imagined a corporate town where offices and living quarters could mix. Plenty of trees and grassy lawns would populate the campus, and it would enable the company to hire bright, young engineers and avoid the inflated Silicon Valley property market. For a while he flirted with flexible hours for engineers, allowing them the freedom to work at home or at the office. When the results weren't up to his exacting standards, however, he shot off a memo: "When I agreed to totally flexible hours, it was with the stated assumption that it was the most efficient way to get a very professional quality of work done. This group has not demonstrated that quality during the past 60 days. Effective tomorrow everyone is required to be in by 10 A.M., no exceptions."[3] However, it was still Apple—10 A.M. is pretty liberal for most nose-to-the-grindstone manufacturing companies.

"Apple was very much like a club," says Phil Roybal. "We would have management retreats at spectacular resorts, like the Pajaro Dunes south of Monterey and right on the ocean. There would be a couple of days of meetings, and at night we would open the bar and dance until we dropped. Apple was asking an incredible amount of us. We were working around the clock. At the very least, we had to give everyone a sense of mission and purpose. We decided to try and quantify what we all believed in. It was called the Apple Values project."

In 1979 and 1980 "Apple Culture," and the definitions of it, were a focus of attention in the company. Up to then it had been an unwritten set of rules that only Apple could ever have tried to write, to quantify, and they did as part of the Apple Quality of Life Project. They created memos that included lines such as the following, which were mainly quotations from Chairman Steve:

> One person, one computer.
> We are going for it, and we will set aggressive goals.
> We are all on the adventure together.
> We build products we believe in.
> We are here to make a positive difference in society as well as make a profit.
> Each person is important; each has the opportunity and the obligation to make a difference.

We are all in it together, win or lose.
We are enthusiastic!
We are creative; we set the pace.
We want everyone to enjoy the adventure we are on together.
We care about what we do.
We want to create an environment in which Apple values flourish.[4]

As the company developed an extraordinarily relaxed corporate culture—a culture with health club memberships, lots of parties, T-shirts, and personal computers at cost for every employee—Steve was becoming more of a monster. He was approaching his 25th birthday as 1980 began, with money, success, unrelenting drive, ambition, and no social graces—or an interest in developing them—to soften the blows that his Zen-trained, reactive mind dealt out. He seemed to have taken half the message of Zen. He took the mental clarity and the emphasis on intuition that was the key to a Roshi's answer to a koan, but didn't weld it to the contemplative and thoughtful personality that could never make a cutting or dismissive remark to another human. Zen Buddhism was a Japanese religious movement, and it was founded on the Japanese personality traits of respect for elders and the timelessness of the universe. Steve was a brash American who had the counterculture's disdain for previous generations—look what a mess the world was!—and an obsession with cramming as much as possible into every day. His was a hybrid Zen master, an American original. He was creating a new kind of "business Zen"—"Zen business." And Apple was his testing ground.

Steve's meddling in the Lisa group finally got to Rothmueller, who made it clear that he wasn't getting on Steve's bus and departed about halfway through 1980. John Couch took over the project. It became apparent that this scheme of Steve's was a real alternative to the way computing was done in the rest of the world, and through the year, more and more of the company's key engineers hopped onto the bandwagon. The company started to believe that this was indeed the proper direction for the Lisa project, and Steve's preaching the gospel didn't hurt.

With the hardware and software teams charting a new course for personal computing, some of the excitement and enthusiasm was transformed into extreme cost overruns.

"We just went crazy," says Hawkins, "everybody, Steve included. Lisa became a kind of kitchen sink where we were trying to do everything that could possibly be done with a computer, and suddenly the cost factor, which in the original plan was set at $2,000, went out the window.

"We made two radical underestimations: how much things were going to cost and how long it would take to do them. Steve was such a biddler, always changing things, that many things were done again and again, because he would get bored with it being a certain way and want to change it, which just produced interminable delays."

As 1980 proceeded, and the Lisa design and engineering teams went through paroxysms of change created by Steve's whims, other people in the company looked on in horror. John Couch was a friendly, low-key person with an unfailingly optimistic mindset and no desire to buck the vice-chairman's unrealistic schedules. He didn't have the personality to stand up to Steve, and as the Lisa's design issues looked as if they were nearly resolved, he and the cofounder started to snipe at each other.

Steve decided he had no time for Couch, who had been his prime supporter in shifting the direction of the Lisa project, and started to dismiss him. He thought that his product vision had now been vindicated and in his inexperience thought that the top management of the company, the executive staff, was ready to hand over the actual implementation of the product line to him. Couch, who was in his late thirties and very good at the politics of a corporation, cultivated another ally, Mike Scott.

The Apple III was announced during the summer of the year at an extravaganza in Disneyland—Apple took over the park for a night—timed to coincide with the National Computer Conference in Anaheim. The machine was plagued with problems. As it neared shipping, there was little software. The hardware, once it started to be manufactured, didn't work well. The circuit board was too complex and the trace lines of solder—the rivers of electric current that make a circuit do its magic—were far too close. The connectors for components didn't seat correctly. Mysterious, unrepeatable bugs terrorized operators. The press and public smelled the problems almost immediately, and the machine was fatally tainted.

At the top of the company it became quickly apparent that the Apple III was not going to be the kind of success that the Apple II had been. If the Lisa were to be the company's savior, they had to do something radical about turning the project into a serious and substantial product group, not just a whim of Steve's. The haphazard, friendly way that the III had been designed was not the way to do it. A new concept had to be put into motion.

Couch plumped for the H-P model of work groups, secrecy, and insularity, a close-knit group that could make all the decisions democratically. Steve was flying off the handle, having wild and amazing ideas, working in secrecy with Atkinson and Page, and making preemptive strikes and unilateral decisions. The Apple III group was nearing completion, and the wheels of product introduction, documentation, and support were turning for that ill-fated machine. Behind it all, the Apple II was continuing to generate cash and profits. In 1980, the company's revenues approached $117 million, every penny of it earned through sales of the Apple II and the burgeoning library of software Apple was publishing. There was urgency in the corridors of Apple. The company was defining the world of personal computers on every front, and everyone was on the firing line. However, behind the bulging coffers, concern was building on many levels.

On his side, Couch wanted to create the semblance of equality in the Lisa group, and that was the last kind of arrangement in which Steve was interested in working. Up until then, Apple had always been driven by the edicts of a few, especially Steve's. Something had to give.

"Steve had an incredible ability to rally people," says Hawkins, "towards some common cause by painting an incredibly glorious cosmic objective. One of his favorite statements about the Lisa was, 'Let's make a dent in the universe. We'll make it so important that it will make a dent in the universe.'

"On its face, that is a completely ridiculous idea. But people would rally around stuff like that, especially engineers who had spent their lives bottled up in a lab somewhere missing out on all the fun. He had a very charismatic style of communicating, and it works because deep inside, he really wants to make a massive contribution. You have to admire that. A lot of capable people are just looking for their own security, the trappings of wealth. That's the way the American system works."

As Couch tried to make sense of the ever-changing demands for an entirely new generation of computers and the sudden elevation of the Lisa from just another project to the company's "great white hope," he and Steve found themselves increasingly at odds. Then another set of events occurred that made the young founder even more difficult to control and swelled his youthful head. In the summer of 1980, the publicity engine of Regis McKenna's agency was introducing a new ad campaign that would thrust him into the public's eye as the boy wonder. It would also position Steve as the creator of personal computing, the new field that was sweeping the country as the bad news from Iran continued to come in. It was a new field that was all-American, homegrown, and almost magical.

Dick Cavett, who was fighting a losing war of ratings with Johnny Carson for America's late-night television audience, had been hired to be Apple's spokesperson in 1979. The first ads in the campaign were friendly and chatty, in Cavett's particular style. By 1980, their focus had changed from home applications to the business of business, and scenes such as interviews with housewives running steel mills reinforced the point that the company and its agency wanted to entice buyers with: Apple computer provided solutions for business, but with an individualistic, humanistic touch.

The success of the firm was starting to create rumblings about a public stock offering. It seemed like the time to develop an "institutional" advertising campaign aimed at influencing professional investors. This would be the initial step in going public.

"It was the *Wall Street Journal* campaign that really put us in the public eye," recalls Fred Hoar, Apple's first director of corporate communications, who was hired in 1980. "The most famous headline was 'When We Created the Personal Computer, We Created a Twenty-First-Century Bicycle.' The first one featured Steve, with an extensive quote about computers."

Here, in part, is what the ad said:

> What is a personal computer? Let me answer with the analogy of the bicycle and the condor.
>
> A few years ago, I read a study, I believe, in *Scientific American*, about efficiency of locomotion in various species on the earth, including man. The study determined which species was the most efficient in terms of getting from point A to point B with the least amount of energy exerted. The condor won. Man made a rather unimpressive showing,

about one-third of the way down the list. But someone there had the insight to test man riding the bicycle. Man was twice as efficient as the condor.

This illustrated man's ability as a tool maker. When man created the bicycle, he created a tool that amplified an inherent ability. That's why I like to compare the personal computer to the bicycle.

The Apple computer is the twenty-first-century bicycle, if you will, because it's a tool that can amplify a certain part of our inherent intelligence. There's a special relationship that develops between one person and one computer that ultimately improves productivity on a personal level.[5]

It went on in that vein, filling a full page in the *Wall Street Journal*. Following that series, the company was suddenly in the public eye, and Steve was high-tech's poet. In the photo of him that accompanied the ad, he had a beard and looked very much like a modern-day John the Baptist. The campaign made some outrageous claims, such as "Steve Wozniak and I invented the personal computer." Although the idea that Apple had invented the personal computer could be seriously debated, style is always more important than substance in the advertising world.

The ads were written by Arlene Jaffe, a copywriter at the McKenna agency (who ironically would later write the Charlie Chaplin ads for IBM). They were filled with the extravagant yet compelling claims that Steve was used to making in the company, but they were now directed to the business public. One, for instance, compared a mainframe computer to a passenger train and the personal computer to the Volkswagen. It was a perfectly timed, deftly designed campaign, and Steve captured the imagination of a number of editors.

The mood in America was turning from introspection to business. Ronald Reagan was coming on strong as the challenger to the mild and liberal Jimmy Carter. Students were flocking to law and business schools instead of liberal arts. It was the time for the "Me Generation" to make its move, and the story of the astronomical success of one of its members fit right into the increasingly conservative trends of the country. Apple captured the swell perfectly.

"The line that the personal computer was a twenty-first-century bicycle," explains Hoar, "came from some article that Steve had read in

Scientific American about the efficiency of locomotion, and the bicycle was high on the list. He took it as a slogan, and then the agency itself took it and refined it.

"But Steve wasn't sure about it. He was never sure about what was right, particularly in advertising. He would believe different people at different times, and in a sense it was the last person he had talked to. He always had an insecurity born of his inexperience about whether a thing was in fact good or not."

The second ad, which also featured Steve, was headlined, "When We Created the Personal Computer, We Created a New Generation of Entrepreneurs," which was guaranteed to hook everyone who hadn't read the first one. It was a brilliant series of advertising moves that lifted Apple out of the obscurity of electronics, from the hobbyist world of Apple IIs into the consciousness of America's mainstream of business. It also gave Steve a swollen sense of self-importance, especially since it was only at the last minute that they had changed the copy from "I" to "we." The original idea had been to make the campaign personal to him. Woz was furious. Even though he had slipped out of the mainstream of Apple life with the completion of the disk drive in 1978, he was still around enough to be consulted. Hurriedly, the agency people added Woz into the prose, but it was plain that in his heart Steve Jobs believed that it was indeed he alone who had taken Apple over the top as a company. And he was probably right. Regis McKenna remarked once that "Woz designed a great machine. But it would have sat on the shelf had he not discovered an evangelist."[6]

In 1980 benchmark marketing testing showed less than 10 percent name recognition for the company in the public at large, but Apple was just beginning to come out of its cocoon. The first enormous "event," which was to become an ongoing part of the emerging marketing strategy of the company, had been held for the Apple III's introduction at Disneyland. It would be a year of firsts for Apple: the first event marketing extravaganza, the first ads in the *Wall Street Journal*. It was also the first for something else. Just as Steve was riding high, featured in a smashing series of ads, at the helm of a new line of computers, and with the company that he had founded making oodles of money, his wings were clipped. The only person at Apple who could cut him down to size did just that.

Mike Scott watched Steve's ego inflation with growing distaste.

Scotty was a complex person who prided himself on cutting through the bull. He had no time for the childish concerns that Steve and his cronies espoused. He was a pragmatist, concerned with getting computers out the door, and the airy-fairy intellectual ideas and pretensions of the company cofounder left him cold.

Apple had also grown too large and was unwieldy in its present haphazard, unstructured form. Scotty, in concert with Markkula, decided to reorganize the firm in anticipation of taking the company public, a decision that had been made at the August 1980 Board of Directors meeting. Over the following weeks, in secret, with only a couple of key managers involved, the two plotted a new structure for Apple. The business would be divisionalized. The first was the Personal Computer Systems, which comprised the Apple II and Apple III product lines, to be run by Tom Whitney. The new Lisa computer was to be the flagship in a new Professional Office Systems division. But instead of putting Steve at the helm of it, Scotty put John Couch in charge. Finally, a third division, the Accessories Division, handled all other items—printers, add-on circuit boards, and especially the new disk drive that Apple was developing at Steve's insistence—and would be headed by another former H-P manager, John Vennard. None of these divisions were to be run by Steve Jobs.

The plan to reorganize was first revealed to the company, including Steve, at an executive management retreat in September held at a golf course in Carmel Valley. Steve was shocked. He had not been consulted. And the Lisa project was no longer his.

"After setting up the framework for the concepts and finding the key people and sort of setting the technical directions, Scotty decided I didn't have the experience to run the thing," recalled Steve. "It hurt a lot. There's no getting around it."[7]

At that point, Lisa was Steve's baby. He had more personal involvement in it than anyone else and handing it over to Couch was a slap in the face. He had assumed that he would be the vice-president of new product development, handling all new products, especially the Lisa, until they were complete. This unforeseen reorganization removed him from any day-to-day operating role doing what he loved to do: building new machines. Scotty and Markkula made Steve chairman of the board, knowing that having a 25-year-old at the head of a $100 million company—especially one with such a seductive manner—

could only be good for the stock offering. Scotty tried to soften the blow by telling him that it was done to free him for the publicity that the public offering would generate.

Steve felt abandoned. It was products that he loved, that made him feel loved, and he had been hit right where it hurt the most. Even worse, John Couch, feeling his new corporate oats and determined to make the Lisa team in his image, not Steve's, made it clear to him that he didn't want him meddling in the affairs of his division any longer. The Lisa project was gone for good.

"Steve was real unhappy about all of that." says Hawkins. "He was unhappy about the way that Scotty had pulled this stunt without informing or consulting him—it was his company, after all!—and he was upset about losing direct involvement with Lisa. And he didn't particularly like the choice of John Couch to head it. He was really bent out of shape."

Steve accepted the role of chairman to marshal the company through the most successful public stock offering in history. He told himself that it was good for the company, but all the while his bitterness smoldered. Within six months he would get back at Mike Scott, and then, with the power that he had consolidated, his actions would in turn destroy the Lisa, the computer that he had created and named after his child.

But he couldn't live on vindictiveness alone. Steve needed a project, a new crusade to make him whole, to pour his energy into. Apple was a chaotic place with projects always starting and being canceled. A great idea, and enough enthusiasm, could convince one of the leaders to offer three months of development time to work something out. If a usable concept came of it, great. If not, as was nearly always the case, there was so much money rolling in the door that it made no difference to the bottom line. In the fall of 1980, cut loose from the Lisa, Steve started to look around for a new computer to pour all his passion into, a new machine he could make the world love. Luckily, he didn't have to look far.

11
Going Public

While America was watching the hostages in Iran, Voyager I was sending back spectacular photographs of the rings of Saturn, demonstrating clearly America's technological strength. But just in case anyone in Silicon Valley in 1980 thought that humankind was on the verge of controlling the universe, Mother Nature sent an unequivocal message about the real ruler of the roost with the eruption of Mount St. Helens.

The big movie of the year was *10* featuring Bo Derek as every nerd's fantasy. In the presidential election that fall, Ronald Reagan swept to victory. Sushi had become the craze of America's urban and suburban cognoscenti, the latest in a spate of Japanese successes that included cars and corporate management techniques. The country was in a bad temper, and with the end of a decade that included the near impeachment of a president, the ugly conclusion to a disastrous war, and the continuing erosion of America's influence in the world, good news was hard to come by. Then, on December 8, 1980, four days before Apple's stock was offered for sale to the public, ex-Beatle John Lennon was murdered by a crazed fan. It plunged the world into a week of mourning. For everyone under the age of 40, hearing that news became one of those moments that they would always remember, such as learning about Kennedy's assassination 17 years earlier or seeing the first moon walk.

For Steve, the event was part of a week that seemed to have no anchor. He owned 7.5 million shares of Apple's stock, valued at the offering price of $22. He was trying to come to grips with what it would be like to be worth nearly $150 million. He was already wealthy, with a net worth of something in the tens of millions of dollars, but this was an entirely more rarefied platform that few people ever reach. He was about to become one of the country's richest self-made men.

In the most oversubscribed initial public offering since the Ford Motor Company went public in the mid-1950s, on December 12, 1980, a Tuesday, Apple Computer's 4.6 million public shares were sold within an hour. On the New York Stock Exchange ticker tape, the stock closed that day up $7 at $29 per share. Steve was worth $217.5 million dollars. He had moved into the lofty territory of storied wealth.

"Visibility," Steve reflected later when asked about the impact of his newfound wealth. "There are tens of thousands of people who have a net worth of more than $1 million. There are thousands of people who are worth more than $10 million. But the number who have more than $100 million gets down to 100."[1]

He was the youngest of the super-rich, with a wonderful new technology, a winning smile, and an exuberance that was still a little coarse—but that was one of his charms. It would not be long before he smoothed that out, too.

In Cupertino he wasn't the only millionaire, not by a long shot. On that December day, more than 40 people suddenly became very wealthy, all Apple-made millionaires, but the distribution of stock had been anything but equitable. Apple was a fiefdom run by the erratic and emotional Steve Jobs and the equally tight-fisted Mike Markkula. People who had been instrumental in the company's early success, such as Allen and Elmer Baum, the father and son who had loaned Steve and Woz $5,000 during the summer of 1976, were told that outsiders couldn't buy stock. But certain outsiders could buy stock if they had the right connections and if selling them stock was deemed to enhance the corporate image. Through 1979 and 1980, while some were being denied, Fayez Sarofim, an Egyptian investor operating out of Houston and a close friend of member of the board Arthur Rock, bought more than 100,000 shares. Other buyers were the chairman of United Technologies, Harry Singleton, and the wife of the vice-chairman of Intel, Ann Bowers, who was Apple's first female vice-president as the head of human resources.[2]

The way stock was given out was not necessarily equated with ability or the value of contributions to Apple and had much to do with good timing and an individual's ability to negotiate for stock options.

Each share of stock distributed prior to April of 1979 was known as a "founder's share" and split five times before the date of the public offering. Each was worth 32 shares of public stock by December of 1980, and 1,420 shares of founder's stock made you a millionaire.

The press coverage of the day's stock offering was extraordinary. It was as though the entire nation was rooting for the upstart computer company in Cupertino. For a time, the plan had been to erect a thermometer in the street between the two rows of low-slung Apple buildings along Bandley Drive to follow the anticipated rise in the stock price. The day was a holiday for the company, and a ticker tape machine in the building lobby spewed out the minute-by-minute changes in the stock price. Dozens of Apple II computers linked up to the Dow Jones network through the company's *Dow Jones News/ Retrieval* software charted each 15-minute update.

The amounts of money that were suddenly part of the net worths of some of Apple's people were astronomical. Steve was at the head of the list with $256.4 million, and Markkula came next at $239 million. Wozniak was worth $135.6 million, and the venture capital firm Venrock had a $129.3 million stake. Rod Holt, the analog engineer, had $67 million, Tom Whitney, the head of engineering who had been fired by the time of the offering, was worth $48.9 million; Gene Carter, the head of the company's sales force, found his stock translated to $23.1 million; and John Couch, who was heading up the Lisa project and had stood up to Steve, was worth $13.6 million overnight. Even Woz's estranged wife found that her share of her ex-husband's stock was worth $42.4 million.

Engineers had been given stock options, but hourly technical employees had not. As the company expanded through 1978 and 1979, stock options were dangled like carrots in front of potential recruits. Animosities were hard to conceal when newly hired managers found that their employees were worth much more than they were. It was an untenable situation, and in perpetuating such inequities, the man-child who had cofounded Apple and watched over its meteoric growth was showing his dark side.

Steve was tight with his money, the kind of person who never paid for a meal, no matter how wealthy he was. He carefully guarded his stock and was equally careful about who was given options. He sat at the head of the Compensation Committee that doled out the light gray envelopes filled with lucre and found that the situation gave him the opportunity to settle some scores. Up until then, he had only been as strong as his ideas. If he couldn't convince the executive staff to go along with him, his ideas bit the dust. With stock options he had another weapon for his arsenal. He understood the power of greed, and he used it.

He denied options to many of his peers who had founded the company with him. It was a bizarre action that set in motion deep-seated, hard currents of anger and disgust among the crew who put in the labor necessary to make the company successful in the early days. Bill Fernandez, the company's first employee, was also the first to leave when he realized that he wasn't getting stock while newly hired engineers were. "I felt I was doing all the donkey work and that I would be a technician forever," says Bill. "It didn't seem that I would get stock. I didn't think the company was loyal to me."

Chris Espinosa and Randy Wigginton didn't receive any options from the company either. Luckily for Wigginton and Fernandez, Woz was a generous soul, and in 1980 he started a private sale and giveaway of his stock called the "Wozplan," which distributed about one-third of his shares—80,000—to his family and a long list of deserving and undeserving friends and acquaintances, including a real estate developer who had befriended him.

Steve was offended. "Woz ended up giving stock to all the wrong people," muses Steve. "Woz couldn't say no. A lot of people took advantage of him."[3]

Although Steve felt that Woz had given shares to the wrong people, Steve had an even stranger attitude toward the shares that could make his family and closest friends fabulously wealthy. He gave none to Colleen or Lisa and made sure that the legal agreement calling for him to support his daughter was signed a few weeks prior to the public offering. Whenever Colleen called to ask for a little extra cash, he invariably refused. He gave his parents 25,000 shares out of 7.5 million, but he kept control of them and asked his parents to scrape off the Apple decals from their cars and unlist their telephone numbers. The riches enabled Paul and Clara to take cruises for their holidays, but they refused to move from the modest suburban Los Altos house where Apple had been founded.

"I still don't understand it," Steve says, referring to handling his riches. "It's a large responsibility to have more than you can spend in your lifetime—and I feel I have to spend it. If you die, you certainly don't want to leave a large amount to your children. It will just ruin their lives."[4]

Among many examples of his inconsistency in giving out shares, one of the most revealing involved his long-time friend Dan Kottke. Kottke, who had journeyed to India and had shared a house with him, was still a technician at Apple in 1980. He had become a superb bench technician and was the primary builder of Apple III prototype circuit boards for the engineers designing them. While the two were sharing their Cupertino house, Kottke had asked Steve about stock options a few times.

Steve's response was that he had nothing to do with them, recalls Kottke. "He told me to go see my supervisor. But he was the guy in charge of the options. As it became clear later on, it was Steve who was stopping it. It turned out that Rod Holt had suggested that I be given options several times at the Compensation Committee meetings, and it was always Steve who said no."

According to another Apple employee, "Holt remained bothered by the fact that Kottke had no stock. One day he approached Steve and suggested that they give Kottke some stock by matching each other's contribution. By doing it privately, he thought they could get around the restriction of not giving technicians stock.

"Steve turned to Holt and said, 'Great! I'll give him zero.'"

Later Steve tried to explain his lack of generosity to his closest friend. "Daniel generally tends to overrate his contributions. He did a lot of work that we could have hired anybody to do, and he learned an awful lot."[5]

Kottke was so distraught over the situation that, as the countdown to going public started, he went to Markkula and Scotty, who finally granted him 2,000 shares. All the rank-and-file engineers, the guys who had come in after Kottke, had been given 1,000 shares of "founder's stock" which, after splitting several times, amounted to 32,000 shares on the day of the public offering. Steve had intentionally kept his friend from receiving any. It was as if he needed to withhold something from Kottke to demonstrate the power he had over him, to prove that he really was the boss.

For the next year, Kottke was unhappy—he carried the burden of betrayal on his shoulders. One day in mid-1981, he decided it was time to have it out with his old friend, so he spent the better part of an afternoon waiting for Steve to appear at his office.

"I just wanted to have a talk with him, the old Steve Jobs I had known," says Kottke. "I didn't even want to bring up the stock. But Steve was so cold. I got all choked up. I started to cry, I couldn't even talk with him. I was so sad. I never even brought up the subject. The past was dead. We just weren't friends anymore."

Steve was getting rid of the past the way a snake sheds its skin. As the publicity for the offering erupted on national television and in the financial pages of newspapers across the country, he was increasingly visible. It changed his life, even as he made fun of the new wealth. He toyed with sharing the ownership of a private Lear jet with Markkula but eventually decided against it. The two did share $200 bottles of wine on occasion. He still wore jeans and running shoes, but he found it hard to keep his head when the *Wall Street Journal* called him for comments on the latest industry developments.

In the months following the December offering, a number of people sold their stock and retired, but they were looked upon as traitors. Jef Raskin sold his entire stake, which amounted to many millions. Steve accused him of betrayal, but Raskin said, "I didn't want to have to open the paper each day to find out how much money I had."

As the holiday season came in 1980 and his worth had risen astronomically, Steve was feeling more alone than ever. He had just signed his child support papers and had yet to see his daughter. Although he was in the midst of a stable relationship with Belinda, he was personally unsettled. He bought a house in Los Gatos but could never seem to finish the remodeling. The house remained nearly empty of furniture and interior decorations. Steve could make snap decisions about aesthetics at work, but when it came to his personal life, he was indecisive.

The shock of losing the Lisa project left him at loose ends. He had enjoyed the publicity of the public offering, with the interviews, the reporters, and the opportunities to explain the vision of personal computing that he had carefully rehearsed with Regis McKenna. As the rush of publicity fell off, however, and he returned to Cupertino for the new year, he found that his new role as company whiz kid without a portfolio was not particularly thrilling.

If he had been 50 and burned out, he might have been able to take the loss of day-to-day operating responsibility without reacting. But he was not. Luckily, a computer in the R&D phase caught his attention— one that he had tried to bury several months before.

Jef Raskin led a group that was building an experimental machine. Apple was always forming small research teams to develop new product concepts. Raskin had been thinking of a small, inexpensive computer for the masses since late 1978, and by late 1979 he had formed a small, two-member group to build some prototypes. With amazing speed, they produced a working prototype over the Christmas holiday of 1979. Raskin named his invention Macintosh, after the apple, but he had misspelled it.

Raskin's vision of a computer was as a complete, "canned" solution. He had very strong ideas about ease of use. You should be able to turn on the machine and begin working immediately without having to maneuver through complex procedures or an operating system. The easily portable machine also had to sell for around $1,000, which meant that Apple had to be able to build it for about $300.

Most important, Raskin had a different idea from anyone else at the company about how software and hardware should interact. He was convinced that the two had to grow hand in hand. The hardware engineers had to work closely with the software system programmers. All computers up to then had been developed by a hardware team. The software team came in later—separately—to do its thing. He wanted to test his idea of software/hardware synergy on a machine that would come with all its software built in, for both cost reduction and general ease of use. And as part of this complete solution to computing, he wanted to design a new programming language—APL (Apple Programming Language)—to replace BASIC and Pascal as the standard program development language for the new computer.

His group's Macintosh also specified a cassette tape system for program storage, a Motorola 6809 microprocessor, and a bit-mapped, high-resolution, nearly square, 256-by-256-pixel monitor. The circuit board was engineered by Burrell Smith, a gnomish, self-taught digital hacker. Smith had been recommended to Raskin by Bill Atkinson, who ran into him working in the company's service department. Secretive and aggressively self-assured, the blonde-haired engineer was all of 25 years old in 1980, born the same year as Steve. He was cut in the mold of Woz, whose machine Smith absolutely revered, and was a designer in the hurry-up mode. Once he started on something, he didn't stop until it was finished. He also had the raw mental capacity to keep all the elements of a circuit board design in his head at once, and then to minimize. This was the magic art of digital design. Smith's design skills were disdained by the "professionals" in Lisaland, but he was just the type of eccentric on whom Raskin liked to gamble.

And since they were working on the fringes of the corporate freight train that was Apple by late 1979 and 1980, spiriting parts and scavenging components out of engineering labs in the dead of night, they attracted a few other like-minded souls. One of them, Apple II hacker Andy Hertzfeld, brought the first images up on the screen of the prototype in an all-night session the same day he saw the earliest Macintosh, in February of 1980. In the first demonstration of what would always be the irreverent spirit of the computer, Hertzfeld was able to display an image of the cartoon character Scrooge McDuck with a handwritten line, "Hi Burrell," scrawled across it. Although he wasn't then free to join the team, Hertzfeld instantly became one of them in spirit.

The Macintosh had been in and out of favor for the better part of a year. Raskin's pipe dream would be canceled and then reinstated. He was very casual, very slow, about producing anything tangible. Raskin's background was as an academic, and his Macintosh project progress reflected the pace of a university research program. Steve, who had no tolerance for slow progress, had been one of the first to abandon the project in mid-1980, when he was in the midst of the design of Lisa as a real product.

"Jobs said, 'No you can't do this,'" recalls Raskin. "'This is wrong, and it is not what Apple needs. Apple needs Lisa and this will interfere.'" Steve lost the battle, and Scotty kept the R&D project alive.

The Macintosh project was sequestered in the same suite of offices where Apple had started. The space behind the Good Earth restaurant on Stevens Creek Boulevard had remained in the company's hands after the move to the rows of low-slung, adobe tilt-up buildings along nearby Bandley Drive that were in constant construction after 1979. The advanced Lisa project had used the space for start-up in 1979, and by mid-1980, when that computer had been officially launched as a product and the team moved to their own building, the Macintosh group took over the space. It was known as a cauldron for advanced projects.

By the following fall of 1980, not much more had occurred on the Macintosh project. Smith had a working prototype based on the underpowered 6809 microprocessor, but there was little else. In the September 1980 reorganization that saw Steve ousted from the Lisa project, the Macintosh was canceled again. Raskin went to Scotty shortly thereafter and begged for three more months to get something going. Scotty acquiesced and gave Raskin an extension until the end of the year.

The Macintosh project was given a temporary green light, but it was flying in the face of new technological directions at Apple. The Lisa user interface that was based on the work they saw at Xerox and the Motorola 68000 family of microprocessors had been agreed upon by the company as the standard for future products. That autumn a debate raged in the Macintosh group about whether they should adopt the 68000 and redesign the board. Although it was cheap, the puny 6809 processor in the original Macintosh didn't have enough horsepower to create Lisa-like windows, icons, and menus. Nonetheless Raskin was dead set against the new processor. He had developed an almost slavish, philosophical attachment to an 8-bit bus (8 bits of information processed at a time through the machine) coupled with 64 kilobytes of memory. The 6809 met his requirements perfectly, and by then he had a very specific idea about how the computer should look and act. The Lisa interface didn't fit his dreams.

For several years he had collected all his thoughts about the product in a black, loose-leaf notebook that he called the "Macintosh Papers," which he shared with anyone who evinced the slightest interest in his project. Raskin was a writer first, and he had a reverence for characters and typing. He envisioned a computer that started up with a screen as open to possibilities as a blank sheet of paper. If you started to type text, you were word processing. If you typed in two numbers separated by a plus sign and then pressed return, the numbers would add up. He saw no need for graphics and certainly no need for a mouse. Of the system he saw at Xerox, all he liked were the windows. He thought the electronic simulation of a desktop was superfluous and would interfere with a naive user working on the computer. Raskin saw his Macintosh as a "toaster," a self-contained appliance with no add-ons. What you bought was all you needed.

About the time the debate over the microprocessor was going on in Raskin's group, Steve began meddling. He was looking for a new product into which to pour all his energy, and Raskin's "Macintosh Papers" caught his eye. He was intrigued by the concept of an appliance computer that was as easy to use as a toaster, but he started pushing for the adoption of the 68000, which annoyed Raskin. Steve saw the potential of a cheaper Lisa and realized that the project leader had a team already in place, which meant the project could get moving fast if someone with power at Apple got behind it. Raskin had recently hired a marketing person, Joanna Hoffmann, another child of 1955 and a graduate student in an obscure branch of archeology. He also brought on yet another former UCSD student, Bud Tribble, a reserved, self-taught programmer who was Atkinson's best friend, to take over software development.

Much to Steve's delight, Tribble almost immediately wrote a case for switching to the 68000 microprocessor. This would allow the new computer to adopt Atkinson's LisaGraf routines and consequently many of the Lisa's graphics capabilities. Steve understood the power of the 68000 and shortly thereafter unilaterally decreed that they build a new prototype with it. Raskin dug in his heels at the idea of creating a little brother to the bigger Lisa, but Steve pulled rank on him, went directly to Burrell Smith, and challenged him to bring a 68000-based version of the Macintosh up by the end of the year. Smith thrived on that kind of impossible challenge. Raskin was powerless and could do nothing but smolder inside.

Steve's input inspired the Macintosh team, but it was a double-edged sword. On December 12, 1980, one of the members of the team sent Raskin a memo in which were outlined some of their concerns about the increasing involvement of Steve Jobs in their cozy Macintosh project. In part, it said:

Your ability to mix play and work further helped reduce the tension and increase the fun of the job. I came to work on the Macintosh largely because I wanted to be in that work environment again. However, since the Macintosh has lost its research status, and especially since management has begun being split between you and Steve Jobs, I have felt this relaxed, free-to-concentrate-and-work-hard atmosphere to be in jeopardy. Steve Jobs seems to introduce tension, politics, and hassles rather than enjoying a buffer from those distractions. I thoroughly enjoy talking with him, and I admire his ideas, practical perspective, and energy. But I just don't feel that he provides the trusting, supportive, relaxed work environment I need.[6]

But stopping Steve was like trying to dam the leak in a levee with a finger. Steve had already decided there was a computer in the Macintosh group yearning to be set free, and once he caught wind of it, all bets were off. By Christmas of 1980, Smith, assisted by Howard, had a working 68000-based Macintosh running. Raskin, although he still resisted the idea, projected that the new Macintosh could be manufactured for about $370, and its size and weight offered a degree of portability. It would have a subset of the much more expensive Lisa's capabilities and could cost a quarter of the price.

Just after Christmas, Smith was in the labs working on his newly created prototype when Steve came by. Smith was a tireless worker, driven by the madness of engineering perfection. Steve, always a workaholic, appreciated employees who stayed late or worked weekends and holidays. The sum total of Steve's vacation in the preceding year had been five days in Yosemite. Smith explained to Steve that his little brother of a Lisa had a clock speed nearly twice as fast as its sibling. This meant it could perform a similar feat of computing in about half the time. When he heard that, all the bells went off in the company cofounder's mind.

Looking at the crude working model that Smith had produced, it was suddenly clear to Steve that the Macintosh could be the Apple II of the eighties, a computer that could deliver the technology of the future—the ease of use that a graphic user interface and mouse heralded—at a remarkably low cost. Steve knew that cutting the cost to around $1,000 would mean he'd sell a lot more machines than the Lisa group had ever dreamed of. Just as the Apple II put an affordable computer into the hands of software hackers and hardware engineers, the Macintosh could be a computer for the next generation of intelligent consumers who would soon take the plunge into computing.

The digital design that Smith had come up with by January of 1981 was extraordinary. The Lisa, which by then had been in development for two years, was a planned product with a team of 24 hardware engineers and countless software programmers. A single working prototype of the Lisa machine existed in a closed lab in one of the Apple buildings along Bandley Drive, and the computer was slated for release in mid-1982. To work, it needed five circuit boards and a number of custom components. Over a tiny suite of rooms in another building, separated from the rest of the company, a long-haired, 25-year-old engineer had made a new computer in a few weeks that was twice as fast and could be sold for one-third the price. It relied on a single circuit board and contained nothing but off-the-shelf parts.

It was the kind of feat that Woz had pulled off with the Apple II when he crammed more features into fewer parts and components than anyone had believed possible. "It didn't take long, once you saw the gleam in Steve's eye," recalls Joanna Hoffmann, "to see the writing on the wall for Jef. Steve was going to get what he wanted, and the question was whether our loyalty to Jef outweighed our allegiance to the amazing potential we saw in Burrell's prototype."

Steve was attracted by more than the hardware, however. The little band of five people working on the Macintosh had an enthusiasm and renegade spirit that separated them from the rest of the company, an attitude that Steve could relate to. For the past several years, he had tried to subjugate his outlaw spirit to the corporate process, but all he had to show for it was his unceremonious departure from the Lisa project. Here, suddenly, he had discovered a pocket of passion in the heart of his company. These were engineers who thrived on the impossible. This was the force and the spirit that had been with the founders of Apple. The project was tailor-made for Steve.

Working in a forgotten corner of a building, he would show the guys at Lisa, Scotty, the whole company, and the entire world that he could lead this team and produce a computer more successful than the Apple II. He would create a computer the way that Apple should be doing it, not the way that the bloated bureaucratic company had mismanaged the Apple III and threatened to mishandle the Lisa. He made his decision, set his sights, and leaped into the project with all his guns blazing, setting off a two-month battle for control of the Mac project.

On January 20, 1981, Ronald Reagan was inaugurated as President of the United States, and 63 hostages were released by Iran. The day marked a new start for the country. It also coincided with Steve's building a team for the new machine. He made formal overtures to Raskin, telling him that the Macintosh seemed like the way for the company to go and that he wanted to get more involved in the project. Raskin was flattered but worried, having already butted heads with him over the 68000 microprocessor.

When he had started working for Apple in 1987, Raskin had been Steve's mentor. He provided stimulation and perspective from the front edge of theoretical, academic computing. In the ensuing years, he had

had run-ins with Steve and knew how difficult he could be to work with. By late 1980, they had a love-hate relationship. He realized that having Steve's seal of approval meant that what had been a pipe-dream of an advanced research project was suddenly viable. Raskin was more comfortable with ideas than the hurly-burly world of products, and he wasn't prepared to have his research project suddenly shift into fifth gear and take off from underneath his feet.

The differences between Raskin and Steve were indicative of the way the computer would evolve. Raskin was an intellectual, a careful thinker with the kinds of analytical skills that allowed him to see the sweep of history and identify ways that the computers of tomorrow might change. A tinkerer, an inventor of model airplanes and computers, a concert-level musician and conductor, his was the kind of mind that could create an entirely new type of computer. He also had a researcher's lack of concern for producing commercial-quality products on back-breaking deadlines.

Steve was the opposite—emotional, impulsive, self-taught, diamond in the rough with a silver tongue that could sell anything. Steve liked to think in terms of millions of units and always let the latest technology drive his decisions about what to build. Whereas Steve found the mouse a compelling and seductive idea, Raskin was dead set against it on intellectual grounds. For the one, it felt right to point instead of type. For the other, the keyboard was synonymous with the mind and intelligence. Once Raskin lost that battle, he found it impossible to keep his dissatisfaction to himself.

As Raskin complained to Scotty about Steve's interference, the company president realized that it would be better to sacrifice Raskin if it meant separating the disruptive Steve from everyone else. At the corporate level, Markkula and Scotty were only too happy to let Steve get involved in Raskin's project. After the events surrounding the transfer of power in the Lisa group, they knew that it was only a matter of time before Steve found something else in which to dabble. The Macintosh group was housed in an isolated location, a decision originally made by Raskin, Markkula, and Scotty precisely to keep the group away from Steve. Now, nine months later, the isolation of the Macintosh project could work perfectly to keep Steve away from the rest of the company.

Scotty willingly provided new office space for the Macintosh group when Seve came asking and was only too willing to let them do their work with a minimum of interference from the rest of the company. "I just decided that I was going to go off and do that myself with a small group," said Steve. "Sort of go back to the garage, to design the Macintosh. They didn't take us very seriously. I think Scotty was just sort of humoring me."[7]

The chances that they would produce a viable product were extraordinarily slim. As long as Scotty was at Apple, Steve would have nothing to do with any new products the company released. When Steve asked to have the Macintosh elevated to "product" status so that he could bring a few of the old-timers on board, Scotty agreed.

Steve moved in from the sidelines according to plan and started to take over the group. One of his first acts as general manager was to hire the key people who made the Apple II happen; Rod Holt, Woz (although this choice was primarily to lend legitimacy to the team), Randy Wigginton, Jerry Mannock (who had designed the Apple II case), and even Dan Kottke and Bill Fernandez. The Apple veterans joined Smith, Tribble, Brian Howard (a Stanford electrical engineering graduate and one of the few formally trained computerists in the project), and Joanna Hoffmann on the infant project. Steve commandeered new space. They took over part of a floor in another building that Apple was leasing nearby called Texaco Towers, so named because of its proximity to a gasoline station.

That January the entire group moved in and began to work on turning the Macintosh prototype into a bona fide computer product. Steve was convinced that they could build an affordable little brother to Lisa in a year. It was a ridiculous timetable. He was sure that his team needed only 12 months to tansform the prototype with no operating system and only a few demos into a working machine ready for the market. And his staff believed that his timetable was right.

Steve had a reality distortion field that the Macintosh team quickly identified. Charisma, confidence, and a clear, compelling vision combined to produce an overpowering aura. Whenever he wanted to bring someone around to his point of view, the intense company founder used his personal magnetism to manipulate. Over the years, he honed his technique to an extraordinary fineness.

"He has the ability to make people around him believe in his perception of reality," said Bud Tribble a few years later. "It's a combination of very fast comeback, catch phrases, and the occasional, very original insight, which he throws in to keep you off balance."[8]

Steve wanted to be general manager of the group. So did Raskin.

He and Raskin were at loggerheads. Raskin saw the machine as his and resented Steve's presence. The original concept of a small, neatly packaged, affordable personal computer came from Raskin. But the impetus to get it to market was Steve's.

When Steve joined the project, it gained something that no one else would have been able to bring to the machine—an evangelist with the mantle of celebrity that made everything he did seem a little bigger than life. Steve had the religion of personal computing, and he was a true apostle. He could rattle the windows, shake the pulpit, and make the congregation stand up and shout "Praise the Computer!" The dream of computing burned in his heart, and his sermons on behalf of the dream came through loud and clear.

He also had the glamor of wealth, celebrity, and, best of all, power. Even though Scotty had given him the Macintosh product to keep him out of the way, Steve could make things happen at Apple. He could get funds and support services for the project and protect his team from other managers. "All we had to do was complain about someone," one of the team members said once, "and it was like unleashing a doberman. He would chew the guy's head off so fast that our heads would spin."9

All through January of 1980, Raskin and Steve sniped at one another with memos, incandescent arguments, and clandestine meetings. Then, early in February, Woz crashed his airplane on take-off from a local airport and was seriously injured. The company waited breathlessly as he moved in and out of consciousness. Steve hired a limo to ferry Woz's distraught parents to the hospital.

Steve decided to relegate Raskin to publications director for his new project, and since he wasn't moving out of the way fast enough, told him so bluntly. The mild-mannered Raskin started to seethe and spent his first date with the woman who would become his wife railing about "this guy Steve," she recalls. "I couldn't believe there was anyone quite that obnoxious at a nice and progressive company like Apple."

Once Steve had decided to take over the group, his next step was to present his plans to the company's executive staff, which he did without Raskin's knowledge or presence. To make the project his, he renamed the Macintosh "Bicycle" and distributed a long memo to the executive staff, cribbed closely from Raskin's most recent project descriptions, that detailed his plans. At a key staff meeting, Steve reportedly told the executive staff that Raskin was a dreamer and didn't know anything about actually making a product. Everything was coming to a head. There could be only one ruler of the Macintosh team, and Steve knew who he wanted.

Raskin knew nothing about the meeting, but he received a detailed report about it from a sympathetic attendee. When Steve told Raskin that the executive staff had already decided to give him the Macintosh project and that he had decided to take over both hardware and software and change them as he saw fit, the older computer scientist was furious. Two days later, Raskin was scheduled to give a company "brown bag" presentation on the Macintosh. These were informal lunch-hour discussions where anyone was welcome. On the morning of his presentation, Steve called him and told him that the meeting had been canceled and forbade him from talking about the Macintosh anymore.

Depressed and hurt that two years of his life were slipping away, Raskin decided to walk over to the auditorium just in case the message hadn't been relayed to everyone. He found the room filled with Apple employees waiting for him to give his talk. The meeting had never been canceled. Steve had set him up to simply not show up and thereby look like a flake. Raskin gave a presentation extemporaneously. Steve heard about it and that afternoon fired him.

Raskin had been through this kind of episode with Steve before, so he said he would wait before clearing out his desk. Sure enough, an hour later Steve had changed his mind and asked Raskin to stay. But he had already pushed Raskin too far. That afternoon the mild-mannered former professor wrote a confidential memo to Mike Scott. It was a bitter piece that ran four pages and cataloged a litany of Steve's personality and managerial problems. Two days later, Scott gave a copy to Markkula, who in turn gave it to Steve. He hit the roof. In its entirety, it follows:

To: Mike Scott
From: Jef Raskin
Date: 19 Feb 81
Re: Working for/with Steve Jobs

EXECUTIVE SUMMARY

The following examples show that Steve Jobs has not performed adequately as my manager, and that he has demoralized or damaged other employees and some projects vital to the company. The recommended actions are to have me work for some other supervisor, to find another leader of the Macintosh project, and to assign Mr. Jobs to duties in keeping with his demonstrated abilities, where his problems will not adversely affect productivity and morale.

INTRODUCTION

While Mr. Jobs's stated positions on management techniques are all quite noble and worthy, in practice he is a dreadful manager. It is an unfortunate case of mouthing the right ideas, but not believing in or executing them when it comes time to do something. I have always liked Steve personally, but I have found it impossible to work for him and retain much enjoyment in my work.

I am not alone in these feelings but am braver than most in regard to writing them down, or even stating them.

Here is a list of a few specifics that, I believe, would more than justify removing a person (if it weren't Mr. Jobs) from project leader status. I do not think we should have a double standard and believe that it is in Apple's interest, and in the best interest of our shareholders to immediately replace him as project leader on the Macintosh project, and see that he gets management training before being allowed to manage other company projects that involve creative work.

SPECIFIC PROBLEMS

1. Jobs regularly misses appointments. This is so well known as to be almost a running joke. It is not funny, hurts Apple's image when he does it to outsiders, and wastes our time and energy when it is done to another employee.

2. He acts without thinking and with bad judgment. An incredible example was his behavior at the excellent demonstration of a touch-sensitive CRT panel that Mr. Pohlman arranged. The facts are well known (in front of 20 people he told Pohlman that he had no "right" to call such a meeting; he told the entire group that they were wasting their time; when a few of us objected to his manner he justified his actions by saying that "Taylor hasn't been doing a good job lately. . ." which he shouldn't have said at all). It is true that Jobs admitted he acted badly afterward—but it is unfortunately his pattern to quickly admit to an error and then to continue

doing it. His admissions of error are, in the main, a tactic to take the heat off. As many examples show, his contrition is often short-lived.

3. He does not give credit where due. This is an especially damaging trait in a company that depends on innovation for its survival. Very often, when told of a new idea, he will immediately attack it and say that it is worthless or even stupid, and tell you that it was a waste of time to work on it. This alone is bad management, but if the idea was a good one he will soon be telling people about it as though it was his own. Proof that he really believes these ideas to be his own is that he sometimes comes back to the originator of the idea with Jobs's "original" thought. This has happened to me many times.

It is another running joke that the way to convince Jobs of something is to tell him about it, listen to him reject it, and then wait a week until he comes running to tell you about his latest idea.

4. Jobs often reacts ad hominem. When a person is in Jobs's ill favor, any idea from that person will be rejected. On the Macintosh project we have occasionally experimented by trying the same idea on Jobs, but attributing it to a different person (one in favor at the moment), whereupon Jobs tends to accept the idea.

Jobs also has favorites, who can do no wrong—and others can do no right. He will uncritically dismiss an idea saying: "Oh, that's X's idea. His ideas aren't worth anything." Similarly he will take a half-formed idea of one of his favorites and promulgate it before even the originator knows if it is a good idea, often making the originator look silly in the process.

5. He makes absurd and wasteful decisions by trying to be paternal. One day I was going over to Bandley I, and I was asked to bring back the paychecks that were in Pat Sharp's office. When I got there, Pat started to give me the checks but Jobs said that I couldn't take them over because he wanted to be the one to hand them out even though that meant a delay of a few hours and there was one person who was leaving early and wanted their check sooner.

He also annoyed Smith and Tribble by handing them their notification of raises even though he was not their manager at the time.

6. He interrupts and doesn't listen. This happens all the time: for example yesterday he brought a number of people from marketing to see the Macintosh prototype, and he asked Bud to explain the software and Burrell the hardware. As each of them was talking he talked right over them, rudely interrupting them.

Often, at presentations, he asks questions that have just been answered by the speaker. I remember one visiting speaker saying: "The linearity is .25%, the overall accuracy, which is not important in these applications, is about 2%." Steve then interrupted him saying (loudly and in an imperious manner) "What we at Apple are interested in is not the accuracy! What is the LINEARITY of the product? That's what's important!". The speaker was, to say the least, puzzled. I am sure he went away with the impression that we have rather boorish management. Again this is a well known problem of Jobs's that makes him a difficult person to work for.

7. He does not keep promises or meet commitments. The most recent example (which occurred during the writing of this memo) was his rescinding of his agreement to fund the Macintosh Software I have been designing—in support of his "decision" he cited Mssrs. Rosing and Daniels as recommending this action. He compounded his broken promise with misreporting their opinions. For example, Rosing said that I should be given an opportunity to produce a detailed document on the software, and the document evaluated. Daniels also believes that such a document would be desirable and that I should be given the opportunity to produce it. It is very difficult to work for someone who systematically distorts the facts.

8. He makes decisions ex cathedra. In moving the Macintosh group he did not come to us and say: Here is the proposed layout and room assignments, what do you think? Instead, he did it all himself and then said: Here's where you'll be. Even if his layout was satisfactory (it was not) his method of

presenting it is bad managerial technique. His dictatorial methods are also very expensive to the company since some of what he does either must be redone, or causes employee dissatisfaction.

Another example is the memo put out two days ago describing the Macintosh project. It was done without consulting any of the people doing the work; and aside from annoying the entire group, it contains many inaccuracies.

9. Optimistic estimates. Jobs was wrong on his Apple III schedule, wrong on the LISA schedule, wrong on the cost and price estimates, and he will be wrong on Macintosh. He is a prime example of a manager who takes the credit for his optimistic schedules and then blames the workers when deadlines are not met. His cost estimates are often based on unrealistic assumptions about the elasticity of prices of parts.

10. Jobs is often irresponsible and inconsiderate. An example is the brown bag seminar I was scheduled to give on 17 February. In January, he first canceled the seminar, but then he agreed that I was to give it. Two hours before I was to give the talk he called me to say that he was canceling it again. His reason was: "I canceled it because of the reorganization in PCS." However, Jobs did not tell the seminar's organizer about the cancellation, nor did he place any notices announcing the cancellation.

At noon, fortunately, I made a last minute decision to go over to the seminar site, where I discovered a crowd of over 100 employees waiting to hear the seminar. I announced the cancellation myself—and then I gave a talk on my current work and interests at Apple, instead.

Imagine the result if I had not happened to go there: over 100 employees would have been annoyed at ME for not showing up. Jobs would have put me, his employee, in a bad light, and Jobs would have wasted the time of over 100 people for a half hour or so each.

Any supervisor who would do this kind of thing to a person working for him, and to the morale and happiness of a large number of employees, is clearly of borderline competence. I also point out that he chewed out Taylor Pohlman for allegedly "wasting" the time of 20 employees in the demonstration mentioned above (when in fact those employees

KING Library

Orchard Ridge Campus
Telephone: 248.522.3525

ate Due _____

08 7.1

CK

thought that the demonstration was informative and thought-provoking). At the very least he is hopelessly inconsistent.

11. He is a bad manager of software projects. I started the APL project, but Jobs took it over. He did not know what he was doing and Walters & Kelly soon realized that they had no supervision from Apple and did their own thing (on our money). In fact, I was prevented from and told not to deal with Walters and Kelly even though I was the only person in the company at that time who knew APL, and had a good working relationship with them. When I saw that it was being botched and said so, Jobs told me that it was none of my business.

The Notzo BASIC project was going poorly until I stepped in and wrote a spec, but Jobs's inconsistent behavior and obvious lack of knowledge (which did not stop him from trying to make technical decisions) soon alienated Shepardson Microsystems, me, and everybody else connected with the project.

When I brought Pascal to Apple he was strongly opposed to it, and it wasn't until Atkinson had it implemented (all this work was done on our own time and at our own expense—including buying PDP-II equipment and paying for the UCSD software license) that the company realized I was right.

His present "design" of the Macintosh software and his schedules for it should be greeted with extreme caution.

SUMMARY

These instances are sufficient evidence that Jobs has not performed adequately as my manager, and that he has demoralized and damaged other aspects of the company. The recommended actions are to have me work for some other supervisor, to find another leader of the Macintosh project, and to assign Mr. Jobs duties in keeping with his demonstrated abilities, where his problems will not adversely affect productivity and morale.[10]

That afternoon Markkula, Steve, and Raskin held a no-holds-barred meeting. Steve was in tears—he was always quick to cry when he couldn't have his way—and said that he couldn't possibly work with

Raskin any longer. Raskin, much more composed, said that he couldn't work for Steve. They came up with a mutually acceptable solution. Raskin would take a vacation, and Steve would take over the Macintosh. It was a couple of days before his 26th birthday.

The slowly recovering Woz, still suffering from lapses of consciousness and amnesia, and the original Macintosh creator Raskin weren't the only casualties of that month. Apple had grown meteorically by the winter of 1980–1981. A swollen bureaucracy, fueled by the continuing onrush of cash generated by the venerable Apple II, by the effort to release and then fix the Apple III, and by the engineering of the Lisa, put the company's employee count at nearly 2,000. No one had been formally fired at the company yet. The firm was four years old, and it still behaved as if it belonged to the people who worked there, not the owners. On a dark and rainy day in February of 1981 that came to be called "Black Wednesday" in Cupertino, 42 employees were terminated with a one-month severance paycheck and a security guard escorting them off company premises.

"I knew something was wrong the minute I walked in the door for work that morning," says Andy Hertzfeld, the Apple II programmer fanatic who was working on software for the ill-fated III at the time. "There were little groups of people standing around, looking worried, and something was in the air. I knew right away that something was up."

Hertzfeld had missed that morning's meeting. At 7:30 A.M., Scotty went around telling people that a company-wide meeting was being held at 8 in a parking lot underneath one of the buildings. Donn Denman, a programmer working with Wigginton, had been there all night working and attended the event. Most of the software team worked late and rarely appeared at work before 10.

"There were hundreds of folding chairs set up in the underground parking lot," Denman recalls. "And Scotty stood up and starting talking about how Apple had grown too fat and he was going to have to fire some people. He was going to be calling people into his office through the morning, he said. And then he dismissed us. The whole place suddenly went silent. Who was on the list? None of us had any idea if we would make it through the day or not."

The firings happened in spurts, and no one knew who would be next. Some of the names on the list seemed appropriate, but others were purely arbitrary. Lists had been quietly circulated for weeks, since Markkula, Scotty, and Steve decided at a meeting in early January that the staff needed to be taught a lesson. The company had too much fat, and too many new hires were taking it easy, assuming that Apple would never get rid of anyone. In the Valley, working at Apple was considered a guarantee of lifetime employment.

If a department head were fired for incompetence, so were all the people working for him, no matter how good their latest performance reviews might have been. The New Product Review/Quality Assurance group was wiped out in its entirety because the head of it was axed and no one else stood up for any of his employees. It was the arbitrariness of the list that frightened the employees. Even though many who were let go were considered weak, marginal performers, the way the firings were handled sent shivers through the firm. If Apple could fire these people on the spur of the moment, was anyone safe?

That afternoon Scotty hosted a beer bust in the basement of one of the buildings. He tried to make light of what had been a devastating event for most of the remaining employees. He lost whatever sympathy he might have gained by a show of remorse with his jocular manner. People were shell-shocked. Steve, who had acquiesced to the firings earlier, tried to distance himself from the proceedings, putting the blame on Scotty. Chris Espinosa told him that it was not way to run a company, to which Steve replied, "But how do you run a company?"

Overnight Apple changed. No longer were the employees insulated from the harsh realities of the corporate world. Incompetence was a sin, but so was being in the wrong group. It was one thing to fire incompetent people, but it was another to conduct a wholesale massacre and then make light of it at a party that evening. The temper of Apple turned sour.

"It was the end of Camelot," says Bruce Tognazzini. "It was the end of loyalty. If they could treat us like that, why should we care about Apple?"

A few days later the following anonymous flyer was posted around the company:

APPLE EMPLOYEES!!

Are you
Tired of being pushed around by an arbitrary management?
Bothered by the lack of morale?
Disgusted at the recent capricious mass firings?
Angry at the way it was done?

Annoyed at being treated like children?
Then DO SOMETHING about it! We are forming the
COMPUTER PROFESSIONALS UNION (CPU)
so that we can keep Apple's management IN LINE. The thing
they fear most is concerted employee action, the tactics they
use are divide and conquer, and threats of economic reprisal.

THEY CAN'T GET AWAY WITH IT IF WE UNITE!

Apple was once a good place to work, management preaches
to us about the "Apple Spirit." Let's show them what a little bit
of real spirit is like and ram it down their throats!
We have real issues: job security (don't you think some of the
recent firings were spiteful rather than motivated by concern
for productivity?), working conditions (a majority of workers
and the committee of employees DID NOT WANT open
offices and NOW they tell us we can't talk unless we're sitting
down—what is this, a grade school?), and paranoid management (how do you like being yelled at in public?).
Soon a meeting and time will be set up. YOU CAN'T BE
FIRED FOR GOING TO A MEETING. TELL YOUR FRIENDS.[11]

Nothing ever came of the flyer, but it demonstrated the change in
mood at the company. Hertzfeld was devastated. His cubicle neighbor
and software project manager, Rick Auricchio, was one of the 40. Were
they going to fire him as well? How could he go on with his project
when the other guy working on it was gone? He went to see Scotty the
following morning and told him that he was leaving. Scotty, who was in
the midst of fielding questions from board members who had heard
about the events in the morning newspapers, was filled with a kind of
frightening glee. He finally asked Hertzfeld what could make him stay.
The young programmer mentioned several projects, but the only one
that mattered to him was the Macintosh.

IV

Let's Be Pirates

12
Takeover

The afternoon after Black Wednesday, Steve came breezing into the hacker's gallery. Located on the left side—left handedness was always a mark of belonging to the inner circle at Apple—of Bandley 3 was a set of cubicles that belonged to Donn Denman, Woz, Andy Hertzfeld, Randy Wigginton, and, until three days earlier, Rick Auricchio. This was the heart of the Apple II hacker's universe at Apple as it existed in 1981. These were the company's prime wireheads, 1981 style, the guys who worked with computers because they loved them.

On this particular day, February 26, the merry band of prankster programmers at the core of Apple was reeling. Woz had been released from the hospital, but there was no way of knowing whether he would ever put it back together. He had moments of lucidity combined with fits of paranoia. He had been released against the wishes of some of his doctors, and all of Apple, including Steve, was on tenterhooks. Steve was in the midst of his "That's not the way Woz would do it" mode, and in the wake of the accident his admiration was at its closest to hero worship. Although he would bad mouth Woz in private moments, he still understood that without the burly engineer, he would have had nothing. When he went to look for the right guys to create the Macintosh, he naturally came to Woz's team.

This was his only bullpen, these were the guys who had it. Then Black Wednesday removed one of them. Furthermore, Wigginton and Denman, both young clean-cut hackers in their early twenties, had just seen their last two years' work, BASIC III for the Apple II, go down the

219

tubes as the company decided to go with Pascal, the language of the Apple III. The presence of the Apple III infringing on the Apple II made the traditionalists feel like second-class citizens at Apple.

"In the company, it was 'Give up the old, get out the new,'" says Wigginton. "Most of that came from Steve. Woz was gone, and no one was defending the Apple II."

Apple had definitely turned against the core of old Apple hackers. It was trying hard to be a more marketing-driven company, trying to calculate all the angles and choices on the basis of business school formulas at the expense of exuberance and intuition. The new Lisa group headed by Couch wasn't interested in hiring any of them either, since the team of hackers didn't exactly fit their idea of what a programmer looked or acted like.

Shortly after Hertzfeld met with Scotty the previous morning, the company president relayed to Markkula and Steve what the bright programmer had told him. After lunch Steve came over to Hertzfeld's cubicle, and immediately started talking: "Scotty tells me you want to work on the Macintosh with Burrell? Are you any good?"

That afternoon Hertzfeld wasn't ready for a cheerful, upbeat conversation with the perpetually turbo-charged Steve Jobs. He was unhappy and on the verge of quitting. Hertzfeld was an intellectual sprite, the ultimate amateur who wrote programs on computers for the fun of it—it was his art form. Raskin, the former head of the Macintosh group, had no time for him, contemptuously calling him a "hacker in the worst way, a patcher of programs," but he had the spirit of personal computing in every cell of his body.

Short and bespectacled, with a square face, a serious demeanor, and brutal honesty, Hertzfeld was a 28-year-old from Philadelphia. He had discovered the Apple II at Berkeley while he was a graduate student and teaching assistant in computer science. Smitten by the machine and what it allowed him to do, he experimented with fonts and graphics, eventually designing a ROM chip that could be plugged into the main circuit board to add lowercase letters to the Apple II display. He had tried to sell it to Apple in 1979 and in the process met Steve, whom Hertzfeld found exceedingly charming when the company cofounder agreed to buy it.

"A few months later, however, I had a call from one of Steve's flunkies," remembers Hertzfeld, "telling me that they had changed their mind and the sale was off. That was typical of him. He had somebody else do the dirty work for him." While Steve usually avoided doing the uncomfortable work, he also had no memory of the event. It was as if his mind was wiped clean. Over the next few months, Steve called Hertzfeld several times, never mentioning the former incident and asking if he'd like to come work for Apple. After a short period of hesitation, Hertzfeld did. The archetypal hacker joined the Apple II group in 1979, early enough to participate in the stock derby.

"So, do you want to work on the Macintosh or not?" asked Steve. Hertzfeld didn't reply. He wasn't sure if he even wanted to work at Apple, let alone on a specific project. He was still dazed from the summary firing of his programming partner. Moreover, he had designed a number of products on his own, knew he could make a living lots of places, and had enough stock to take his time about choosing a next step.

"Yeah, I guess. But I'm not real happy about Apple now. I may be leaving, Steve. Rick's firing has me really upset. It was wrong."

Hertzfeld was direct. He let everyone know exactly how he felt and what was on his mind. Like Steve, he held strong opinions and had little social tact. He believed passionately in the dream of personal computers. He was the kind of person who would listen very politely while a boss told him that he couldn't do something, and then go right ahead and do it anyway.

"Okay. Come on, you can start right now," Steve said.

"What?"

"Yeah, you can come over and start working in the Mac group today."

"Well, wait a second, I've got some things I need to finish. It'll take me a few weeks to tidy up the loose ends."

"No, I need you to start right now." And with that Steve leaned over, switched off Hertzfeld's venerable Apple II, piled the disk drives and joysticks on top of it, unplugged the machine, and picked the entire thing up in his arms. "Come on, I'll take you over there right now. If there's anything else you need, come back and get it later."

With that Steve took off at his typical high-speed walk and headed out of the cubicle, down the corridors, and outside to his Mercedes, which he had driven over to Bandley 3. Hertzfeld trailed along behind him protesting, but to no avail. Steve opened the trunk, set the computer inside, and drove the bewildered programmer three short blocks to the Texaco Towers building where he was creating the

Macintosh. Walking in, he looked around the nearly empty suite and then, quickly making up his mind, headed for one desk and plopped Hertzfeld's machine on top of it.

"Here. This is where you work from now on. Welcome to Macintosh." With that the company's cofounder disappeared. Hertzfeld was dazed. He walked around the suite and said hello to Burrell Smith and Dan Kottke. He headed back to the desk. The desk didn't look empty; files and papers were on top of it and scattered throughout the drawers. Its previous occupant hadn't taken anything with him when he left. Hertzfeld had been given Jef Raskin's desk.

The takeover was complete. Steve and the embryonic Mac group were beginning a long, often frantic journey.

From the start they had to fight against extraordinarily tough limits. Steve demanded that the machine come out in 12 months, and he wanted every bit of the Lisa's on-screen graphics. He was infatuated with Atkinson's LisaGraf routines, soon to be renamed *QuickDraw*. So was everyone else who saw them. This was the programming watershed that allowed the Lisa and Macintosh screens to be faster by factors of many times Xerox's own office computer system when it was released that year. So they had to work on the Mac as well. "Porting" them over was Hertzfeld's first project.

Atkinson had Steve's ear, and by early in 1981 he was growing disgruntled with the decisions in the Lisa group. "Everything was by committee," he says. "The machine was getting more and more expensive. And without Steve there wasn't the same level of care, that passion for excellence. Things started getting sloppy."

Atkinson stopped by the Mac group whenever he could to grouse with his best friend, Bud Tribble, manager of the Macintosh software group, about the decisions being made over in Lisaland. Since they often met in the evenings, he would also run into Steve, who made it a habit to come by the Texaco Towers suite then, after his corporate duties were completed. Atkinson's personal loyalty to Steve was tied to a day the previous year when he was building the feature known as "regions" into the *QuickDraw* package, after seeing what he thought was a similar idea at Xerox. (This allowed him to grab groups of pixels at once instead of having to meticulously program for every single dot inside a circle, for instance.)

By then Atkinson, the mad scientist of Apple, was doing much of his programming work at his home in Los Gatos. Like all possessed programmers, he would labor through the night when a particularly thorny problem was before him, working until he solved it. One morning, after an all-night session when he had made major break-throughs, he dozed off in his car on the three-mile drive to Apple's Cupertino headquarters, slammed into the back of a big rig, and sheared off the top of his sports car.

When he came to several hours later in the hospital, Steve was sitting by his bedside. "Are you okay?" asked the young company founder, worried that amnesia like Woz's might have struck Atkinson as well. "Don't worry, Steve, I can still remember how to do regions," replied Atkinson, but he was pleased that he rated personal attention from Steve.

Atkinson joined the informal design pow-wows at Texaco Towers that covered every minute detail of the new computer they were creating. Everyone had strong egos, and the arguments raged about how the screens should look, what shape a window should have, how big the computer should be, what the name ought to be, who would buy it, and how much it should cost. Steve was passionate about every detail of the machine. So was everyone else, or else they were speedily booted off the crew. You had to love the computer with a fervor to match the boss's or you would never survive the cut.

"Steve believed in hands-on management," says Denman, who was brought in early to work on a Macintosh version of BASIC that would be called *MacBASIC*. "He would march into your cubicle, invade your space, sit right down, and start playing with whatever you were working on. He would make comments and suggestions about making something easier to use or better looking off the cuff, depending on his mood that day. He didn't really know what you were doing on the technical level, but he was real interested. Then he'd be gone, and you wouldn't see him for a long time.

"We were working for each time he'd come around. And you never knew when it would be, but the goal was to do something neat to show him by the next time he blew in." Steve was the guru of the group, the Zen master, the professor checking on the work of his students. He was the inspiration, the inquisitor, and the executioner.

As Steve took on the leadership role, he wanted several things for the Macintosh immediately: new demo programs to show what the Mac could do; the Apple II disk drive working with the machine; and a sleek packaging that would make it a real product, not just some bench-rigged skeleton. Hertzfeld soon became his key programmer. The hacker had written the original demo for the previous Macintosh, the 6809 prototype, a year before, and was willing to work for days on end to create new demo programs. Smith and Hertzfeld rapidly became friends—a strong asset in a project that was going to require simultaneous development of hardware and software. By early March, Hertzfeld had a bouncing ball demo program running that was faster than anything anyone had ever done on the Lisa. The disk drive wasn't much of a problem for him either. He had been fascinated with the Apple II disk drive when it was released and had taken the first one he bought completely apart in 1978 to learn every nuance of how it worked. Getting it to work on the new Mac was a piece of cake.

For the design of the case, Steve turned to Jerry Mannock, who had designed the Apple II and subsequent Apple products. By early 1981, he was the head of the company's industrial design group, and when Steve came to him, he assigned draftsman and product designer Terry Oyama to the project.

Steve's style of problem solving was to think about it constantly, to meditate upon it. If you started a conversation with him, or more likely he started one with you, he would immediately launch into a question about how you would solve his particular problem of the day. As soon as you reacted, he either decided that you knew nothing significant that could help him solve the dilemma, which meant he would say no more, or that you had some insight into the situation. His reply to you in either case was usually some variation on the phrase "that's shit," which was his stock reply to almost everything. The difference was that if he thought you a worthy person, he would go on to explain why your ideas were "shit" and his was the only right way to look at the situation, challenging you to convince him otherwise. He could change his mind, but only if someone on his "A" list made a really strong case.

He often showed a haughty superiority, and bolstered by the remarkable success of the Apple II by 1981, he had developed an acute sense of his own unerring judgment. But he was growing in other ways as well, albeit slowly. One day he pulled his Mercedes up outside the tiny house Colleen and Lisa were sharing in Menlo Park. She was still so poor that she had only a bicycle, no car. His daughter, who was then three years old, had no idea who he was. It was an uncomfortable moment. He indicated that he had been passing by and thought he'd drop in. He and his former girlfriend sat idly talking on the steps outside—the house was too dingy for him to go inside. And then, just as quickly, he was gone. They wouldn't see him again for another year or so, when he dropped in unannounced again. As he grew more and more secure in his career, he was able to start wrestling with his personal demons. He started to make some headway. But success also cemented other traits into place.

Steve always had a love for the unconventional. He always wanted to be in on the latest thing, he liked being different, and he tailored his entire persona to impress that upon everyone he met. Since he had $200 million in the bank, he could afford to be unconventional in ways that the rest of the world simply could not. His perception of himself as a unique individual was rooted in the isolation of being an orphan, encompassed his vegetarianism, acid tripping, and Zen Buddhism, and produced his Zen Crazy managerial style in which he used the off-the-wall comment to test people's mental acuity and keep them off balance. By 1981, he was far along this path. At the age of 26 and the possessor of fabled riches, he was fighting hard not to become like the conventional upper-middle-class of suburbia, the milieu that he was from but was desperately fighting to escape.

One of Steve's keenest regrets was that he didn't have the natural individuality of a great artist. He was the proselytizer, the advance man for the fellows with the "true gen," as Hemingway called it. He was not a real innovator like Woz or Atkinson. He was a middle-class American salesman who had been singed by the heat of the counterculture and the youth movements of the late sixties and seventies. That fire made him determined to follow his own path and his own drummer, even if that meant grabbing onto unconventional ideas because they were different rather than necessarily better. Steve threw his arms around the new, the different approach, the unlikely solution, with an aggressiveness that betrayed his deep-seated need to be different.

A few months after Steve took over the Macintosh from Raskin, Xerox finally released its first computer. The $15,000 Star was aimed at the same office environment as the Lisa and introduced the world to the idea of on-screen windows with different documents inside them, icons representing different programs and files, a high-resolution bit-mapped screen, and the mouse. The system was large and cumbersome, expensive and slow. It made little impact on the computer community.

Anyone else might have been chastened by this indifference. After all, the Xerox effort was the crucible for the ideas the Macintosh group was refining in glorious isolation at Texaco Towers and in Lisaland. But not Steve. He knew that his path was right, his cause just, and the glory would be his. Steve and his cohorts in the Mac group dutifully trouped down to their local Xerox dealer and took a close look at the system, but they were relieved to see just how unwieldy a product it was.

The first and most fundamental problem facing the group was what their $1,500 computer should look like. The more Steve thought about it, the more he became convinced that the machine had to look different from every other personal computer the world had yet seen.

For a while Steve had championed the name Bicycle for the Macintosh, even going so far as to write a memo officially changing its name. No one else followed his lead, so he eventually dropped the idea. But he was always a big thinker, with a knack for the inspiring analogy, and he soon started to think of their computer as the next telephone, a device that could thoroughly change society, just as the telephone had decades before. As he thought about the machine, meditated on it, and considered his options, he spent hours staring at telephones on desks and in houses. The more he stared, the more he was struck by one thing: Many telephones sat on top of the telephone directory, and that seemed to be the maximum space that a computer should take up on a desk.

One day he came into a design meeting with a telephone book under his arm and threw it on the table. According to one of the early team members, he told them that the Macintosh should be the size of the book. The people in the meeting took a look at the book and blanched. It was smaller than any computer yet built by a factor of about three times, and it meant they would have to create a vertically organized personal computer, as opposed to the horizontal orientation that was already the standard. Burrell Smith thought it was impossible. But Steve was adamant, so Smith rose to the challenge. He had chosen his people well—none of them believed that anything was impossible in the wild and wonderful world of electronics.

Steve had already decreed that the keyboard be detachable. Now he had decided that the "footprint" of the machine, the amount of space it took up on a desk, had to be no larger than a telephone with a directory underneath it. It may have been done for all the wrong reasons, but as time went by, the decision was critical to differentiating the Macintosh. The vertical orientation reinforced the idea, for all who worked on the machine, that they were breaking new ground with the

Mac, that they were producing a revolutionary little computer like none other that had ever been built, even though little in it was truly new. It was not so much revolutionary as innovative. The magic of the Mac was in the packaging, the mix of features. That mixing and matching, the shuffling and recycling of old ideas into a new package, was always Steve's strong suit.

Throughout the spring, Terry Oyama designed mock-ups, which were lined up daily in the Texaco Towers suite of offices the team inhabited. Everyone had a turn at discussing the good and bad points of each. Battles raged over aesthetics, but one voice always prevailed— the final decision was Steve's. Everyone on the team knew it and accepted it. Soon, by mid-May, the look of the computer was fixed. Once the basic design of the machine was set during the spring of 1981, it changed very little. As with the Apple III, new features then had to be squeezed into the box that Steve had decreed was the right size.

Slots were Steve's Achilles heel. He had argued with Woz about them on the Apple II, and with the Macintosh project under his complete control, he decided that the knockout diagnostic port—a way to put in a slot and get around around FCC regulations that Smith and Raskin had built into the original Mac—had to be eliminated. If the Macintosh was going to be the low-cost computer he had in mind, he didn't want people adding all sorts of other devices and gumming up the elegant design. The idea was that the hardware was fixed, so that software could be written knowing the exact capabilities of the machine. The Mac was a computer for the general public, not for the sophisticated—it would have no slots. If you wanted a machine with slots, you could buy a Lisa.

Steve opposed slots and that was that. Nobody could change Steve's mind, no matter how vociferously he or she argued, once he had made a decision. While his vision could be breathtaking and expansive in one direction, it could also be parochial and stifling in another. By dictating an absence of hardware expansion for the Macintosh, he threatened to kill the enormous peripherals industry that had blossomed with the Apple II.

He was able to dictate terms because, during March and April, Steve's power within the company as a whole took a quantum leap. In the wake of Black Wednesday, a whispering campaign was launched against Scotty, who was taking the blame for the firings in February. The campaign was spearheaded by Ann Bowers, the human resources vice-president, a woman who operated in a liberal, self-realization mode and couldn't stand the way Scotty ran over people in meetings, along with John Couch and Trip Hawkins.[1] Scotty was having a tough time anyway, trying to fight off a serious eye infection that his doctors feared might blind him for life. The pressure, a "that was just the beginning" comment made on Black Wednesday, as well as his peremptory manner of looking over a cubicle wall and asking "Are you working your ass off?" combined to seal his fate. The company needed a scapegoat for the poorly handled firings, and he would be the sacrificial lamb.

While Scotty took a vacation in Hawaii in late March, Markkula conducted a trial by executive staff meeting. Some of Scotty's strongest supporters were not invited, and the vote went against the company's president. Steve was one person who voted for Scotty's removal. There was no love lost between them, especially not since the secret reorganization the previous September. When Scotty returned, he found a message from Markkula on his answering machine. At a Sunday evening meeting at the president's house a few blocks from Apple, Markkula told him that the executive staff had requested his resignation. Markkula would take over the presidency.

For Steve and his Macintosh project, the decision couldn't have been better. With Scotty gone, Steve would have a much freer rein. Although Markkula was a shrewd man, he never could stand up to Steve's drive and ambition. Steve knew that as the Macintosh developed he would be able to twist the new president around his finger, and he was right. The removal of Scotty made both Steve and Markkula look like heroes to the rest of the company and gave them greater support.

Steve grew more determined that they be able to ship the Mac by early 1982. He even bet Lisa project manager John Couch $5,000 that the Mac would ship first, although the bigger computer had been in development for three years and the Macintosh project was just starting. It only made the atmosphere in the Texaco Towers offices all the more frenzied and insane. If they were going to get the computer out as quickly as the Lisa, they had a lot of work to do. After bringing the *QuickDraw* code over, Hertzfeld turned his attention to the operating system, the programming code that kept house for the computer and made it possible to write programs that worked on the Mac hardware. The first printed circuit board for the machine appeared that summer, and Steve promptly decided that he didn't like the way it looked. It had to be redone. Burrell went back to the drawing board.

With the Xerox Star, they had seen pull-down menus and a desktop metaphor in full action for the first time, and by May of 1981, Tribble and Hertzfeld created on-screen examples of a similar desktop look that they were thinking of using. They were going to make their decisions about the look and feel of the Macintosh by testing their ideas first, unlike the Lisa crew, which was discussing everything to death.

As they toiled feverishly to make a working computer out of their digital dreams, Steve made a design decision that would have a significant impact on the ultimate success of the project. He decided, on the basis of encouragement from Atkinson and Hertzfeld, to include within the Macintosh a standard set of programming tools. The idea was that although all the necessary software would be contained inside the Mac, the machine would also include a predefined set of tools inside the ROM for building the same user interface. Developers would all produce the same look for every software application created. As Steve and the other Apple II hackers saw it, this would be their software version of the hardware expandability success that the Apple II had had. The internal tools would force every program written for the machine to use the same shaped windows, icons, and menus. Like the Lisa, the Mac would have a carefully controlled operating environment that would be "radically easier to use," a phrase that was one of Steve's favorites on the mashed potato circuit when he was asked where he thought the next innovations in computing would come from. But to make their scheme work, they had to make the tools so easy and convenient that software developers would follow their lead.

The difference between the two projects was that the Lisa had been in progress for years and all the software—spreadsheets, word processors, databases—was being written in house at Apple. The Macintosh, with its outrageous schedule, had no such luxury. They needed programs to run on the computer quickly, and there was little interest in building a sweatshop of software writers. Steve had watched how the bloated Apple III and Lisa divisions operated and had seen that as they grew larger he was able to exert less and less influence. He was determined to avoid the same problem with the Macintosh, and that meant enlisting other companies in the industry to help write software for the machine. Providing outside developers with a standard

Toolbox would compel them to use the Macintosh look and make it easier for them to write programs. It would also enable him to keep the Mac group small enough to remain his personal division.

The first company Steve turned to was Microsoft, headed by Bill Gates, the young entrepreneur who co-wrote the first versions of BASIC for personal computers. Gates was a young whiz kid in the industry who had more technical prowess than Steve but who lacked his bluster and showmanship. Gates had a very close relationship with IBM in 1981 since he had talked his way into writing PC-DOS, the operating system software, for Big Blue's (an industry nickname for IBM) first personal computer, which was finally about to be released. Rumors were flying about it, and although Steve didn't know exactly what it would be like, he was contemptuous and had an idea that it would break no new ground. In early 1981, Steve invited himself to Microsoft to look around and see Bill Gates and his partner Paul Allen at their offices in Bellevue, a suburb outside Seattle, Washington.

Gates was slightly younger than Steve and came from a household where both parents were prestigious lawyers. He had been a programmer mischief-maker in high school, bringing entire computing networks in his home town of Seattle to their knees. Steve had become fabulously wealthy with the previous winter's stock offering, and Gates very much wanted to be rich. He could also appreciate Steve's wild, swashbuckling style, although only from afar. Although it wasn't his own style, he did have a streak of the daredevil about him. The show-off in him always liked Steve's willingness to say the unconventional.

At a meeting in early spring, they discussed the future and where their companies were going. Then Steve spun the Macintosh dream. He didn't have anything to show, however; they would have to go back to the Cupertino labs to have a look at the real machines. But he waxed poetic about accessibility, low prices, the mouse, and the desktop metaphor. The two young whizzes disagreed violently about the market for the personal computer. Steve foresaw a loose intellectual coalition of college students and educated, progressive home buyers, combined with a fuzzy constituency of middle managers and secretaries. Gates, on the other hand, was strongly influenced by IBM's centrist point of view. Computers were utilitarian business tools, and there was no room in that view for the kind of emotional attachment to computers that Steve had. However, Steve could create a vision into which listeners would want to crawl. He outdid himself for the guys at Microsoft.

"It was about how he wanted to put a factory for this new kind of computer he was designing by the side of a beach," recalls Jeff Harbers, one of the original team from Microsoft briefed on the Mac. "Sand, for the silicon in chips, would go in one door and finished computers would come out the other side."

The guys in Bellevue thought it was a pretty crazy idea. But you couldn't just dismiss Steve Jobs. They code-named Steve's project Sand. It was only one of many projects on Microsoft's plate. IBM's order for an operating environment had given Microsoft instant credibility. The IBM PC had yet to reach the market. There was no telling how successful it might be. They wanted to keep their options open. Apple, after all, was still the most successful personal computer company.

The deal with IBM showed how sharp Microsoft was. Gates and his long-term partner, Paul Allen, had licensed the guts of the DOS program from a pair of local programmers, with an exclusive lease in perpetuity. Then, even though they were a gnat to IBM's elephant in size, they finagled a nonexclusive deal with Big Blue. This opened the door for Microsoft to license IBM's operating environment to all comers. In addition, the pair still controlled a license for BASIC, an empire that they had carefully consolidated during the late 1970s. Among the licensors was Apple, for routines incorporated in Applesoft BASIC, which was still incorporated in ROM on the circuit board of the Apple II and the Apple III. Although they had a long-standing relationship with the Cupertino company, Steve questioned whether they were willing to make the major commitment he wanted: a spreadsheet, a chart program, and BASIC for the Mac, ready for shipment with the machine in just over a year. It was the kind of challenge he could always throw out to inspire the best and the brightest.

After Steve left, they discussed it among themselves and decided to go for it. They were too sharp not to play both sides of the fence. Lisa looked like it might be a winner, and to be in on the ground floor of a low-cost version was very attractive. Who knew what might happen to the IBM computer? Even if it were successful, why not have a part in Steve's wild-eyed scheme as well? The next meeting was in Cupertino a few months later, and there, amid nondisclosure forms, Steve introduced them to the Macintosh team and their machine. Burrell Smith demonstrated his prototype hardware. Andy Hertzfeld led them through a technical seminar in which he laid out the plans for the computer: the operating system, the size and shape of the screen, the proposed modular programmer's Toolbox in ROM, the consistent user interface, and how Microsoft could program it. Gates and company left convinced that Apple was onto something special.

Now that Steve had a computer and some software in the works, he focused on drawing up the right marketing plan for his machine. He knew that the key to convincing Markkula and the rest of the company's more professional business people was to present a compelling business plan for the new machine. And that meant identifying who was going to buy the Macintosh, and why.

Steve had come to have complete faith in his own intuition and his feel for the personal computer marketplace. "You make a lot of decisions based on the fragrance or odor of where you think things are going," he said once.[2] "We think the Mac will sell zillions, but we didn't build the Mac for anybody else. We built it for ourselves. We were the group of people who were going to judge whether it was great or not. We weren't going to go out and do market research."[3]

As he started to have a nationwide publicity presence after the public offering in 1980, Steve also began a series of lectures on campuses. He liked to meet and mingle with his contemporaries, and he discovered that it was a fertile recruiting ground for drawing the best and the brightest business students, those with a desire to change the world. It also helped him identify his best market.

In July of 1981, Steve completed the first draft of the Macintosh business plan. It called for the introduction of the computer in mid-1982, at the same time as the Lisa, and a new model Apple II, the VLC (Very Low Cost). The Mac 1 would be followed two years later with the Mac 2. This machine would be smaller and less expensive and would incorporate a flat-panel display. The price of the Mac 1 was $1,500, without a printer but with software; that of the Mac 2 was $1,000. The VLC Apple II would come in at about $1,000, and two years later would be superseded by another, even cheaper machine. The same strategy was planned on the Lisa's timeline. By mid-1984, there would also be a Lisa 2 on the market, and it too would be less, rather than more, expensive.

Since this product-and-price timeline would have brought out newer, improved machines at lower cost that their predecessors, it would have made Apple the only manufacturing company in the world to reduce their income over time. Steve wanted to sell more powerful computers at ever lower prices. The fact that no company in the world could realistically do that and still continue to innovate and support their products eluded him. The plan confirmed that Steve was working on his own, with minimal supervision, and the rest of the company was humoring him. He had little idea how to forecast and plan prices, and since the group organization chart showed him as the head of the marketing group, he was going by the seat of his pants. When Joanna Hoffmann, who had also never done a sales forecast before, based her preliminary figures for that early Mac plan on the Apple II curve, Steve took one look and told her to throw it away. He wanted bigger numbers; as she sat there, he dictated 500,000 to her. For years, until the machine was released, that was the projected figure for Macintosh sales in the first year upon which the entire company based its budgets.

A more troubling problem with the plan was in the marketing segmentation. It was clear from the first document that the key market for the Macintosh was the same office environment at which the Lisa was squarely aimed. That didn't seem to faze Steve, however. In that preliminary plan, dated July 12, 1981, he identified three potential market segments:

> "Every Manager's Tool"
> Every day more managers rely on computers to help perform their functions more effectively and efficiently. MAC makes it possible for any manager to experience the automated office with minimum investment of time and money. MAC will be a rewarding first computer experience.
>
> "Little Lisa"
> MAC will substantially increase the productivity of every manager by providing some of Lisa's advanced capabilities at an entry-level price.
> 1) With promotion and associated increase in responsibility, a manager will be ready to graduate to a Lisa.
> 2) Managers already using Lisa can use MAC when away from the office (traveling, home).
>
> "Low End Clerical/Secretarial"
> MAC can help every secretary grow into an area associate. With Macintosh secretaries can take on more interesting assignments and more responsibility which can make the manager more productive.[4]

It should have been obvious that unless there were some compelling reasons to buy Lisas, the Mac was going to undercut that machine's marketplace severely. Having two computers come out at the same time aimed at the same markets was a disaster in the making. But who was going to tell the emperor?

Steve was concerned with two other key markets as well: the college and high school educational area; and the consumer home and home business segments. Nothing based in reality could have supported the outrageous sales predictions that the first plan detailed: that over half a million Macintoshes would sell each year from the day the machine was introduced in 1982. The total sales of the Lisa were projected at 300,000 over four years; 500,000 Macintoshes per year was completely ridiculous. The cost of the project was also unbelievable, since Steve was predicting a shipped computer in just over a year. His total cost for the development, engineering, manufacture, and support of the Macintosh was just under $5 million. It would end up being closer to 25 times that, and the machine took two additional years to bring to market.

In any case, the special task force Steve was heading was no more than a test program. His figures didn't have to be on target: He was just playing anyway. A month after he rolled out the predictions that July, IBM introduced its version of the personal computer. It was exactly the kind of computer that everyone on the Mac team was expecting. It was large and clunky and introduced no new technology. It was difficult to learn to use and was the furthest thing possible from the Lisa or the Macintosh. The guys in the Macintosh project bought one as soon as it was available late in August. Then they tore it apart. All of them were relieved to find it inelegant and unwieldy. They were sure that their new computers would destroy IBM's challenge as soon as they were announced the next year.

There was a smugness on the Macintosh team, in part produced by Apple's early success, in part by the youth and arrogance of the team, in part by Steve's faith in his own instincts. IBM was bigger, but Apple was always smarter.

"We looked very carefully at their PC when they released it," says Chris Espinosa, whom Steve had enticed back from college to head the documentation effort on the Macintosh. "At first it was embarrassing how bad their machine was. Then we were horrified by its success. We hoped the Macintosh would show people what the IBM PC was—a half-assed, hackneyed attempt at the old technology."[5]

For his part, Steve saw IBM's presence in the market as a call to battle, a race to save the world. It felt right for him to be the underdog, the unlikely David to IBM's Goliath. "It is coming down to Apple and IBM," he said once. "If, for some reason, we make some big mistake and IBM wins, my personal feeling is that we are going to enter a computer Dark Ages for about 20 years. Once IBM gains control of a market sector, they always stop innovation—they prevent innovation from happening.

"If you look at the mainframe marketplace, there's been virtually zero innovation since IBM got dominant control 15 years ago. The IBM PC fundamentally brought no new technology to the industry. It was just a repackaging and slight extension of Apple II technology.

"Apple is providing the alternative."[6]

Although Steve downplayed the technology of IBM's computers, Apple also took out an ad in the nation's newspapers that combined an elitist sense of the company's destiny with an overblown style of prose:

WELCOME IBM.

SERIOUSLY.

Welcome to the most exciting and important marketplace since the computer revolution began 35 years ago. And congratulations on your first computer. Putting real computer power in the hands of the individual is already improving the way people work, think, learn, communicate, and spend their leisure hours. Computer literacy is fast becoming as fundamental a skill as reading or writing. When we invented the first personal computer system, we estimated that over 140,000,000 people worldwide could justify the purchase of one, if only they understood the benefits. Next year alone we project that well over 1,000,000 will come to that understanding. Over the next decade, the growth of the personal computer will continue in logarithmic leaps. We look forward to responsible competition in the massive effort to distribute this American technology to the world. And we appreciate the magnitude of your commitment. Because what we are doing is increasing social capital by enhancing individual productivity. Welcome to the task.[7]

It was a self-righteous, smug ad, especially coming as it did from a firm less than one-tenth the size of IBM. But as events would work out,

IBM's release of a personal computer was the best thing that could have happened to Apple. It legitimized the market. It brought enormous amounts of publicity to Apple as the only real competition to IBM. It gave the company the appearance of the underdog, a role that many wished to identify with, and set them up as the only substantial alternative in this now suddenly legitimate business. In terms of name recognition, 1981 was the watershed year for Apple. As the year started, less than 10 percent of Americans knew what Apple was. By the end of the year, after IBM's announcement and the resultant publicity, that figure was up to 80 percent. The IBM PC gave the Macintosh and Lisa teams even more reason to make sure that they brought out their revolutionary new machines soon, to show the world just how stodgy IBM was—and how brilliant Apple was by comparison.

By November of 1981, the group's first true business plan was complete. Steve was marshaling all the forces he needed to bring the machine to market as a real product. Since seeing the IBM PC that previous summer, he had refined his ideas about what made the Macintosh unique, and he had come up with the idea of the "Crankless Computer." The plan, written by Steve himself, described it in this way:

> Personal computers are now at the stage where cars were when they needed to be cranked by hand to be started. They are now at the same stage as washers were before the invention of the spin cycle, when the wringing of the wash was done manually. The personal computer still requires a great deal of human intervention and effort to be fully operational. Personal computers are simply not complete, as cars were not at the crank stage.
>
> The crank for personal computers is the awkward human interface. Users need to learn a host of quite unnatural commands and operations in order to make the computer do what they want it to do. These commands are a function of the computers' crude internal architectures.
>
> The turn of this decade saw a lot of manufacturers, some very big ones, jump on the personal computer bandwagon. Some personal computers have more memory than others, some have more mass storage, some have color, others have more columns, but they all need to be hand cranked.

There is only one crankless computer on the market, and that is the Xerox Star. It is a crankless Rolls and affordable to the very few.

Since 1979 Apple has invested millions of dollars and thousands of man-hours in the development of a consistent user interface that will take the crank out of the personal computer. The outcome of this mammoth undertaking can be summarized as follows

- a nearly modeless user interface, based on familiar concepts and models (such as a desktop) that relies heavily on graphics and visual cues
- a pointing device (the mouse) that allows the user simply to point anywhere on the screen
- a system which is generally intuitive to users.

This superior user interface was developed in the context of an office system: Lisa. Lisa is Apple's crankless Mercedes: It is beautifully engineered for a specific market that can afford to pay for its fine features.

Macintosh adopted the conceptual advances of Lisa's user interface and tailored them to suit a general purpose, low cost device.

The philosophy behind Macintosh is very simple: in order for a personal computer to become a truly mass market commodity, it will have to be functional, inexpensive, very friendly, and easy to use. Macintosh represents a significant step in the evolution of the mass market personal computer. Macintosh is Apple's crankless Volkswagen: affordable to the quality conscious.[8]

The idea of the Macintosh as the crankless Volkswagen caught fire in the boardroom when Steve presented his plan. The group had expanded, and he had added a finance person to help him with the projections, but they were still as unrealistic as ever. For the November 1981 plan, they were now predicting development costs of about $30 million. Apple's cost had risen slightly—from $387 per Macintosh in the original plan to $408—but the sales projections stayed at almost exactly the same level. Steve had made up the 500,000 per year figure from thin air, and now he was using it as gospel to prove that his new machine would be very valuable to the company.

Steve presented his case to Markkula with a virtuoso performance. The report glossed over the obvious similarities between the markets for both machines, similarities that were dismissed in the plan with the brief phrase, "Macintosh is aimed at the markets Lisa does not address." The power of Steve's vision and the rightness of selling an inexpensive machine with all the power and features of the Lisa carried the day. The executive staff and the company's board approved the go-ahead for the project. In December of 1981, the Macintosh was a real product. Steve was almost vindicated. He could produce real products: first the Lisa and then the Macintosh. Now that his nemesis, Scotty, was out of the way, he was effectively in charge at Apple and could get his way.

The first shipment date had been pushed back to October 1, 1982, but the schedule was still as unrealistic as ever. By the fall of 1981, they had much of the graphics package that Atkinson had done for the Lisa running on the Mac, and it seemed only a matter of months before they could have the entire machine and operating environment completed. They even had a first operating environment, Monitor, and a first prototype application, MacSketch, a drawing program that demonstrated how the bit-mapped graphics world might work. The hardware was about to be finalized—it had been redesigned several times during the year—and everything was in place for the computer to be signed off to go to manufacturing.

Everything, that is, except Mike Scott. At Apple's annual meeting that year, nine months after the company's first president had been demoted, he mounted an effort to add two new directors to the board.[9] Steve, who found out about the attempt as the public meeting proceeded, was furious. He thought that it was being done behind his back and without his approval. The company cofounder erupted and publicly attacked his former president. Apple's stock, which had risen as high as $29, had settled back to $22 by the end of the first year of being a public company. The Apple III launch and recall, combined with the executive level shakeup that occurred after Black Wednesday, had cautioned investors. The Apple III had been re-released that fall, and the machine was being retargeted to businesses as a complete solution, but the market was wary. Although profits were strong from the Apple II, and the company was having an excellent Christmas sales season, Apple's management still seemed a little chaotic to the conservative brokers and investors of America.

When Steve told the press after the annual meeting that "someone was trying to destroy Apple,"[10] he believed it and did nothing to shore up the company's early reputation. However, what was seen publicly was only the tip of the iceberg. To many of the company's own people, the advent of the Macintosh project and its enthusiastic adoption by the top echelon at Apple was the worst thing that could happen. Far too much power was given to Steve, and with no one to rein him in, he was going off the deep end. Steve was trying to destroy Apple, company malcontents grumbled. During the next year, he did his best to prove that they were right.

13
The Kids Can't Wait

The attempted coup at the 1981 annual shareholders' meeting failed. Scotty was unable to make a comeback, and Steve was free to take the Macintosh to the people. In October, his face appeared on newsstands around the country gracing the cover of *Inc.* magazine above the bold caption, "This Man Has Changed Business Forever." He was sitting atop a company that had a stream of money rolling into its coffers the size of which increased every month. Although the IBM PC was making a run for their market, there wasn't much fear in the Cupertino corral in 1982. Steve was convinced that Apple would beat back Big Blue's challenge by offering a new style of computing that, he was fond of saying to the press at the time, "could reduce the time it takes a new user to get up to speed on a personal computer from 40 hours to 20 minutes."[1]

Steve was convinced that he was on a holy quest that justified any means. He had started the project by targeting the best people in the company and stealing them away to work on the Macintosh. Since they were plundering the Lisa project and the Xerox Star for anything worthwhile, taking the best ideas that had been worked out by that team over three years while discarding the rest, he soon came to see his

Macintosh crew as a gang of pirates and himself as the pirate king. The team was about 25 strong by early 1982. They were all opinionated, dedicated, and convinced that they could do almost anything better than anyone else. They shared one other attribute: They cared more about building an amazing computer and shocking the world with it than they did about anything so ordinary as money, career paths, or tradition.

They worked in splendid isolation and were doing so at a pace that put the rest of the company, and even the rest of the computer industry, to shame. They were going to bring the greatest computer to market in less than two years. So they thought.

Like Steve, they were suburban brats who had been deeply influenced by the waning days of the counterculture and the movies of Steven Spielberg and George Lucas. They proudly wore self-imposed chips on their middle-class shoulders and wanted to prove that they were different and superior. It was what had lit their flames in the first place: the individuality that was suddenly possible for a computer scientist with an Apple II, a computer for an individual. In the Macintosh, they would find their own expression of disdain for tradition and the lemming-like values of the rest of the computer industry.

"We were mavericks out to blow people's minds," says Andy Hertzfeld. "We wanted to overturn standards, create new standards, not to do things like everyone else."

Steve also looked outside the company to find people who in his eyes had the right stuff and then stopped at nothing to get them. He personally recruited a quiet, reclusive woman who he had heard was a European office-products giant's best 68000 programmer. (The company was rumored to be preparing a 68000-based microcomputer for the office market.) In October of 1982, he flew to the Hanover Computer Fair, Europe's largest show, where the woman was demonstrating the prototype that she was working on. With his considerable charm and unrelenting single-mindedness, he convinced her to work on the Mac team. She would join Hertzfeld in building the operating system for the computer. Getting her to work for Apple did nothing but build Steve's ego. It reinforced the idea that he was a corporate pirate who could sail throughout the world capturing any person or thing he wanted.

With his power at Apple consolidated after a year without Scotty, and the focus of the country and the region's media on him as an archetype of the new entrepreneurial touch that was making a strong comeback in Reagan's America, he felt no compulsion to follow the same rules of behavior that limit the rest of the world. He was loose on the high seas. The business of personal computers was going through the roof, and he was its leading spokesman.

At the same time that he was successful in increasing his R&D budget to $38 million—an increase of 81 percent—and consolidating his power by keeping Markkula in the president's seat, he was dealt a serious blow. In the aftermath of the 1981 annual meeting, the company lost one of its first superstars. Randy Wigginton had been one of Scotty's inner circle. The self-taught programmer had created Apple's BASIC and for a year had been working on *Mystery House*, a spreadsheet program for the Apple III that had been requested by Scotty to reduce Apple's dependence on *VisiCalc*. He decided to leave and wrote a letter of resignation that was almost a carbon copy of Scotty's, which had appeared several months earlier. In it he attacked "yes-men, empire builders and a cover-your-ass attitude," which were the same words that the company president had used when he resigned the previous July. It was a major blow to Steve and the Macintosh.

Wigginton had been one of the first recruits to the project, but he had become fed up with the unrelenting pressure and Steve's personality quirks. Like his mentor Scotty, Wigginton was rooted in the practical and the concrete. He found Steve's flights of fancy unconvincing and his brow-beating of programmers appalling. Furthermore, his hero, Woz, was recovering from his airplane crash and wasn't involved with the company any longer. With counsel from his good friend Scotty, Wigginton decided to resign.

The problem for Steve was that Wigginton was slated to develop the word processing package for the Macintosh, then called *MacWriter*. In order to ship the Macintosh by October of 1982, which was still Steve's plan, he had to have some applications available for the machine. Atkinson had been working on a computer drawing program based on his earlier *MacSketch* demo that demonstrated his graphics routines for the Lisa. He called it *LisaDraw* and was planning a similar program for the Mac. Since he'd adopted the Macintosh group from the start, he had promised to make *MacSketch* a working program by the time of the Mac's introduction. But a drawing program wasn't exactly the kind of powerful business-oriented tool that the Macintosh needed to penetrate the office environment, which Steve considered the computer's primary marketplace.

Word processing and spreadsheets were the key programs. Microsoft had committed to a version of a spreadsheet called *Multiplan*, which they had previously created for the Apple II and were in the process of refining for the IBM PC. They also planned a business charting program called *MacGraph*. They refused to buy into Steve's outrageous schedule and agreed to commit to having it done one year after the hardware and operating system were completed. In late 1981, neither was finalized yet, and it was obvious that Microsoft's programs weren't going to be ready for release nine months later. *MacWriter* was the only other application that could be ready for release. When Wigginton walked out, Steve was faced with the prospect of having to hire an outside firm to write it or finding someone within Apple to do so.

At first he toyed with the idea of stealing the programmer who was doing the Lisa word processing application. But the word from Atkinson and Hertzfeld was that *LisaWrite* was a mess—slow and with convoluted code that was a nightmare to debug. Going outside Apple had one serious drawback: No one else would agree to Steve's unrealistic deadline. Within the company, he could distort reality enough to convince others that his deadlines could be met. Besides, he was signing the checks, so the final decision was his. If he wanted to set an unrealistic deadline and then keep slipping it, that was his business. Outside the little kingdom he had no such power. The only solution to the dilemma over *MacWriter* seemed to be to convince Wigginton to do it, even if he were no longer with the company. So he did.

Wigginton had left Apple because of Steve, so when the chairman came to see him in December and offered a deal, the programmer was initially uninterested. But he added, as a kind of lark, that he would do it for $1 million.

"I figured that for $1 million I could put up even with Steve," he says. Steve rejected that idea, saying that if he paid Wigginton $1 million, what would the rest of the Macintosh team feel? Wouldn't they all want that much? At that point, Steve was paying the lowest salaries for engineers in the company. For all his idealism and product vision, no one in the group was making more than $30,000 a year. They were expected to give their all for that, while he was pulling down $250,000 a year in salary as chairman of the board. However, as he ruminated on the situation and agonized about it for weeks, he realized that he had little choice if he really wanted the program written in the incredibly short time—one year—allocated to produce it.

Steve went back to Wigginton and offered him a deal. If he delivered the word processor by the date of the release of the Macintosh, Apple would pay a royalty of $2 per Macintosh sold, up to $1 million, and provide half of that in advance. As Steve pointed out, that was equivalent to one year's sales, since he was projecting sales of 500,000 Macs per year. The deal also included a future revised and improved release of the word processor and Apple's ownership of the rights. Wigginton thought that was fair, as long as Apple agreed never to sell it, only to give it away as part of the bundle of software that accompanied the machine. Steve gave him his word and the deal was made. It was a few days before Christmas of 1981, and the success of that deal made Steve feel better about the loss of Bud Tribble, the group's first software manager, who had just announced that he was going to medical school.

Steve was carefully building the team that he wanted. At first he was determined to keep the number down to 45, then 100. He made sure that every new member passed muster with everyone already in place. The personnel tests were off the wall and unique, as befitted the project as a whole and the group's determination to be different. Two of Steve's standard questions were: "How many times have you taken acid?" and "When did you lose your virginity?" The idea was to weed out the wimps who were no good at thinking on their feet.

"We were very, very selective," says Hertzfeld, "It was very hard to find people to work on Mac software, because on the one hand we had very high goals of doing this research, Xerox PARC-like stuff with uncommon, high technical standards. On the other hand, we had a very inexpensive, limited memory machine.

"All the Xerox PARC-type guys who came to interview said, 'You don't have two megabytes? Forget it. I don't want to work on this thing.' Gradually, we found great people who were turned on by the dream. They came and joined our band, and I guess we reached critical mass."

For the software and hardware groups, another benchmark was how good you were at playing the videogame *Defender*. The game involved negotiating a high-speed spaceship through a world of

Klingons and hyper-bombs. The ultimate player was Burrell Smith, who along with Woz seemed to have an uncanny skill for controlling all elements of the complex game.

"It was as though he could somehow get right inside the game and anticipate what was going to happen," explained Donn Denman, another ace player. "Burrell was beyond good—he was great. If we were going to hire somebody, the final test was playing a game with Burrell."

Early in January of 1982, Steve presented the Macintosh project to a yearly meeting of all Apple's middle managers. Grumblings from the Lisa group that the Macintosh was going to destroy the bigger computer were unheeded in the face of Steve's determination to make the machine a success. The meeting concluded with an enthusiastic affirmation of support for the Macintosh, and Markkula, the company's president, gave Steve the green light to do whatever he needed.

Later that month, Hertzfeld had a mock-up of the Toolbox working, and in the process Steve refined his thinking about the Macintosh. Steve knew more about the cost of parts and components than anyone at Apple, and in knowing the prices and watching the changes, the former Haltek stock clerk had devised a strategy for the Mac that would truly revolutionize computing. The idea was rooted in industry changes that had occurred during the five years since the Apple II was released, and with his knowledge of the business, he was shrewd enough to detect a change in the prevailing winds and design a computer to take full advantage of it.

"When we first started off with the Apple II, the variability—how you customize your machine—was with the hardware: you plugged in a new card," says Steve. "In those days a microprocessor cost a lot of money, maybe $50 or $60 with the RAM and ROM you needed. You obviously wanted to share that cost among the peripherals, which is what the Apple II did, what any slotted system does. So Woz designed slots that used the computer's own processor and power, and increased the cost of the main computer to the consumer.

"But now prices have dropped, and you can buy that micro-processor for about $5. Doesn't it make more sense to add a $5 bill to the peripheral rather than make the consumer pay $100 for slots that will never get used? Customization really is mostly software now. The way I get my machine to do what I want is by sticking in a different disk."[2]

Steve had foreseen the trend toward cheaper peripherals, with their own on-board processors and a diversity of software. Since he was fundamentally opposed to hardware add-ons, he did nothing to make it easy for them to be connected to the Mac. He saw the future expansion path for consumers of his personal computers in providing an open door for the development of lots of diverse software along with a few cable connections to "smart peripherals" that could have their own microprocessors. Software was the wave of the future for the Macintosh, not add-on hardware. His theory was that because of the programmer's Toolbox, tons of software would appear that would allow users to customize their computers.

Although the modular Toolbox that Hertzfeld devised allowed an easy way to create "Macintosh-style" applications, programmers would find learning how to program the Mac a prodigious task. And closing the Mac's hardware to outside developers ran the risk of putting the machine out to sea without a paddle. Undaunted, Steve, the kid who had never worked in a real office situation, who had no real under-standing of the struggle of the common worker, believed that he understood both computers and the consuming public with such clarity that he could single-handedly decide on the configuration of the machine. By then his ego and personal certainty were such that field and market testing were not a part of his makeup. He had done his market research by looking into the mirror, and the rest of the group was willing to agree.

Supported as he was by his cohorts, who all shared a contempt for the "bozos"—anything normal or traditional—he got away with it. It was part of the blindness of a small group who had purposely set themselves apart from the masses. While the isolation may have been necessary to create a product as good and as focused as the Macintosh, the pitfall was in the endemic belief spread throughout the group that they knew what was best for the hypothetical "public" that would buy a Macintosh. Their attitude turned the rest of the company against them and would eventually lead to the downfall of both their cozy little gang and their captain. It was an arrogance born of youth, inexperience, and public adulation.

By early 1982, Steve was flying high and felt he had the golden touch. Shortly after the beginning of the year, he had calls from *Time* and *Life* in rapid succession. The former wanted to put him and the

Apple II on the cover of a February issue on "Striking It Rich—America's Risk Takers." It appeared the week before his 27th birthday and was a piece of fluff journalism. Steve was easily the most prominent and intriguing of the series of entrepreneurs profiled, and the article read like a prescription for the success of the Macintosh. A month later he was pictured in *Life* with a serious mien while sitting cross-legged on a conference table. Again, the text was a public relations dream. How could he be wrong if the nation's press thought he had all the answers?

In February, Steve took the Macintosh team to Pajaro Dunes, a posh seaside resort about 100 miles south of Cupertino, for the first of the project's retreats. These were a long-standing tradition at Apple, and in later years memories of the Macintosh retreats would be imbued with a kind of nostalgic magic for all participants. At each retreat Steve created a slogan that was his interpretation of the main point of the meeting. The sessions generally lasted two days, with a bus leaving from Cupertino on the morning of the first day, followed by meetings that afternoon, a guest speaker at dinner, and more meetings the next morning. The sessions began with each group in the project presenting a precis of the work they had accomplished and their goals. Steve would generally remain silent during the presentations.

Then, during the second day's morning session, Steve presented his synopsis of what he had heard and where they were going, and led a discussion of the key points and issues that had to be resolved. At that first retreat he handed out T-shirts with the date May 16, 1983 emblazoned across the back. The brute force of reality had finally made Steve change the introduction date for the Macintosh. On that date at the National Computer Conference (NCC) in Anaheim he would announce the Macintosh, and the team would present their creation to the world. The 25 people present at the retreat were of one mind and would follow Steve wherever he led them. The Lisa was scheduled for introduction early that year, and the Mac would follow shortly after. He had it all orchestrated. May 16, 1983 was the slogan of the first retreat.

Raskin had resigned a few weeks before, in early 1982. After he had taken his leave of absence, he hung around the Macintosh group for a while as the publications manager, but he grew steadily more depressed. Twenty-year-old Chris Espinosa took over the publications group. Wigginton, a 21-year-old who swears he had never used a word processing program before, delivered his first mock-up of *MacWriter*, and it soon became apparent to all of them that the display width of the

Macintosh screen was a serious problem. The prototype that they were working with then, already expanded from the square 256 by 256 dot screen that had been specified by Raskin, had 384 dots across, but that wasn't enough to display a line of text properly. The big topic at the retreat was how to squeeze more dots out of the Mac.

"The thing that really drove us was 80 columns, the standard width of a sheet of paper," says Atkinson . "The first thing anyone would ask us was 'How many columns does it have? Does it do 80 columns?' One of the drawbacks of the original Apple II was that it displayed only 40. We were trying hard to get the lines on the screen to break exactly the same place as they would on a printer or a typewriter.

"When we finally had a word processing demo program to test it with, we realized that we couldn't do it with that size screen. The whole point was that we wanted to have a 'what you see is what you get' [WYSIWYG] display on screen. It wouldn't be a Mac without a big enough screen to go to 80 columns."

Burrell Smith told them that it was impossible to squeeze more dots out of the hardware, but Steve insisted that there had to be a way. It was impossible, the bright young designer continued . . . unless they built a special custom chip for the video.

A custom chip appealed to Steve's audacity—no one had ever done something that technologically aggressive for a personal computer before—and he knew exactly who to hire to accomplish the task. Joanna Hoffmann, the first and still only member of the marketing team at that time, had a boyfriend who was working on the final design and testing of a custom chip for an optical mouse that Xerox was about to introduce. Steve had met him several times as Hoffmann's escort and decided that he was going to hire him. But Martin Haeberli wasn't interested. He found the entire setup at Apple too loose and unprofessional. As a way to break down his resistance, Steve convinced him to come to the first retreat as Joanna's guest.

Haeberli arrived for dinner on the first day. That evening Ben Rosen was the guest speaker at dinner. Rosen, who had been touting Apple for years, was a true believer in the personal computer. At the table that night, Steve asked Rosen how long it would take to design, build, and test a custom VLSI (very large scale integration) chip, to which Rosen said at least one year. Haeberli overheard Steve reply, "Then we'll do it in six months. We'll hire the best guys in the world, pay them twice as much [as they are currently making], and we'll do it in six months." Haeberli realized that he was being offered an opportunity to prove just how good he was. However, he wasn't quite ready to take the plunge.

Steve was at the peak of his power during the retreat. The schedule had not slipped yet, and his nemesis, Raskin, was gone. He had just been on the cover of *Time* and was raiding any company he wanted for the best people and ideas he could find. He was feeling his oats, and as the dinner ended he started conducting a brash, off-the-wall interrogation of everyone at the head table.

"There was this great-looking secretary that we'd just hired," recalls Donn Denman. "Steve decided to go around the table asking everyone the maximum number of times that they had had sex in one evening. He was attracted to her, but she wasn't quite bright enough to hold his attention, so he kept flirting with her.

"When it came time for her to answer the question, she was too embarrassed and refused. He started making fun of her. There was an awkward silence at the table as he continued. Then she excused herself and ran away.

"We were all really embarrassed. He realized that he had gone too far and apologized right afterward. That was always his style."

Apologies were a facet of Steve's personality that kept people working for him. He would destroy someone's ego with a thoughtless remark, ridiculing him or her, and then he'd realize that he'd been too rough and apologize. A few days later he would do the same thing again. He was charming enough to make the apologies believable, but the sharp-edged tongue kept lashing out. His personality drove the intense, highly strung, extremely bright people he surrounded himself with to distraction. Some couldn't take it and left. The ones who stayed became "Steve addicts," says Denman.

"You'd get ripped to shreds. He'd take one look at what you were doing, to analyze what had taken weeks to do, and then tell you that your latest effort was shit and that you can do better. The Steve addicts would work all day and night, through the weekend, pushing themselves to prove that they could do it well enough to pass his muster and to prove that he was wrong.

"And then you'd get this little bit of praise. That was what we lived for. The next time he would come through, you'd have something even more spectacular to show him, something he couldn't help but appreciate. Then the cycle would start all over again."

Perhaps part of Steve's complex personality came from a lack of love and understanding. He poured his love into his machines. As the pace of the Macintosh escalated in 1982, he found again that the product came before love. It might be chance, but not too long after he was on the cover of *Time* and the Mac development project reached a feverish pace, his relationship with Belinda broke up.

"It was like lots of relationships," recalls Bana Whitt, who became one of Belinda's closest friends. "Their combined neuroses were too much for the relationship. They drifted apart. He thought she should be there when he needed her and leave him alone when he didn't—it wasn't much of a two-way street."

If Steve had to choose between a woman and a machine, he always chose the machine. He needed companionship, however, and was unsettled alone. He met a woman in Paris one day, but she didn't show up for the date. He toyed with taking out a full-page ad in *Le Monde* to track her down but decided against it. He seemed incapable of finding the right person.

The Macintosh took up his emotional life, but one or another in a string of girlfriends was always on his arm. Mostly blonde, not overly made up or aggressive, often students at Stanford, they were the kinds of California beauties that a young millionaire might be expected to pursue. He was always the center of attention, and they lasted only as long as he was interested, and only up to the point at which it would have to become serious—then he cut them off.

By the end of the first retreat, while the team debated the size of the new video screen, they had pretty much defined how the rest of the product would look. The case was finished, the machine had one built-in disk drive, and the Toolbox and user interface had both been set. Steve added two programmers to the team around the time of that first retreat to help Hertzfeld finish the system software. Larry Kenyon had a degree in computer science from Stanford, and Bruce Horn was a young programmer who had been one of a group of bright teenagers testing Xerox's Smalltalk throughout its development. The software seemed well in hand, and as long as he could find the right person to design the custom chip for the video display with Smith, the project was home free. He was exhilarated.

The one group that Steve had yet to begin building was his marketing organization. He saw himself as both the general manager of the Macintosh division and the head of the marketing group. With

Apple's adoption of the Mac as an actual product, he knew that he had to bring in some firepower. He hired Barry Cash, an older, seasoned Texan to help out. Actually, Cash was hired as a consultant, but Steve was convinced that he could talk him into joining the project full-time once he started in on him. Cash had been one of the founders of MOS-Tech, the firm that sold Apple the original 6502 microprocessors for the Apple II and had a distinguished reputation in the consumer electronics business. But Cash had teenage children growing up in Dallas and wasn't willing to relocate to Cupertino or take on a full-time role in the project.

For the hands-on, day-to-day work of marketing the Macintosh, Steve turned to someone born a few months after him in 1955, Mike Murray. Murray, an elf of a man with a cheerful, positive attitude, had a knack for slogans and a view of the big picture that matched the scale of Steve's vision for Macintosh, and he could always help Steve articulate it. Like most of the Macintosh team, he had little practical experience. To any other manager, that might have been a drawback, but Steve knew it meant that he could control the project all the better and could build it the way he wanted, without a lot of preconceived notions. Bright, inexperienced, and willing—those were the attributes that the chairman of the board was searching for in his Macintosh team. He found them in his peers, the kids of 1955.

Murray had graduated from Stanford with an MBA in the summer of 1981. The son of a comfortably prosperous rural Oregon dairy farming family, Murray had first encountered Steve the previous spring. Stanford's business school held regularly scheduled brown bag lunches to which they invited prominent business people for informal talks with students. It was part informational, part recruitment.

"This little company called Apple was listed one day, so I decided to turn up," says Murray. "I sat in the back of the room with a newspaper, because these things tended to get boring. I'd look up once in a while to see if something was going on.

"There were three young guys in the front of the room who all had suits on and were giving a fairly straightforward, regular presentation. About 15 minutes into their presentation, a person walked in who I didn't recognize as another student. He had on a strange combination of clothes: Levi's, tennis shoes, and the 'double-vested' look—a button-down shirt, with an unbuttoned suit vest over that, and then over that a down jacket vest. Vest on vest—it was a true fashion risk.

"He walked straight down the stairs of the auditorium, sat on top of the desk on the podium, folded his legs and acted like nothing could possibly have been going on before because he had just shown up. The other three guys faded into the background. Things started when he got there.

"Then he said, 'Hi, I'm Steve Jobs and I started Apple. What do you guys want to talk about?'"

It was his standard opening for the college circuit. As his personal fame rose, Steve found that he was a welcome speaker at colleges across the country. And better, he also discovered that college students listened to his pronouncements and slogans with a rapt awe that he could rarely expect among groups of older people. College students still had the idealism necessary to buy into his vision of personal computers changing the world. He never presented a set speech but fielded questions from the assembled group. It had all the appearance of spontaneity, but after he'd made ten or fifteen presentations he realized that the questions were pretty repetitive.

"I let go of my paper and started listening to this guy," recalls Murray, "and I remember getting a real rush of emotion. This was somebody I could really identify with. He was talking in a way that I talk, he communicated very effectively, and he was talking about things that were very exciting. He didn't seem at all like the other 499 companies parading through.

"I cut classes, went home to my apartment on campus, and called Apple Computer. First I had to find out where Cupertino was—I had no idea. Then I told the switchboard operator that I had just heard a presentation given by one of the founders and wanted to send him my resume. All I knew was that his first name was Steve.

"She said, 'Two Steve's founded this company. Which one do you mean?'"

With that first call, Murray started a persistent campaign by letter and telephone to get through to Steve. This business student had decided that Apple was the company for him, expressing the same kind of passion that the hardware and software hackers had for the Apple II when they first saw it. All the next year he tried to get Steve to offer him a position.

"I didn't want a regular position as a product manager. I wanted something that would challenge me." Eventually Murray met a number of the people in the Macintosh team, including Rod Holt, who conducted one of the classic Apple employment interviews with him.

"Rod came in with a book of professional photos, black-and-white landscapes and shots of people. He would show me one and say, 'What do you think of this photo?' I didn't know what to make of this, so I'd say, 'Well, that's really nice.'

"'No it's terrible, and I'll tell you why' was his response. Then he'd flip randomly to another, and the same thing would happen. Only this time I'd say 'It stinks,' and he would say, 'No, it's great.'"

Nonetheless Steve liked Murray and, after Murray had spent a summer interning at Apple, finally offered him a job in marketing, but he didn't offer him much money—around $30,000. Murray, who had two children and educational loans to repay, was disappointed. He needed more to live in Silicon Valley and Steve wouldn't budge, so the young MBA took a job with Hewlett-Packard in their personal computer division at Corvallis, Oregon. In the summer of 1981, Murray joined the same H-P division Woz had once worked for, assigned to a new 68000-based computer project with a mouse—H-P's Macintosh. He was one of several young guys in the trenches working on the initial marketing plans for it.

In December of 1981, fresh from his successful swashbuckling capture of the Olivetti programmer, Steve called Murray at H-P. "He told me that he had made a mistake," Murray recalls. "He had blown it. He should have hired me, he really needed me, and he wondered whether I would reconsider and come down and work for him."

Murray said no. "We had just built a house and were enjoying life in Oregon, but then Steve implored me, 'Well, just have dinner with me,'" Murray reports. He finally agreed to meet for dinner on a forthcoming business trip. Steve took him back to the lab afterward and showed him the Macintosh.

"It was so much further along than anything we were doing at H-P. These guys were a light year ahead of us, they had a much better understanding of new software technology, and they were doing it, while H-P was only thinking of it."

He threw caution to the wind but asked them for more money than he thought they could possibly agree to—which Steve instantly agreed to pay. Murray accepted and then called a colleague at H-P, another kid born in 1955 and a 1981 MBA from Harvard, Mike Boich. Within weeks Boich joined the marketing team as well.

When Steve introduced both Murray and Boich to the Macintosh team that March, he explained that he had hired "two Mikes to be better than Joanna." It was the kind of unthinking comment that he specialized in. Understandably, Hoffmann was upset, and Murray and Boich spent weeks making her understand that they had no intention of moving her off the project. There was plenty of work for all three.

Murray was an energetic guy with an abundance of ideas and plenty of ambition. He was also a fast learner and quickly sized up the situation vis-à-vis Barry Cash. In a blitz of documents, Murray peppered Steve with marketing organizational ideas and wildly off-the-wall thoughts. Not too much later, Cash resigned and Murray became the head of Macintosh marketing.

Murray pored over the documents that made up Raskin's "Macintosh Papers" and was struck by one word: appliance. In the early 1980s the ultimate kitchen appliance was the Cuisinart food processor. It was small and neat, the design was clean and uncluttered, and it performed a number of kitchen chores more rapidly than pre-existing options. In Murray's mind, the Macintosh would be the "Cuisinart of Computers." It was an idea that Steve enthusiastically embraced, because earlier, in one of his wild-goose chases, he had actually sent someone in the Macintosh design team off after a Cuisinart, which he had seen in Macy's one day. For a while, that was the design look he wanted for the Mac—until he just as swiftly dropped the idea.

As Murray developed the product introduction plan with Steve, and the Lisa group set their product introduction process into motion for the following January, the Apple III fell onto hard times. After its reintroduction the previous November, the machine simply died in the water and plummeted like a stone. By January of 1982, it had become obvious that there was no easy way to resurrect it, and the Apple IIe group—working on an enhanced Apple II codenamed Yoda, after the character in *The Empire Strikes Back*—was given a hurry-up schedule. The idea was to ensure that there would be a new member of the Apple II line to introduce sometime soon, although the original machine was continuing to sell in startling quantities.

Relocated in a five-story building more than a mile from the main cluster of Apple buildings at Bandley, the Apple II group by mid-1982 was thoroughly demoralized. Isolated and ignored, they had been moved out of the heart of Apple's campus lock, stock, and barrel when first Lisaland and then the Mac group expanded and needed more space. Nonetheless, they were still providing all the firm's revenues and were in the midst of orchestrating their superbly designed upgrade to the original Apple II line, Yoda, that would extend its life by at least another five years. Yet all of Apple's attention went to its two new, as yet unproven products: Lisa and Macintosh.

Steve further alienated the Apple II and Lisa groups by pampering the Mac team. Unlike the rest of the company, from mid-1982 on, all of the Mac team members were given permission to fly first-class whenever they were on company business. This made for bizarre scenes and grumbling when employees from other divisions flew on the same flights.

Steve also created the ultimate yuppie environment tailored to the team's style of work. A stereo with six-foot-high speakers blasted constantly. Steve ran into a Japanese shiatsu masseur and made a deal to put him on call for anyone in the group who was working late—to be paid for by the company. Fruit and carrot juice and mineral water were stocked in the Macintosh refrigerator at a cost of $100,000 a year. Steve's adherence to natural juices, especially carrot, became an inside joke when the team made up T-shirts that read "Reality Distortion Field" on the front and "It's in the Juice!" on the back. Catered lunches and dinners were a regular occurrence during endless meetings. The parking lot started to fill up with expensive European cars such as BMWs, Volkswagen convertibles, and Saabs that the company arranged to lease for the Mac team, many with customized license plates such as MacWiz or MacHack.

Steve's passion for the Macintosh, and the team who created it, led to another of the most celebrated events of the project: the signing of the case. Steve considered his Mac team members artists, not computer nerds. One day, as the final mechanical drawings for the plastic case molds were being inspected and passed around, he had a big idea.

"We were artists," recalls Hoffmann, "and since artists sign their work, why shouldn't we? That was all the discussion it needed. He decided we should all sign the case."

Each one of the 30 or so members on the team at that point signed their names on the final shop drawings for the Mac. The handwritten names were made a permanent part of the mold. On the inside of the back plate of every Macintosh produced were the signatures of all the team members as of July 1982. He had deftly captured the underlying reason they were all working on the machine and giving their best years to make this computer the most astonishing one of all time: It was for posterity. Now they would all be immortal, too.

The Macintosh was not Steve's only interest that year, however. He pursued one other passion with the single-mindedness that was both his strongest asset and his worst trait. Every autumn, Apple held a large sales conference in Hawaii. The event was for the company sales force and was the traditional kick-off for the Christmas season, the company's most profitable sales period. On the last day of the previous October's meeting, Steve was sitting in the back of the enormous hotel ballroom, by himself, when he caught sight of Phil Roybal, one of Apple's first marketing managers.

Roybal had been responsible for the company's early emphasis on the educational market with the Apple II and in some ways might be credited with muscling that market into Apple's lap. More recently, he had been involved with the Apple III reintroduction strategy and was a close friend of the company's head of sales, Gene Carter. Steve beckoned him over.

"Steve was not an original thinker. He was great at taking ideas from others and then making them a little better and selling them," says Roybal. "'Look, it's time to get computers into the schools,' he said to me excitedly. 'We've got to do it now—the kids can't wait. I've been thinking about this. Why can't we just give away a computer to every school in the country? We'll get all sorts of good publicity and a tax break, and we'll get our systems in front of hundreds of thousands of kids.' It was the only purely original idea that I heard from him during all the years he was with Apple.

"I started in to tell him that the laws of donations were such that a manufacturer could only take credit for the raw materials involved. I continued until I realized that he had that glazed look in his eyes that he got when he didn't hear anything you were saying because he didn't want to. When I was finished he looked at me and said, 'Then we'll change the law.'"

Which is exactly what he tried to do. Steve set in motion a research effort to find out what would be involved in rewriting the tax law so that a donation of technology could be deducted at full value. He wasn't getting very far, until one day he happened to be on an airplane with Pete Stark, a California congressman. On a cross-country flight, he bent the representative's ear. The result was a bill introduced in Congress, which Apple called "The Kids Can't Wait" bill. Unfortunately, it didn't pass, even with Steve's presence on Capitol Hill as a highly visible lobbyist, but similar legislation was introduced into the California state assembly and in the summer of 1982 became law. The following year more than 9,000 Apple IIs were distributed to California secondary schools.

During the years that followed, this was the program that he often said was his favorite. If there was one group of customers he always seemed to have time for, it was kids. At parties, Steve could be found sitting with a child showing him or her how to run the Apple II, and later the Mac. "Older people ask 'What is it?'" he once commented. "The boy asks 'What can I do with it?'"[3]

In 1982, the big movies were *E.T.* and *Gandhi*. *E.T.* celebrated the triumph of childlike wonder over cold-hearted adult technology in the suburban wastelands where the Mac team had grown up. *Gandhi* spoke to the religious interests that Steve had once so ascetically embraced. The book *Soul of a New Machine* was also all the rage in Silicon Valley. It was an account of the team that created a new minicomputer at Data General Corporation's advanced research facility near Boston. The book described a closely knit engineering project headed by a charismatic project coordinator. It became Steve's model for the Macintosh project for a while, even though he rarely read books and almost never finished any. He was a workaholic immersed in the most important work of his life. Who had time for pleasure?

In 1982, Steve made the transition from an *arriviste*, a young and suddenly very wealthy man without much sophistication, to a much more smoothly groomed and finished young prince. He was named to the California Commission on Industrial Innovation by Governor Jerry Brown, and he started to hob-nob with the likes of the chairman of the board of the Bank of America and his childhood idol, David Packard of Hewlett-Packard. He found that people treated him deferentially, and almost everyone wanted to hear what he had to say. He was considered a great innovator and was invited to numerous symposia and college classrooms as a lecturer on creativity and entrepreneurship.

As Steve's one-time partner distanced himself from the business of computing—Woz returned to college to complete his bachelor's degree in 1982—Steve had virtually to himself the territory that Apple had carved out in the popular and business culture at large. In early 1982, he added another project to his list: giving Apple IIs to prisons to teach convicts programming. The prison idea put him in touch with Mimi Fariña, who ran a prison music and reform project called Bread and

Roses. At a benefit he met her sister, Joan Baez, and was smitten by the folksinger, though they were at least 15 years apart in age.

Baez was an entirely different breed from anyone he had been with. She was indisputably more famous than he and had been involved not only with the beat generation and the early counterculture, but also with Bob Dylan, who was one of Steve's enduring cultural fixations. Furthermore, she was a little wild and dangerous, having publicly announced during the frenzied seventies that she had slept with a woman. For Steve, who was always trying to be as different as possible, she was a real radical respected for her singing and political stances. For Baez, he and his wild crew of young computerniks were an interesting diversion.

The complement to his self-absorption with work was a habit of pouring out his heart to an employee. It almost always concerned a woman, according to Hertzfeld. "He might go on for hours. I'd listen to him talking about his problems with Joan, and try to help him through it. By the end of it, I'd feel like we were real close. Then the next morning it would be as if all that intimacy had never occurred. It was back to business as usual, and he was your boss again. There was no evidence that we had shared anything. And of course, he wasn't interested in doing the same thing for me. He wanted to hear the latest gossip, but that was it."

Part of Steve wanted to settle down and have children, even as he fought the impulse. He had finally begun to see Lisa, his daughter, occasionally, carrying on the drop-in visits that had begun the previous year. But he never celebrated her birthday or spent holidays with her. Nonetheless, he seemed to want to be a father, at least theoretically, if not in practice. He agonized over Baez with part of the team at dinner one night, saying, "If only she were of child-bearing age, I'd marry her."

His relationship with Baez didn't work out. "I think eventually she got fed up with him," says Andy Hertzfeld. "He was too young and immature for her." They remained friends, however, and through 1982 and 1983, she became a celebrity fixture at all the Mac parties.

In a close-knit crew of young, single men and women, affairs were part of the territory. There was one child born to a couple on the team, and a couple of marriages were celebrated. Several other marriages collapsed under the weight of the work required, because few wives could accept the allegiance and intensity required of their spouses by the passionate leader of the team. Just as earlier he had seen the sale of stock as betrayal, he now saw efforts of less than 80 hours a week as a wimp-out.

Most of the team were white and middle class. They were all college-educated, bright, and homogeneous. There were 22 women in the first 70 employees. There were also no blacks, and only a couple of Hispanics and Asians in the early days. The numbers would change later, but Steve was building a team in his own image.

"One of the requirements for employment was a love of pineapple pizza," recalls Chris Espinosa. "We actually asked that. I mean, if they didn't like the same kind of pizza as we did, how could they come out to dinner with us?"

Food fads came and went. Burrell Smith was behind much of the faddism. He was a compulsive who, once he discovered a new sensation, would gorge himself on it for weeks. Sushi was one such craze, pineapple pizza another. The local hang-outs for the team were a hole-in-the-wall falafel joint called ViVi's about a mile down the road and a local pizza parlor that stayed open late and sold pineapple pizzas. The wooden benches, funky atmosphere, and assortment of meatless pita sandwiches made ViVi's a perfect place for Steve, who was careful about what he ate. Although he still professed to be mostly vegetarian, he had started eating meat. One day at a meal in a Los Gatos Mexican restaurant, Steve started bragging about what a good vegetarian he was and how he knew all about nutrition and hadn't touched meat for years, as he ate a plate of rice and beans. When one of the programmers pointed out that refried beans were usually made with lard, which was made from animal fat, he refused to believe him—until he interrogated the waitress and personally inspected the kitchen.

It became a running joke within the group that eating out with Steve was an exercise in embarrassment. First there was the issue of sending plates back. He rarely accepted the first or even the second plate brought to him. It would be "shit," "dirty," or not what he thought the waitress had described, and he would send it back. Something in him had to play out that kind of scenario and make the waiter or waitress grovel. With all the money, power, and adulation that society had showered on him, Steve had never learned humility.

Then there was the strange and ongoing saga of paying the bill. "The first time Burrell and I had dinner with him, we went to a pizza place in Cupertino," recalls Hertzfeld, "and when the bill came Steve said something like 'I don't have any cash. All I've got is a credit card.'

"That was all I had as well, so I said so, and he replied 'Great, you can pay for it.' It took him years before he paid for anything. He never had cash with him, and whenever we went out with him, we had to pay. I think it had something to do with not wanting to be taken advantage of, or maybe he was just a skin flint."

This was all part of the dark side of his personality. He could be charming to the press, to a woman he was interested in, or to other famous people. But with employees and those he didn't have to care about, he was devastating, obnoxious, and in many cases dangerous. Most kowtowed to him, but a few refused to take his treatment. One day an engineer who had been working on a particularly grueling project was treated to the "that's shit" routine. He was so incensed that he turned on the chairman of the board and had to be physically restrained from pummeling him.[4] The engineer lost his job, but Steve never changed.

His insecurity—his determination, according to Donn Denman, to "prove that he was worthy of all this money that had been given to him"—made him unable to see his mistakes until one of his trusted few convinced him of the error of his ways. The energy required to shove him onto the right path sapped the team, burned them out far before their time, and created anxieties and turbulence. At the same time, the threat of his irrational challenges inspired supreme efforts.

"It was all seduction, pure and simple," says Mike Murray. "He seduced us all with the dream, and even when he was at his blackest, when the vindictive, dark side of his personality was at its height, we could say that we were working for something more important than him, more important than anything he could foul up. That kept us going.

"Steve just doesn't have the limits that the rest of us have. Because of his background and his early success, he doesn't have any boundaries, he doesn't know that anything is impossible, because he has always been able to do anything he wanted. For most of us, it would be too scary to get out there where there are no fences.

"But that's all Steve knows. Even as he's being a jerk, he's got this incredibly seductive aura around him that keeps you bound to him, keeps you near the flame, keeps you on the team."

Family was the only thing that could interfere with his vision and power over individual team members. Few of the group had children, and for those who did it was a major problem. "I always went home at five or six o'clock to be with my family," explains Mike Murray, who had four children by the end of the project. "I felt like I was never quite part of the team, because I couldn't stay there all night and have pizza at midnight with the rest of them."

Steve kept his relationships outside the company. That didn't stop him from taking an inordinate interest in matchmaking, however. He rarely liked people's wives or girlfriends. He thought they could do much better, and since everyone working on the Mac was, by his own definition, superb, in his mind they would be better off together. Moreover, if both were working on the Mac, they could put even more hours into the project. Meddling in the love lives of his staff only indicated the dissatisfaction he had with his own.

"Steve can't have a satisfactory relationship," concludes Hertzfeld. "He's too caught up with himself. So he was interested in all of ours." And it wasn't just love, it was friendship that eluded him. He didn't have friends—he had employees and former friends. There were none of the long-time intertwining relationships that begin to define life in one's twenties and thirties. He had no one he hung out with, no one who was his buddy. He had had one in Kottke, but that relationship was all but destroyed by his intransigence over the stock offering—or lack thereof. Nonetheless, it's a measure of his personal seductiveness and charisma that Kottke was working on the Macintosh project, working on the keyboard and taking care of miscellaneous engineering details that Smith was too busy to handle.

In 1982, after *The Big Chill* was released, a group of the old gang from Reed decided to have a reunion weekend. Kottke, Holmes, Friedland, and another friend invited Steve, and he agreed to come. They arranged to rent a house in the Northern California wilderness near Clear Lake for a week. On the appointed day, Steve never called or showed up. He was like Jay Gatsby, isolated in the midst of all his worldly success from any roots or ties he might have had. The only people he spent time with were those whose salaries he paid. He had built the citadel, and he was surrounded by the troops, but there was no one with whom he could share his heart.

Steve Jobs in the living room of his Los Gatos home, 1982.

Steve Jobs holding an informal question-and-answer session at Stanford University, 1982.

A working lunch meeting of the Macintosh design team.

Mike Murray, Macintosh Marketing Director, with some of the marketing materials he created.

Steve Jobs with John Sculley in Manhattan's Central Park, a few days before the official release of the Macintosh in January 1984; the bag contains a Macintosh.

Key members of the Macintosh development team after the January 1984 Apple shareholder's meeting.

Stephen Wozniak, Steve Jobs, and John Sculley at the unveiling of the Apple IIc.

266

Steve Jobs and Stephen Wozniak with the Apple IIc computer at the unveiling in San Francisco, spring 1984.

John Sculley and Steve Jobs at the 1985 shareholder's meeting at which they introduced The Macintosh Office strategy.

Steve Jobs receiving the National Technology Medal from President Reagan, February 1985.

Steve Jobs greets reporters outside his Woodside mansion after his resignation from Apple, September 1985.

The team at NeXT; from left: Dan'l Lewin, Rich Page, Bud Tribble, Steve Jobs, Susan Kelly Barnes, George Crow.

Ross Perot and Steve Jobs announcing the Texas billionaire's investment in NeXT.

© Ed Kashi

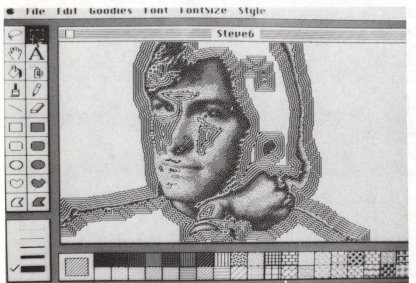

A digitized image of Steve by the Macintosh team, using MacPaint.

© Norman Seeff

14
Evangelism

If the Apple II was the computer that introduced teenagers and grade-schoolers to computing, then the Macintosh was its older brother. By 1981, Steve had decided that colleges were ripe for personal computing, and by the time specific plans were being formulated a year later, the colleges took second place only to the office worker in terms of importance for the Macintosh. After all, it was the only market in which Steve really felt comfortable. College kids could appreciate his sense of idealism as well as his belief that he knew what the world really needed. With the Macintosh being created by a group barely out of school themselves, it was an ideal fit.

Much more confusing was the marketing thrust of Apple as a whole. Isolated in the kingdom of Cupertino, surrounded by the duchies of Silicon Valley, they were convinced by their leader that they had an almost divine sense of the way the market was going—or better, that they could lead and control the marketplace by their actions without regard for the realities of their customers' working lives. Thus, Apple pursued a series of market segments for which their machines were poorly suited. Steve believed that because Apple's machines were more advanced and easier to use than IBM's, their computers would succeed. He undervalued the importance of security and the absence of risk that IBM represented—the FUD principles, "fear, uncertainty, doubt," that they jokingly used to refer to their archenemy's appeal. He couldn't see that his erratic leadership of Apple was not the kind of stewardship destined to inspire confidence in the middle managers of America's corporate armies who made major purchasing decisions. Steve might follow an unconventional company's lead, but would America's businesses?

The marketing issue was confused by the past success of the Apple II with *VisiCalc*. The smokescreen of success for that combination—effectively the only business computer choice when it reached supremacy in 1979, 1980, and most of 1981—blinded Steve to the fundamental distaste most corporate managers had for his youth, elitism, and arrogance: in short, for everything he stood for. Instead of recognizing a powerful dislike for Apple that could only be overcome with a remarkable product, he thought it was only a matter of bringing out another good machine to recapture the market magic Apple had once had—a market magic that by 1982 was starting to move over to the archenemy, IBM.

The company's remarkable myopia must have contributed to its belief that the slow Lisa—the word used by one Macintosh team member to describe its speed was "majestic"—was going to make inroads into the Fortune 1000 marketplace. Add the fact that the two computers in development at Apple had incompatible operating systems and programs that could not share either data or files and any clear-sighted analyst could see a disaster in the making. And of course, the Lisa and the Macintosh were not only incompatible between themselves but with all other personal computers as well. The "Product Introduction Plan" for the Macintosh, authored by Murray in conjunction with the rest of the marketing staff and released in the summer of 1982, continued to predict that the Lisa was going to displace the IBM PC as the machine of choice. Furthermore, the plan mentioned that "the price differential of the two products [Mac and Lisa] will hopefully allow us to explain away the lack of complete compatibility."

The elite Mac group spent much of their time laughing at the follies of the Lisa, but they didn't try to understand why the Lisa people were so unhappy with them. In one memorable meeting, Rich Page, one of the prime architects with Atkinson of the Lisa system, started pounding the table and screaming at Hertzfeld, "Steve Jobs is trying to destroy the Lisa with the Macintosh." Hertzfeld, who loved the Mac like his own child, couldn't understand the attitude. Didn't the folks in Lisaland realize how great a computer the Mac was? What was their problem?

The problem was that the Lisa people realized only too well how great a computer the Mac was, and with the chairman of the board leading the Mac division, it was only too clear who would get the real resources from Apple. The Mac team had all the mistakes of the Lisa in front of them each time they fired up one of their development machines. It gave them not only something to react against and be different from, but also provided them with a learning lab second to none. As they continued to reject the Lisa's solutions, preferring always to go ahead and reinvent a better wheel for their little machine, resentments festered.

A perfect example of the differeing attitudes of the two groups occurred on the day the full firepower of the Mac team showed up in the heart of Lisaland, led by Steve, who was determined to convince his colleagues that square pixels were the only way to go. Because of the rectangular shape of the Lisa screen, that team had settled on rectangular dots. To Steve, Atkinson, Hertzfeld, and Smith, it was obvious that the square dots on the Mac were aesthetically preferable so they brought Macs over to compare the Mac and Lisa screens side by side. But try as they might, they couldn't make the Lisa team understand—it was too late to make the change, they swore, or it didn't really matter, anyway. In desperation, because aesthetics were over-whelmingly important to Steve, they returned to the Mac offices and Burrell Smith set about patching together a demonstration of how square dots would look on the Lisa. He ripped open a Lisa, played with the hardware, and after a weekend of near continual effort, had a working version of something that the Lisa engineers had said was impossible. The Mac team felt that this demonstration proved how great square pixels would look on a Lisa and what a bunch of clowns the Lisa team was. The Lisa engineers believed it was another example of how the Mac team was trying to show them up. When confronted with the demo, they dug their heels deeper. The Lisa was released with rectangular pixels.

One of the big issues in working with a bit-mapped computer was how to print what was on the screen. A character display can use a typewriter-like printer with a print wheel, but both the Lisa and the Macintosh needed something that could also print graphics. Steve had seen a demonstration from C. Itoh, a company that produced a high-quality dot matrix machine which seemed to match the bit-map concept very well. The printhead was made up of a number of tiny pins that pushed out against a ribbon to deposit ink on paper. This technology could reproduce all the bits and pixels on the screen. Steve decided it was the answer to printing. Apple signed a deal with the Japanese firm and then started to look for someone to make it work with the Lisa and the Mac.

They found the people they needed at Xerox, where, not surprisingly, various advanced print technologies, including laser printers, were being tested. Xerox realized early on that going from the bit-mapped screen to paper offered an opportunity for a marriage of computers and copier technology. In the 1970s they had begun working out the principles of office laser printers and by the early 1980s had working laser printers hooked up to their office computer systems. However, as with everything else the company pursued, these printers were expensive, in the $50,000 range once installed. There was little motivation at the company to put them into action with low-cost personal computers.

Owen Densmore was a classically trained computer scientist who had worked on bit-map printing at Xerox's advanced Rochester, New York, research center. One day in 1980, he was delegated to present a seminar on printing to some visiting Apple engineers, one of whom was Bill Atkinson.

"When Atkinson started asking me questions, it was clear he knew what he was talking about," says Densmore. "He really understood the idea of bit maps and what you could do with them on personal computers. Nobody at Xerox had ever said anything like it before. When they offered me a job, I took it."

Just as he had subborned Tessler a year earlier, the wild-eyed Atkinson, filled with the vision of the personal computer, had seduced another Xerox engineering star. Densmore, in turn, convinced co-worker Steve Capps to follow, and by mid-1981 the two had been able to bring laser printing to the Lisa. They were also deeply involved in making the ImageWriter, the name Apple had given the C. Itoh dot matrix printer, work with both computers, as well as supporting the Apple Daisy, a letter-quality impact printer, for the Lisa. When Densmore suggested to Steve that the Macintosh could also run a laser printer, he was roundly rebuffed. The Mac was an inexpensive computer and couldn't be running an expensive laser printer. Furthermore, Steve told him that he didn't want them wasting any time making the daisy wheel printer work with the Macintosh. It was old-fashioned technology by Steve's standards, and he wouldn't have it on his Mac. But in the spirit of Apple engineering, they went ahead and did it anyway—on the sly.

Thus the Lisa printing group was on the distribution list for the latest "build" of Macintosh prototypes, so they could make sure the ImageWriter worked properly. Each "build" consisted of a couple of dozen prototype machines, meticulously wired by hand and carefully doled out to the most deserving. Steve didn't receive one for himself until early in 1983, because programmers and developers were more important in the broader scheme of things.

Densmore's partner, Capps, was a driven, youthful hacker similar to those on the Mac software team. He designed a variation on chess called *Alice* that used the Lisa screen and graphics well. The ingenious game used the character Alice to outsmart a number of characters on a chessboard. When the first of the new Macintosh prototypes were distributed during the spring of 1982, Capps decided that as a lark he would port—or reprogram—the game to the Mac. He did it in one all-night session, and within hours it had made its way over to the Mac group, where Steve decided it was the greatest thing he had seen on the machine. From that day on, *Alice* and *MacSketch*, Atkinson's primitive drawing program, were the demonstration programs that Steve used to show off his baby. And Capps became a marked man—the pirates were going to steal him away from Lisa.

Meanwhile, with Murray trying to create a document encompassing both the target audiences and the elements required for a successful launch of the machine, Mike Boich was pursuing third-party software vendors with a vengeance. As far as the kernel of programmers at the heart of the Macintosh were concerned, Boich was the okay marketing guy and Murray was the "marketing" marketing guy. Boich, the son of a coal mine owner from Pennsylvania, was a hacker from way back—an Apple I hacker, no less. While an undergraduate at Stanford, he bought his first computer from one of the Byte Shops along El Camino Real. He understood software and could keep up with high-powered discussions of heaps, compilers, and recursive loops.

By the time Murray called him at H-P and told him to come to Apple, Boich was a full-fledged hacker and the perfect choice for the group's liaison with software developers. As the Macintosh came into sharper focus over the previous year, the idea of soliciting software development from companies outside Apple became increasingly important. Not only did the Macintosh have to have excellent programs, in a purely practical sense, it was also essential on a symbolic level. If many software packages were either complete or nearly complete and announced on the day of the Mac's introduction, it would provide instant credibility. It was already clear in early 1982 that the Apple II and the IBM PC were two standards in computing; the goal was to make the Mac a third.

Steve and his crew felt that if the Mac could win the hearts and minds of third-party developers, they would be getting resources that would otherwise go to competitors. Working closely with developers was a strategic business decision with strong implications for Apple. Furthermore, because Steve was obsessed with quality—"doing it right"—he wanted to enforce the Macintosh look and feel that the group had devised. The Apple II had been "ruined," in his opinion, by the haphazard hodge-podge of programs and keyboard conventions that appeared on it. With the Mac, there would be no such diversity. By having a group dedicated to interacting with the developers, he could make them hold the party line. Murray coined the phrase "software evangelism" to describe what they had in mind. More than just a description of the marketing group, the phrase characterized the fervor of the entire Macintosh project. Steve was their Elmer Gantry, their preacher, and they were his disciples taking the message to the people.

"The Macintosh was meant to be an open machine, from the software angle, from the very beginning," says Boich. "Steve had this vision that we were going to have a catalog of outside programs that Apple would publish. If they obeyed the user interface, Apple would publish their program in the catalog. I thought it would be a headache, because of all the troubles of policing it and updating the list."

At that time, bundling to Steve still meant putting the software into ROM. Steve had the idea that if you could put the basic programs— word processing, spreadsheet, and business graphics—into the machine itself, you'd have a true appliance. You could buy additional programs, but everything necessary to use the Mac would come with it.

"He was really into minimalist thinking in those days," Boich says. "The consumer would plop it down on a desk and get to work, with nothing else to add, not even a disk."

It was a noble but ill-fated idea. What about the entire competitive subindustry of software development? Steve was going to cut them out of the loop, until Murray and Boich convinced him otherwise. They replaced it with the idea of seeding machines to a few developers to get software going early, so that by release they would have a robust market of software choices. Boich was allocated ten Macintoshes from the first build to seed around the country. Microsoft was already under contract for three applications—*Chart*, *Plan*, and *File*—and Apple had the right to publish them under the Apple label and bundle or sell them with the computer. But this cozy inside track made other developers nervous.

"Jobs liked to call Gates to Cupertino at least once a quarter," says Boich, "and sort of kick him around a little, asking him why he wasn't working harder on the Mac and why they weren't further along—why they were still working for IBM."

Apple was many times larger than Microsoft, and Steve never missed an opportunity to let Gates know who was in the driver's seat. At one point, Steve tried to talk him out of doing any more work on *Windows*, a project Microsoft had launched that brought on-screen windows to the IBM PC. As far as Steve was concerned, it was an out-and-out theft from the Macintosh. Gates disagreed because he saw the idea as originally Xerox's.

"Gates had this slightly self-righteous stance that the *Windows* guys weren't allowed to talk to the Mac programmers he had working for him, so there was zero information transfer," explains Boich.

"Steve said, 'It's kind of like if your big brother punched my little brother in the nose, we'd all run around saying that the Gateses were beating up on the Jobses.' Bill said, 'No Steve, I think it's more like if we both had this rich neighbor named Xerox and I broke in to steal the TV set and found out that you had already stolen it.'"

The big software company in 1982 was not Microsoft but VisiCorp, the firm behind *VisiCalc*. Steve was having a great deal of trepidation about how to bring them into the Macintosh fold—or whether they should be brought in at all. When VisiCorp had first presented *VisiCalc* to Apple, Steve and Markkula turned their noses up at the chance to buy them out and missed the opportunity to make the world's first spreadsheet a proprietary Apple product. Then, after the Apple II was revived by their spreadsheet and they were negotiating for the rights to bundle the program with the Apple III, Steve approached them with an ultimatum.

"He said, 'Either sell us each copy of *VisiCalc* for $10 above your cost,'" recalls Rich Melmon, head of VisiCorp's marketing at the time, "'or we'll put you out of business.'" Not surprisingly, the relationship was not warm. Then Scotty had directed Wigginton to write a *VisiCalc* look-alike, codenamed *Mystery House*, which further deteriorated relations between the two companies.

The fact that VisiCorp was the biggest software company in the world had no influence on Steve. In fact, knowing that almost guaranteed that he would go in the opposite direction—to treat them like an errant vassal. The entire Mac group agonized over whether to turn one of the rare early Macintosh prototypes over to VisiCorp. Finally, a summit conference was set up and VisiCorp proudly showed Steve and Boich and a team of Mac people their latest effort, *VisiOn*. No one from the elite Macintosh project was impressed. Eventually, the president of the company called Steve, who happened to pick up his phone.

According to Boich, "Sorry, but we were underwhelmed," were his only words to the guy before he hung up. VisiCorp never developed a product for the Macintosh.

Another company they went to see was Lotus, which was about to bring out the spreadsheet *1-2-3* (at that point codenamed *Trio*), for the IBM PC. That was no point in their favor as far as the pirates were concerned. In May of 1982, Boich, accompanied by Joanna Hoffmann, flew to Boston to talk to several firms along Route 128, the other great technological corridor in America. At Lotus they saw Mitch Kapor, head of the company, who was a friend of Ben Rosen. The electronics pundit had prepared Kapor, and when Boich walked in he said, "I'd sell my mother to get a Mac."

"He showed us the new program [*1-2-3*], and it looked pretty nice," says Boich, "but compared to the Macintosh spreadsheet demos that Microsoft had running with the pull-down menus and graphics, it was very primitive. All this slash-s stuff. So I said, 'Thanks but no thanks.'"

Kapor was from the same generation as the Macintosh pirates, and he liked to hang out with the team. Whenever he came to the West Coast, he stopped by to visit the Mac group and play ping-pong with the guys. Eventually, he convinced Steve that his intentions were honorable, and Boich let him have a machine. Lotus started producing an integrated program for the Macintosh.

By mid-1982, the rumor mill was active, and calls were coming in constantly from developers. The problem was both the absence of working Mac prototypes and the difficulty Steve had in prying Lisas away from John Couch. All programming for the new machine required a development system based around the Lisa, and that machine was still a year away from release. "Once a month they'd call us up, and when we went over, they'd take a beat-up machine off some guy's desk, replace it with a brand new one, and hand us the trashed machine. Then I'd have to explain to the developer why he was getting a third-hand development system," recalls Boich.

With the departure of the group's first software manager, Bud Tribble, there was a hole in the center of the project. One of the first responsibilities of Apple's newly hired vice-president of human resources, Jay Elliott, was to make sure that they had a large number of candidates for the vacant position. In they paraded, and out they went. The combination of Steve, Hertzfeld, and Smith was enough to make most straight-and-narrow engineering managers run in the opposite direction. During one particularly noteworthy interrogation, Steve suddenly started cackling "gobble, gobble, gobble" in the middle of the candidate's answers. The trio collapsed in laughter as the bewildered man stared in disbelief. Not surprisingly, they had trouble finding anyone they approved of who also approved of them.

Eventually, they settled on an unlikely person, Bob Belleville, who had a breadth of experience managing engineering projects at Xerox PARC and had left in disgust when an inexpensive laser printer he had designed was abruptly canceled. Belleville was the opposite of Jobs in some ways: He was reserved, cautious, and experienced in working with computer science professionals. But Belleville also shared Steve's lack of social skills. He was basically a loner whose idea of a relaxing vacation was hiking through Death Valley alone. He was originally hired to take over just the software, but within a month or so of his appearance, Rod Holt, the early Apple II savior, stepped down to devote his life to designing ocean racing hulls. Belleville became the head of all Macintosh engineering.

Belleville was a complex person who didn't get along with the free spirits of the Macintosh inner circle. He was a manager in the traditional sense. Soon neither Smith nor Hertzfeld could stand him. He expected allegiance, and neither the hardware nor software wizard of Macintosh was about to kowtow to anyone other than Steve. Belleville resented the fact that Steve told the inner circle everything that was going to happen days or weeks before revealing the information to him, and he could never understand the magic of the late-night sessions. Belleville simply wasn't one of the guys. His steel-rimmed glasses and carefully plastered-down hair gave him the appearance of a German storm trooper.

For all Belleville's personal rigidness, he managed to bring a balance to Steve's chaotic managerial style. Methodical and contemplative, he was an ideal foil for the off-the-wall cofounder. He had enough power, in the hierarchy of the Macintosh group, and enough experience at the Oz of computer research centers, Xerox PARC, to be able to stand up to some of Steve's crazier ideas. He was familiar with the latest directions in which Xerox's advanced research center was heading, so he could keep Steve up to date. Besides, Steve had grown enough to recognize that he had a few weaknesses that the reflective manager could help shore up. Otherwise Belleville would never have lasted.

In late summer that year, Martin Haeberli and Burrell Smith were working on the custom chip that had been discussed at the first retreat. Steve had finally been able to convince Haeberli to join the project.

"I always wanted him to like me, and I was charmed by him," recalls Haeberli. "But I never knew how much was real and how much was manipulation. Steve has a remarkable ability to know just exactly what someone wants and then to promise it.

"But he never delivers. It's like the carrot-and-stick."

At first Haeberli wasn't interested in a lateral salary transfer from his job at Xerox to a position reporting to Smith. "Burrell wasn't my idea of the kind of person I wanted to work for."

Steve was insistent, and even after Haeberli turned him down following the first retreat at Pajaro Dunes in early 1982, he refused to accept the fact. Steve took Haeberli into the lab, showed him the digital board, and said, "Think of all these chips that your chip will replace. Think of all the machines that we'll ship. Your work will be famous." Still Haeberli wasn't convinced, especially after they argued about laser disk technology pointlessly for hours.

"I found out the next morning that he had gone back into the lab and argued my side of the disagreement word for word 15 minutes after I'd left," says Haeberli. "It wasn't rewarding arguing with him, even if he did eventually come over to my point of view. He somehow resisted acknowledging that there was anything he could learn."

Nonetheless, when Steve called him again a week later and offered a completion bonus for the chip—tens of thousands of dollars— Haeberli changed his mind. Haeberli wanted to buy a car, and Steve had figured this out by asking Hoffmann. When he offered the bonus, with 40 percent of it in advance, he added, "now you can buy a car." Steve knew how to motivate people, and he had enough clout to get what they wanted.

The custom chip was called the IBM, or Integrated Burrell Machine. By this time, it was going to be the salvation of the Mac. Since Steve knew nothing about custom chips, he decided that it could do everything. Not only would the chip allow them to squeeze more dots onto the Mac's video monitor, but by taking care of a number of low-level "housekeeping" circuits, it would reduce the total chip count inside the Mac by about 20, cutting materials costs significantly. Haeberli was enthusiastic, as was Smith, neither of whom knew a great deal about designing a chip from the ground up. Haeberli's work at Xerox had involved fine-tuning one that was already prototyped. They contracted VLSI Technology, a custom chip design and manufacturing outfit in Silicon Valley, to help complete the device. The deal was for time and materials with a $250,000 cap.

As usual, Steve set an unbelievable deadline. Haeberli started at Apple on March 8, and the final chip was due at the end of June. Although Rosen had predicted one year, Steve was allowing less than four months. Haeberli didn't have enough experience designing chips to say that the timetable was impossible, and because he really wanted Steve to like him, he tried to move heaven and earth to do it. As they started building the mock-up, though, Smith kept adding features. Haeberli, a methodical, classically trained, gentlemanly computerist, found the self-taught and self-styled Hardware Wizard of Macintosh (that was Smith's title on his business card) difficult, if not impossible, to work with. But he didn't put his foot down to stop things from careening out of control.

There was no fixed prototype for the Mac in early 1982. The design constraint was that they had to be able to support both 384 by 256 dots, the original configuration, and 512 by 384 dots, the proposed new arrangement, because Steve had yet to give his full go-ahead to the new configuration and was being indecisive. There were cost limits, design limits, pin limits. It was tedious work. Painstaking, detailed, multifaceted, this was state-of-the-art chip design by two not very experienced designers. It was an aggressive design, and Smith kept changing his mind as he began to realize what was possible.

The master timing logic for the memory, called Burrell's Whiz Bang, was, according to Haeberli, a "brilliant design idea. Burrell wanted to master custom chip manufacture, but he also felt very impatient about it. It was a huge process. You run all sorts of computer simulation tests on all the subsystems, trying to predict what will happen when you actually produce the thing. But Burrell wanted instant gratification, which is hard to come by in chip design."

By the end of June, they had the entire design on a computer, ready for full testing. But in 1982, the business of designing custom chips was still in its infancy. The tools that VLSI Technology had at their disposal were relatively primitive, and the Macintosh custom chip was a test case for them as well. Ready for testing was different from ready in the hand.

"Steve was getting nervous," says Haeberli. "And Burrell was getting nervous because we still had nothing to show. So then Belleville and Jobs asked him to investigate whether he could possibly design a Macintosh using PAL chips that ran 512 dots. Burrell disappeared for about a month with Brian Howard. When he came back he had a working design."

PALs (Programmable Array Logic chips) are programmable chips that an electronic designer can customize himself in about five minutes. Burrell was known as a master of PALs, which had been at the center of his innovative design for the early Mac. As Labor Day came that year, there were two competing choices: the new design by Burrell and the chip that Haeberli had nearly finished. Unfortunately for Haeberli, the first "cut-and-go's" ran about 40 percent slower than required, and a few weeks later Steve, Belleville, and Smith decided to go with the new PAL chip design and to scrap the IBM chip. They neglected to tell Haeberli until a few weeks later, and then he had to continue clearing up the loose ends at VLSI, although he knew that the chip would not be used.

Steve wanted to have a finished machine for the programmers to work on. The machine was due to be frozen in January so they could make the May 16, 1983, introduction date. He couldn't take a chance on an uncertain chip. Haeberli was crushed.

"Burrell wanted his digital board to be the one that flew," Haeberli says. "He wanted to be the hero. And Steve just wasn't willing to give it any more time. By anyone else's standards, it was a success. But Steve had been told three months, and then six, and the thing still didn't work."

Whereas Haeberli was depressed by the turn of events, VLSI was left holding the bag. When the contract was canceled, Steve refused to pay them the $250,000 he had promised in the letter of intent. He offered $100,000 instead, but the chip company had invested more than 50 percent above its budget in the project, because they figured that having a project with Apple would be good for their long-term prospects. Steve was adamant, and VLSI ended up taking a bath on the project. Apple could throw its weight around, since it was still the biggest thing in personal computing. Steve played the bully when it came to his first love. The only thing that counted was getting the Macintosh out the door.

Although Steve had built the software and marketing organizations, he had yet to tackle the crucial issue of manufacturing. From the beginning, he and Rod Holt had been influenced by robotics assembly lines they had seen in Japan, and in keeping with his fundamental drive to make everything about the Mac new and different, he decided to build the most advanced assembly plant in the world. In 1982 he set about doing so.

The very first Macintosh business plan, written by Steve in mid-1981, described this new approach as follows:

> The Manufacturing Plan for the Macintosh differs in some respects from prior practice: Emphasis will be on a designed process rather than one evolved from Apple's early days. A major goal is to greatly reduce the extent and complexity of the material handling chore. This will be facilitated by a direct flow using only a small number of people in direct labor. Automatic component insertion and extensive in-process test will be used. The second major goal is to improve the field reliability and control of the manufacturing process, and more intelligent testing is the means.[1]

To help him design the testing equipment and begin plans for the automated factory, Steve hired Matt Carter, an older, experienced manufacturing line designer who was unafraid to stand up to him. Carter was a top specialist in robotics and automation along the assembly line, and he sat in on most design decisions to ensure that the Macintosh the pirates were building was produceable in quantity.

One of the big issues was whether to locate the plant in Dallas, where there was some spare space in an Apple II assembly plant, or in a new building closer to Cupertino. Steve wanted an entirely new building that was all Macintosh, close to home. The factory issue became a political football that was kicked around between Del Yocam, the company's head of operations, and Steve's Macintosh team. Yocam was offended that they were going to circumvent his organization and manufacture their own machines. Besides, he had no faith in their wild, potentially expensive idea to automate most of the component insertion and assembly subroutines. Carter was certain that he could keep the labor component in the Macintosh equation down to 1 percent. This was unheard of in pre-Macintosh Silicon Valley. No one believed him until two years later when he did.

The concept that particularly peeved the traditional manufacturing guys, however, was the "just-in-time" theory of parts delivery. With close enough control over parts ordering and inventory, a plant could theoretically receive materials every couple of weeks and never have to keep a huge inventory of parts on hand. That strategy reduced inventory costs and allowed orders to be tailored to need, but it required high-quality parts and dependable suppliers. It was an idea that worked well in Japan, with its smaller geographical area and clubby relationships among manufacturers. The traditional American manufacturing approach was to turn inventory over two or three times a year, and Apple was really proud that they were operating the Apple II division with four turns a year. Steve and Carter were proposing new inventory every two weeks! That would mean 26 turns a year.

Markkula recognized the value in Apple's pioneering state-of-the-art manufacturing and slowly joined the Macintosh side. The Macintosh crew finally had their way on the "just-in-time" idea, but they had to compromise on the plant location. The compromise, worked out through ombudsman Markkula, was that they would build the automated factory in the unused Dallas factory space, which was costing the company $325,000 a year. And since this was Apple, with enormous revenues and little debt, they also had to build side-by-side assembly lines: one automated, one traditional. The board wasn't convinced that the Macintosh kids could really do what they promised—they wanted a backup.

During the summer of 1982, Carter supervised a pilot build of 50 more Macs and began to supervise the hiring of operations staff for the Dallas facility. With the hardware only just approaching final state after the decision on the IBM chip, the manufacturing group was preparing to spend more than $10 million on the acquisition of specialized insertion and automation equipment alone. This was up from the $2 million that Steve had so optimistically predicted in his Macintosh budget for the previous year.

By the fall of 1982, the Macintosh group was expanding wildly. New people were appearing daily, and for some, such as Hertzfeld, the end of the dream was near. "The whole mood of the place had changed," he recalled. "It was no longer just a bunch of people out to make the greatest computer ever. Now, it was seen as a good career move to join the Mac group."

By the second Mac retreat in late September, again held in Pajaro Dunes, the team was nearly 100 strong, with an average age of 28, nearly 50 percent of whom were left-handers. At this session, Steve wrote a carefully chosen slogan on the blackboard to open his morning session: "It's better to be a pirate than to join the Navy. Let's Be Pirates!" Everyone in the meeting room stood and cheered. They all wanted to be pirates, and they were pledging allegiance to their pirate king. The slogan keenly defined the attitude of all the key players and the reasons they were willing to put their all into the Macintosh. It summed up the spirit that Steve was able to imbue in the team, the spirit that drove them, the spirit that encompassed their outlaw personas and their belief that they were working on something that was more important than mere ordinary morals and ethics.

They were finally large enough and had a real product. It then became important to Steve to keep the spirit of mediocrity, which he was convinced was ruining Apple, from infiltrating their little world. Insularity became even more important.

Steve was still shooting for the May 16, 1983, ship date at the NCC in Anaheim. The strategy was to release the Lisa at the shareholders' meeting that coming January and then surprise the world with the Macintosh four months later. The guts of the Toolbox were finished, and it looked as if they could really start giving the machines to developers. Hundreds of details were yet to be resolved, but the spirit was willing.

In Steve's presentation at the retreat, he added a little flourish to the roar of approval he had produced by writing the slogan on the wall. He added another phrase underneath it: "Working 90 hours a week and loving it!" Then, with a showman's touch, he reached into a box he had brought with him, pulled out a sweatshirt that had the phrase emblazoned on it, and pulled it over his head. Everyone at the retreat was given one, and again, it served to reinforce the pirates theme and the group's sense of camaraderie.

No one pretended the crew was a democracy. A handful of sweatshirts also had a tiny line of type over the left breast that underscored the point: It read "Macintosh Staff." Of course, Steve's had it, as did Hertzfeld's, Smith's, Coleman's, Atkinson's, Murray's, and Belleville's. They might have been a merry band of pirates, but there were still those who swabbed the decks and those who ate at the Captain's table.

Indications that there might be problems with the ship date planned for the following spring started when the group returned to Cupertino from the retreat that fall. The programmer Steve had hired away from the European company, and the only female programmer on the early team, didn't work out. The operating system work she had been doing—the fundamental input/output routines that allow data to be stored and retrieved from disks—needed revision. When she left, Larry Kenyon had to redo the code. It was a severe setback, but Steve would let nothing stop him. They were going to ship the Macintosh the following May no matter what happened.

That fall he was feeling extremely good about not only the Macintosh but also Apple. The Lisa was prepared for release, and the reaction from journalists who were given sneak previews was very positive. The new graphics-oriented interface was called revolutionary, and the machine looked as if it could be a big success. Apple II orders and sales were leapfrogging ahead of any other Christmas season, even as the company readied the Apple IIe in the wings. Revenues continued to soar, and Steve was in the midst of his infatuation with Joan Baez. Things were going very well for the young man who had cofounded Apple a few short years earlier. Nonetheless there were still two loose ends troubling him: the matter of the presidency of Apple, and the trademark to the name *Macintosh*.

Markkula wanted to step down and take a less active role in managing the affairs of the company. Although Steve thought he had the skills necessary to run the multimillion-dollar corporation, no one else on the board or in the company thought so. Apple paid a prestigious search firm to locate a suitable candidate. After more than a year, they had yet to come up with the right person, and Markkula was growing anxious. Finally, late in the year, a feeler was put out to John

Sculley, the president of Pepsi-Cola. The recruiter handling the search told him that working in Silicon Valley was the equivalent of being in Florence during the Renaissance. A luncheon was arranged in Cupertino with Markkula and Steve.

"Steve was very quiet," recalls Sculley. "He listened to what I had to say. At the end of it, I was telling them about my ideas, how I approached marketing and business. I think he was somewhat intrigued by the fact that I was not caught up in the hierarchy or traditional things associated with corporate America."[2]

Although intrigued, Sculley rejected the offer. However, he did indicate an interest in meeting Steve again and continuing their talks, so the door wasn't completely shut.

What made the situation all the more urgent was that as Steve looked back on the year, he could recognize that Apple's stronghold in the personal computer market was eroding; 1982 was the year of the IBM PC, as that computer gained about 20 percent of the market on sales of nearly 200,000 machines. Portable computers, led by Osborne, Kaypro, and Compaq, opened a new market, and it looked as if the future of the business computer might be in reduced size, which dovetailed perfectly with the machine he was readying. The real competition for Apple, however, was in the home. In 1982, Texas Instruments, Atari, Radio Shack, and Timex all slashed prices to around $100 for a full-fledged computer. The enforced competition from off-shore manufacturers drove American factories out of business, and by the end of the year, Atari, with its rock-bottom prices, had captured 50 percent of the home market and was starting to zero in on the much more expensive Apple II's educational market.

The Apple III had failed miserably. Its combination of price and bundled features proved unattractive to businesses that could choose between it and the expandable, open-ended IBM PC. It was essential for Apple to strike back with a success. The company's hopes were riding on the Lisa, and shortly thereafter, the Macintosh. Bringing in a respected corporate president would help add credibility in the financial world and could probably clinch some sales in the Fortune 1000 market they were targeting for both machines.

By now the Macintosh project was attached, both emotionally and actually, to the name *Macintosh*. Several months earlier Mike Murray had requested a trademark search and discovered that the trademark to the name Macintosh was owned by an American manufacturer of high-quality hi-fidelity gear, McIntosh Laboratories. With his belief that he was on a holy war to bring a new kind of computer to the people, Steve fired off a letter to the president, Gordon Gow, requesting a worldwide release for the name Macintosh.

"We have become very attached to the name Macintosh," he wrote. "Much like one's own child, our product has developed a very definite personality." The letter was rather formal and high handed and included a description of the Macintosh and its market as Steve saw it then. It was a "desk appliance, providing tools and solutions to professionals, managers, small businessman[sic], and college students whose productive hours are spent at a desk. We expect at least 70 percent of our units to end up in an office environment. Target customer is 35-50 years old, male, professionally trained knowledge worker. In many instances, the end user's employer will purchase the product, that is, it will not be bought with discretionary funds."[3]

The letter aptly demonstrates the blindness that the head of the Macintosh team had about prospective customers. Apple had always sold to individuals, not to office workers, and their attempt to sell to this group was the kind of misguided marketing thrust that youthful inexperience could generate. None of them, least of all Steve, had any idea what life was like for a manager in a mid-sized corporation. Nor did they have any handle on how the market perceived Apple. This was the blind leading the blind.

But that wasn't as important as Gow's response. The president of McIntosh Labs had a trip planned to San Francisco for the Thanksgiving weekend and said he would stop by. He was a white-haired gent in his seventies who took the tour hand in hand with his wife. Afterward, he concluded to Murray, "It's very interesting what you boys are up to. Very interesting." Of course, with the absolute confidence that everyone in the Macintosh project had, a confidence that filtered down from Steve, they were sure that he would sign the release as soon as he returned to the East Coast.

Unfortunately, such was not the case. A few days before Christmas, Steve and the Macintosh group received an unwelcome present. Gow, on the advice of his firm's legal counsel, rejected their request. It was a bitter loss for the group. For years they had been working under the code name Macintosh. It had come to symbolize everything they had dreamed of—every difference between their computer and every other one. As the holidays came, a pall settled over the entire group that even the appearance of the first production prototypes of the wide screen—512 by 384 dots—Macs couldn't dispel.

As the year came to an end, Steve heard that *Time* magazine had named the personal computer "Machine of the Year" for its traditional New Year's issue, formerly always the "Man of the Year" issue. For several months, the magazine's San Francisco correspondent, Michael Moritz, had been working on a book about Apple and had been given carte blanche and the run of the company. Steve and everyone else at Apple were sure that the issue would feature the company prominently and could do nothing but help propel the introduction of the Lisa.

On New Year's Eve, the final day of 1982, a remarkable year that had taken the Macintosh from a research project to an incipient product and that had started with Steve's face on the cover of *Time*, he was couriered the first copy of the magazine to appear on the West Coast. As he flipped through the first 15 pages of the 40-page special feature, he looked in vain for his name and started to despair. Then he turned a page and was confronted with a full page portrait of himself and a headline that read "The Updated Book of Jobs." He was the only computer industry person to have a separate piece on himself. By the placement of his article, readers couldn't help but see him as the real Man of the Year, no matter what the cover said. He took a deep breath and started to read the article that he expected to extol his virtues and his single-handed role as the promoter of personal computing to the masses.

As he started to read it, though, he realized that something was very wrong. Phrases such as "prime advance man for the computer revolution" and "smooth sales pitch and a blind faith that would have been the envy of the early Christian martyrs"[4] seemed to be making fun of him. When he came to the first quotes from his former friend, Woz, the cofounder of Apple, his cheeks must have started to burn.

"Steve didn't do one circuit, design, or piece of code," the article quoted Woz as saying. "He has not really been into computers and to this day he has never gone through a computer manual."[5] The article went on, growing, if anything, worse. Again quoting from the *Time* feature: "As a boss, Jobs is admired for courting long chances, but, as a friend, 'something is happening to Steve that's sad and not pretty, something related to money, and power, and loneliness. He's less sensitive to people's feelings. He runs over them, snowballs them.'"[6]

If that wasn't enough to throw him into a tailspin and bring the tears to his eyes, the article went on with quotes from two other Apple people: "He would have made an excellent King of France" said one.[7] Another pointed to a "technical ignorance he's not willing to admit."[8] A brief thumbnail sketch of his life followed, including a recounting of his sorry episode with fatherhood and the early denial of his responsibility for Lisa. Here it all was, in its sordid glory. The *Time* writers painted the picture of a man without creative or design skills who skillfully made his fortune on the backs of others—rock promoter in the land of high technology.

The story was accurate to anyone but Steve. It was as though no one had ever told the emperor he had no clothes on, and he had to find out in a weekly magazine with a circulation of 15 million. Steve was devastated and canceled his New Year's plans. He stayed home and spent the night ruminating. But he was no quitter. He was a fighter. He wouldn't let it get to him. He would prove they were wrong. He would bring out the Macintosh, and they would eat their words.

At 8 A.M. the next morning, New Year's Day of 1983, he called Jef Raskin. He wanted a shoulder to cry on, and Raskin's was the one he chose. It gave him no pause that Raskin was the man he had forced out of the Macintosh project after a bitter fight and the man who had compared him to the autocratic kings of France in the *Time* article. For Steve, the past was irrelevant—only the present mattered. Only the present according to Jobs.

He was 27. He had learned little from his past.

15
Superstars

Steve swallowed his pride and tried to put the *Time* article behind him. "I know what it's like to have your private life painted in the worst possible light in front of a lot of people," he said. "I've learned what it's like for everyone you meet to have preconceptions about you."[1] But he had a mass of publicity appearances scheduled for the next month and couldn't hide. It was the other side of the role he had chosen to play. He couldn't beg off because of a headache. Steve had to grin and bear it.

A few days before the management team was to leave on a round of press conferences prior to the annual shareholders' meeting late in January, when the Lisa would finally be introduced, a disaster occurred. It caused their plans for the Macintosh introduction to change for the first time in over a year. The Mac had long been slated to use the new "Twiggy" disk drive developed by Apple's peripherals division for the Lisa. It was so named because the disk drive prototypes were very thin and reminded the design engineers of the rail-thin 1960s "mod" model Twiggy. From the beginning the project had been plagued with problems, and now, as they neared the home stretch for the release of the Mac, it derailed all Steve's carefully orchestrated plans.

May 16, 1983, was one day before his daughter Lisa's fifth birthday. For more than a year it was the date that Steve had pinned all his hopes and dreams on. The date was written in stone—or at least on T-shirts—from the time of the first Macintosh retreat in early 1982.

The drive project had been in the works even longer. It was launched by Steve in 1980 while he was still heading the Lisa project. He had been piqued by Apple's prime supplier of disk drives' continuing failure to deliver drives in sufficient volume for the Apple II line, so for his new machine he decreed that Apple would build its own drives. His decision evidenced what had become a part of life at Apple, the NIH syndrome: "Not Invented Here." It grew out of Steve's over-arching egotism and confidence. He believed that Apple could do a better job than anyone else—at anything. It also grew out of his megalomania; he wanted Apple to be the world leader in everything, to reinvent the wheel if need be, and disk drive technology seemed like the kind of field that the company could handle with ease.

The project was dogged from the start by the lack of experience that characterized most of the other operations of Apple, deficiencies that could be glossed over when the market was expanding geo-metrically. A disk drive has complex problems of synchronization. The feat of making one work has been compared to flying a 747 across the country one inch off the ground. Apple was never able to lick the troubles, and as the clock ticked through 1982, it became increasingly obvious that the fundamental design of the drives had serious flaws. They were never able to hike the yield of working drives above 50 percent, and, worse, a working disk taken out of one drive and then inserted into another couldn't always be read. Some even showed no data present. This was a fatal flaw in any machine, but especially for a computer meant to form the backbone of an office computing envi-ronment.

By then the Lisa, its design, and its introduction, were too far along to change the drive, so they were saddled with the product that Steve's whim, and subsequent stubbornness, had produced. Steve and his engineering manager, Belleville, had no such requirement. He wasn't about to bring the Macintosh to market with an inferior disk drive, even one that he had rammed through to production.

Finally, in a pow-wow early in January, Steve and Markkula made a decision: The errant drive would be re-engineered and built by another disk drive maker, the Japanese company ALPS. The Lisa would be introduced on schedule a few weeks later, but they would not start shipping until the new drives were ready, forecasted for May. There would be no change in format; it was still going to be a high-density 5¼-inch floppy system. With a crash program, at high cost, ALPS promised that they could supply the needed 10,000 drives for the introduction of the Mac as well, within six months. Sadly, and with great disappointment, the introduction date of the machine was moved back to August 15, 1983. It was an enormous letdown for the Mac team, which had been working feverishly to finish all the software and hardware for the January 15 "freeze" date.

A few days later, Steve headed for the East Coast with a new set of suits and a fresh mustache-less appearance. He was due to conduct a series of press briefings to reveal the Lisa to the influential media headquartered in Manhattan. He was sequestered in a $575-a-night suite in the Hotel Carlyle, with a bevy of Lisas and a team of managers who had spearheaded the computer's development. It was the company's first attempt at an orchestrated product introduction—both the Lisa and the Apple IIe were being unveiled—and it was a fiasco.

It was not that the machine was unpopular. Far from it—the media gushed over the icons, interface, mouse, and the ease of use. It was called "revolutionary" and a "breakthrough product" by industry analysts and observers. The problem was Steve's lack of self-discipline. He couldn't help but tell reporters all about his new baby, the Macintosh. For instance, "when it comes out, Mac is going to be the most incredible computer in the world—another Apple II," he was quoted as saying in *Business Week*. Since he was proudly describing its features as "like the Lisa" but with a cost of $2,000 instead of $10,000, it was not surprising that buyers felt like waiting to see what was coming before making a decision. And in a major strategic mistake by the company's spokespeople, they admitted that the two machines were not going to be compatible—the kiss of death. What was so obvious to the rest of the world had been ignored by the inner circle at Apple.

It was too late to change horses. The company had made its mistake two years earlier when it allowed Steve to keep his Mac team separate and to develop a computer with all the best features of the Lisa but without a path for sharing. They were now stuck with two office computer systems, and the less expensive one was faster and being actively touted by the ebullient and highly quotable chairman of the board at the same time that he supposedly believed in the Lisa.

Steve's unconcealed mistakes were compounded by another disastrous choice that the company made. The goal was to sell the Lisa as an office system, rather than as an individual personal computer, which was where Apple's strength had always been. The sales department decided to change the way they sold the Lisa and created both a national accounts team to sell the machines directly to Fortune 1000 customers and a core of "qualified" dealers. Not surprisingly, this alienated the bulk of the company's dealers, who also found themselves being wooed by IBM. Within months, Apple found that its dealer strength had seriously eroded, and by the end of the year the company's distribution channels were in trouble.

Another of Steve's business decisions was coming back to haunt him and seriously prejudice the market's attitude toward the Lisa. VisiCorp was actively leaking word of their new product *VisiOn* for the IBM PC. It was the same product that Steve had dismissed, and the same company that he had vowed to put out of business one day. The new program they were showing had many of the same graphics features as the Lisa desktop interface and ran on the IBM PC. Since the PC cost about half as much as a Lisa and was supported by hundreds of software programs as well as the security blanket of the letters IBM, the supposedly impending release of *VisiOn* further dampened customer enthusiasm for the Lisa. The guys at VisiCorp felt no allegiance to Apple anymore and did their best to undermine support for the Lisa. (Ironically, *VisiOn* was a failure when it was eventually brought to market nearly a year later and very nearly bankrupted the once highly successful software house.)

Apple had taken the high ground of technological innovation in the personal computer business with the introduction of the Lisa and its easy-to-use look, but they were also admitting that its success was crucial to the company's fortunes.

"We're really banking on Lisa's revolutionary technology," said Steve, but then he added, with an air of studied insouciance, "If Lisa fails we'll just be another half-billion or billion-dollar company."[2] He saw the arena of the multibillion-dollar personal computer industry as his playing field and was willing to wager the future of the company against his personal vendetta with John Couch. The result was a fragmented product strategy that no one had been powerful enough to stop.

The divisionalization of the company initiated by Mike Scott three years earlier had been a mistake. Without a strong captain at the helm, Apple was divided into competing product divisions where most of the key functions such as engineering and marketing were duplicated. The left and right hands didn't talk to each other, and personalities ruled the day. Whoever yelled the loudest at executive staff meetings prevailed. Steadily rising revenues hid the internal chaos at the company. Lisa was quite possibly doomed with its performance and price problems. As far as Steve saw things, the Apple IIe (Yoda) was nothing but a stopgap measure, and the Apple III had been a disaster from the beginning. Now the only hope for the company would be the Macintosh, which was exactly as Steve wanted it. He would either sink the company with it or be the hero Apple needed. Of course, as they introduced the Lisa, none of this was yet clear.

Apple was still looking for someone to take over the presidency, and the way that Sculley had rejected their offer had left some room for negotiation. While they were in Manhattan for the Lisa introduction, Steve met Sculley for dinner at the Four Seasons. The meeting went well, and the young prince found the soft-drink industry marketing whiz, the man who had orchestrated Pepsi's strong challenge to Coca-Cola during the 1970s, a receptive audience. The two decided to pursue the matter further.

After returning home from the Lisa introduction, Steve's first order of business was leading the third Macintosh retreat, set this time not at Pajaro Dunes but in a hotel in Carmel. The pink and white, mock-Spanish hotel built around a tiled swimming pool and covered with cascading bougainvillea had the kind of fairy-tale appearance in which both Carmel and Apple specialized. It belied the worries haunting the team. The change in the ship date, the problem with the disk drives, and the apparent loss of the name Macintosh had combined to cast a pall over the youthful group's spirits. Steve knew that he had to do something to bring their spirits back up. As everyone assembled in the large meeting room at the hotel, Steve sat quietly in his room and tried to meditate on what he was about to say. There was a knock on the door, and Bill Atkinson entered, accompanied by an unwilling Andy Hertzfeld.

Atkinson was fuming. He had gained Steve's trust years before when he stood up during a meeting in which Steve was spewing ridiculous statements, yelled "Steve Jobs, you're an asshole!" and walked out. The next day Steve invited him to dinner and they became close friends—as close as Steve ever allowed anyone to become.

"That day in Carmel Bill told Steve that he was quitting," says Hertzfeld, the only witness to the scene that erupted. "He was upset because in all the publicity about the Lisa, in the hours of interviews, the pages of articles, there hadn't been a single mention of his name. Bill was the guy behind it. Without him there would have been nothing. Without his *QuickDraw* routines to allow us to quickly and easily draw the screen, there would have been no Lisa or Macintosh. But it was as though he didn't exist as far as the publicity was concerned.

"The guys who managed the project—John Couch, Wayne Rosing, Larry Tessler, and Bruce Daniels—did all the interviews and took all the credit. With everything else that had been happening, it seemed like we had come to the end of the dream."

Atkinson knew that Steve had been in control of every detail of the introduction. If he had taken a moment to consider the guys in the trenches, he could have brought the programmers into the loop. Steve argued that if he had been overlooked, the same wouldn't happen with the Macintosh. Hadn't he let them all sign the inside of the case? A few minutes later, when it was apparent that they couldn't resolve the problem easily, according to Hertzfeld, Steve screamed, "I have 100 people out there waiting for me, depending on me. I can't let one person get in the way," and brushed past Atkinson and out the door.

Atkinson was exhausted. There was nothing more to say. The two software magicians—Atkinson was the brains behind both computers and Hertzfeld was the heart and passion behind the Macintosh—sat in misery.

Steve took a deep breath and burst into the meeting room. It was filled with his entire, carefully selected team. He was always a master of compartmentalization, of keeping his mind focused on one thing and ignoring everything else, and this was a moment that would test that skill to the maximum. On display for the first time was the machine they were going to ship. It was a critical milestone, and for the first time they had working versions of the key programs as well.

When he walked onstage, he first went to the blackboard and wrote his homily for the retreat. This one was "Real Artists Ship." As he completed it, the assembled crew murmured a faint hum of approval. Then he turned back to the crowd and in one moment of cosmic understanding, realized what he had to do. Lifting a half-empty bottle of Perrier that he had picked up on his way in, he walked over to a working Mac sitting on a table to one side of the podium.

"I've just been talking to the folks at McIntosh Labs," he lied glibly to the assembled masses, "and we got the name. I christen you Macintosh." With that he poured the bottle of mineral water over the machine, and the room erupted in pandemonium. Everyone stood and cheered. It was absolutely the right thing to do. Of course, he hadn't been talking to McIntosh Labs. He wouldn't until a few weeks later. But Steve knew that he needed the big gesture, the big moment, to galvanize everyone for the final stretch. From somewhere deep inside him, he found it.

Down the hall, Hertzfeld and Atkinson heard the roar and the cheers and decided to see what was going on. They walked out of a room filled with despair into the pandemonium of a revivalist meeting. Steve was standing on the platform grinning, and all around him people were shouting and cheering. "It was surreal," explained Hertzfeld.

It set the tone for the rest of the retreat. They had a party that lasted all night. They went skinny dipping in the hotel pool. They danced to ear-splitting rock music and boogied on the beach, watching the sunrise. They had an "insanely great" computer, an "insanely great" team of people, and, as Steve was fond of saying, they were on the way to "making a dent in the universe." It was just what the team needed.

The rest of the meetings flew past, and they returned to Cupertino ready to bring the Macintosh to life. Within a couple of weeks, Atkinson was named an Apple Fellow, in part to make up for his lack of recognition. The appointment carried a sizable salary, a hefty stock option, and freedom to pursue whatever interested him. Furthermore, Steve and Hertzfeld had decided early on that every program released for the Mac would carry the name of the programmers, hidden under a special "Apple" menu that provided information about the software along with the requisite copyright notification. Atkinson was given one other perk. His drawing program, renamed *MacPaint*, would display the line "MacPaint by Bill Atkinson" each time the program started, giving him widespread exposure. He also got a promise from Steve that when it came time to dole out the praise for the Mac, he would be one of the superstars.

When they reached Cupertino, another superstar was in for a shock. Hertzfeld was given a highly critical employment review. Three years before, almost to the day, Hertzfeld had been ready to quit. The negative review that he received from his boss, Bob Belleville, coupled with the scene that he had witnessed between Steve and Atkinson, made Hertzfeld ready to leave again.

Belleville was a traditional manager, and he expected his underlings to submit to his authority. A few months earlier, when Belleville had wanted to fire a programmer because the guy had taken time to do something that he had forbidden him to tackle, Hertzfeld had stood up for the young man and interceded with Steve on his behalf. Belleville had been overruled and never forgave Hertzfeld for going over his head and meddling. Hertzfeld worked for love not money. He never did anything because it was a good career move or was politically expeditious. He was not about to keep quiet when he thought something was a bad idea or a misguided plan, and because of his remarkable relationship with the chairman of the board, he had enormous power. Belleville took him for a walk around Apple's buildings, and in Hertzfeld's recollection told him that he had "too high a visibility and a lack of respect for authority, and thus you are being given a poor employment review."

Hertzfeld, who had been putting in 100-hour weeks for two years, couldn't believe what he was hearing and burst into tears. His life was the Macintosh—he loved the computer and had given it everything he had. Belleville couldn't understand how anyone could grow so attached to a machine. "There'll be another computer next year," was one of his favorite phrases. For Hertzfeld, there was only the Macintosh, and like Steve and Burrell Smith, he lived, breathed, and slept the machine.

After the bad review, it took all of Steve's legendary charm to make Hertzfeld stay. But Belleville would have no role in managing him. Nonetheless, Hertzfeld decided that he was leaving just as soon as they pushed the machine out the door. The Macintosh project had changed. The career engineers and marketing MBAs were taking over.

It was no longer a band of iconoclastic pirates out to do their own thing anyway they had to, in spite of the company or the world. "We're not the Navy" had been one of Steve's early phrases to rally them around his flag, but as Hertzfeld saw it, by early 1983, they were. Since the Navy was the enemy to this merry crew and could represent either IBM or the rest of Apple, depending on context, that change in the prevailing winds was the kiss of death.

While Hertzfeld and Smith were feeling the loss of innocence and the departure of the gilded age of the Macintosh, the new band of young turks who were joining the parade had no such feelings. For the most part, they were fresh out of grad schools and colleges and felt privileged to be part of the most important project that Apple had ever mounted. They hadn't known the "good old days" so they had nothing to compare the present to. And the heady ambience, the startling unconventionality of Steve's managerial personality, with its dictates and mercurial passions, drove them on to prove themselves the way the inner circle already had.

None of them questioned the $100,000 a year that was being spent on carrot and fresh fruit juices in the refrigerators. None of them questioned the need to spend $1 million remodeling the building along Bandley Drive—Bandley 3, it was called—so that it would be the right Herman Miller landscape in which to do "insanely great" work. None of them questioned the need to hire 75 members of the San Francisco Symphony for a Macintosh Christmas party. After all, they needed a common room with a giant atrium, ping-pong tables, video games, a compact disc player, soft, luxurious sofas, and meeting rooms designated by the names da Vinci or Picasso. Steve wanted to make their environment feel right, make them all feel part of a team, and he had no sense of limit.

Steve was always a technophile, and whatever the latest piece of electronic gear, the Mac group had it first. In the fishbowl, the glass-doored set of cubicles where the software programmers were sequestered in the new building, toys, robots, tiny televisions, Sony Walkmans, video cameras, trashed computers, and Mac prototypes fought for space. On the walls were printouts from early drawings done with *MacSketch*, invitations to the Punk Party, a ROM Freeze Picnic, or a softball sign-up sheet. The group's software bug reports were festooned with thousands of drawings of bugs. It was an environment designed for producing creative engineering work, and it looked more like a college dormitory, where all the students had money, than it did a high-tech computer company.

Around the time of the third retreat, that February, two key people joined the Mac team. Steve Capps, the author of *Alice*, the game that had early on caught Steve's eye, was one. Steve ran into him one day the previous fall and had told him that he wanted to "steal him." Capps, who shared a broad streak of pragmatism with Hertzfeld, thought it was a pretty weird thing to say, but by the time he joined the team, he understood the concept and became an enthusiastic pirate.

At the same time, Hertzfeld had been pushing the group to hire someone artistic to design fonts for the Macintosh since the computer had been built to use different ones. One of his long-term interests had been computer typefaces, and he was particularly insistent that they get to work creating the library of typefaces and styles for the machine. He suggested a woman he had gone to high school with, Susan Kare, who was working in a high-tech design store in Palo Alto.

Both instantly fit into the group. Capps was a burly, energetic hacker born in 1955 whose standard outfit was a pair of shorts, "Vans" brand highly decorated sneakers, which were all the rage in the skateboard set, and a white, button-down shirt hanging out. He liked to work from noon (or later) to midnight (or later) and, of course, he was a superb player of *Defender*. He was also a bright programmer who was, in his words, "the relief pitcher. I came in and took on whatever little jobs still had to be done." It was an essential role. Someone had to glue all the pieces of the operating system and the first applications to the ROM routines inside the Mac. He hadn't been burned out yet, the way Hertzfeld and Smith were in danger of becoming by working under Steve's unrelenting gaze, and he had every bit as much talent.

Kare brought a different quality to the final year of the Macintosh development work. Softspoken and dedicated, she was an artist by training and had little interest in computers per se. Her interest was in making everything that appeared on the computer's screen—the user interface—look beautiful. The graphic touches she added made the Mac seem a little less intimidating, a little less a computer, and a little more a friend. Her work was reflected in the small things, such as the design of the title bar in a window, the appearance of the icons that resided on the Mac's desktop, and the choice of the font that displayed the menus. It was a new job role for a computer project. Engineers had never had their work humanized and finessed by an artist. Steve was very much an advocate of the user interface, the way the Mac "felt" to a naive user, and he was willing to invest whatever it took to make it look and feel right. It was he who insisted that file folders onscreen have rounded edges, because that was the way they looked in real life.

"We just wanted to build the best thing we could build," Steve says about the Mac. "When you're a carpenter making a beautiful chest of drawers, you're not going to use a piece of plywood on the back, even though nobody will ever see it. You know it's there, so you're going to use a beautiful piece of wood. For you to sleep well at night, the aesthetic, the quality has to be carried all the way through."[3]

Steve's sense of aesthetics carried over to merchandising the Mac. About a year earlier, he saw the work of French poster artist Folon and decided that he was the person to create a look for the Mac. Folon's work is primitive, almost naive, with a little top-hatted character who is his trademark. Steve went to one of his shows in New York, met him, bought a print, and discussed the project with him. Folon then sent a number of sketches that adorned a chest of drawers in Steve's house. Creative director Tom Suiter took the sketches and created a series of posters, T-shirts, decals, caps, cups, advertising mockups, and merchandising goods based on them. Murray was going to offer the artist a contract of $1 per Macintosh sold, and they agreed to an advance of $30,000. The printed circuit boards in the build that came out of Carter's prototype factory late in February all had little Folon "MacMen" emblazoned on them.

But then Steve changed his mind. One day he decided that the friendly, light-hearted image was too lightweight for the Macintosh. He had realized that the Lisa was dying in the marketplace and that if they were to succeed, the Mac couldn't look like a toy. He abruptly canceled the contract, paid Folon his $30,000, and told Suiter to come up with something more sophisticated. Suiter turned to the Macintosh art director, Tom Hughes, who within weeks created the "Picasso" look that adorned the packaging of the Mac: a few brightly colored brushstrokes suggesting the distinctive shapes of the Mac. Steve liked it. That was all that counted. They used it.

On February 24, 1983, Steve was 28 years old. The Mac team, led by Murray, bought a billboard along the Saratoga-Sunnyvale Road, the main path between Steve's house and Apple. On it they wrote: "Happy 28th Steve. The Journey is the Reward. The Pirates." It was the kind of swashbuckling gesture Steve himself might have thought of. The Mac team was trying to show him their love. Unfortunately, Steve had a cold that day and stayed home so he missed it.

At the same time, another event occurred that symbolized the spirit of the project. On the wall of their newly occupied building, someone had tacked up a Jolly Roger pirate flag, complete with skull and crossbones. In place of its one eye, Susan Kare had put the Apple logo. One Sunday night, Steve Capps, who was working late along with Kare, decided that they should fly the flag from the roof of the new building. He climbed up onto the building, rigged the flag to a spare board that was lying around, and hoisted the pirate flag. The next morning it caused a sensation as the "regular" Apple employees showed up for work.

Although the flag delighted the pirates, it seemed like a very public slap in the face to all the rest of Apple, especially to the Lisa team located across the street. A few weeks later, a small band of Lisa people stole the flag. By then the point had been made. As the year continued, Steve grew more aggressive and powerful and, for the other groups at Apple, less willing to compromise on anything.

Steve had started the Navy analogy by using it to refer to IBM, but he soon extended it to the rest of Apple as well. As 1983 progressed, the atmosphere inside Apple grew more poisoned as Steve promoted the Macintosh as the only hope for Apple. At one point, he addressed a meeting of Apple II managers as "the dull and boring product division." He got a perverse pleasure out of rubbing their noses in the muck, especially after the *Time* article had come out and given him no credit for that machine. And his attitude was completely insulting, because while the Lisa had been a bomb and its introduction a mishandled disaster, the Apple IIe was a marketplace success whose introduction had gone like clockwork. On the day of the introduction in January of 1983, they were ready to fill orders and ship, and every dealer in the country had a model of the new computer on display. Throughout 1983, as he continued to denigrate the Apple II at every chance, key managers from the Apple II division departed and revenues from the six-year-old computer continued to soar.

Perhaps there was no better example of his technological blindness and misguided impulses than the story of the adoption of the disk drive for the Macintosh. For the people who worked around him at the new Mac building, where he took the only corner office, one of the running jokes was that the way to get Steve to agree to a new idea was to say, "Hey Steve, you've just had a great idea!" They learned to keep things from him until they were finished so he wouldn't forbid them from working on those projects. In the months after the first disk drive disaster, when he was convinced that Apple could have its 5¼-inch drive manufactured by ALPS, others secretly started working in another direction. George Crow, who had designed the analog power portions of the Mac, became convinced that the right answer was a new type of disk drive being manufactured by Sony. It was a 3½-inch drive and was first introduced more than a year earlier. It offered several significant advantages, including greater disk storage capacity and small disks completely encased in plastic that were virtually indestructible.

But they had been designed in Japan, and that was enough to seal their fate as far as Steve was concerned. Steve's "that's shit" attitude hadn't changed by the following spring. Although he had a respect for some of Sony's products, he had a thorough disdain for the Japanese when it came to electronic, computer-related design. One of his favorite responses, when asked about the challenge for Apple from the land of the rising sun, was that "the Japanese have hit our shores like dead fish. They will get something that has already been invented and study it until they thoroughly understand it. In some cases, they'll understand it better than the inventor. Out of that understanding they will reinvent it in a more refined second-generation version. That strategy only works when what they're working with isn't changing much, like the stereo industry or the automobile. When the target is moving very quickly, they find it difficult. As long as the definition of what a personal computer is keeps changing, they will have a very hard time."[4]

After the February retreat, Steve, Belleville, and Crow headed for Japan to evaluate both ALPS and Sony. They took along a Japanese-American who spoke Japanese, but whose role was to pretend he didn't. The idea was that the translator would listen in to the private conversations the Japanese were having and then later tell the Apple team what was being said. Sony showed them a working 3½-inch disk drive, a completed product, that was already being shipped to H-P for inclusion in that company's personal computers. But Steve was convinced that they were lying to him after hearing his translator's clandestine reports of their conversations. ALPS presented a prototype motor for the new drive that was to be built from Apple's own design but nothing else. However, they did not "lie" according to Steve's auditory spy. He unilaterally chose ALPS as the supplier, against the recommendations of his colleagues.

When Crow was rebuffed, he decided to pursue the matter with Sony on the quiet. One day it led to a scene that might have come straight from a Moliere farce. The drive's chief engineer, a proper Japanese gent in his fifties, accompanied by a junior, was visiting the Mac group, trying to iron out a problem Apple was having with the test drive that they were using. Suddenly, word came that Steve had driven up and was heading into the building. Crow, thinking fast, pushed the engineers into a nearby closet, where they waited while Steve made a perfunctory round through the engineering lab. Then, after the chairman disappeared into his office, they were hustled out the back door and sent on their way.

By summer, ALPS still had nothing tangible to show, and to release the Mac, Steve needed 10,000 drives by the fall. Eventually, after endless broken promises, Steve adopted the Sony drive at the last possible moment and, better yet, made a deal with Sony for Apple to buy them at manufacturing cost, since their appearance in the Mac would make them an instant industry standard. The superb negotiator had another remarkable coup.

The team knew how to handle him, and they all cooperated in the effort to keep the erratic chairman on the right path. He had the right instincts. He wanted a machine for the masses, and he wanted it to be friendly, inexpensive, and easy enough to use that no one could be intimidated by it. But he often traveled down roads that led away from the route that he had staked out. As Matt Carter described it, "Half the time Steve didn't know what he was talking about. He liked to go fishing with hand grenades."[5]

One thing Steve did know was that he wanted John Sculley to help run the company. In early March, he returned to Manhattan, where he had decided to buy an apartment in the prestigious Dakota Apartments overlooking Central Park, the apartment building where John Lennon had been shot. On a brisk, cold day, Steve and Sculley whiled away the hours with a long walk through Central Park, an afternoon in the Metropolitan Museum of Art, and time spent lingering in a cafe. The next day the two took a drive to IBM's Armonk, New York, headquarters. Steve wanted to see the enemy up close. Sculley was almost convinced, especially when Steve asked him the final question: "Are you going to sell sugar water to children for the rest of your life when you could be doing something really important?"

Something else was gnawing at Sculley. The chance to run Apple was a chance to get out from under the shadow of his former father-in-law, Arthur Kendall, the strong-willed chairman of the board at PepsiCo. By training, Sculley was an architect, had been educated at Eastern prep schools and Brown University, and had only joined Pepsi at the urging of Kendall after he married the man's stepdaughter. Sculley stayed on after the couple's divorce. No matter how well he did, however, there was always an undercurrent at Pepsi that he had only risen to the top because he had married the boss's daughter.

In the end Sculley decided to make a stop at Apple on his way to Hawaii for a vacation. He came by the Mac offices on a day when Steve was in Japan comparing Sony and ALPS' disk drive operations. The group was unimpressed by the short, gaunt, compulsive jogger they met. They had no idea that he was being considered for the presidency.

He was supposedly just another of Steve's celebrity friends out to take a gander at Steve's baby.

Later that month, while on his way to the McIntosh Labs, where he was going to secure the rights to the name Macintosh with a payment of a reported $100,000 in cash, Steve made an offer to Sculley. The deal was $1 million a year in salary, a $1 million bonus for accepting, and up to $1 million in stock options, performance incentives, and low-interest loans to enable him to purchase a suitably opulent house. Sculley took it. Apple had a new president and, not insignificantly, a new president who worshipped Steve.

"If you can pick one reason why I came to Apple, it was to have the chance to work with Steve," he said, shortly after the announcement was made by Mike Markkula late in April. "I look on him as being one of the really important figures in our country in this century. I have the chance to help him grow. That in itself is exciting."[6]

The change from the technocratic entrepreneurs to mass marketing businessmen was approved by the investing public. In spite of a declining market share and falling profitability, Apple's stock boomed to a high of $63 per share in the wake of the Sculley announcement. While the stock market was bullish on Apple, inside the company it was soon apparent that the Lisa was flopping big. In March, IBM slashed the price of the PC by 20 percent, further pressuring the costly Lisa. Initial orders of Apple's new computer were strong, and the computers that were finally shipped in May were quickly sold out. But as the months wore on, there was no more than a trickle of new orders. Inside the company, projections for the Lisa, which was supposed to sell 50,000 machines the first year, were revised steadily downward to less than 10,000. It was a sobering reality. It looked as if Apple, after the failure of the Apple III, had another disaster in the making. Perhaps Sculley could save the company from keeling over.

Creeping optimism was part of Steve's evangelical fervor, and it affected Sculley as well as every staffer who had to deal with him. As Lisa sales fell, every month the sales forecast meeting would come up with a higher figure for the projected number of Macs that were going to be sold the first year. Figures jumped 10 to 20 percent from month to month. In his first executive meetings in May of 1983, Sculley was projecting 600,000 Macintoshes sold during the first year, which was even higher than Steve's best and most optimistic projection that he had pulled out of a hat in 1981. Steve realized that if he could get the new president to buy into his outrageous figures, he could push the numbers even higher. By July he was throwing around the figure of 750,000 computers, which was the equivalent of more than 2,000 computers a day for each and every day of the year from day one.

"When I joined the group, I heard these ridiculous projections of 70,000 computers in the first 100 days, and 500,000 Macs in the first year and I thought it was crazy," says Joe Shelton, a marketing manager who managed the Apple label software products for the Macintosh at its introduction. "But within a few months, I found myself saying the same thing—and believing it. Steve had the most remarkable effect on all of us. We knew what he said was impossible to achieve, but emotionally he had us all wanting it so badly to come true that we came to believe it."

Sculley would later deny that he, too, was mesmerized by Steve. He claimed he was "biding his time" before taking over the reins. But he was clearly enraptured by the personality of the chairman. A year after arriving at Apple, Sculley described his relationship with Steve to a Harvard University business class:

> We had to first see if there were any similarities between us, since we came from such diametrically different experiences in our lives, Steve having grown up in Silicon Valley and I from East Coast corporate America, and 16 years age difference. We discovered incredible similarities in the way we thought, the respect we had for ideas, and the respect we had for not compromising.
>
> We were quickly tested after I was here, because strategy tends to be idea driven. And I am a person who believes in the power of great ideas. Steve is the same type of person. We found we're very visual. We think and describe things in visual terms. The way we talk is to go up to a blackboard and start writing. That gave us a very quick shorthand. Plus we tend to talk in half sentences. We talk in phrases, and we jump from subject to subject. In the span of five minutes, we cover six or seven subjects, not completing them, and then we loop back. We often debate and argue with one another. Switching sides is not unusual. We pound on the table and then turn around and take the other person's position. So we work an issue to death.[7]

Sculley and Steve became inseparable for a time. The group came to monitor the handicapped parking spots outside the Mac building, because that was where Steve always parked his sleek, silver-blue Mercedes. A black Mercedes of the same model—the SEC, a two-door coupe with a high-performance engine—in the other handicapped spot meant that Sculley was also present. It didn't matter if there were other spots available; this was where the two big-wigs parked.

In 1983, Steve was too busy for much of a social life. He had all the social activities of being chairman of a nearly billion-dollar corporation, combined with the overwhelming number of decisions to be made daily on the Macintosh. He wanted to have the last word on nearly everything, so he would regularly stay late into the night reviewing the day's developments with his staff. And since he genuinely liked the software programmers working in their glass fishbowl, he hung out there, sitting on the sofa, bantering with them. This was his family, and he poured all his emotional and intellectual energy into them. There simply wasn't time to pursue relationships with outsiders.

As the projections for the number of machines to be sold during the coming year reached the stratosphere, the importance of the Mac factory working absolutely perfectly grew. By May, however, with continuing uncertainty and indecision about the disk drive, it became clear that the Mac wouldn't make it out by late summer, and the date of the release shifted to the next annual meeting, scheduled for January 19, 1984. Even to make it happen that quickly, everything had to go perfectly at the manufacturing end.

From the beginning, Steve was determined that they design an easily manufacturable, single-board computer. The Lisa had five separate circuit boards and proved to be labor-intensive and costly in assembly. The Macintosh was going to represent the state of the art in American manufacturing know-how, and as such he devoted a lot of energy to it. But as with everything else he dived into, he brought both imagination and chaos to the project.

One day in February of 1983, Steve decided to cancel the "conventional build" assembly line for the Macintosh. Markkula was taking little active interest in day-to-day matters any longer, and Steve decided that he would take charge of the situation. At a meeting, he laid down the law.

"Apple needs to become a manufacturing company, and the Macintosh product is the vehicle for an offensive manufacturing strategy," he told the senior managers. "With regard to some of the manufacturing options being discussed, I don't believe in alternatives. I believe in putting all my eggs in one basket and then watching that basket very carefully. Then I either succeed or fail colossally."[8]

With that settled, Matt Carter ordered the steel and assembly line equipment for the Dallas facility. But that Christmas, Apple IIe orders had gone through the roof, which seemed to indicate an end to the recession that year. Suddenly, the Dallas facility was needed to build Apple IIs again. The Macintosh plant would have to be located near Silicon Valley, in a building that Carter had previously negotiated to lease in Fremont. Equipment was already on the road to Dallas when the decision was made and had to be rerouted to California. Apple counsel Al Eisenstadt, a tough corporate lawyer who never allowed himself to be buffaloed by Steve, refused to sign the letter of intent on the space that the owner required before allowing the equipment in the door—he wanted the deal to go through the proper corporate channels, not be part of a decision by the youths in the Mac group. Instead, Steve, as an officer of the company, took matters into his own hands and signed the letter of intent himself, unilaterally. They got the building and started moving equipment in the next day.

The factory was a source of friction within the group. Steve had hired another guy to be Carter's boss and run the Dallas plant. Dave Vaughn was an older and seasoned line boss from H-P, but Carter sorely resented having someone over his head. It was bad enough from a distance, but when the plant was relocated back to California, so was Vaughn.

"Steve turned on me because I fought him too much," opines Carter. "I was trying to do the right thing, and I was one of the few people who would really stand up to him, yell and scream, and fight tooth and nail. He really didn't like that.

"He wanted people to do a great job, but he wanted them to be subservient. He would push a lot of people to failure because he would go after them and keep thinking up crazier things, or more aggressive goals if they were doing good, or if they were achieving their goals he wanted them to do more. He just couldn't stop, he had to push you to the edge."[9]

While you can change artwork or software up until the last moment before a computer ships, a factory is like a giant freight train barreling down the tracks. There was custom equipment and a massive assembly line to be coordinated. Steve had a problem with making up his mind.

"He always wanted the factory to be beautiful, a showplace," explains Carter. "We even got big-name interior designers and decorators involved and went through all this crap and hassle over what colors the factory equipment, and the inside of the factory, should be."[10]

Carter tried to accommodate Steve's whims, but he had his priorities. Finally Steve couldn't make a decision about what color to paint some of the factory equipment. He thought he wanted the colors of the Apple logo reflected on the tiers of equipment that were to fill the block-long room, but he was indecisive. The steel and equipment for the factory was sitting on the docks in Japan ready to be shipped, and it was starting to rust because it hadn't been painted. Carter couldn't wait any longer and ordered it painted beige. When the gear appeared, and Steve took a walk through the plant, he objected to the color Carter had chosen. He demanded that it be repainted. Carter tried to explain that much of it was precision equipment, and taking it apart might make it unable to perform to specification again. Steve insisted, and Vaughn buckled to him. One machine was repainted blue. It never worked again and for months sat on the side of the factory floor, a pile of bright blue machinery that cost hundreds of thousands of dollars and was known as Steve's folly.

"It took so much energy to fight him, and it was usually over something so pointless that finally I had had enough. First you get to fight the guy tooth and nail, and then you make him successful in spite of himself. It was too crazy. I gave him my resignation. The next day, Vaughn turned in his. Steve called me every two weeks for more than a year, begging me to come back, but I'd had enough."[11]

Suddenly, no one was around to run the plant, and it was midsummer of 1983. The factory had just completed the prototype build of 200, and they were scheduled to ramp up during the next few months for the January introduction. It was a few days before the summer retreat, this time a one-day event held at a local historical mansion because everyone was too busy to go away overnight. The mood was solemn.

"We all worked so hard," recalls Joanna Hoffmann. "We had everything ready to go: the machine, the software, the media plan, the advertising. And now we weren't going to be able to ship because the factory people had squabbled with Steve and there wasn't anybody around to make the machines. That was absolutely the lowest point in the whole project."

Steve led off the session with a description of the problems he was having at the factory, but he wasn't worried, he lied to them. He had everything under control. He held up a prototype of the ALPS drive and claimed that this was the one they were going to use. (A week later he changed his mind for the final time when the company still couldn't deliver a working model.) But these were little details that were easily swept under the carpet when he turned on his charm and captivated the room. He emphasized that they had to work together as a team and that with the Macintosh they were moving the computer industry into an entirely new realm. Service and support were no longer part of the equation. They had built a computer that was so reliable, so well designed and engineered, that they didn't need a service plan. Macintoshes would never break down. The team believed him. In the audience was John Sculley. He believed Steve, too. They all believed the glib kid from the Valley, and suddenly the sun began to shine again.

That began the parade of group leader reports: engineering, manufacturing, marketing, finance, and human resources. On this day, six months from the projected launch of the machine, the tenor of the meeting was subdued. The presentations were serious, with none of the light-heartedness of previous retreats. This was the real thing, and with the troubles at the factory, no one was in the mood for joking.

The group's young and ambitious financial controller, Debi Coleman, presented the numbers: Apple had spent $78 million to date on developing and creating the Macintosh. The cost of a Mac to the company was $500, although that price would drop to closer to $400 once the factory had ironed out its bugs and was up to speed. That consisted of 83 percent cost of materials, 16 percent overhead, and 1 percent labor. Carter might have taken a hike, but his projections from 18 months earlier were dead on. It was one of the few parts of the Macintosh project that had never changed.

A month later Coleman, a heavy-set young woman with a degree in economics and no manufacturing experience, stepped into the factory breach. At a Pajaro Dunes executives-only retreat, she buttonholed Steve during a walk along the beach and convinced him to let her run the factory. Another inexperienced but ambitious and willing kid from the class of 1955 was given a chance to prove herself on the Macintosh.

The other interesting presentation that day, new to most of the team, was from the creative director of the Apple account at Chiat/Day, Lee Clow, and the key copywriter, Steve Hayden. Late in the previous year, Mike Murray had started working with the creative team from the agency on an ad campaign to bring the Macintosh to the public's attention. That day they introduced the advertising themes and strategy that they had created for the new computer.

Located in a brick building in San Francisco, with offices around the country, Chiat/Day was renowned for its creative finesse and remarkable campaigns, especially for Apple. The account had gone to Chiat/Day when Regis McKenna decided to sell off his advertising accounts and concentrate on public relations in the early 1980s. Since then the account had stayed with the new agency, in large part because of close relations among Jay Chiat, his head creative whiz, Lee Clow, and Steve. Over the years, they had won numerous awards, and they shared a vision of excellence that involved creating advertising that was striking in its difference from anything else in the field. That attitude of being aggressively different was always essential to Steve's world view and was all the more important with the introduction of the Macintosh.

At the beginning of 1983, one of the agency's writers suggested to Murray that they do something with George Orwell's "1984" theme the following year, turning it inside out and making it work for Apple. Murray immediately agreed, since everything that Apple was doing with the Macintosh spoke of breaking down the faceless mechanized behemoth that the public saw as computing. By playing off the 1984 idea, he thought they could make a strong statement. Steve instantly agreed. It was exactly the vision of himself that Steve held: He was an outlaw, spitting in the face of the forces of conformity. The Macintosh was his weapon, and he wanted the public to see it as the victory of the small guy over the forces of Big Brother, the perfect analogy for IBM.

With the introduction of the Macintosh scheduled for January, Apple had purchased advertising time for the Super Bowl telecast, a few days before the announcement. The idea was to make a major 60-second teaser ad that would capture the attention of the nation at the most watched television event of the year. Super Bowl Sunday was four days before the annual meeting, and a startling ad shown then would reinforce the hype and hoopla scheduled for that event. Subsequently, another campaign would start, focusing on the Macintosh itself. The advertising budget alone for the first 100 days after introduction was $10 million, and for the first year, $20 million. Steve controlled the purse strings of Apple through his manipulation of the board.

"Steve had us convinced that the Macintosh would be a smash by then," recalls Phil Schlein, the CEO of Macy's and a long-time Apple board member. "He was powerfully seductive, and since Lisa was failing, we felt the company had to put everything behind the new machine to ensure its success. We basically gave him a blank check."

Sculley was Steve's equal when it came to spending advertising dollars. The new president had been involved in an extraordinarily expensive and successful Michael Jackson campaign for Pepsi just before he resigned, and he understood the value of spending money to create brand-name identification. The thrust of the Macintosh introduction was to make the Macintosh a household name immediately. Not an easy or inexpensive task in America in the eighties.

By that summer retreat, the storyboards for the teaser ad were finished, and production was about to begin in London. As for everything else relating to the Macintosh, Steve was very picky. Over the months, he and Murray had rejected dozens of ideas and innumerable drafts of copy for print ads, brochures, and television advertising. They finally settled on a futuristic TV spot to be directed by Ridley Scott, an English film director who had made *Alien*. They were looking for an other-worldly look, a frightening "East German socialism failed look," explained Steve Hayden, the man who wrote it.[12] Into this police-controlled world, they would introduce a young woman wearing a Macintosh T-shirt, who could represent Apple's challenge to conformity. Because of the exorbitant cost of building the sets and creating the right look in the United States, they went to England for the actual shooting. Nonetheless, the 60-second spot, planned to be shown only once for maximum marketplace impact, cost more than $400,000 to make, and the advertising time on the Super Bowl ran another $500,000. It was going to be a million-dollar minute.

At the retreat, the Chiat/Day team showed the storyboard art and described the thrust of the ad. It was an immediate hit. They described their print ad brochure, a 20-page advertising insert that was going into several major magazines the week of the introduction, including *Time* and *Newsweek*, and showed mock-ups of the dealer brochures as well. However, they were still uncertain about the campaign for the follow-up after the Super Bowl and were toying with three themes: a series of ads with business people having trouble at IBM-style computers. "Syntax error . . . syntax error . . . syntax error . . ." beeps at them on screen, and, growing frustrated enough, they pull out sledgehammers and shotguns to destroy the computer. Another was a series of interviews with the key creators of the Macintosh talking about what the computer meant to them. A third idea was a graphic description of the number, weight, and size of manuals required to use an IBM PC, compared with the much smaller ones for the Mac, punctuated by the line, "Now you decide which is more sophisticated." They were all potent ideas; the only question was which ones to use. Steve, with his indecision about things, ordered them all produced, adding hundreds of thousands of dollars to the Mac's advertising costs. He wanted the whole team to have a vote, but of course the deciding vote would be his.

At the end of the meeting, Steve began to talk about the future products that the division would introduce. In the midst of all the madness of planning for the Macintosh, changing the disk drive, and creating the campaigns for introduction, Steve, Belleville, and Sculley had been planning new products to keep the line alive. They were developing their new product strategies for the next year.

He told them that when they introduced the Mac, there would be new Lisas as well. The new Lisas were going to use the new disk drive, the one he had held up and showed the group that morning, and would come with various hard disks. Furthermore, a program was being developed that would allow the Lisa to run Mac software, but that was still a few months off. Sculley had finally forced Steve into trying to bring the two computers closer together. More important were the future Macintosh products that he wanted them to start thinking about and working on soon. While out of one side of his mouth he was saying that the Lisa was a viable machine, his new product strategy belied it.

First, there was the Big Mac, a large-screen Macintosh with a display the same size as the original Lisa; one megabyte of RAM memory, the same size as the Lisa; a single double-sided disk drive, which stored the same amount of data as a Lisa; and a networking port so the machine could be linked in an office network like the Lisa. The Big Mac was a Macintosh Lisa, even though Steve insisted that there were major differences. He was the only one who saw them.

Then there was a reduced-cost Macintosh, the Mac 2. This machine would cost no more than $1,500 to the consumer and have fewer chips. After much debate, the price of the Mac had been set at

$2,495. The plan was to drop the cost to $1,995 after the first 100 days, but to sock the first buyers with the higher premium price. Amazingly, Steve, who for years had been pushing $1,500 as the price of the machine, was behind the $2,500 cost. Sculley had held out for the $2,000 price tag, but as usual that year, Steve prevailed.

The other products that he saw on the horizon were high-speed modems for telephone-based communications, more sophisticated software, double-sided disk drives, hard disks, and three distinct types of "servers" to expand the Mac's power in the office. The FileServer would offer mass storage capability for a number of users; a communications server, CommServer, would allow access to a modem and telecommunications connections by an office full of people; and a LaserServer would let a number of computers share an expensive laser printer that he had decided Apple would build. The laser printer proved to be a crucial development that ultimately snatched the Mac from the precipice of defeat.

Laser printers were developed at Xerox as part of their attempt to define a solution to the office printing needs of large companies. Owen Densmore, who had headed the Lisa and Macintosh printing group, tried to convince Steve of the value of laser printing when he first arrived at the company two years earlier, but to no avail. Finally, in early 1983, Bob Belleville introduced to Steve a couple of ex-Xerox guys who had just founded a tiny company to write and sell a "page description" language. This software technology potentially allowed a page with a mix of text and graphics to be printed at any resolution. The text-and-graphics-oriented Macintosh seemed like a good match for a page description language that could turn the dots on the screen into near-typeset-quality printed output. Early in 1983, Steve became convinced that laser printing might be a technology that Apple could co-opt, if they could only bring the price down.

By then Steve had annoyed and alienated so many people inside Apple that any idea he had, no matter how good, was instantly fought. Laser printing, with its high cost, was an immediate red flag to the Apple II group. Steve grew more excited about the possibilities of the technology, but the rest of the company resisted. The company of ex-Xerox thinkers, called Adobe, originally had the idea to sell a complete package, including the printer, as a printing and typesetting station. About the time they lit a fire under Steve, they were starting to think that it might be smarter just to license the language they were writing and let a computer manufacturer such as Apple or DEC build, sell, and market the machines—especially since they knew that Canon and a few other Japanese manufacturers were close to introducing prototypes of much lower cost laser printer "engines" than Xerox's cheapest $15,000 machines.

"Steve fell in love with the technology," says John Warnock, one of Adobe's founders. "It was painfully clear that they couldn't go into the serious business market with this computer [the Macintosh] and the ImageWriter, and we told him so. Our technology was the first full-powered graphics technology that could support the graphics that they had built into the machine and compete with letter-quality printers for text."

Steve, in cahoots with Burrell Smith and Bob Belleville, decided that the best way to do it was to build a new 68000 circuit board and put that into the laser printer itself. Apple would license the engine from Canon and the page-description language, *PostScript*, from Adobe. With a circuit board designed by Smith inside the printer, the Mac could send a page of text or graphics to the printer, where the page would be "imaged" and printed. But instead of licensing the language, Steve decided that he was going to make an investment in Adobe, a struggling company that needed cash to finish their work, in exchange for rights to *PostScript*. The only problem was that he needed board approval.

"When he first proposed that Apple build a $7,000 printer for a $2,000 computer, the entire board thought he was nuts," says Schlein. "It flew in the face of everything that Apple was trying to do. But he wouldn't give in, and he came to each one of us individually and showed us what it could do, how Apple had to take the lead, and how we had to make this new technology ours. He sold us on the dream and the vision, and a few board meetings later, we agreed to do it.

"By then he could get us to agree to anything."

By the time of the final retreat, Steve had pushed the laser printer idea through against the objections of almost everyone in the company. "This was an incredibly aggressive machine," continues Warnock. "It relied on 256-kilobyte memory chips, of which there were none. It used a 12-megahertz 68000 chip, which was rare back then. Steve's entire focus was, 'We are going to go through and prototype this machine, and when we announce it, we assume that the prices are going to drop and the parts will be available.'"

The only problem was that Steve had set an announcement date for the following summer, again an impossible schedule. A few weeks after the summer retreat, when Smith, who had completed his hardware work for the release of the Macintosh, returned from a vacation with Hertzfeld in Martinique, he moved over to designing the circuit board for the laser printer. When Steve announced the project to the troops that July, little had been done, and it wasn't even certain that the machine he had outlined would ever work—yet he was basing his entire future strategy on the new technology. Steve told them that the advent of affordable laser printers made letter-quality printers obsolete, so they would not support them with the Macintosh. It gave him the justification he needed to flout conventional wisdom again.

In 1983, other than "IBM compatible," the only computer-related phrase most people knew was "letter quality." Since the invention of the typewriter, business correspondence in America has been based on letter-quality printing. Furthermore, the print shop guys at Lisa had even written a driver that allowed the Mac to work with Apple's own letter-quality daisy wheel printer, which was sold for the Lisa. But Steve was adamant. He knew better than every office manager in the country what was good for them. His Macintosh wasn't going to support a daisy wheel printer.

The great loss for the group was that they were trapped in the cul-de-sacs into which Steve had led them. By not supporting a letter-quality printer, Steve thumbed his nose at corporate America. The laser printer was a better technology and a much better fit for the Macintosh, but supporting letter-quality printers was a small detail that would have cost nothing and kept open the doors to the markets they were aiming for.

Steve couldn't see it. He loved the new and the unconventional, and he was determined to force it on the public. The same thing happened when the programmers developing the word processor, *MacWrite*, tried to put cursor key support into their program. Steve ordered them to take it out. They argued that fast typists don't want to take their hands off the keyboard to move a mouse.

"What difference would it make?" Wigginton said to Steve. "Why not just add that little feature to make it easier for secretaries? But no. We couldn't have them. 'We have to force the issue—make people use the mouse. It's better for them,' was what he told me."

Although the Macintosh team may have been willing to accept their leader's pronouncements as gospel, the rest of the company was not. A few weeks after the summer retreat, a draft of the Macintosh product introduction plan was circulated through the company for comments. The reaction from the folks who were keeping Apple afloat on a sea of Apple IIe money was vicious. Here are some examples:

- "The Macintosh PIP [Production Introduction Plan] shows that little market research or critical thought has gone into developing either the Mac positioning or its marketing communications strategy."
- "I cannot believe that the corporation has allowed them to get away with what they are calling positioning."
- "An Apple II will do everything a Macintosh will do. Why do we think everyone in the world will want to buy one."
- "Mac marketing seems hopelessly hung up on this inane 'product positioning' statement about the Cuisinart for the desk. Let's stop this silly proposition and just cut the crap!"
- "There is a real lack of substance in this plan, which the author tries to hide with smoke and mirrors. I feel the marketing messages were written by someone who doesn't understand the market."
- "Saying a product is all things to all people isn't positioning."
- "My hat is off to anyone who can sell a computer in a five-minute demo, and I've always wanted to see a product sell itself."
- "'The marketplace for the Macintosh is desks. Primarily desks of achievers.' Such statements are ludicrously simple-minded. Didn't we learn anything from the Apple III? We are again selling all things, all people, everywhere, every time, always. Instead of focusing on someone we can sell to, we don't focus at all."[13]

Steve dismissed the comments as sour grapes. Murray was stung, and he organized a number of focus groups to try to identify the marketplace, but it changed nothing. It was far too late, anyway. They would put the machine out into the world, say that it was for this new group of customers that Murray called "knowledge workers," and the world would beat a path to their door. They all knew it would happen that way—it was the way Steve had predicted it. The entire effort was based on simply showing how "insanely great" the Mac was, because that was all the world needed. The idea of building solutions and entire focused marketing efforts aimed at specific customer groups was not Steve's way. The company was maturing in many ways, but Steve was not. He was still the same Zen-Crazy pain in the ass.

In the only focus groups they did conduct, two comments came through loud and clear. People who knew little about computers repeatedly asked two salient questions: "What will it do for me?" and "All these graphics are very nice, but will it do *VisiCalc*?" The message was plain. Customers didn't care how neat it was, who built it, or about drawing with it. They cared about what it would do for them, what business problems the computer could solve. Although the Mac did a lot for Steve and the team, all those fancy features seemed less than appealing to the potential customers in offices.

The spate of critical memos was the first sign that something might be wrong with Apple and the Mac. In early September, the group did the final ROM release for the machine. This meant that the internal programming of the Mac was set for shipment. The days leading up to that September 12 freeze date were hectic, especially since Hertzfeld, who had written the ROM routines in the first place, had only returned from his vacation a few days before. Finally, with everyone staying up for days on end, it was completed. They were in the home stretch.

Steve was feeling confident, even as the price of Apple's stock plummeted from $63 a share to $21 in the wake of the company's admission that the Lisa was not selling anywhere near their projections and that the firm was not going to show a profit for the final quarter of the fiscal year that ended in September. In response, his net worth dropped, in a matter of weeks, by a quarter of a billion dollars. The money didn't matter to Steve. The Macintosh was going to save the day, and he still had more money than he could give away in his lifetime. However, a group of shareholders wasn't quite so sanguine about the future. A few months later, they filed a lawsuit accusing Apple's officers of artificially inflating the price of the stock by making optimistic pronouncements even when they knew sales couldn't support them.

By then, with the failure of the Apple III and the Lisa in succession, Steve had come to see the introduction of the Macintosh in starkly apocalyptic terms. "It's kind of like watching the gladiator going into the arena and saying, 'Here it is.' It's really perceived as Apple's do or die. And it goes even deeper," he concluded, in an interview that autumn. "If we don't do this, nobody can stop IBM."[14]

Yet he was still the same ebullient and optimistic Steve Jobs he had always been. In the next breath, he could continue, "The Mac stands for what we are as a company—taking technology that's out of reach of the people and making it really great. That's what we did with the Apple II, and that's what we're going to do again with the Mac. Computers and society are on a first date in this decade, and for some crazy reason, we're in the right place at the right time to make that romance blossom.

"I don't want to sound arrogant, but I know this thing is going to be the next great milestone in this industry. Every bone in my body says it's going to be great, and people are going to realize that and buy it."[15]

In September, as the pressures mounted, so did some unforeseen problems. Third-party software developers were up in arms about Apple's decision to sell Microsoft's software products for the Mac under the Apple label. It seemed to them, especially to Mitch Kapor of Lotus, who was working to develop a *1-2-3* type program for the Mac, that it was an unconscionable advantage to give a competitor. If Apple really wanted to stimulate market development of programs, shouldn't everyone be on equal footing?

The Apple-label software was a throwback to the Lisa and Apple III concepts of providing a family of software for the machine. It was also rooted in Steve's determination to provide a selection of programs with the computer so that the buyers would be able to do something with the Mac as soon as they opened the box. But including *MacPaint* and *MacWrite* in the box caused serious arguments in the group. Murray, the marketing chief, was opposed to it. He felt that they could sell the programs, thus providing some income to the dealer as well as stimulating other developers to create competing products.

"The real benchmark of a computer for most users is word processing," Murray explains. "If we were giving away a perfectly good word processor, why should anyone else try to write one that costs real money?"

Steve was adamant about bundling *MacPaint* and *MacWrite*, and they stayed in the box. He had no such emotional attachment to the Microsoft products. Besides, Microsoft was late with their software, and it looked as if they might not even be ready to ship by introduction. He ordered Murray to send a letter to the Washington-based company, rescinding the agreement and cutting Microsoft loose to sell the products on their own. Gates was furious and claimed that Apple couldn't do that to him three months before the Mac was to come out. A careful reading of the contract, however, showed that Apple could indeed change its mind. Microsoft had to scramble to produce a duplication and distribution strategy by January. They made it, but the early versions of BASIC and *Multiplan* were riddled with bugs. The episode left a bitter taste in Gates' mouth, and in turn he felt no compulsion to push a Macintosh version of the word processor Microsoft sold for the IBM PC, Microsoft *Word*, out the door the next year.

During the same month, Steve made another choice that demonstrated his lack of tact and sowed further dissension, this time in the ranks of his beloved Macintosh team. Steve had decided that the company should do a series of commercials in which the creators of the Macintosh talked about what it meant to them. One day in early September, a group of six of the Macintosh team members drove up to a deserted warehouse in San Francisco to become movie stars for a day. To the rest of the 97 people dedicated to making the Macintosh a reality, the six became the superstars.

They were Smith, Hertzfeld, Atkinson, Murray, Crow, and Kare. The first three were no real problem. Everyone realized that they had done the ground work upon which the Macintosh was founded. The last three were a mistake. It wasn't that they were undeserving, just that they were not that much more deserving than anyone else on the team, at least not in the eyes of the other members, who were giving their hearts and souls to Steve's computer. Kare was a real shock. She had been with the team for less than six months and was doing something considered relatively peripheral, or at least no more essential than the work that another fifty or so of the team were slaving over night and day.

Steve liked her and that was all there was to it. He never listened to anyone else anyway, and certainly didn't hear the whispering that started as soon as the list was made public. Steve was always a favorites person: You were in or out, and the list could change depending on his mood for the day. This was his way of doling out the credit that he thought was important. He showed up at the filming, but no matter how hard they tried to get him to do one of the spots, he refused. In the end, the ads weren't used. They were too self-congratulatory and indulgent for a serious computer meant to attract business people.

This was yet another of Steve's wild and expensive ideas that didn't pan out. As it happened, it very nearly sank the project, because the guy doing arguably the most important piece of software, as far as a user is concerned, was so upset by it, along with the pressure he was under, that he nearly dropped the ball. By the summer of 1983, Bruce Horn had been assigned to write the Finder, the set of program codes creating the desktop environment when the computer is turned on. This was the code that allowed the user to organize files and documents stored on a disk. It was the first thing a user saw, and it had to work effortlessly because it was the essential road map to working with the computer. Horn was incensed that Kare had been chosen before him for the ads, and he simply stopped doing any work. It took a week to realize that he had stopped turning out anything, but by early October, the software project manager, Jerome Coonen, knew he had a major problem on his hands. Without the Finder, there could be no release of the Macintosh. They had a real crisis on their hands.

The press sneaks began in earnest that October. Magazines have a several month lead-time for publication, and to make the cover of the maximum number by January, Apple had to offer the information in October. But every time a reporter showed up and started interviewing one of the superstars, Horn was upset all over again. It got so that he started complaining the minute he saw an interview begin and kept it up loudly and volubly for hours afterward. His attitude was disruptive and unproductive.

Mac staff meetings were held to determine whether they should fire Horn and put someone else in charge of the project or keep him. Finally the staff decided to separate Horn from the rest of the crew and give him a partner who could hopefully keep him on track. There was only one person to choose: Steve Capps. They were given a spare office in the back of a building across the street from the Mac building, next to the Xerox machines. They had 100 days to complete the program. They worked seven days a week, on Thanksgiving, on Christmas, and on New Year's. A sofa was moved in, and they took turns sleeping on it. They released version after version of the Finder, including a Turkey Day Finder and various beta versions. Finally, early in January, they completed it. Steve gave Capps a medal for his work. Horn retired to fly airplanes and eventually to return to college. Still, neither man received much credit in all the hoopla of hype that accompanied the release of the computer. It had been a superhuman effort on both their parts, but Steve couldn't see beyond his hand-picked crew of superstars.

The marketing campaign that Murray had put in place over the past year was about to bear fruit. He had read an article about the work of George Lucas's organization on the movie *Star Wars*. They had built a marketing campaign a year ahead of the release of the movie, arranging for merchandising and events related to the release, so that when the movie was released "it seemed like a newsworthy event," explains Murray. "There were all these little explosions going off, and folks saw them and decided that they had better go see the film or they would miss the boat.

"We wanted to do the same thing with the Mac. We wanted to make it seem like a news event, so that on the nightly news there would be an item about how 'Apple Computer released a new computer today.' That way the public wouldn't think they had been manipulated, even though of course we had orchestrated the whole thing. It was event marketing at its very best."

Part of the scheme involved having a magazine devoted to the Mac come out on the day of its introduction. Computer magazines had become big business over the years, and both the IBM PC and the Apple II were supporting several. Murray approached the biggest publisher in the field, Ziff-Davis, the company behind *PC* magazine, and asked if they were interested in making a proposal. As an afterthought, Steve decided to extend the invitation to the original creators of *PC* magazine, a San Francisco publishing company that, in a bitter stock and ownership dispute, had broken off from Ziff and formed a competing IBM PC magazine, *PCWorld*

"The Ziff proposal was extremely professional," recalls Murray. "They were really slick. The two guys from *PCWorld* were not. They were kind of funky and unprepared but were really enthusiastic. Afterward I said to Steve, 'Well, it's obvious who we should go with, isn't it?'

"We both agreed. The guys from *PCWorld* were Mac-type people, and it would mean a lot more to them than it would to the conglomerate at Ziff-Davis. We chose the local guys."

The magazine was *Macworld*, and the founding staff were the first journalists allowed to work with the Macintosh outside Cupertino, but not the first to see it. Early in 1983, when they had the first "final" prototypes, Steve decided, in concert with Regis McKenna, that they should sneak the machine to a few influential opinion makers such as Esther Dyson who wrote the influential newsletter *Release 1.0*, or the Bay area bureau chiefs at *Newsweek* and *Business Week*. (*Time* was given the cold shoulder after its "Machine of the Year" article.) These were conducted under strict nondisclosure terms.

"Sure, we'd let them see it, with all these caveats and warnings about not telling anyone," says Murray, "but we were really hoping that they would tell everybody in the world about it as soon as they left the building."

In November, the Super Bowl "1984" ad was completed and screened in the Mac group, where it was an instant success. All the plans for their Macintosh introduction were put into motion, and the reaction from the press was better than they could have hoped for. As Murray described it, "Reporters under about 35 seemed to really get it. The older ones were much less likely to respond, but the younger ones were very enthusiastic. As we watched the reactions, we knew we had a winner."

Unfortunately, the entire board of directors at Apple was over 35 years old. During that November board meeting, Steve planned to present all the elements of the roll-out to the group. As part of that, he wanted Murray to come in and show the spot.

"I was really proud of it," says Murray. "This was my crowning achievement, and I was finally going to be recognized for my contribution. After we screened it, I looked around the room and Phil Schlein had his head on the conference table and was banging his fist on it. I thought, 'Wow. They really liked it.' Then he looked up at me, and I realized that he hated it. Right there they voted to have us sell the time and pull the ad. The board thought it was the worst ad Apple had ever made." There were only ten days or so before the final deadline, and reluctantly Steve ordered Chiat/Day to try to sell the block of time. As the days ticked by, however, there were no buyers. No one at the agency or in the Mac group wanted to pull the ad, but they felt bound by the board's wishes. Finally, the deadline passed and Apple was committed. Steve was ecstatic. It was all going his way.

That same month, John Sculley announced that the Lisa and Mac groups were going to have to be merged into one after the introduction of the Mac. There were too many inefficiencies, and the Lisa wasn't pulling its weight. The head of the new division, to be called the Apple 32 family, was to be Steve Jobs. At first Steve resisted the idea, but then it grew on him. He had shown the businessmen that he could run a project and bring a product to market. He had Sculley in his pocket, everyone agreed that the Mac was the greatest computer ever built, and he was going to head a large division. He was 29 years old, and he had everything.

As 1983 drew to a close, it was all over but the shouting. He had orchestrated the most amazing new computer introduction in the history of the industry. There was only one tiny thing left: the buying public's reaction. He knew they were going to embrace the Mac. How could they not love it? He knew what the world needed in a computer, and the Mac was it. Anyway, it was his baby, his flesh and blood. How could the world not love him?

V

Hubris

16
1984

T he orchestration of the Macintosh introduction was everything Steve wanted and more. As the seconds ticked away in 1983, the only question remaining was whether the software would be completed. An internal memo describes the feelings of the marketing team: "The software is still questionable for release. Especially the Finder. This is THE BIG QUESTION. When will we be comfortable enough with it to release it?"[1]

The answer, as it turned out, would come at 6 A.M. on the morning the so-called Golden Master had to be hand-carried to the factory so production could begin. Everything else was perfectly arranged, although the factory, under its new leader Debi Coleman, was having a number of shake-out problems. A few days into January, Steve, a team of executives, and Mac team demonstrators took off for a series of product introductions to the dealers and the press. Called the Roll-Out, the tour would take them to key cities throughout the United States and was the first time that a roomful of Macs could be seen at once. It was a religious experience for those participating. Finally, the machine was real and could be unveiled to the people who would actually be selling them.

On Sunday, January 8, a conference call was scheduled between the East Coast product introduction team and the West Coast software programmers and testers. The discussion was not whether the Mac would be introduced, but whether the software that was shipped with the Macs to dealers would be labeled "demo." By noon Sunday, the West Coast team had realized that they would not be able to make the deadline for disk duplication: Monday, January 16. They wanted to be let off the hook for producing absolutely final "final" code.

Steve wouldn't hear it. He didn't react with anger, as they were all expecting. He started telling them how great they were and how all of Apple was counting on them. He told them that they could make it happen and that sending out demo disks was impossible because of the signal that it would give to the marketplace. Then he hung up before there was a chance to argue.

Everyone in the conference room in Cupertino was stunned. They looked at one another. They were already exhausted, but Steve had done it again. They would make the deadline. He had challenged them to rise to the occasion, and he had chosen his people well. They wouldn't let him down. There was little to say. Silently, they got up and went back to their cubicles.

Few of them slept that week. Out in the field, Macintoshes were being revealed to dealers in crowded hotel rooms, while back in Cupertino the programmers were working madly. Finally, in the wee hours of the morning on the 16th, they had the software finished. Then Capps discovered a tiny bug and fixed it. *MacPaint* and *MacWrite* started to crash. They were only hours away from the deadline. Bill Atkinson and Randy Wigginton started working feverishly to correct the last problems, but each version of *MacWrite* Wigginton created was worse than the one before. At last, with 15 minutes to spare, they had a working set of programs. Fifteen people put the programs through as much testing as they could cram into 15 minutes, and at the designated hour, the software project manager Jerome Coonen put the top down on his sports car to keep himself awake and headed for the factory. They had a computer.

On the East Coast, Steve was in his element, talking to the press and glibly selling the Macintosh dream. The other key participant in the week's activities was Sculley, who had by then been at Apple for eight months. Sculley was "one of the boys" as far as the financial analysts and Wall Street press were concerned, and it was important that he be present to explain just how sold on the company he really was. There had been a great deal of skepticism on Wall Street when Sculley's appointment was first announced. The veterans predicted that either he or the brash chairman would have to go. It hadn't happened, although the company's stock had taken a beating during the past few months, falling by 60 percent of its value in the wake of poor Lisa sales.

Now, as the pair of them faced the press and lunched with every opinion maker the Regis McKenna agency could rustle up, it was obvious that they actually liked each other.

It could have all been PR hype, but it wasn't. Sculley was fascinated with his younger partner and had taken on a number of Steve's evangelical phrases. As the pair fielded questions, sitting side by side for the most part, they seamlessly finished each other's sentences. As Steve described the automated factory and the components of the Macintosh, Sculley dutifully pointed to the appropriate sections on a blow-up poster of the Mac behind him. It was a smooth and effortless performance that won them not only astonishing press coverage for their product a week later when it was formally introduced, but also the appearance of corporate stability. The financial world may have respected Steve's flair for innovation, but they were never comfortable buying stock from a firm that had such an unpredictable, inexperienced chairman of the board. Sculley was one of them, and his presence gave Apple the unmistakable air of belonging.

Seeing the Macintosh itself only reinforced the impression of stability and promise. Two months before in November, IBM had introduced its long-awaited Peanut, a low-end computer formally named the IBM PC Junior. With limited power, an unpopular keyboard, and severely proscribed options for upgrading so as not to interfere with the business market for the IBM PC itself, the machine was labeled a loser before it even shipped. With the Macintosh coming on its heels, priced a little higher but showing real innovation in the personal computer field with its graphics and mouse, Apple was suddenly in a better position than ever.

Between mid-January and early February, the Macintosh hit the cover of more than 20 magazines. Articles in computer magazines were expected, but the machine and its team also appeared in *Rolling Stone* and *The Atlantic*. The infrastructure that Murray had so proudly put in place meant that the computer was mentioned on the nightly news of all three networks and was covered by all the major papers and wire services in the country. For the first time, the announcement and introduction of a computer was considered major news. Some of the more extensive stories gave others credit: Smith and Hertzfeld had their day in *Newsweek*; Atkinson and Kare made it big in *Rolling Stone*. But in every line of prose, every moment of coverage, Steve clearly was the prime motivator for Apple's innovation.

Steve was, after all, the cofounder of the company and the interesting multimillionaire in the story. His consistently hallucinatory prose, analogies, and descriptions also captured the imaginations of reporters. In the weeks leading up to the formal announcement, which would come at the stockholders' meeting on January 24, he gave more than 200 interviews and posed for countless photos. Over and over they repeated his theme for the month, a story that he had honed to perfection but that he could always deliver as if it were just coming to him.

Again and again he described the machine that he had spent three years of his life perfecting and cajoling into existence:

A hundred years ago, if somebody had asked Alexander Graham Bell, "What are you going to be able to do with a telephone?" he wouldn't have been able to tell the ways that the telephone would affect the world. He didn't know that people would use the telephone to call up and find out what movies were playing that night or to order some groceries or call a relative on the other side of the globe. But remember that first the public telegraph was inaugurated in 1844. It was an amazing breakthrough in communications. You could actually send messages from New York to San Francisco in an afternoon. People talked about putting a telegraph on every desk in America to improve productivity.

But it wouldn't have worked. It required that people learn this whole sequence of strange incantations, Morse code, dots and dashes, to use it. It took about 40 hours to learn. The majority of people would never learn how to use it. So, fortunately, in the 1870s Bell filed the patents for the telephone. It performed basically the same function as the telegraph, but people already knew how to use it. Also the neatest thing about it was that besides allowing you to communicate with just words, it allowed you to sing, to intone your words with meaning beyond the simple linguistics.

And we're in the same situation today. Some people are saying that we ought to put an IBM PC on every desk in America to improve productivity. It won't work. The special incantations you have to learn this time are "slash qzs" and things like that. They're not going to learn "slash qzs" any more than they're going to learn Morse code. The current generation of computers just won't work any longer. We want to make a product like the first telephone. We want to make mass-market appliances. That is what the Macintosh is all about. It's the first telephone of our industry. And, beside that, the neatest thing about it to me is that the Macintosh lets you sing the way the telephone did. You don't simply communicate words, you have special print styles and the ability to draw and add pictures to express yourself.[2]

Insanely great! It was the kind of performance that the press loved. As the Macintosh was released, Steve went from being an interesting figure within the computer and high-technology world to a major American cultural hero. The garage-to-riches Macintosh story catapulted him into the public's eye, and, combined with the Mac's slap in the face of convention by not being IBM PC compatible, it was the underdog tale gone high-tech. He was already rich—which was always America's prime yardstick of success—and he was showing his individualism, another trait that the country prized. Sure you might still buy an IBM PC, but you were pulling for the brash young kid with the big dreams to make it, because that was the American way. And both he and his older, mentor-like company president were talking about "betting the company" on the new Macintosh. Talk like that was guaranteed to appeal to an America where the go-for-broke mentality was always a birthright.

In the third quarter of Super Bowl 18 (in which the Los Angeles Raiders defeated the Washington Redskins by the score of 38 to 9) Apple's controversial "1984" ad aired. The company served notice that it was indeed going for broke in a way that few other companies would have dared. That year the Super Bowl telecast was estimated by the television rating firm A.C. Nielson to have reached 46.4 percent of the households in America, a full 50 percent of the nation's men and 36 percent of the women. They were treated to an ad that was unlike anything they had seen before, something akin to the rock videos that were just starting to appear on the new cable television channel MTV.

The ad opened with an off-key musical chord, which quickly segued to a soundtrack combining an uncomfortable rhythmical sound with that of thousands of trudging feet. In a bleached-out gray world, rows and rows of shaved-headed people—whether they were slaves, prisoners, or citizens was unclear—tramped in endless succession. Above them a giant face on a video monitor—Big Brother himself by implication—dispassionately delivered a faintly audible speech. Every few seconds a quick intercut showed a young, attractive, blonde woman wearing red shorts and a Macintosh T-shirt, the only colors in this otherwise drab world, running through the labyrinthine building where all this was going on. Surreally, she carried a sledgehammer and was being pursued by a gang of lumbering, helmeted "thought" police. Eventually, she reached a large auditorium where more of the affectless hordes were gathered, sitting on rows of wooden benches staring up at the face of their leader. As she neared the wall-to-wall screen, she suddenly stopped, whirled around, and tossed the sledgehammer into the middle of the giant video monitor. A strong fresh wind blew across the massed audience. Superimposed over it all came a line that the narrator repeated: "On January 24th Apple Computer will introduce Macintosh. And you'll understand why 1984 won't be like *1984*."

Even in a football game where the third quarter was producing all the scoring that Los Angeles needed to win the game, the ad was a show stopper. All over the nation conversations came to a standstill as people couldn't believe what they had seen. In an advertising business built on sameness and follow the leader, it was a powerful statement of Apple's willingness to lead the personal computer industry. A diversity of reactions followed, but one thing was certain: It had created waves, which was exactly what Steve wanted. All of a sudden, millions of people were aware of something called the Macintosh.

The day of the unveiling, the January 24, 1984, annual share-holders' meeting, was one of Steve's finest. He had been up until 3 that morning with the software wizards, trying to iron out the last bugs in the demonstration software he was to use. That morning he started with his best bow tie and wore a double-breasted, black tuxedo jacket. Then he watched from backstage as the Flint Center Auditorium at De Anza Junior College, a stone's throw away from Apple's growing collection of buildings, filled up. In the first few rows were the members of the Mac team, wearing their Macintosh T-shirts and bubbling with the enthusi-asm they all shared. The music that blared from the speakers as the audience gathered in their seats was the theme song by Vangelis from the film *Chariots of Fire*, a movie sweeping the nation whose theme was the success of an underdog. This wasn't just a computer introduction; it was a revivalist meeting in the grand American tradition of evangelism.

This one was all about believing that the little box of plastic, metal, and silicon that was about to be unveiled could change the world. But how, and to what, no one was certain.

Steve had created and honed this pseudo-religion, the concept that the world needed computers and that computers would make life better. But never, ever, was it clear just how this was going to happen or exactly what they would do to improve the world so dramatically. That was part of his crowd-swaying tactics, part of his power. He baffled and inspired his audience with big, poetic concepts and let them imagine the multiple uses of the machines. Electronics was good. It was new. It was American. It was "clean." Ergo, personal computers were good. And the Macintosh was better. It was faith, and he was the preacher.

Finally, the lights dimmed and Steve appeared at the podium in a spotlight. He opened the meeting with a shrug of his shoulders and a strangely unmodulated recitation of a few lines from his favorite poet, Bob Dylan. In his faintly high-pitched voice, a voice with a touch of the squeaky kid to it, he started the meeting:

> *Come writers and critics*
> *Who prophesize with your pen*
> *And keep your eyes wide*
> *The chance won't come again*
> *And don't speak too soon*
> *For the wheel's still in spin*
> *And there's no tellin' who*
> *That its namin'*
> *For the loser now*
> *Will be later to win*
> *For the times they are a-changin'*[3]

It must have been the first time that Bob Dylan's lyrics opened a shareholders' meeting. There was a smattering of applause from the Macintosh partisans in the front, but bewilderment from the shareholders in the rest of the audience. A knowing cynicism came from the press, who were used to the techniques of crowd manipulation employed by Apple's boy wonder.

With that out of the way, a multiple-projector slide show came on screen, accompanied by the pulsing sound track song of the movie *Flashdance*, rewritten for the occasion. The song was based on the line

"Apple, oh what a feeling!" and featured hundreds of images of the computers being used by good, solid yuppies, the Apple market that the company could discover by looking in the mirror. Next came the stolid Al Eisenstadt, Apple's general counsel, to dispose of the business of the annual meeting.

He was followed by Sculley, who presented the company's balance sheet, profit, and earnings information, detailing the firm's rise to a business with gross sales of $983 million in fiscal 1983, a company poised on the brink of becoming a billion-dollar corporation eight years after its founding in a garage. He was greeted with hearty applause as he described Apple's strong cash position, with no long-term debt, and the reorganization of the company into two product families: Apple II, and Apple 32, which comprised both the Lisa and the Mac. Furthermore, he revealed that sales of the Apple IIe had broken all records in December, giving the company strong momentum even as they prepared to introduce new products a month later and glossing over the fact that the final quarter of the previous fiscal year had been Apple's first ever nonprofit one. Then, speaking of "developing a relationship with Steve Jobs" as the greatest thing that had happened to him since coming to Apple, Sculley reintroduced Apple's chairman.

Steve appeared with a carrying case that he carefully set on a table. Then he started, in darkness lit only by a flashlight, by recounting the history of computing from a pro-Apple, anti-IBM point of view. "The year is 1958," he began, bringing a breathless sense of urgency to the recitation that one wag called his Edward R. Murrow imitation, "and a small company has succeeded in perfecting a new technology. It is called xerography. IBM has the opportunity to acquire rights to the new technology but elects not to. Thus Xerox is born."[4]

From there, with a mix of cutting sarcasm and hype, he moved through the minicomputer business—here DEC became a giant and IBM again refused to get involved—to the personal computer business and Apple's founding. Then he mentioned the introduction of the IBM PC and finally jumped to 1984. The "1984" ad played. To tumultuous applause, the lights came up, and the visionary of computing finally described the features of the Macintosh with slides—still without actually having shown its distinctive shape. He ended with a quick comparison of the chip in the IBM PC, the Intel 8088, and the Mac's Motorola 68000, that he punctuated with, "and it eats 8088's for breakfast."[5]

After a jaunty walk across the stage, he silently lifted the machine out of its carrying case, turned it on, and inserted a disk that had been produced the day before by Hertzfeld and the crazies of the software brigade. Big letters spelling out M-A-C-I-N-T-O-S-H slowly floated across the computer screen and slid along the enormous projection screen behind him. The audience went wild. A standing ovation lasted several minutes. The 100 Mac team members started cheering and crying. For all of them it was a catharsis. Steve's eyes glistened as he stared at his team in the front rows, and he told the audience, "The folks who built the Mac are sitting in the first five rows. They must be feeling pretty good right now."[6]

Then, with the applause still ringing, he told the gathering that he had done enough talking. Now it was time to let the Mac talk for itself. With a prototype voice synthesis program, the Mac gave a little speech written by Hertzfeld and Capps. In a tinny, computer-generated voice, the Macintosh addressed the assembly:

Hello, I am Macintosh. It sure is great to get out of that bag. Unaccustomed as I am to public speaking, I'd like to share with you a maxim I thought of the first time I met an IBM mainframe: Never trust a computer you can't lift!

Obviously I can talk, but right now I'd like to sit back and listen. So it is with considerable pride that I introduce the man who's been like a father to me, Steve Jobs.[7]

Again, the auditorium erupted. With that Steve went into his full-power sales pitch, talking about the 25 million "knowledge workers" in small- and medium-sized offices at whom the Mac was targeted, and the 11 million college students who were "the knowledge workers of tomorrow." Over and over, he talked about how the Macintosh was the computer "for the rest of us," and the sales campaign was off and running. He also introduced three new Lisa models as well as a number of peripheral devices for the Mac: the printer, the disk drive, and the numerical keypad. It was a performance as flawless and seamless as any he had ever given. It carried on throughout the events onstage and in the press conference that he and John Sculley held afterward, when premier issues of the slick magazine *Macworld*, with Steve on the cover, were distributed to everyone at the meeting. *INC.* magazine described him as the "missionary of micros. Steven Jobs may, in fact, be the microcomputer industry's first rock 'n' roll superstar."

Sure there were a few discouraging words in the avalanche of press coverage that followed: complaints about memory size and the lack of expandability, doubts about the size of the screen or the dependence upon Lisa technology, which had been disgraced by the failure of that computer in the marketplace. Cynical reporters asked whether Steve and the Mac team had done any research into what the public might want or need in a personal computer. "Did Alexander Graham Bell do any market research before he invented the telephone?" was always his off-the-cuff reply. "If Mac's sales are just average, then our vision of the world is significantly wrong."[8]

Steve was self-assured when it came to Apple Computer. The 28-year-old millionaire was the personification of the "Me Generation," the very symbol of success to a generation who, in the shadow of Ronald Reagan's conservatism, wanted to make money more than they wanted to stop the arms race or follow a spiritual journey. The irony was that Steve had started the whole enterprise with a very idealistic attitude that was shared by his elders, a countercultural value set that by 1984 had all but been rejected by the nation's youth, the blossoming generation of yuppies, his peers. By then he, too, had lost sight of his starting point and had severed the roots that had originally nourished the dream.

The Mac was an instant success on campus. The Apple University Consortium, announced on the same day as the machine itself, included some of the country's leading universities. Harvard, Stanford, Princeton, Brown, and eight other universities contracted to spend more than $2 million each in the coming two years buying Macintoshes at greatly reduced prices, which they could in turn sell their students cheaply. The announcement caused rumblings in the dealer channel, since thousands of sales would bypass local college town computer dealers. However, the problems with the strategy were more than made up for by the establishment of a massive beachhead in a market that was critical for the long-term success of the computer. And, not unwittingly, selling directly to the universities, even at reduced cost, was a highly profitable coup for the company. The contracts called for little follow-up support from the company, meaning no costly hand-holding or sales support to eat up profits.

The other major flank of their strategy—the third-party software seeding effort—looked more successful than it actually was as the machine was introduced. Other than Microsoft's BASIC and *Multiplan*, both of which were riddled with bugs and quickly withdrawn to be re-released a few months later, no other third-party software was available on the day of introduction. To cover themselves, the McKenna agency had Mitch Kapor, Bill Gates, and Fred Gibbons (of Personal Software, another successful software house) standing by to lend credence to their development efforts on the Mac. Gates even went so far as to say that he expected half of Microsoft's revenue to come from Macintosh products during the coming year. The three men gave the machine a stamp of approval that made other software companies want to start developing for the Mac.

Dealers were enthusiastic, and customers flocked to shops to see for themselves what all the hype and hoopla was about. Orders poured in, and the critical first 100 days—Steve repeatedly talked about the "window of opportunity" they had to exploit during the first 100 days— saw the 70,000 sales he claimed were essential to making the Macintosh a viable alternative to the IBM PC. The first $10 million in advertising included the series of extensive magazine inserts and a big television campaign. The ads that hit the Winter Olympics telecasts a few weeks later featured the soft music of Windham Hill Records and a graphic demonstration of the difference in size of the training manuals for the PC versus those for the Mac. They were a sophisticated and warmly comforting series that contrasted strongly with the harsh and frightening images of the Super Bowl ad but were nonetheless just as effective. Within a year, the style that this series ushered in became something of a cliche in the advertising world, just as "1984" carried all the top honors in the advertising industry's CLIO Awards sweepstakes. Having a computer company's advertising at the top of the heap was unprecedented.

The strategy that the Mac marketing team and Steve had launched was an extraordinary success, but there was a dark side to it. The danger in creating such a ground swell of media attention and acclaim is that it becomes impossible to separate the true market messages from the hype. During the first 100 days, there was so much noise, so much advertising, so many people crowding so many stores, and so many orders backlogging the production capability of the Fremont plant that the machine appeared to be an enormous success.

By 1984, however, several things had changed in the personal computer marketplace since the early days of the Apple II. Steve and his crew didn't see the changes. First there were more "early innovators," to use a "psychographics" term popular in Apple's marketing meetings, than anyone had imagined. The years of Apple II and IBM PC sales had produced a large subculture of affluent, sophisticated computer-literate people who wanted to be the first on their blocks to have the latest in "whizzy" technology, i.e., a Macintosh. The orders that they placed, combined with a new generation of computer-interested people who were drawn into the stores to see the Mac, but not necessarily to buy one, contributed to the success of the introduction.

Second, working computers didn't have the short half-life of many consumer products. Once you had invested your money, there had to be an extraordinarily compelling reason to buy another machine, especially if the original one did what you needed. Although the IBM PC may not have been at the cutting edge of technology, it was better than adequate at performing the tasks most business buyers required: spreadsheets and word processing. The Macintosh's ease of use, mouse, and graphical user interface were an advantage for naive users, but in 1984 they weren't the ones buying computers.

Steve's megalomania and the reinforcement he always received from his insular band of like-minded pirates made him certain that the Mac would instantly make headway in the business market. "We thought we had the most precocious child in the world," says Steve Capps, the group's software relief pitcher. "People would see the machine, fall in love with it, realize that we were right, and instantly buy it." Unfortunately, hordes of business users didn't shove IBM PCs off their desks to make room for the Mac.

And finally, Apple had thoroughly underestimated the power requirements of users, even the unsophisticated knowledge workers they were after. "I thought people would fool around with it for a year before needing more power," explains Chris Espinosa, the "guardian of the user interface" and head of the documentation group. "But apparently, while we were locked away in our ivory tower, the world outside was moving very fast."

The 64 kilobytes of ROM, 128 kilobytes of main RAM memory, and the single-sided disk drives simply weren't large enough to handle the requirements of a graphics-intensive system like the Mac. The machine's limitations were especially obvious when developers tried to create the types of sophisticated software programs that could make the machine a success. The potential was there in the hardware, but the computer Apple had delivered was still a weakling.

In Cupertino the problem of creeping optimism was raging, and soon the chairman's predictions of 750,000 units for the calendar year 1984 seemed, if anything, conservative. If they could sell that many Macs right away (70,000), the sales figures would theoretically increase monthly and go right through the roof. Sculley was so captivated by Steve's vision in the wake of what looked for all the world like the hottest computer introduction of all time that he provided no brakes. And in any case he had no experience in big-ticket items such as computers. He went right along with the forecasts, and when Floyd Kvamme, the executive vice-president of sales and marketing, and Ken Zerbe, the executive vice-president of finance and administration, both started to raise doubts, they were removed and reassigned, respectively. The Macintosh would be the company's savior after the disaster of the Lisa, and in 1984 Sculley was Steve's biggest supporter.

A couple of days after the Macintosh introduction, Steve was getting ready to take over the reins of the newly merged Lisa and Mac groups. The seeds of the merger of both teams into the Apple 32 division had been sowed six months earlier at a dinner meeting with Steve, Sculley, Jay Elliott, and Wayne Rosing, head of the Lisa group. The meeting had been called to try to devise a strategy for the future of the Lisa, and the others were surprised when Rosing, with no argument, offered to disband the Lisa team in exchange for support in developing an educational computer system that he wanted to build. With no advocate, Sculley quickly decided that the Lisa team had to be merged into the Macintosh group and that Steve was the guy to head the combined division. Steve didn't want to run a big, unwieldy division in those days, however, and at first resisted the idea. Then, as he listened to Sculley telling him that he was the only one who had what it took, he changed his mind and decided that managing a large group would be a good learning step for him. They kept the whole thing quiet until after the introduction hoopla was over, and then one day Rosing invited Steve and his team to the Lisa building to make the merger official.

Steve turned in one of his most aggressive and obnoxious performances. Riding on the crest of the Macintosh's success, emboldened by the dawning realization that Sculley was under his thumb, and unbridled by the absence of the one corporate officer who could always bring him up short, Jay Elliott, Steve cut loose. With both groups gathered in the atrium of the Lisa building, according to one who witnessed the events, his first words to the Lisa people were, "You guys really fucked up." It went downhill from there. He accused them of creating a shoddy computer that never worked, and was too slow and too expensive. He told them they were "a bloated division. I'm going to have to lay a lot of you off." Then he contrasted the Lisa project with the great success of the Mac and the small team that had done it. Finally, as if he hadn't done enough to destroy the morale of the entire division, he added that the Mac people would be their managers, and that although the Mac team was welcome in the Lisa building, the Lisa people "can only come over to Bandley 3 [the Mac building] if specifically invited."

It was an incredible performance. Some on the Mac team were appalled by his remarks. "I was embarrassed to be part of Macintosh," says Donn Denman. "I looked over at the Lisa people as he was going on with his tirade, and there was pure hatred in their eyes. I couldn't blame them." That, however, was by no means the only reaction. Others thought that Steve's comments were absolutely correct. "I thought it was his finest hour," says Hertzfeld. "It was just what he needed to say. They had screwed up."

Although the new division was officially known as the Apple 32 division, colloquially it was always called the Macintosh division. Steve's performance was an astonishing harbinger of things to come, of the inhumanity at the core of Apple and the loss of the values upon which the company had supposedly been founded.

Steve was forever talking about his ideas for an untraditional corporation. "As companies start to grow in sales to several billions, they start to turn into vanilla corporations," he once explained. "Ten to fifteen years ago, if you asked people to make a list of the five most exciting companies in America, Polaroid and Xerox would have been on everyone's list. Where are they now? What happened?

"Companies, as they grow to become multibillion-dollar entities, somehow lose their vision. They insert lots of layers of middle management between the people running the company and the people doing the work. They no longer have an inherent feel or a passion about the products. The creative people, the ones who care passionately, have to persuade five layers of management to do what they know is the right thing. The great people leave, and you end up with mediocrity. The way we will not become a vanilla corporation is to put together small teams of great people and set them off to build their dreams. We are artists, not engineers."[9]

Steve had neglected to recognize one of the fundamental aspects of a progressive work environment: humanism. Although he had the vision and drive to spur his artist-engineers to do superb work, he had never developed the empathy of others' feelings that can then make those exceptional people continue to produce exceptional work for decades. Steve's style chewed up talent and spat it out. Taking over in the merger of the Lisa and Mac teams was the first step in what Steve saw as his next evolutionary leap: He was meant to run all of Apple, and the time for it was fast approaching.

The change was closely watched by Jay Elliott, the only other member of the Mac team besides Steve to sit on the company's executive staff. Elliott was Apple's vice-president of human resources and was a keen student of corporate organizational strategy. He watched the relationship between Sculley and Steve with growing apprehension during the first few months of 1984. "John was the president," says Elliott, "but all the power was with Steve. At executive staff meetings, all you had to do was watch the body language. Steve and John would talk to each other, but everyone else who was supposedly reporting to John spent all their time talking to Steve. He was in charge."

What had happened was simple: Now that Macintosh was a real product, it needed the support of all facets of the company. This meant that for the first time Steve was intimately concerned with the distribution of computers, the entirety of marketing, sales, manufacturing, sales support, and service. He lacked expertise in coordinating all these functions since he had no experience handling them—he had always been involved in the more dramatic new product efforts at Apple—and that meant certain chaos unless he was steered in the right direction.

Always a meddler who was decisive in attacking a solution espoused by another, Steve was strangely indecisive when faced with a number of options. "Steve is like a good poker player," said one Mac team member. "He'll go around to five or six people with the same idea, as if he's already made up his mind, but he's watching their eyes to see how they'll react." Although he often made snap judgments, he also had a streak of insecurity. In areas where he knew very little, he always doubted himself even as he bluffed his way through. That insecurity drove him to make his designers and engineers modify and rework their designs until he was able to fully understand what they were doing and what it was that he really wanted. At the top of a corporation, that indecision and bluster hiding a lack of real knowledge was paralyzing and created enormous amounts of wasted effort.

Sculley had been hired to make those decisions, but he wasn't the strong-willed, decisive leader Apple needed. He was quiet and somewhat retiring, almost a diffident president who did not stand up to Steve. He was calculating and cunning but not forceful. Executive staff meetings ended up being free-for-alls, with the loudest voice winning and Steve, as the undisputed founder and guiding light of the company, usually taking precedence. As the months passed, Sculley was "unwilling or unable," according to Elliott, to rein in the wild and moody chairman of the board, and Steve grew more and more powerful.

By the spring of 1984, Sculley had been at Cupertino for one year, but he had shown no signs of learning how to fight. Steve only respected those who stood up to him and fought him off. In fairness to Sculley, it must have been nearly impossible to call down Steve, a man whose appointment calendar was filled up months in advance. A man who hobnobbed with the powerful and famous. A man who by early 1984 had become a major media star whose face was widely known and whose opinion was sought daily.

Now that the pressure of the Macintosh introduction was past them, it was time to turn the company into a well-oiled machine. Steve grew increasingly disenchanted with Sculley's leadership style. His fawning, almost adoring respect for the young product visionary turned the tables. "We hired John to be Steve's mentor," explains Elliott, "and it ended up being the other way around. It was Steve who taught John."

The increasingly important Macintosh group started to treat Sculley as a kind of joke. For instance, late in 1983 the president started pushing for an MS-DOS compatible disk drive for the Macintosh. Sculley realized that having such a capability would greatly expand the Macintosh's acceptability in the all-important business market. He asked Bob Belleville to work on developing one, and Belleville agreed. Thereafter, at each staff meeting he asked Belleville how it was coming along, and each time Belleville mumbled that he was working on it.

But he wasn't. Steve, who was not about to offer IBM compatibility on the Macintosh, had told Belleville to string Sculley along. There was no MS-DOS drive in the works, and eventually someone else on the staff had to tell the president that it didn't exist.

Sculley's marketing instincts drew mixed reactions. "PepsiCo owns both Pepsi and Frito-Lay," says Murray, "and both of them sell through the same outlets—supermarkets—without competing with each other. To him, that was the same as us having the Apple II and Macintosh families selling through the same computer stores. But we all thought there was something fundamentally different about computers from soft drinks and potato chips."

In the weeks after the Macintosh introduction, Steve received two strong endorsements: BusinessLand and Sears Business Centers signed up to carry the Mac. When the sales figures started to come in, showing that they had sold more than 70,000 computers, there was an occasion for celebration. The occasion he chose was the product introduction event for a new model of the Apple II, the IIc. The "c" stood for compact, which reflected Steve's vision of what the II should have been all along. It was small, easily portable, and completely self-contained, with no room for expansion slots or hardware add-ons. This was Apple's version of a Sony Walkman.

The impetus for building this computer came from another of Steve's sudden brainstorms. Late in 1982, just before the Apple IIe was introduced, he had stormed into Peter Quinn's cubicle. Quinn was the chief engineer on the IIe and a man who had fought Steve tooth and nail for the company resources he needed to make the IIe a success. Their battles, and his machine's subsequent success, meant that Steve respected Quinn as he respected few others in the Apple II division. Without any preliminary pleasantries, Steve dropped a IIe circuit board onto the middle of Quinn's desk, a new low-profile keyboard that he'd just discovered on one side, and an Apple II disk drive on the other.

Quinn recalls that Steve said imperiously, "That is a great product. Do you want to do it?"

Quinn knew that when the chairman was on a tear, it behooved him to clamber aboard. "Sure Steve," he replied unctuously, looking at the already created parts. "We're half done."

"Great. Then do it." Away he went, and that was that. The compact machine was a "go" project. The only part of it that Steve had anything further to do with was the design of the case. He wanted something really sexy for this one since it was aimed at the home market and consumers would buy the machines through department stores such as Macy's. He'd recently met the German designer of the Sony Walkman,

Hartmet Esslinger, at a design conference and decided that Apple should have a similarly portable computer. So he gave Esslinger's firm, Frogdesign, this project to cut their teeth on, and they created an elegantly portable Apple II with no expansion capabilities. Everything was built in. Steve finally had his way with Woz's Apple II. It went hand in hand with his no-expansion Macintosh. Steve's personal product vision was supreme, and he could finally feel that he had exorcised the demon of Wozniak from his system.

To introduce the machine in April of 1984, the company rented the Moscone Center, San Francisco's new underground exhibition hall, and put on an extravaganza. In the middle of all the acclaim for the Apple II family, which was highlighted by the theme "Apple II Forever," Steve gave a little speech about his Macintosh, bragging about how the 100-day sales had exceeded his wildest hopes. He went on to say that the Mac was the Apple II of the eighties. The audience roared its approval, and next-day coverage of the event generally highlighted the exceptional sales of the Macintosh and mentioned how Apple was trying to breathe life into its obsolete and dying Apple II family. Steve had struck yet another blow against Woz's machine.

Because of the way Apple's financial accounting system worked, Steve was constantly brought face to face with his old nemesis, the Apple II. Each division was a "profit center," and the Apple II and Apple 32 divisions vied with each other for better monthly results. Steve was extremely competitive, and the monthly staff meetings turned into detailed comparisons of the profits of each group. His mood was entirely dependent upon whether he won or not, regardless of what was good for Apple.

After the IIc introduction Steve went into conference with Belleville and Murray to dream up a new marketing strategy for the family of products that they were going to have the following year. First was the FatMac, a standard Macintosh with 512 kilobytes of RAM instead of the 128 kilobytes of the original machine. The only things holding it up were the availability of inexpensive 256 kilobyte chips and Steve's opposition. He had fought the expansion of memory for months. He continued to cling to the ancient Raskin doctrine of one version of the computer, but he finally washed his hands of the matter and let his people make the decision. The price floor was dropping out of the memory chip market, and it looked as if they might be able to announce the new machine as early as the fall.

The rest of the product strategy came from a single-page memo that Belleville had written a year before, which effectively espoused the entire Xerox office computing strategy he had helped develop albeit at a lower price. The LaserWriter, Apple's laser printer, was well along the road, although its introduction had recently slipped from the summer NCC in Anaheim and now looked definite for the 1985 annual shareholders' meeting. Then there were the AppleBus/AppleNet communications protocols, which would allow Macs to be linked in office work groups. This system, eventually renamed AppleTalk, was nearing completion. Belleville was also promising a pair of servers that would extend the power of a group of Macs: The ImageServer would be used with the LaserWriter; and the FileServer, an all-purpose device, would be used to store shared files in a work group.

All in all, it was an impressive collection of equipment that could really extend the power of a Macintosh in small groups. In the wings were also a number of other products, including *MacPhone*, a joint project with AT&T that promised to marry a telephone with the power of the Mac; *TurboMac*, which was Burrell Smith's idea for bringing an internal hard disk and increased performance to the Macintosh family; the *Big Mac*, which had a larger screen and color as well as an internal hard disk; a new, higher quality, dot matrix printer codenamed *Express*; and a number of hard disk storage systems developed by several outside manufacturers, one of which the company would select and sell under the Apple label. However, there was little product strategy, no matter how much Sculley liked to talk about making Apple's product strategy cohesive. As they talked about the new product mix, they tried to come up with some identifying name for the whole group.

Throughout the introduction of the Mac, Steve was haunted by IBM's shadow. In all his appearances, he continually attacked Big Blue and what he called their mainframe-based approach to personal computers. He wanted a dogfight between Apple and IBM, because that at least meant that Apple had decimated all the smaller competition. With the apparent success of Macintosh and a bevy of products that his engineering manager told him were on the horizon, he and Murray felt that they could make the final move in the chess game to crush IBM once and for all and to show the giant corporation who was really boss in the personal computer business.

At the height of Steve's power, with what he perceived as the success of Apple's newest products, he decided to launch a frontal attack on IBM. Suddenly, he had the inspiration he needed. They would call their next family of products *The Macintosh Office*. It would show the world that Apple had the kind of office appliances that every office and office worker needed.

Steve was ready to rattle the world's cage in earnest. He was railing at the gods. Now David wanted to bring Goliath to the mat. He was convinced that he could do no wrong, that his instincts were infallible. Although Steve's was a story rooted in the twentieth century's Silicon Valley, the ancient Greeks had a word for what he was exhibiting. They called it *hubris*, the insolent pride that a human exhibited when he thought he could challenge the gods. And the gods' response was always the same: They would strike down the arrogant human with a bolt or two from the heavens.

17
Bluebusters

In late 1984 Steve moved into his new house in Woodside. It was a two-story Spanish-style mansion overlooking seven acres of woodlands for which he paid $1.6 million. Moving in was something of a misnomer. Steve never believed in having much furniture, and the new house, which was still being remodeled a year after his purchase, was no exception. Dark and somewhat forbidding inside—an impression he tried to dispel with several interior decorators and a stream of craftsmen—the house had its own water supply from a nearby well, a long private driveway, and lots of empty rooms.

For a while, a pair of huge Bosendorfer pianos occupied the living room. Steve was trying to decide how to put one of the $10,000 pianos in the atrium of the Mac team's building without inciting a riot from the rest of Apple. Subtly, Elliott had taken him aside one day after the Lisa team debacle and suggested that he needed to "cool it" with the perks for the Mac team. He had bought the piano with his own money, he contended, so what business was it of anyone else's? Eventually he had the piano and his BMW motorcycle carted to the atrium in Bandley 3 to be put on display. Steve was convinced that just having superb products hanging around influenced the team in their own designs, but even he realized that the Bosendorfer was a bit much. Every once in a while, they invited Liz Story, a Windham Hill pianist, to play the instrument, but otherwise it languished next to the pair of six-foot-high speakers. It was the video games—*Defender*, of course, and *Joust*—that were played.

Bringing in high-priced products did not stanch the flow of Macintosh people out of the company. There were the burn-out cases like Hertzfeld, who had decided he was going to leave long before the Mac was released and only waited out of loyalty to the product. Others, like Bruce Horn, needed a break. The real shock to most of the team came after the Mac and Lisa merger, when the Mac members suddenly found that they were being paid only a fraction of the amounts their Lisa counterparts were making. Engineers in the Lisa division were routinely drawing salaries in the $50,000 a year range, while only Hertzfeld, Murray, Belleville, and Smith rated that in the Mac constellation. Steve had been able to create allegiance to the concept of the Mac and paid salaries in the $30,000 to $40,000 range for work far beyond the call of duty. The merger created not only "extreme depression among the engineers,"[1] as one Lisa manager wrote in a memo, but also a minor uprising among the Macintosh folks, who found themselves supervising personnel who brought in much higher salaries.

Steve attempted to solve the problem by awarding generous bonuses to his Mac people—bonuses equal to a year's salary weren't rare after the Mac's introduction in 1984—but that only rankled the Apple II division. The Apple II was still paying the way for all of them at that point, and no one had given them such bonuses after the success of their Apple IIe introduction a year earlier. Jay Elliott tried to console the different factions, explaining that the leased cars, the first-class business travel, bonuses, nannies, and other perks made things equitable between the Mac and Lisa groups even if financial compensation was at different levels.

Elliott's reasoning didn't do much good. The dedicated Mac people felt betrayed and used by Steve, and he was never able to regain their trust. The prevailing feeling was that they had given their hearts and sold their souls to Steve and the Mac, and he had treated them poorly and underpaid them for the privilege to boot. Just as when Apple had gone public and he had had a chance to reward his loyal followers but didn't, Steve showed that he was still a scrooge at heart. Although he often professed that money meant little to him, his employees felt as if money was the only way that he could really show his gratitude. The situation made them question their involvement in his schemes, and the grumbling in Bandley 3 started to become audible. By mid-1984, Steve had isolated himself in the executive suite with his group leaders, and the grumbling went unheard.

A few days after the Apple IIc introduction, the first of several red lights started flashing in the Macintosh division. As is often the case, it was a financial alert. Susan Barnes, who had been elevated to the position of group controller when Debi Coleman took over the factory, noticed that project budgets were getting out of hand. This was especially true in engineering, where suddenly dozens of projects, with little central coordination, were in the works. While it was by no means a crisis yet—they were still forecasting sales of 40,000 units per month—it was a matter for concern. Both Belleville and Murray warned their teams that closer attention had to be paid to the financial aspects of the decisions they were making. Budgets had to be realistic, for one thing. It was the first time that strict cost accounting was set in place in the Macintosh division. But it was realism, Apple style. Murray's marketing budget alone for the second year of the Mac was $60 million—better than a million dollars *a week* in the hands of a 29-year-old two years out of business school.

Another growing problem had to be confronted that May. Software and hardware products for the Macintosh from third-party developers were not appearing as quickly as developers had promised. The joke that made the rounds with the introduction of the Mac was that four programs were available: *MacPaint*, *MacWrite*, *MacPaint*, and *MacWrite*. *Multiplan* and Microsoft BASIC were re-released with bug fixes, but Microsoft *Chart*, *Word*, and *File* were delayed again and didn't appear likely until the fall. Writing code for the machine was much more complex than they had hoped. At least 200 projects were in development, but only a handful neared shipping. They received information from Lotus that their as yet unnamed project was delayed again and instead of appearing in the summer of 1984 might not make it out until sometime in 1985. Having software for the Mac was crucial to the credibility and success of the machine in the business world, and the success of *Lotus 1-2-3* for the IBM PC had made that company's integrated program for the Macintosh a kind of bellwether for the market's acceptance of the computer. Delays at Lotus seriously hurt the Mac's credibility.

Guy Kawasaki, a charming, hale-fellow-well-met type, took over the third-party evangelism role from Mike Boich, as the original marketing coordinator turned his attention to co-writing a communications program, *MacTerminal*, with Haeberli. Kawasaki crisscrossed the country stoking the fires of enthusiasm at every hole-in-the-wall software operation he could find. As a strategy, Steve hit on the idea of offering financial incentives—matching marketing funds or bonuses— to some key developers if they could bring their products to the market early. The primary recipient at that time was supposed to be a word processing program called *MacAuthor*, developed by a group in Seattle that included former Mac software manager Bud Tribble. In 1982, concerned that he had all his word processing eggs in one basket with Wigginton's *MacWrite*, Steve decided to second-source the product. Second-sourcing was the development of alternate suppliers, primarily in the hardware component world, so that a manufacturer could not be held hostage by one supplier. Steve had long been an advocate of it, and with Apple's clout, they had been able to fund a number of small electronics companies with backup contracts.

In that spirit, Steve gave the green light to Tribble's group. To hide their real intentions from Wigginton, who claims he didn't find out about the other word processing program until after the Mac was introduced in 1984, the *MacAuthor* team was officially creating a spelling checker program for *MacWrite*. By the summer of 1984, they were nearing completion of the project, or so they reported. Steve and Murray decided that if they were offered a substantial incentive such as $10,000 they might be able to get it finished for the fall. Then the program could join three internal projects that were nearly finished: *MacProject* for project management; *MacDraw*, which was a drafting program; and *MacBASIC*, the long-delayed BASIC language for the machine.

It wasn't just software that was hurting them. Steve also thoroughly miscalled the need for better storage solutions. One of his major mistakes was not providing compatibility with a hard disk, a mass storage device with the capacity of many disks, on the original Macintosh. Then he also refused to provide help to hardware manufacturers who saw the Mac as a viable business opportunity. Companies such as Tecmar, Corvus, and Davong tried to make their equipment work with the Mac, but because of the design of the Macintosh hardware system and the lack of aid from Apple, their equipment was unreliable and had to work in decidedly un-Macintosh ways in order to function at all.

The Mac's single internal floppy disk drive configuration also caused serious disfavor among users. Disk swapping—the need to alternate a pair of disks interminably in a single disk drive when saving a document or transferring a file—was unbearably tedious. Inside Apple, where many external disk drives existed as prototypes, that was not viewed as a big problem. Customers, however, didn't get an external disk drive until the summer of 1984, and even then only in limited quantities. Users had to go through contortions to make the Macintosh work, and the Mac team was oblivious to their problems.

The public was saddled with Steve's original dream machine while he and the rest of the team were charging ahead with a fresh set of horses, the next generation of products. Although its innovations were spectacular and forever changed the way personal computers would be viewed, the Mac as introduced was an underpowered machine, with too little memory, and an unwieldy disk storage situation. The lack of controlled final testing—and the long hours and intense deadlines before release—had resulted in buggy System and Finder software. Early users encountered system crashes and locked files. It was not a situation likely to instill confidence in the business world. Isolated in the Silicon tower of Apple's four-story Cupertino headquarters, Steve was oblivious to the problems of his machine. He was working on the future products of the company and couldn't pause to see that his baby had serious imperfections.

All of Steve's huffing and puffing couldn't keep the sales figures from dropping dramatically as June of 1984 came around. At first Steve refused to believe them, but when the figures for the second month in a row showed the downward trend continuing, a low-level panic started to set in. First the company lowered the retail cost of the machine to $1,995 from the introductory $2,495, but the price reduction had no significant impact on sales. Then they decided to accelerate the introduction of the 512K Mac to September, and Murray devised a "Test Drive a Mac" program, which Steve enthusiastically endorsed. None of it worked. As the months churned by, the Apple 32 division, which was nearing 1,000 people, was in no way supported by income, and widespread resentment set in within the rest of Apple. The much-vaunted product of the aristocrats of the company—the Brahmins—was floundering, and yet they were still not reined in by Sculley or the board.

Steve ordered a massive market research test to find out why the Mac was stalled. The results were chilling. They used the "mystery shopper" concept as well as traditional focus groups. The former consisted of shoppers entering a computer store to see how salespeople presented options. They found that sales people always introduced the IBM PC first, even if the shopper asked about the Mac. They were losing with the salesmen. In the focus groups, it turned out that customers loved the graphics, the clarity of the screen, and the ease of use of the Mac, but they disliked its closed architecture, small screen, and lack of color even more.

All the glamor of innovation, all the concentration on vision and idealism, all of Steve's personal charisma and celebrity status had suddenly turned out to be a serious liability. People bought computers not out of emotion but out of need. While Apple was admired for its industry leadership, it was distrusted because of its erratic history and the off-the-cuff comments of its chairman. IBM was safe and secure; Apple was an incandescent rocket. IBM sold to businesses; Apple to individuals. And most important of all, computer store salespeople consistently sold the IBM PC.

Steve took that research as a slap in the face and, in typical fashion, didn't turn the other cheek but declared war. The Macintosh Office was going to be the answer. He decreed it to be so, he decided that all the pieces would be ready when he needed them, and his key advisors agreed with him. He would will it all into existence if need be. He would conjure it up out of thin air. The next year he would finally have the right combination of items to tackle IBM head to head, he told his people, and he would lead the company into battle. He was convinced that his destiny was to prove to Big Blue that Apple was the greater force, and by extension that he could prevail. This was the last line that "Big Brother'" had uttered on the video screen before the young woman threw the sledgehammer during the "1984" spot: "We will prevail!" Inside Apple, the wags in the Apple II division had twisted the meaning of that ad and had seen it as depicting Steve. He was Big Brother, and the Apple II team was trying to throw the sledgehammer to free the company from his tyranny.

As he continued to watch the sales figures for the Mac drop, Steve became even more convinced that he was on a religious quest to rid the world of the dreaded Big Blue. They were the ones who were destroying his Mac, wringing all life and innovation out of the personal computer revolution that he had started nearly ten years before. He had to bring The Macintosh Office into existence for the good of mankind. It was high noon at the OK Corral, and the young gunslinger was ready to attack. In his mind, he was wearing the white hat. He wasn't just fighting for Apple, but for the good of the country. He saw it as a noble political quest. He started to talk about running for the U.S. Senate one day, even though he had never bothered to register to vote.[2] He saw the fight with IBM as his election campaign, and his victory would be the primary.

His absolute, unswerving passion for his own point of view made him ignore the warning signals he heard when Belleville couldn't deliver even a working prototype of the FileServer. This device supposedly would be at the heart of the work group concept upon which Apple was basing its entire next year's marketing program. The LaserWriter was almost finished, but it was a $7,000 item. It was not clear to anyone but Steve that it would sell. "I'd buy one," he shouted at one particularly heated meeting about it. "Great! But 28-year-old multimillionaires aren't exactly a large market for us, are they," rebutted one of the more fearless marketing guys. AppleTalk, the network product that allowed a number of Macs to be linked in a small work group, was progressing well. It would allow the LaserWriter to be shared, but that was only a small portion of the concept behind the work group office strategy that Barbara Koalkin, as the manager of The Macintosh Office roll-out, was supposed to be promoting. Fundamentally, she was selling the idea that files and work and electronic mail could be shared electronically with Macintosh computers as smart terminals, but without a FileServer to act as a repository for the documents, her sales pitch was an unwitting sham.

All the ethics and carefully publicized values of mock-humanistic Apple went out the window as they were faced with an impending crisis. The continuing delays in production of software threatened to topple the carefully orchestrated launch they had devised. Instead of paying bonuses to stimulate programs, Steve decided to try a more treacherous approach.

"We would tell the market about all the software that was about to appear—making it seem ready, not the vaporware that much of it was—and in that way bring people flocking to buy machines," explained the head of special projects marketing, Alfred Mandel. "Since the machine really was terrific, the end justified any means.

"One day Steve got hold of a magazine for the IBM PC called *LIST*, that was sort of like a buyer's guide, and he simply decided that we should have them do one for the Mac. I called the guy who published it and guaranteed him that Apple would buy 450,000 copies at $1 apiece if he would get the magazine out in two months. He did it, and we gave them away to our dealers. Unfortunately, it didn't do much for sales."

It was a $450,000 effort at pulling the wool over the public's eyes, but it didn't work. The company was getting desperate by then, and anything was worth a try. Anything that Steve thought of, that is.

While Steve was raging, Sculley was standing by, unable to correct the flaws in the plan. He was like "a lover so in love with his beloved that he could see none of Steve's faults," says Joanna Hoffmann. "John wanted to be like Steve, he wanted to talk like Steve, he wanted to act like Steve, he wanted to be Steve."

Nonetheless, Sculley had sensed that he would have to check the chairman of the board over something if he were to build his control of Apple. Their first major difference of opinion came over the Laser-Writer. By mid-1984, with sales of the Mac plummeting, the entire company had turned against the idea of a $7,000 printer. No matter how great the output looked, it was simply too expensive a product for a company that had built its reputation on inexpensive machines. By then Steve had located a small company in Washington, Aldus, that was working on the first desktop publishing program—software that would allow a Macintosh and laser printer to lay out and produce profes-sional-looking, near-typeset-quality documents such as newsletters or brochures. He was adamant about the potential for this kind of personal publishing, and when Sculley started siding with the critics, he took the issue straight to the board of directors. He won the vote and lost his confidence in John Sculley.

"Steve didn't have the confidence that I could run Apple," said Sculley later. "Because he didn't think I knew enough about product operations."[3]

In early November, Ronald Reagan was reelected President of the United States in a landslide. Mondale's running mate, Geraldine Ferraro, had stumped the Silicon Valley and made a campaign speech at Apple. Steve had been absent. "I am not political," he said later when asked about his preference. "I am not party oriented. I am people oriented. I was not inspired by either candidate."[4]

Rambo, *Indiana Jones*, and *Beverly Hills Cop* were the popular movie blockbusters of the year, while *Amadeus* was the critic's choice. The world was thrilled by pop-star Michael Jackson, and when his 19-city tour ended in Los Angeles, Steve presented the begloved singer with a Mac backstage. Jackson seemed a bit nonplussed by the machine, and it was quickly carried off by an aide. The big book of 1984 was undoubtedly Lee Iacocca's autobiography, and he was dutifully invited to provide a leadership seminar at Apple.

The president of Chrysler was only one of a group of celebrities that Steve and Mandel approached with an offer of the free gift of a Macintosh with no strings attached. The group reflected the circles that Steve was traveling in and wanted to travel in: Kurt Vonnegut, Ted Turner, Milton Glaser, Mick Jagger, Andy Warhol, Stephen Sondheim, Jim Henson, David Rockefeller, George Lucas, Francis Coppola, and Steven Spielberg, among others. If they agreed, their pictures were put into the annual shareholders' report to provide a measure of credibility for the machine.

Some of the recipients were also people he wanted to meet, usually glamorous, beautiful women. "Steve wanted to meet Brooke Shields," says Mandel, "so he gave her a Mac as a calling card. The same for Diane Keaton." Such were the perks of being Steve Jobs. In the group of celebrities highlighted in that year's annual report was also Maya Lin, the young architect of the Vietnam Veteran's Memorial who became Steve's girlfriend for a time. He had decided that he liked "young super-intelligent, artistic women. I think they're in New York, rather than Silicon Valley."[5] He was spending more and more time in his Manhattan flat, where, true to form, he was having endless troubles deciding on the way he wanted to decorate the Dakota pad. He reportedly spent more than $1 million before changing his mind and starting over. He was losing touch with whatever last bits of the common man might have been in his psyche. He took to calling his division staff meetings to order in New York rather than in Cupertino. It was a prerogative that the chairman of the board could exercise, and since the Mac division always flew first-class and stayed at the luxurious Hotel Carlyle, the cross-country trip wasn't such a hideous burden on the staff.

Sculley might have been infatuated with him, but by late in the summer he started preparing various scenarios. As one high-level executive remarked, "Sculley is a professional hit man. He knew how to maneuver, and plan, to get rid of guys at upper management levels who'd been at Pepsi for 25 years, without so much as a peep out of them. He knew how to build his power, marshal his forces, get all his ducks in a row, and work with the board—and Steve was a rank amateur by comparison. John might have looked ineffectual late in

1984, but he was making sure that he came out smelling like a rose no matter what eventually happened."

Nonetheless, Steve was in the driver's seat of the company's entire strategic effort, and though the annual report for 1984 showed a drop in net income, with a near doubling of the firm's marketing and distribution costs, it also sounded a familiar theme, one that he was obsessed with by then. On the inside front cover, in white type on a black page, a quote was reprinted from IBM's annual report:

> . . . While the PC has been a good contributor to 1984's growth, we fully expect large processors, mainframes, storage devices, peripherals and software to carry their share of IBM growth now and beyond 1984.[6]

That was contrasted, on the facing page, in black type on a white page, with Apple's corporate goals:

> The personal computer is the heart of Apple. We don't view the world through the eyes of a mainframe. Since we don't have to protect other parts of our business, we do not have conflicting priorities that force product compromises.
>
> We have just one goal: to lead the industry in innovation. For those who use personal computers daily—and especially the millions who have never used a personal computer—we want to provide the most flexible and technologically advanced computer solutions available.[7]

Steve kept trying to convince the public that IBM was to be feared while Apple was the good guy. He was still fighting the street battles of the sixties and seventies but in the complicated mazes of the eighties. Steve was pounding the stump about Big Brother and contrasting it to the personality of Apple. But the public had realized that it wasn't a choice between good and bad, dark and light, right and wrong, human and inhuman, man and machine. It just wasn't that simple.

The Wendy's hamburger chain showed a TV commercial in 1984 called "Where's the Beef?" That was exactly the question that might have been asked about the Mac. The first 100 days had stood up on sizzle and flash, but then the promotion gave out and people began to realize the machine had no substance. Little software was available for it, though it was competing with a computer supported by thousands of programs. Hardware couldn't be hooked up to it, but the IBM PC offered an open architecture. (IBM had ironically taken its cue from the Apple II.) The Mac was seen as a toy, a cute machine that a person could love but wouldn't buy. The public was selecting IBM PCs because, in the Reagan-era America of the mid-eighties, it was productivity, doing the job, that counted more than the look and feel of the product. They had a choice between a computer that worked, that was a complete business solution, and one that wasn't complete, and their decisions surprised no one but Apple. As the fall came, Apple was diving deeper into a hole that Steve was wildly digging. Buttressed by his success, insulated from the real world, supported by a weak president, and surrounded by inexperienced managers afraid to call him on the carpet, he steamrollered Apple into a disastrous policy that nearly lost the farm.

In September of 1984, Steve and Mike Murray traveled to the high desert north of Los Angeles, where they met a film crew to create a sales training film for the upcoming Hawaii sales meeting. The title of the black-and-white war film that the two 29-year-old Apple crazies produced and wrote was *1944*. Inspired by every Saturday-afternoon war film ever made, the short represented another take on Steve's obsession: the war against IBM. The idea was that the Macintosh army had secured a beachhead and now intended to take the battle to the countryside. It was an elaborate exercise in communication. The bill would be nearly $80,000 for the eight-minute video, with dozens of extras, uniforms, and even an orchestrated "fly-by" with a couple of World War II fighter planes.

The film included a number of inside jokes, such as a fat corporal called FatBits and a new weapon known as the LightWriter (an interim name for the LaserWriter). A number of Macintosh marketing folks were used as extras. Murray was the General, while Steve played "The Chief"—F.D.R. himself—with his hair slicked back and a cigarette in a holder.

It was a high-quality, sophomoric production, and psychologically it was another part of the puzzle that he believed had to end with his battle of destiny: the confrontation between himself and IBM. One line, uttered by the actor who portrayed the leader of the troops, said it all perfectly: "The enemy is strong . . . but we are smart."

When they presented the movie at the Hawaiian sales conference a month later, it was a smash hit. The conference had kicked off with a wild dancing and light show extravaganza featuring a troupe of show dancers undulating to a musical knock-off of the theme from the hit movie *Ghostbusters*: "Who you gonna call? Bluebusters!" It was one of Murray's touches, something he had come up with after seeing the film on a transcontinental flight. "Bluebusters" would be their tongue-in-cheek theme for the attack on IBM. It was stamped on T-shirts sporting a Charlie Chaplin clown (IBM's advertising symbol) inside a red circle with a slash through it.

The sales force loved it. In the wake of the "mystery shopper" results during the summer of 1984, Steve ordered Apple's sales and marketing department to create a new national sales force to go out and "fire up" the retailers. This new sales group stomped and whistled as they watched the movie. Bill Campbell, the ex-Columbia University football coach Sculley had brought in to head Apple's sales and marketing organization, gave a rousing speech. He was followed by Steve and Murray, who presented a kind of Mutt-and-Jeff demonstration of the new Macintosh Office, most of which didn't exist and was unlikely to be ready at all during the next year. The film was a total success, and The Macintosh Office was apparently an inspired strategy.

Even the hand-picked reporter invited to attend was snowed. Deborah Wise, a *Business Week* reporter who came with a photographer, had been secretly allowed in to watch the events in return for a cover story. Her title read: "Apple's Dynamic Duo . . . and their bold plan to take on IBM in the office." The article appeared in the November 26 issue of the magazine and featured Steve and Sculley on the front cover.

But behind the scenes, things were not quite so wonderful. "Steve was incredibly depressed," recalls Jay Elliott. "He couldn't understand why people weren't buying the Mac. But worse, he thought John was screwing up. He was going to have to take charge of the company because John didn't 'get it.' It was a phrase which Steve used over and over. As Steve saw it, John didn't understand the business."

In Hawaii, Sculley was still on the honeymoon. Murray accompanied him for a walk one morning and was contemplating raising a few of the concerns he had about Steve staying on as the head of the Macintosh division. The marketing director of the Macintosh division was rapidly coming to the conclusion that a reorganization was necessary for the good of Apple and had started discussing his ideas with Elliott. But as they walked along Diamond Head, the company's president confided in him: "'You know, I keep thinking someone is going to pinch me one day. This job is a dream come true.' I didn't feel it was the right time to talk to him about everything that was wrong at the company," recalls Murray. It wasn't the right time to shatter the dream.

Steve was in the middle of a manic period. He was having astonishing mood swings and was seeing everything as a win-lose situation with his Macintosh teetering on the precipice. Every morning he would pull up the company's latest sales figures on the firm's MIS system and decide whether he was losing or winning. If the figures were good, he was happy. If they were bad—and by the fall of 1984, they were almost always worse than the day before—he would be upset for the rest of the day and search for scapegoats. Steve started to become frightened that his Macintosh was going to be a failure. It would be the third strike against Apple: the Apple III, the Lisa, and now the Mac. He started to look around the company and realized that the organization was a mess. Sculley was doing nothing, so he had to do something.

At that Hawaii sales conference, a series of executive meetings were held. A month earlier, there had been a leadership conference at Apple with the president of Federal Express, Fred Smith. His ideas about centralized shipment and overnight delivery had struck a responsive chord in Steve, who figured it was a perfect way to distribute Apple's computers. He unilaterally decided the company should investigate this new way to distribute product. The sales and marketing executive vice-president, Bill Campbell, and the vice-president of distribution, Roy Weaver, were opposed, since they had large organizations already in place to take care of distribution. Of course opposition had never fazed Steve. At a sales conference meeting, he proposed that they change the system from the ground up and fire a number of people. An enormous fight ensued, with Campbell pounding the table and storming out. Sculley wasn't saying anything, and because he wasn't, Steve ran wild with the ball. Perhaps he wasn't trying to radically change the distribution system, only trying to shake things up, but his tactics were driving a stake into the heart of the firm.

"Steve made me realize that we were in deep trouble early in 1984," explains Jay Elliott. "He thought we had an enormous spare tire of managers insulating us from running lean. We were walking along Bandley Drive one day and he said 'I think we're about 2,000 people over head count. Let's go fire them.'

"We had built in all these marketing people, all these manufacturing people, all these distribution people, and with the Lisa going down there was no way that it could be supported. We were bloated."

Apple executives were scared. Steve had started diving into all the details of the business with his inimitable style. The executives allowed themselves to be driven by Steve. "Whole days were spent trying to answer the question, 'What am I going to do with Steve?'" says Elliott. "Meetings would consist of holding on to the status quo. Ideas weren't being nurtured. No one wanted to be responsible for an idea that 'was shit.'" New plans were shot down because of the scatter-shot personality of a chairman who was also the head of the Apple 32 division. There was no leadership at the very top of the company. Sculley wasn't providing the backstop that Steve's off-the-wall remarks required.

The Macintosh division lacked cohesive strategy. The TurboMac was way behind schedule. This was a machine that would have a hard disk inside it along with a new and better set of ROM routines. Once Steve had decided to do the product, he also decided to set up a "TurboTown" where the software would be written. This was his attempt to recreate a Mac-like fervor in a small group, but everyone was already burned out. Joanna Hoffmann was assigned to the group as manager, and when she realized that they had done nothing much and were far behind in the schedule, she called a meeting at which she read them the riot act.

"The meeting was at 3 in the morning," she says, "because that was the only time I could get all the prima-donnas together. TurboTown was a joke. They weren't doing a thing. And no one was making them."

Steve, whose strength was in motivating and driving a small group of dedicated people, was now consumed by his activities on the corporate side of the fence, and the TurboMac development effort had been left to Belleville, the engineering chief. Belleville was not the kind of person to inspire the superhuman effort that the original Mac had required. TurboMac floundered and the FileServer never got going. Even though Belleville was telling the company that it would be ready a few months hence, the project had never gone beyond the paper stage. He kept promising it, but he did nothing about it. And no one called him on it. That was how out of control the managerial process was late in 1984 in Steve's Macintosh division.

As the sales figures continued to slide, Steve grew deeply depressed. While he at least tried to find answers inside Apple, Sculley became convinced that the only solution for Apple was in forming a strategic alliance with another major company. The idea had its roots in an approach to Apple from Wang, an office systems company frightened by the market dominance of IBM. Their contact had come in the spring, but Steve had decided that it would make more sense if they made a deal with a company much bigger than Wang. A deal with Wang wasn't "sexy" enough. If they were going to do it, he wanted deep pockets, large cash reserves that would allow Apple to weather the temporary period of slowness in Mac sales. They went looking for bigger fish.

The first and most serious suitor was AT&T. The telecommunications giant wanted to take on the computer business, and it seemed like a perfect alliance. Steve loved the telephone, considering it the ultimate business machine, and no one had deeper pockets than the phone company. A contact was made at the board of directors level, and throughout the fall of 1984 long, sleek limousines appeared at Cupertino on the weekends. Button-down AT&T executives would emerge to mingle with the engineers in Apple's advanced product development teams. The Mac software and hardware guys thought they were bozos, and eventually the deal fell apart because AT&T wanted to own controlling interest in the company. Steve wasn't willing to give up that much control over Apple.

For a while Apple had a relationship with General Electric, or at least their credit arm GEICO, which provided the muscle behind an Apple consumer credit card program. Steve was also interested in letting them handle manufacturing, but there wasn't much interest from GE unless they could own the company. Sculley contacted the head of marketing at Coca-Cola, Sergio Zyman, a charismatic Brazilian who had jumped ship from Pepsi-Cola a few years earlier. Together they looked at launching a co-merchandising program, a national program to give away computers partially underwritten by Coke, and from there they escalated the whole arrangement to encompass a possible investment. Nothing came of it, however.

General Motors was also considered as a mate. Steve invited Roger Smith, the company's CEO, out to tour the Macintosh division and the factory, which was of great interest to Smith. He was in the midst of setting up an automated plant in Tennessee that would use many of the same techniques on an automobile assembly line. Steve suggested a strategic alliance, and Smith told him that since he knew very little about computers, he would send a member of his board out to talk with them. The emissary was Ross Perot, who showed up a few weeks later and was taken on the tour by Steve. Although they were an odd couple, the mercurial, Zen-Buddhist-influenced Steve and the strait-laced Texan patriot Perot got along like a house afire.

Perot, of the giant computer data firm Electronic Data Services (EDS), became successful by servicing only one client: General Motors. He turned EDS into a billion-dollar company by providing mainframe computing systems to the giant automaker. His company had provided the software, but he was starting to look for workstations to bring into General Motors. The Macintosh seemed a likely possibility.

"Although three or four people were in the room for the meeting, Perot talked only to Steve," according to Elliott. "Sculley wasn't even in his line of vision. Perot thought Apple had the right ideas, especially at the factory, but it was hard to see how to fit them into General Motors. Unfortunately, in the final analysis, Perot didn't believe the Mac would make it and thought that IBM was too dominant in the marketplace. We couldn't strike a deal."

By late in 1984, everyone was scrambling. The initial Apple IIc rush had died out. Eventually, 200,000 machines had to be liquidated through a bartering company. Apple was stalled and sinking. The Test Drive program that Murray had devised—dealers would lend Macintoshes, with software, to potential customers for a "test drive"—was a marvelously designed promotion but had no impact on sales. The timing was wrong: Christmas was the worst time of the year for a promotion like that because it was lost in all the noise. If anything, sales were flatter than ever. They were desperate by then. Steve had lost all respect for Sculley, the strategic alliance deals weren't bearing any fruit, The Macintosh Office strategy was coming unraveled before it was launched, software for the Mac was still delayed, and the Mac just wasn't selling.

The stock was in the tank, hovering around $20 per share, earnings were down, and Steve too had become convinced that the only way the company could survive was to have a corporate sponsor, a vote of confidence from corporate America. None was forthcoming.

"Steve had thousands of ideas, and Sculley was so insecure he didn't know how to modulate it," explains Elliott. "It was panic all around. John had bought a lot of stock on margin, and by late in 1984, as the stock price fell, he was a quarter of a million dollars under water."

In mid-November, Steve accompanied Elliott, Belleville, and Burrell Smith on a trip to Japan. They wanted to investigate new products and lock down the deal with Canon, the firm that was supplying the printing engine for the LaserWriter, which was to be introduced a couple of months hence. Steve always wanted to be the first on the block to know about new technology, and he was also starting to think about creating a portable Macintosh. He needed to find out what the best Japanese companies had up their kimono sleeves.

One morning they were to visit Epson, whose offices were located a couple of hours outside of Tokyo. Dutifully, a driver from the firm showed up, and they started out, only to find that the road had been closed because of an avalanche. "Steve was in a foul mood anyway," says Elliott. "He started to chew out the driver. He thought the guy should have known about the problem and taken them another way. The guy had only been on the job for a few weeks, and he started sweating. Here he had the very important Steve Jobs, who was yelling at him from the back of the limo.

"The driver finally figured out that he could get us back to a train station, which he did, and we got going again. Only the train couldn't get through either. By then Steve was off his rocker, really steaming, and this poor chauffeur was sure that he was going to get fired."

Finally, they made it through and arrived at Epson late in the afternoon, nearly eight hours later for a journey that should have taken two hours. Waiting for them were all the Epson managers and vice-president lined up in the lobby. Steve was furious, and the first thing he demanded was food, rattling off a list of sushi. Factotums were sent scurrying to scare it up.

The president of the company then took them all into their boardroom, where they had carefully set up all their latest products. A spokesman started explaining what each one was and its special features. After about a minute, Elliott reports that Steve turned to the president of the company and said, "This is shit. Don't you have anything good?" and with that he marched out. The self-effacing Japanese were shocked and had no idea how to react. The team from Apple made a hasty departure.

A couple of hours later Steve and Elliott were back on the train heading into Tokyo. Steve started to talk about the problems he was having with his latest flame, Yale architecture student Maya Lin. "He couldn't understand why things were always so difficult for him," says Elliott. "He didn't care about the little scene at Epson—that had meant nothing to him. He had forgotten it as soon as it was over. What really counted was love, and he couldn't understand why he couldn't make it work."

As the streets of Japan sped by in the darkness, the multimillionaire founder of Apple poured out his heart. He was afraid of the future. He was nearing his thirtieth birthday and wanted to have a family. Finally, he turned to his confidant, the only other member of the Mac team who wore the twin hats of the Macintosh team and Apple's corporate inner circle, and grasped him by the arm.

Elliott says he recalls the moment vividly. "Steve was almost desperate, and said to me, 'I'm just an ordinary guy. Why can't they understand that?'"

18
Rough Sailing

Upon returning from Japan in late November of 1984, Steve headed for Pajaro Dunes and another retreat. This time the group was smaller and included only the key characters in the Apple 32 division. On the agenda was only one item: making the Macintosh succeed in the marketplace at any cost. The cool and blustery weather out on the dunes surrounding the meeting center matched his bleak mood. The only bright spot was the cover story in *Business Week* that had appeared a week earlier. But as numerous folks came up to congratulate him on his picture, and the full page of "Quotations from Chairman Jobs" the article included, he found himself only more depressed. No one but Murray, Elliott, and Coleman seemed to understand that Steve believed the company was going down the tubes, and no matter what he did he couldn't seem to find the right solution to prevent it. The article was a sham, and now it appeared that all the products in The Macintosh Office were delayed. Apple would be announcing a product group with nothing available for purchase until three months later. The momentum the annual meeting generated would fizzle out before the merchandise made it into the stores. He had sworn he would never do that again after the fiasco of the Lisa introduction, yet he was doing exactly the same thing two years later.

Macintosh sales were down even further, dipping below 10,000 units a month. The aggressive "Test Drive" ads running nationwide were creating a ripple of protest. They had finally decided to use the alternate commercials Steve had ordered produced that showed business users sledgehammering recalcitrant IBM PCs. But the public was divided on their efficacy. Apple was probably the only company in the world that had such loyalty among its users that no matter what move they made, there were sure to be dozens of letters in the mail the next day taking both sides. Mothers complained of the inherent violence in the ads and chastised the company for teaching bad values. Businessmen complained about the implicit attack on IBM and the perception that they were making fun of office workers. Students and early purchasers wrote in to support them.[1] All in all, the marketing campaign was too polarizing to be a success.

The real problem facing the group at the retreat was what to do about the Lisa. The computer was basically an orphan. Total sales of the Lisa, nearly two years after its introduction, were less than 50,000— one-tenth of the forecast figure. Late in 1984 a new program, *MacWorks*, was completed that allowed the Lisa to run Macintosh software, but even that had no effect on sales. The machine was a failure, and Steve wanted to drop it, no matter how bad it would look to the business world. There was no point in supporting a product that was losing money daily. At Pajaro Dunes, he prevailed.

During the following month, December, as it really sank in that there were not going to be any new products to introduce at the annual meeting, Steve changed his mind, or at least a portion of it. The Lisa was already canceled, and they had stopped ordering new parts for it. Steve's brainstorm was to turn the Lisa into a giant Macintosh clone and rename it the Macintosh XL. It was a simple no-cost solution that could provide an easy answer to the lack of a tangible product to sell. The machine had been canceled, but that didn't matter. There were plenty of Lisas available in the inventory pipeline, and when they ran out a new, more powerful Macintosh could take its place. At least they could offer the appearance of a new product at the shareholders' meeting.

Steve went into his frenzied high gear, calling Belleville and Murray to tell them his idea. Belleville thought it was a good one, but Murray was shocked. "Here we were going to tell all the folks who trusted us to run out and buy a new Mac XL," he explains, "with the implication that this was a new upgrade path and our product for the future. Yet we had already canceled the project internally."

But Steve had made up his mind. In the first few days of the new year, 1985, Sculley held an executive meeting off-site. Steve made his official presentation, and Sculley nodded his head in agreement. The

Macintosh XL it would be. Steve was running Apple. At the retreat, it became even more clear that the Apple 32 division was on an acquisition binge, taking control of company-wide functions such as advertising, PR, distribution, and peripherals. It was the only way that Steve could be sure that the "right" steps would be taken. It was his last-ditch attempt to save the company, and he was genuinely convinced that he was doing the right thing.

At the same time, Steve was pursuing a remarkable new technology that had come his way. One of the Mac team members, Steve Capps, had run into a firm called Woodside Design headed by an eccentric engineering genius by the name of Steve Kitchen. Kitchen, who had designed various games for Activision, including a Space Shuttle simulation, had a prototype of a flat-panel monitor display that instantly captured Steve's attention when he was shown versions of it in November and December.

The display was about 1½ inches thick in total, and through the presence of thousands of tiny transistors on a kind of mesh embedded in a glass vacuum, was able to create a high-resolution screen display that was as crisp as the Mac's but had no size limits and could conceivably produce color. The only other flat-panel displays he had seen to that point had very poor low resolution and were small. It was a remarkable technological breakthrough, and thus extraordinarily attractive to the technology-sensitive Steve. It also fit into his thinking about the portable Macintosh that he had been contemplating for years. According to Kitchen, by late December Steve had offered to buy out the company for $1 million and told him, "You've just made my Christmas. I'm going to make you very rich."[2]

However, it was only one of the many things on the chairman's increasingly fragmented mind. The annual shareholders' meeting was scheduled for January 23, and again Apple's advertising agency Chiat/Day had created some event advertising for the Super Bowl telecast. This year's ad was very different from the previous year's "1984," however. Both had a somewhat dark world view, but the ad for 1985, entitled "Lemmings," made contact with something much more frightening and foreboding in most viewers' psyches. A seemingly endless line of thousands of blindfolded business people trudged over a hillside. The world they inhabited was painted in muted grays and somber browns. With one hand on a predecessor's shoulder, they dispiritedly whistled a disembodied version of the Disney classic

"Whistle While You Work" off-key as they trudged toward a precipice. One by one, they reached the cliff edge and tumbled off into the void. Finally, one drone reached the edge and, instead of following and diving off the cliff, raised his blindfold, took a peek around, and stepped out of the queue. This was the Apple user in an IBM world. That message was clear, no matter how garbled the rest of it was.

Reactions to the spot within Apple had been mixed from the first screenings. Steve liked the ad instantly—it perfectly expressed his view of the world. He saw himself in a fight with IBM for the hearts and minds of the earth's citizens, and if he lost they would all surely die. Sculley was opposed to it but wasn't ready to stand up to Steve yet. The board of directors unanimously opposed it. "But we had been opposed to '1984' the year before, and it turned out to be an enormous success," said Schlein. "Maybe we were wrong again. This time we swallowed our tongues, sat on our hands, and left the decision up to Steve and Mike Murray."

Murray hadn't liked the ad, and his gut reaction was not to run it. Because the ad caused so much dissension, it was shown to the Macintosh inner circle one night, and everyone was asked to vote on whether to run it or not. The vote came out decisively against it. A few weeks later, Steve and Murray had dinner with the Chiat/Day folks in Manhattan. "I allowed myself to be influenced by Lee Clow [creative director at Chiat/Day]," recalls Murray. "I had learned most of what I knew about advertising from him, and he felt very strongly about running it, so we did."

The ad certainly stopped traffic during the 1985 Super Bowl as the San Francisco 49ers were defeating the Miami Dolphins. The game was being played at the Stanford Stadium in nearby Palo Alto, and Apple had supplied 100,000 seat cushions for the crowd. While the ad again generated plenty of conversation about the company, the difference was that this year most of the talk was negative. An irate survivor of Auschwitz called the company, certain that Apple was making fun of the concentration camps. Office workers were incensed—the ad seemed to be poking fun at 90 percent of the country's workers. It was a terrible miscalculation. The ad only reinforced Wall Street's conception of Apple as a mismanaged company with an elitist attitude.

The annual meeting that followed the running of the ad by two days continued the misguided strategy that Steve had settled upon. The nonexistent products of The Macintosh Office were somehow going to sweep the misgivings of corporate America aside, and the computer professionals in the Fortune 1000 were going to start buying Macintoshes en masse. IBM would be dead in the water, torpedoed by Apple.

This year none of the electricity that had surrounded the previous year's event was evident, although the corps of reporters was abuzz wondering whether a significant new machine was going to be announced. Rumors had a new model of the Macintosh near completion, but that's not what they were shown that day. The Macintosh Office was unveiled with a cute routine between Steve and Sculley standing at two Macs onstage and sending a chart from one Mac to the other. The AppleTalk network, with its $50-per-computer price, was, along with the Macintosh XL, the only product ready to show. The LaserWriter was due out in April, the FileServer in the fall, and the add-on circuit board that supposedly allowed an IBM PC to join an AppleTalk network, wasn't given a date any more firm than "later in the year." It, like the FileServer, was still in an early design stage, and in fact neither would appear for more than 24 months.

The public, press, and shareholders, of course, didn't know about the problems inside Apple's new product development groups. They didn't know the onstage demonstration was a carefully designed one-time operation and couldn't be duplicated anywhere outside Cupertino. Dutifully, they applauded vigorously for their leader when he made the kind of bold comments for which he had become famous. "We're calling for detente with IBM," was one. Another centered on a story about a "six-year-old boy who sent me a letter recently. 'I was filling out a crossword puzzle recently and the clue read: as American as Apple "blank." I thought the answer was computer, but my mom said it was pie.'" [3]

In many ways Steve gave his ultimate performance that day because he was really selling snake oil. He knew that few of the products were ready and that the company was in deep trouble, approaching its first losing quarter ever and coming off a quarter in which Sculley had been forced to cancel profit-sharing contributions to employees. Yet Steve could still put on the pancake makeup and go out on stage to pump up the troops.

Apple was starting to burn, and Steve was still fiddling. At the press conference afterward, he answered all the questions while Sculley sat growing visibly impatient as his partner hogged the limelight. Sculley couldn't escape the realization that something was very wrong with the company. For months Steve had been telling him that the products for The Macintosh Office would be ready, but they weren't. For months he had watched as Macintosh sales fell and the software that was promised to be just around the corner didn't appear. For months Campbell and Yocam had been telling him in private that he had to do something about reining in Steve, but he had put it off. For months Elliott had been suggesting that Apple restructure, with a different unified organization based on business functions instead of product lines, and he hadn't listened.

A week after the 1985 annual meeting, most of Apple's executive staff headed for Phoenix, Arizona, where Ben Rosen's annual Personal Computer Forum was being held. One morning, Mike Murray found Sculley and Regis McKenna sitting in the back of a session. He told them that it was crucial that they meet privately. His tone was urgent, so the two agreed to go up to one of their rooms to hear him out.

As they were about to get on the elevator, Steve popped out, heading for the day's sessions. He asked what the three of them were up to. Murray told him they were going to have a meeting, and Steve asked if he could come. For the first time in three years at Apple, Murray said no to Steve. Steve was insistent, but Murray stood his ground, and eventually they left the chairman standing outside the elevator.

Up in Sculley's hotel room, Murray told the president of the company that he thought his boss, Steve Jobs, had to be removed from his position at the head of the Macintosh division. Sculley and McKenna listened carefully as Murray, an insider, a loyal subject to the prince, delineated his reasons that the change had to be made. If Murray, who was perhaps closer to Steve than anyone other than Belleville, was insisting that Steve had to be removed from the top of the Macintosh division, surely something was seriously wrong.

Murray told them that he was convinced the product divisions had to be stripped of profit responsibility, so the company could streamline its operations and stop the debilitating competition between the Apple II and the Macintosh. He handed Sculley a list of eight suggestions that spelled out a way to reorganize the company. Sculley read it and handed the paper back to him. He never kept papers, always handed them back. Murray remembers that Sculley said, "It's interesting, but I'm not going to do anything about it right now."

As the two older men returned to the seminars at the conference,

Murray felt his world collapsing. The Macintosh marketing director was at his wit's end. The blame for the unpopular "Lemmings" commercial had been laid squarely at his door. When Apple, in response to the firestorm the ad unleashed, sent out a press release on the Monday following the Super Bowl, it was Murray who was made solely responsible. Deep undercurrents of unhappiness in his marketing group were surfacing in endless private counseling sessions he was having to hold for his people. A week before the annual meeting, he had written a long letter to Steve in the wake of a particularly vicious staff meeting at which his alleged marketing strategy failures were identified as being at the heart of the failure of the Mac. The letter detailed his fears for the future of the Macintosh division:

I spend the bulk of my time in counseling sessions. Our greatest asset must be our people, yet we slap them around like nonessential commodities. We call them names (both behind their backs and to their faces). We tear them down. We attack their integrity. We reinforce management by character assassination. We permit them to say no, but never yes. And then we change all our plans and start it all over— again, and again, and again. What a lousy way to run a hotel.[4]

Steve told him that he was overreacting and that everything would be fine.

But it wouldn't be fine. Two days after the annual meeting, Murray learned that a top Pepsi marketing manager, Jeff Myers, who had been involved with the Michael Jackson advertising campaign for Sculley's previous company, decided not to take the job Apple had offered him. The reason he cited was the arrival in his mail of three letters, all written on Macintoshes, thanking him for the Michael Jackson jackets. Each of these also suggested in various ways that he didn't know what he was getting into by coming to Apple. The letters were unsigned. Murray circulated this troubling story to his staff in a memo and begged that the authors come forward. No one did.

A cancer was eating away at the Macintosh division. What had started as a tight-knit group was now a "mondo-division" of 700, unsupported by sales and driven by an unpredictable, abrasive leader.

Things had flowed Steve's way since the Apple II was introduced in 1977. Quarterly sales had always shown significant increases. Now, when they were faced with a crisis, he couldn't understand why, and in turn, he didn't know what to do. Suddenly, it was going to be supremely difficult to turn things around and, like most kids of affluence, he wasn't prepared for the hard slog this effort required.

Steve and his team believed in one person, one computer; Apple always sold to individuals, tailored all their marketing to the individual, to making a person feel good about taking the choice to go with Apple. In the final analysis, when the "rubber hit the road" as Steve loved to say without ever understanding the phrase, that didn't matter, because groups bought computers for their offices based on analysis, not emotion. Steve worked the emotional side of the road. The mechanics of getting to the vision he espoused, the sweat, grease, and noise of the grindstone, were alien to him. "He could see that horizon out there, a thousand miles out," explained Jay Elliott. "But he could never see the details of each little mile that had to be covered to get there. That was his genius and his downfall."

Steve's team was too young and powerless either to stand up to him or put their fingers on what was wrong. Steve believed the fault couldn't lie with the machine—it was, after all, his own flesh and blood. He started looking for scapegoats everywhere and held staff meetings at which he blamed everyone else for the failure of the Mac. He was emotional, illogical, and unfair. His moods swung daily, hourly. Steve was out of control, and no one inside Apple could stop him. Luckily for the company, there were a few people outside who could.

Shortly after the Phoenix event, Steve and Woz went to a White House function where they received a medal from the president for their contribution to American technological advances. These were the first National Technology Medals, which ironically the pair shared with a trio from IBM who had worked on the design of the IBM/360 minicomputer system. It was an uncomfortable moment for both Steves—neither liked the other any more, and they could scarcely conceal their dislike.

When Steve returned from the East Coast, he found out that Woz had publicly quit the company. In a blast of uncensored comments, Woz berated Apple for its lack of support for the Apple II product line and the company's chaotic management. In a clear dig at his former friend, Woz criticized the fact that the company had made no mention of the Apple II at the recent annual meeting, even though it was the firm's only money-making product. Furthermore, he was incensed that the project he was working on, an advanced Apple II with powerful features, had seen its budget cut for the new year and that there seemed to be no support at the top for the machine that had started it all.

When reached by reporters, Steve made the ungracious comment: "Woz hasn't done anything much for years."[5] By then the two had nothing more than a public version of a friendship anyway. Steve considered Woz's misguided effort at rock 'n' roll promotion—the US Festivals of 1982—a joke and had said so.[6] And Woz's comments about his cofounder in the 1983 *Time* Magazine "Machine of the Year" issue had cut Steve to the quick. In recent years, Woz had spent most of his time in his hilltop home, raising his children and a menagerie of exotic pets such as llamas. He made infrequent appearances at Apple and acted as a kind of public spokesman for the firm, trotting out to Apple II gatherings, groundbreakings, and other events. The two cofounders no longer fraternized.

The press had a field day over Woz's resignation. Persistent rumblings of trouble inside Apple sent the stock, which was hovering around $25 a share, down further. In the following days two other key employees resigned: Ken Zerbe, a long-time key operations officer, and Joe Graziano, the company's chief financial officer. They joined Woz and a long list of others who quit early in 1985. The list included the directors of corporate communications, advertising, Apple II marketing, Lisa marketing, Macintosh peripherals, Apple II engineering, and retail programs. The exodus was becoming embarrassing, and the board of directors demanded that Sculley, not Jobs, take charge of the company and make a public statement.

"Apple is a big business now," Sculley said to the *Wall Street Journal*, which ran a half-page article about "unrest" at Apple a couple of days later. "That's a fact of life. Some people can't adjust, and as a result we've lost some good people. But Apple can't stay in the garage forever. The company has to adjust to a changing industry. I'm trying to bring in the strongest successors I can find."[7] And the president was trying to take control of some parts of his sprawling empire. He had instituted daily 7:30 A.M. executive staff meetings and taken to rating employees as A, B, or C "team" players. By early 1985 he had already replaced more than 50 percent of the executive staff he had inherited in 1983. He understood that as an outsider brought in to help the company, he would be held accountable if Apple's tailspin continued. The big question was what to do about the chairman of the board.

A few days later, in mid-February, the first all Macintosh Exposition—the *Macworld* Expo—was held in San Francisco, and it was a desultory event. Business software was still promised but not delivered. The mood on the exhibition floor was guarded. The stranglehold that IBM had on the business world was now all but complete, and it looked likely that the Macintosh would be an interesting curiosity, a great footnote to the history of computing, but no real competition. Furthermore, *Jazz*, the integrated business software from Lotus that had been rescheduled for release at the Expo, was delayed a few more months. Apple was slipping deadlines, big software houses were slipping deadlines, and in the wings were two new competitors, both based on the same 68000 processor and sporting graphics interfaces that threatened to steal Mac's thunder. First was Atari's Mac-killer, nicknamed the "Jackintosh" after the company's tough president Jack Tramiel, and Commodore was due to release the Amiga within months. And both would cost half as much as the Macintosh.

Steve didn't show up at the Expo that week, although he did appear at a few private dinners with Fiona Rojas, his current girlfriend. Bright, blonde, and beautiful, she was known in the Mac team circles as "the marvelous Fiona." She seemed a good match for Steve. She had worked in the industry, was strong enough to tell him off, and she had a lack of pretension that was admired among the old Macintosh hands. To those who cared about him, like Bill Atkinson, it seemed as if he might have met the right woman at last.

During that week, Steve also played an exacting game of poker with Bill Gates. For months Apple and Microsoft had been negotiating over the renewal of the license for Microsoft's BASIC, which was an integral part of the ROM in the Apple II. The original license was up at the end of 1985, and both computer industry moguls were acting tough. Steve wanted Gates to drop his development project for a Macintosh-style operating environment on the IBM PC called *Windows*, even going so far as to threaten a lawsuit over it. Gates scoffed at him and counter-threatened to pull the license for Applesoft BASIC if he was sued, which would mean Apple would have to redesign all the programming for the Apple II.

Gates had another hot button, BASIC for the Macintosh. Steve's Mac team had been working on a version of BASIC to run on the Mac for years and were on the verge of shipping it. *MacBASIC* was finally scheduled to come out in the summer three months hence. Microsoft currently had the only BASIC for the Macintosh, and Gates wanted to protect his product. He also had another product that he had somehow been able to keep relatively quiet. It was called *Excel*, and it was shaping up as a spreadsheet powerful enough to make a big difference in the business acceptance of the Mac.

Steve had been careful to keep from favoring either Microsoft or Lotus, but he was fed up with Lotus' endless delays. When Gates showed the latest version of *Excel* to him, he conjured up a deal. *MacBASIC* wasn't essential to the success of the Mac. Why not agree to cancel it in return for the Applesoft BASIC license and a commitment that Gates would keep *Excel* from ever appearing on the IBM PC? Gates went for it. Even though Apple had spent millions developing *MacBASIC*, it was lost in an afternoon poker game. Steve won a renewed license on Applesoft BASIC for a number of years plus an agreement that *Excel* would not appear on the IBM PC for at least two years. He made the deal himself, unilaterally, without checking with anyone, and never even bothered to tell Donn Denman, who had written Apple's version of Macintosh BASIC. A few months later, when Denman found out, he was devastated.

In February, Steve also unilaterally canceled the TurboMac project after Burrell Smith had worked on it for months. Steve wanted to build a Macintosh version of the Dynabook, a small portable computer first proposed by the Xerox thinker Alan Kay. (Kay had since been recruited by Steve to Apple and was one of the firm's handful of Apple Fellows.) Smith was convinced it was not yet possible even using the new flat-panel display that had Steve so enthused. The man who had redesigned the Macintosh at least five times to incorporate changes dictated by Steve, who had crammed 80 percent of the functionality of a Lisa, which had five circuit boards, onto a single board in the Mac, and who had created the internal workings of the LaserWriter in less than six months, had finally had it. Steve had trampled on him one time too many. Smith quit.

That same week Murray told Steve that he wanted to leave his position as director of marketing. He was burned out and fed up with being blamed for the failure of the Mac. He was disgusted by the changes he had witnessed in the Mac group, changes that had made the friendly team he knew and loved into a bitter, secretive, and fractious group. As Murray saw it, the only hope was to remove Steve as head of the Macintosh division. Somewhere in the back of his mind he thought that only by making a grand gesture could he force the chairman to realize how dire the situation really was.

By that February, Murray wasn't the only one who felt that Steve had to move out of the way for the good of both the Macintosh and Apple. Jay Elliott, the human resources and corporate organization strategist, had come to the same conclusion. Whereas Murray was in close contact only with Steve, Elliott had both Steve's and Sculley's ears. The big question was who could fill those Birkenstocks? Elliott and Murray were close colleagues, and between them they decided that the only person within Apple with the combination of marketing muscle and vision to take over from Steve was a 41-year-old Frenchman by the name of Jean Louis Gassée.

Gassée was the head of Apple-France and a charismatic spokesman for high-tech. He was also the head of the only international operation for Apple that was solidly in the black. Early in 1985, while Macintosh sales were soft everywhere else, France was a bright spot in the Apple constellation. Gassée was the major part of that success.

A trained mathematician, the elegant and animated Gassée was a kind of self-anointed future thinker with a book of murky pop philosophy under his belt and a penchant for making visionary statements. He liked to describe the personal computer as a "magic carpet for the mind" and was a favorite of the Mitterand government's charismatic minister of culture, Jacques Levy. He had worked his way up in the French marketing departments of a couple of American computer companies before taking over Apple-France. Gassée was often described as an older version of Steve Jobs, and indeed the two men genuinely seemed to like one another. Paris was always one of Steve's favorite working vacation stops, in great part because of the fascination that the French media had for the "weez-keed of Seeleecon Vallee."

But there were still substantial differences between the two. Gassée had a firm grasp on the retail consumer business he was in and no sympathy whatsoever for The Macintosh Office strategy. He rejected its application to the situation in France. He continued to concentrate on dealers tucked away on side streets, in market centers, whose storefronts were designed to look like Macs.

Elliott suggested Gassée to Sculley as someone who could take over the Macintosh division, which would allow them to put Steve back in charge of a new product division, where he obviously thrived. With the president's blessing, but without telling Steve, the human resources vice-president broached the subject with the Frenchman and found some interest. Meanwhile, Sculley tried to decide what course of action to pursue.

When Steve asked Murray who he thought could take over the role of director of marketing from him, Murray suggested Gassée. The recommendation for Gassée from Murray finally got through to Steve, and he called the Frenchman that day. Gassée understood only too well both the political verities of life at Apple and the personal upheaval he would have to go through to bring his family to California. He didn't mention his conversation with Elliott; he also realized that a boardroom struggle was going on and that he was a pawn. To protect his interests, he wanted to make sure that any deal was structured his way. Gassée wanted to be assured that he could head the entire Macintosh division, not just be the director of marketing. But Steve was not quite ready yet to abdicate, even though Murray was urging him to do so. In line with his interests, Gassée wanted a written commitment specifying the date on which he would be elevated to general manager of the group, and Steve was uncomfortable with that demand. He thought that Gassée should first win the respect and trust of the division, prove himself, and then be promoted. The conversation ended indecisively, and a few days later, when Murray asked Steve how it had gone, he indicated that they hadn't been able to work it out and he was looking for someone else.

But Steve was also starting to spin another future for himself. On a Sunday in February, he met Kitchen, the designer of the flat-panel display, at his firm's offices in Palo Alto. In an afternoon of talk during which they continued to pursue the details of their deal, Steve started to dream of setting up an Apple research lab that he decided should be called AppleLabs. During a walk, they saw a vacant building, and on the spot Steve decided that this was where the facility should be located. Steve would have his office there; it could be a new skunkworks for Apple.[8] When he took the idea to Sculley a few days later, the president apparently encouraged him. An R&D facility was just where Steve should be. It could neatly solve all Sculley's problems with the headstrong chairman of the board.

On Sunday, February 24, 1985, Steve turned 30. He threw the kind of birthday bash that only multimillionaires and heads of large companies can successfully create. In the ballroom of the St. Francis

Hotel in San Francisco, he treated 1,000 of his closest friends and employees from around the world, including Gassée, to a black-tie dinner dance with entertainment by Ella Fitzgerald. She was a strange choice for a man who revered Bob Dylan. He had asked Dylan, but the poet-rocker had a conflicting engagement and turned down the invitation. On stage, he and Sculley bantered lightly, avoiding the undercurrents that were rippling through the company. The cover of the invitations had said as much about him, and where he had come to, as anything: "There's an old Hindu saying that goes, 'In the first 30 years of your life you make your habits. For the last 30 years of your life, your habits make you.' Come help me celebrate mine."

Turning 30 is a watershed for everyone, and Steve had his share of trepidation as he approached the date. "People get stuck as they get older," he said then. "Our minds are like electrochemical computers. Your thoughts construct patterns like scaffolding in your mind. You are really etching chemical patterns.

"In most cases, people get stuck in those patterns, just like grooves in a record, and they never get out of them. It's a rare person who etches grooves that are other than a specific way of looking at things, a specific way of questioning things. It is rare that you see an artist in his thirties or forties able to really contribute something amazing."[9]

The night was a success, if a little forced, as the chairman of the board emceed the festivities at his own celebration. He worked the crowd from the front of the room with a microphone held deftly in his fist. His life was Apple, his world a company that had brought jobs and success to thousands but at the expense of true friendships. He had come a long way in those 30 years, but he was blind to the fates that were stalking him, ready to shatter the complacent and smug world he was inhabiting.

That month he was also the featured interviewee in *Playboy* magazine. He described a future that was ironically self-confident and that echoed with reverberations that would only become comprehensible six months later:

> I'll always stay connected with Apple. I hope that throughout my life I'll sort of have the thread of my life and the thread of Apple weave in and out of each other like a tapestry. There may be a few years when I'm not there, but I'll always come back. And that's what I may want to do. The key thing to

remember about me is that I'm still a student. I'm still in boot camp. If anyone is reading any of my thoughts, I'd keep that in mind. Don't take it all too seriously. If you want to live your life as an artist, you have to not look back too much. You have to be willing to take whatever you've done and whoever you were, and throw them away. What are we, anyway? Most of what we think we are is just a collection of likes and dislikes, habits, patterns. At the core of what we are is our values, and what decisions and actions we take reflect those values. That is why it's hard doing interviews and being visible: As you are growing and changing, the more the outside world tries to reinforce an image of you that it thinks you are, the harder it is to continue to be an artist, which is why a lot of times artists have to go, "Bye, I have to go. I'm going crazy and I'm getting out of here." And they go and hibernate somewhere. Maybe later they re-emerge a little differently.[10]

Or maybe not. The habits of a lifetime are hard to change. Steve was a big thinker, an inspirational motivator, but not a day-to-day manager. What was sad was that he could not see it.

"I tried to talk to him about it privately, I tried to convince him that he really didn't want to run a big company," said Phil Schlein, the long-time member of the board and the CEO of Macy's. "But he just wouldn't hear it. Early that year [1985], he had gotten it into his mind that he was going to have to run Apple. Nothing less would do.

"It was so obvious that he was the last person you'd choose to do that. To think up new products, to inspire a small group, to be a visionary, I'd never met anyone his equal. But to run a billion-dollar company? Never. It was so obvious to all of us, but not to him."

The day after his birthday, Steve wrote a memo to his troops in the Macintosh division that detailed a series of changes that needed to be made to keep the project on keel. It was partly in response to what he could sense were problems with his leadership of the group, and partly the financial woes that were about to sock Apple on the chin. Although Steve thought he was addressing the issues in the memo, he was missing the point. The problem was with him. It was too little, too late, and too mild. Steve was attempting to cut out the bruises on the surface of the Apple, but the fruit was rotten at its core.

To: All Macintosh Employees
From: Steve Jobs
Date: 25 February 1985
Subject: Rough Sailing Ahead

As many of you know, this is the year we must make Macintosh successful in business as the alternative to the IBM PC. Two things are currently threatening our success: Macintosh business software doesn't arrive in full force until April/May, and we are currently in a serious industrywide slump.

As a result, we in Macintosh are falling far short of our sales goals and are not pulling our weight within Apple. What can we do?

After having given much thought, I wish to make the following changes, some of substance, some symbolic, effective today:

1. Let's eliminate the free beverages until we return to an acceptable profit level. We can survive on water for a while.

2. Let's hold all retreats on site. We can save quite a bit here. I will personally approve a very low-budget alternative if you propose one (a church, sleeping bags in a closed elementary school . . . ?)

3. Let's eliminate all catered food (Delectables, George, etc.). Our prospective customers will be impressed more by our quarterly profits than a catered lunch. Schedule more non-lunch meetings.

4. Let's all fly business class for awhile. Unless we're traveling internationally, let's cut first class air expenses.

5. Let's eliminate overtime. We're all exempt at heart.

6. Let's delay moving into DeAnza II. Bandley 2 & 3 kind of grow on you.

7. Let's cut down on all our purchased services (mostly consulting). I'd like a 50% cut within 60 days. If the consultants we used last year were so smart, we would be selling more Macintoshes now.

8. I'd like you all to cut 50% of our discretionary expenses. These include business lunches, seminars, out of town meetings, etc. Postpone that quality seminar until we are

building 40,000 Macs a month, schedule more nonlunch meetings, and rediscover the benefits of "brown-bagging" it.
9. I'm limiting hiring to critical openings only. All previously approved open req's are now canceled. We are now a division of over 700 people. Seven hundred of us should be able to run our current business and plan for the future. If we need some reallocation of people, let's do it. All hiring will need my personal approval before an offer is extended.

Macintosh sales momentum is slowly building, and I am confident that we will come out of this industrywide slump stronger than we entered it. But for now, we must **batten down the hatches** and get ready for some rough sailing ahead.[11]

That was his bold prescription for holding the fort in the Mac division until times improved. To him and the rest of the team still following his flag, it was only a matter of time before the public decided to start buying Macintoshes. But inexorable forces had already been set into motion that would rock the empire. Steve was already privy, on the day he wrote the memo, to a decision that would send the company's stock plummeting even further. Excess inventory after a Christmas season of lower than expected sales forced Apple to announce week-long furloughs at each of its Apple II manufacturing plants as well as at the Fremont Mac factory. The announcement sent the stock down more than $2, and analysts immediately revised their income forecasts for the company downward.

It was part of the out-of-control sales forecast situation, which had occurred for years but was only then being acted on. For instance, the forecast sales figures of 128K and 512K Macintoshes for the week of March 11, 1985, were 4,447 and 15,703, respectively. The actual number of machines sold were 606 and 1,853—just over 10 percent of the projection.[12] The forecast errors continued throughout the product line; external disk drives, carrying cases, programs such as *MacProject* and *Alice*, and even blank disks were all forecast at least ten times too high. It was impossible to professionally manage a firm when the gulf between wishes and market reality was so broad.

Sculley was finally forced to take some kind of action by an increasingly unhappy board of directors led by investor Arthur Rock.

Had it not been for the excess inventory of Apple IIs, it is unlikely that the situation would have been addressed. Luckily for the company, a few days after announcing the enforced plant closings, IBM announced that it was ceasing all production and promotion of the PC Junior computer—the "Peanut"—which had been a flop from the start. The resulting press distracted from the focus on Apple's woes that had prevailed for months.

As the announcement of the plant closings was made, Murray distributed a memo describing his fears to key members of the executive staff. He finally decided, against better judgment, to go public with his predictions for the company. Under the banner of "Do not circulate, copy or share," he described what he saw as the company's major philosophical problems:

---

1. Apple, an unorthodox company, is caught in an irreconcilable paradox where the more we impose the structure and process necessary to run a multi-billion-dollar company, the more we constrict the creative, spontaneous lifeblood that has made Apple what it is today.
2. The defined rules for divisional behavior (i.e., who owns profitability) are in conflict with the structure and reality of the market and thus create very predictable organizational dysfunction.
3. We have little or no inter/intra divisional trust, thus teamwork is not an option.
4. Whether the *cause of* or *because of* the dysfunction, Steve Jobs now controls a seemingly impenetrable power base, disproportionately large given his role as general manager, fueled by the current rules, served by extremely loyal (perhaps naïve) aides, and perceived by most as maniacal machines bent on espousing vision—be it product vision, distribution vision, or channel pricing vision—at the clear expense of corporate survival.[13]

With that, Murray went on to detail a corporate restructuring that would basically bring the business functions of Apple back into control and keep the products subservient to the overall company's operations.

One of the first people he showed it to was Steve, who was still willing to discuss the issues with the elfin director of marketing. He wasn't threatened by Murray, and throughout March they had endless meetings. Steve's moods were swinging wildly between a belief that he should move out of the way and head for AppleLabs and a new start within Apple, or try to oust Sculley for the good of the company. By now Steve was telling everyone on the executive staff about his doubts concerning Sculley. He himself was growing more certain that the only way to fix the company was to take over in a major new reorganization. One day he would agree to bringing in someone new to head Macintosh; the next day he rejected the idea. He was holding on to the dream of what the Macintosh team and spirit should be, and he didn't believe that anyone else could capture and retain it.

Murray wouldn't go for it and argued with him continually. He believed that the only answer was to put someone else at the head of the Macintosh division and to give Steve a new role in an R&D project such as the proposed AppleLabs. It would be an R&D project the way the Macintosh had been three years earlier, when things were better, when they still had their passion, when they could soar without worrying about managing 700 people and a mature product.

The Macintosh division was going down in flames. Not only were there mass defections, but the FileServer was delayed until at least the end of the year. Sculley wasn't pleased. He thought he had been misled by Belleville and Steve. Sales weren't picking up, and he commissioned some research that showed that the Macintosh was perceived as a yuppie computer, not a serious business machine. Sculley demanded that they change the emphasis of the group's marketing communications, and he told Steve that he thought Gassée should be brought in to take over. Steve responded by telling the president that he didn't know anything about computers. They had a fundamental disagreement about how Apple should be run.

"Steve's view was that it had to be decentralized," explains Sculley, "Because the only way to hold on to entrepreneurial-type people was to give them the chance to, in effect, run their own little business inside a larger corporation.

"My sense was that a more overriding issue was to have one Apple. We were competing too much with ourselves. We had to have an organizational approach that would centralize the process of management by making sure that product development was working on building products for the market place and not competing with other parts of Apple."[14]

But while Sculley was willing to give, Steve was growing more and more intractable. Finally, late in March, he appeared at the offices of Frogdesign to look at some new design work they were doing for Apple. Lying around on the drafting boards were a series of designs the firm was doing for Woz and his new company, Cloud 9. Woz was working on a universal remote control device that could run any television or stereo equipped with infrared signaling capability. When Steve saw the designs, he hit the ceiling. In a rage, he demanded that they either send the artwork to Apple or destroy it. Apparently, a clause in Apple's contract allowed the company to approve Frogdesign's high-tech clients, and his former partner wasn't acceptable to the chairman of the board.

The blowup was immediately covered in the press and reflected very poorly on Apple. "It's not personal. We don't want to see our design language used on other products," Steve explained to the *Wall Street Journal*.[15] The virulence of his reaction and the impressions of everyone else involved, however, spoke of a much deeper resentment than Steve's words suggested.

"Steve Jobs has a hatred for me," explained Woz.[16] The manager of the Frogdesign office, Herbert Pfeiffer, added, "It's a power play. They have personal problems between them."[17]

Steve was under enormous pressures and couldn't control himself. One day while the events were being covered in the newspapers and threatened to blow up into a full-scale scandal, he appeared at Andy Hertzfeld's house in Palo Alto to explain himself to the seminal programmer who was also a long-time Woz worshipper.

"He stood in the doorway and tried to make me understand what he was doing," said Hertzfeld. "But he wouldn't come in. The more he explained, the worse it sounded. I let him keep talking, because he obviously needed to explain to someone. But he was not making much sense.

"He had made a mistake, but he couldn't admit it. That was the sad part. He had to justify himself. I felt sorry for him."

19
Lobotomy

April Fool's Day of 1985 was nine years to the day after the two Steves signed their agreement to start Apple Computer in Woz's one-bedroom garden apartment. On that 1985 anniversary the company had 5,700 employees but no Steve Wozniak. Although the previous day the Macintosh had been named "Product of the Year" by an industry trade magazine, the company was struggling to stay in the black. Nonetheless, some of the old values still remained in the kingdom of Cupertino. As Bob Geldof's Live Aid concert raised funds for the starving in Ethiopia, Apple's employees raised $71,000, which was promptly matched by the corporation. Apple still had a heart, although the next few months would sorely test it.

The beginning of the end for one of the company's other cofounders came when Sculley heard through the grapevine that Steve was questioning his competence. Sculley felt he had been loyal to him and was upset that Steve was not reciprocating. At a meeting he confronted Steve with his back-stabbing, telling him to cease and desist. Steve, although contrite at the time, dismissed the whole affair later as a "lover's quarrel" to his closest associates and quickly forgot about it. He misread how important the meeting was to Sculley, and that was a mistake.

"I told Steve that I was going to tell the board I didn't think he ought to be general manager of the Macintosh division," says Sculley. "I thought he ought to be the chairman and focus on setting the vision for the corporation. He should create the next base of technology and maybe lead a team that would build the next great products, as he had done with the Macintosh.

"I told Steve I was going to bring this up with the board and I wanted him to know it ahead of time."[1]

In mid-April, matters came to a head when the board finally decided to take action after Sculley did indeed raise the subject. They were led by Arthur Rock, the taciturn investor who had been there from the start. Rock was a silent, stout, silver-haired man with a taste for the finer things in life and was known to cut short discussions of new products with terse comments such as "But what good is it?" Along with Markkula, Rock was the power behind the throne at Apple. Because of Apple's vociferous corps of stockholders, there was always the chance that something untoward might happen at an annual meeting, and the board was always alert to the possibility of a coup. At annual meetings, Rock was usually seen hovering in the wings to help provide the necessary quorum and to lend the voice to second Al Eisenstadt's slate of company-approved motions.

For months Rock had been putting up with Steve's blue-sky forecasts, but now, faced with a string of resignations, huge unsold inventories of both Apple IIs and Macintoshes, and Mac sales below 10 percent of forecast levels, he felt compelled to take charge. At the previous February board meeting, he had made it clear to both Steve and Sculley that their positions were on the line. Unless things turned around soon, the board was going to have to initiate a sweeping reorganization of Apple.

At the April 11th and 12th board meetings, a number of key issues were decided. The first was to cancel the Macintosh XL. Inventories were nearly depleted. Just as Steve hoped, the announcement of the Lisa as a large Macintosh spurred sales. Everyone in the boardroom agreed that one of two advanced Macintosh research projects in development at that time—the Big Mac, led by Rich Page, one of the designers of the Lisa, or the Little Big Mac, a less ambitious project— would be able to fill the high-end needs of customers 18 months out. The kernel of the TurboMac project, an expanded ROM set and a high-speed connector for hard disks and other peripherals, was now part of the Macintosh Plus, which was scheduled for release the following January. There seemed no point in playing a game with the Macintosh XL any longer, and the Lisa was dead for good.

At this point Steve brought in Kitchen to make a presentation about his flat-panel display.[2] Board member Harry Singleton, the head of United Technologies, was concerned with the manufacturability of the units and asked a number of pointed questions about the projected $20 million in costs that Steve was espousing. Singleton thought that the flat-panel project would more likely run double that before completion. Nonetheless, they allegedly approved a limited go-ahead for Apple to create the AppleLabs project since it was apparent to all of them that this was exactly the kind of project they needed for Steve.[3] He was excited about it, and they gave him the go ahead to start building a research facility.

The board then turned to more pressing matters and told Sculley to take charge of the company. They met privately with each of the contenders for the control of Apple. Steve had the opportunity to present his case first. He argued that he should take over, that Sculley was mishandling matters, but he was resoundingly voted down. Rock made it clear that he had no time for Steve's foolishness, and even the chairman's strongest supporters, such as consumer advocate Schlein, were finally forced to abandon him.

"I'd tried and tried to make Steve understand that he had to do what he was best at, and that wasn't running the company," recalls Schlein, "but he had a blind spot a mile wide. He thought he was the only guy who could save Apple. He was so stubborn that no one could make him see it wasn't going to happen."

Sculley, sensing the changing winds and realizing that he was close to being cut loose, decided to lay his cards on the table when his turn came to present his case to the board. He was upset that Steve was bad-mouthing him in front of the board and decided that he had to make a power play. He said he found it hard "to act like a CEO when you're meant to boss the chairman of the board."[4] He avowed that he could only turn things around if he was given the authority to handle the company the way he saw fit—without interference from Steve.

"I felt this company was going to get into serious trouble and it was impossible for me to carry out my job," Sculley explains. "So I was, in effect, telling the board that they were going to have to make a choice.

"I wanted Steve to continue to be chairman. I wanted him to lead a new-product team, focus on new technologies and let me run the company, which was what I had been hired to do. And when I recommended it to the board, they agreed."[5]

After hearing out both men, the board took a vote on moving Steve out as general manager of the Macintosh division. Within minutes it was over. The board voted to consolidate power behind Sculley. Furthermore, they agreed to support a reorganization and restructuring of the company to be orchestrated by Sculley and to extend an offer to Gassée to take over the Macintosh division. Steve would be in charge of AppleLabs, but he wasn't going to have a line managerial position.

"He [Steve] agreed—reluctantly," recalls Sculley. "He wasn't very happy about it, to say the least. He asked for as much time to make the transition as possible. I felt that that was only fair, because he was a co-founder of the company and the principal visionary."[6]

The events of the day left Steve in a state of shock. The board had always been a rubber stamp for him, and now they were suddenly asserting themselves and cutting him out. He was bitter toward Sculley. He believed the attack was unprovoked. Even though he was free to attack Sculley, Sculley wasn't free to attack him. Nonetheless, he agreed to do whatever they said for the good of Apple. But the honeymoon was over. Afterward, when Sculley tried to be conciliatory, Steve brushed past him and left without saying a word.

That night Steve called Jay Elliott at home. The human resources vice-president was hosting a small dinner party and decided not to answer the phone, letting his machine take the call. However, he had neglected to turn down the volume on the speaker. With half a dozen people sitting down to dinner, the voice of Steve Jobs, sobbing, came out over the speaker. "I've lost the support of the board, Jay," the chairman cried, thoroughly distraught. "Help me win them back!"

Elliott was torn. For months he had been counseling both Steve and Sculley. He thought that Steve had to step down from managing Macintosh for the good of Apple, but he also believed that Sculley was too weak and had let key decisions slide. Elliott had been preaching the same organizational structure to both, but where Sculley could see a place for Steve, the company cofounder was now only interested in kicking Sculley out.

Elliott didn't have to choose sides immediately because Steve headed back to Japan a few days later, looking for the components to build new models of Macintoshes that were perennially on the drawing boards. In the meantime, Sculley was composing a confidential memo scheduling strategic planning meetings, first with the executive staff and then with the senior managers. It wasn't the president's first effort at reorganization; in his first year at Apple he had consolidated the

Apple II division under a single manager and had brought the Lisa and Macintosh teams into a single organization. Although some thought that Sculley lacked muscle, others saw him as a careful, meticulous manager always concerned that he identify the company consensus before making decisions. For managers accustomed to Steve's chaotic style, Sculley's reasoned and analytic style might have appeared to be weakness, but it could also be labeled prudent.

By the time Steve returned from Japan in late April, Sculley was proceeding along the road toward reorganization. His version of what the company needed was being distributed in a memo to the senior staff:

> Apple has built it [sic] success story by becoming a great innovative product marketing company. We have strong franchises with enthusiasts in education, individuals, and small business which we primarily reach through dealers and direct education sales channels.
>
> As the growth in the personal computer industry has shifted towards professional markets where systems and solutions are becoming more important, we have found it hard to adjust to get an important share of the business market. A tremendous amount of management, technical, and marketing energies are being used up in our efforts to compete with IBM in the largest corporations. We are losing our focus with our traditional users (e.g., the enthusiasts) as we set out to conquer new markets.
>
> It is important that we make sure we are focusing on the "right markets" for Apple over the next several years, and once we determine what those "right markets" are, then we must have the best products and marketing/sales efforts to be successful in these "right markets."
>
> It is also important that we step back and consider how our strategic goals tie in with what we believe are Apple's unique strengths as well as how these goals and strategies fit in with the values we feel are important for our people.
>
> The industry is clearly in a slump and we are in a cost-cutting mode. Under the pressure of these difficult times, we have got to make sure that we are thinking clearly and making the right decisions for Apple.[7]

The same day that the memo was sent around the upper echelon of the company, Steve and Murray were trying desperately to come up with their own strategy that would make all the reorganization plans moot. While Sculley was looking for synthesis and a carefully crafted organization, the two younger men wanted to capture the excitement again. They were looking for the kinds of big ideas that had made Macintosh such a big success in its first 100 days, even though those flashy marketing ideas had proven to be without legs.

In the two weeks after Steve returned from Japan, he opened up conversations with General Motors again, trying to find a corporate sponsor. Coca-Cola was ready to take part in an aggressive summertime joint promotion for the Apple IIc to give away nearly 100,000 machines. And Compaq, the makers of IBM-compatible portable computers, had approached Apple looking for investment. With all that in mind, the two 30-year-olds formulated a strategy as bold as it was ill advised. They called it the *Phoenix Project*, as in rising from the ashes. In part it was inspired by work that Murray had commissioned from Pat Caddell, a presidential pollster, and Scott Miller. The two Democratic Party strategists had a corporate consulting firm in New York called Flying Fortress that Murray was using as his war cabinet. Murray wrote up a draft plan for Steve:

DAY 1 - Apple cancels National Account program; announces it is returning to its roots of small business and education; announces that it will OEM Macs to companies like Tandem for reaching large organizations; announces 31 small business accounting packages and the appointment of a VP Small Business Marketing.

DAY 2 - Apple buys 30% of Compaq, but refuses to answer all press inquiries as to why. The industry is mystified by this unusual action.

DAY 3 - Apple purchases in rapid fashion (at 30¢ on the dollar—to be paid in Apple stock if possible): Computerland (612 outlets), Entre Computer Centers (236 outlets), Valcom Computer Centers (160 outlets), and MicroAge Computer Stores (140 outlets), for a total of 1148 outlets. We would announce the formation of a wholly owned operating company: "Apple Stores" and would introduce the operating company's president: John Sculley.[8]

It was certainly a bold scheme, but the real goals were to offer an IBM-compatible choice alongside the Mac for businesses and to put Steve atop the entire company again. The plan continues:

Organizationally, we may have a real win: You could essentially have four companies if you wanted, with you being the bona fide Chairman: (1) Apple Stores (John Sculley, Pres)—a marketing company with two missions: build and maintain a dominant small-business franchise through a dealer base of 1000 stores and maintain a dominant education franchise through an educational sales force that works either in selected Apple Stores or as a central Apple Stores function. All marketing programs and funds for these programs would be controlled by Sculley. He would be a profit/loss center. (2) The Macintosh Company (Jean Louis Gassée, Pres)—a product development company responsible for the design, development, and manufacturing of the Macintosh product line. The products could be sold through Apple Stores or the Macintosh Company's direct sales force. (3) The Forever Company (Del Yocam, Pres)—a product development company responsible for the design, development, and manufacturing of the Apple II product line. The products could be sold through the Apple Stores or mass merchandisers if appropriate. (4) The Compaq Company (Rod Canion, Pres)—a product development company responsible for the design, development, and manufacturing of the Compaq product line. The products could be sold through the Apple Stores and the Macintosh Company's direct sales force.[9]

It was a completely outrageous plan, both financially—their own estimates were that it would cost $1 billion—and organizationally. Steve had agreed to relinquish the Macintosh division, but the board had not specified a date. As the weeks passed he had seemed to forget his promise and started to talk about taking over the company again. Now he had an action plan. Steve would head the new organization, and Steve and Murray thought that they had a chance to make the rest of the company go for it.

As it turned out, they never even got the chance to present their ideas. Two days after they had hatched the idea, it started to come unraveled when Murray showed up early on Saturday morning for a big meeting with a large retailer whose chain of stores was about to go bankrupt, a circumstance that threatened to leave Apple with millions of dollars in unpaid accounts receivable.

That Saturday, May 11, as Murray walked to his office, he was surprised to see Jean Louis Gassée sitting outside Steve's as yet unoccupied office. In the two months since Murray had suggested the Frenchman as Steve's replacement, he had heard no further discussion of the matter and assumed that there had been no further action. Surely Steve would have told him if Gassée were about to replace him, thought Murray. After all, the two of them had been meeting daily for weeks and in just the last few days had come up with the Phoenix Project.

Murray stopped to ask what Gassée was doing there. Gassée was surprised Murray didn't know. "We're working out the final details of the job, Mike," the Frenchman told him. When Murray stared at him quizzically, still not comprehending, Gassée added according to Murray, that "There must be some kind of mistake. I'm taking over from you as director of Macintosh marketing. I start on Monday."

Murray felt faint and rushed to his office to sit down. His head was spinning. He couldn't believe that Steve, whom he considered a close friend, could have forgotten to tell him. It was inconceivable. Worse, he knew what was going to happen. He had seen it happen to dozens of other executives at Apple. "Someone takes over their job, and suddenly they just don't exist anymore," he explained. "There are lots of euphemisms for it—consulting, leave of absence, new position—but everyone in the company knew that it really meant the person had done a bad job and was being terminated.

"We hadn't even figured out a good cover story, and it was Saturday. They were going to announce Gassée taking the job on Monday, and I would just disappear into oblivion."

Murray sat through the meeting to decide the fate of the endangered chain. He was in a daze as Apple agreed to bail out the retail operation with an infusion of cash. After the meeting, he walked into Steve's office and found the two men talking. Gassée had brought a letter with him that spelled out the terms of the deal he wanted, and Steve was about to sign it. Murray told him that they had to meet that afternoon. When they finally did, Steve couldn't believe that Murray was so upset. He told him it must have slipped his mind. Murray wouldn't buy it and told him he was resigning on the spot and that he thought he had been treated shabbily for giving his loyalty to the chairman.

That night Murray had a call from Sculley, who told him that he was too valuable to lose and that Apple had to find an important role for him. The president invited him to Steve's Woodside mansion the next day to work something out. Sunday morning the three of them paced the grounds behind Steve's house. It was a beautiful day, and as they walked across the rolling lawn and back into the wilder woods behind, they came up with a new position for Murray as vice-president of business development.

Throughout their walk, Steve had scarcely been able to contain his dislike for the mild-mannered Sculley. He rolled his eyes and kept giving Murray pointed looks of disgust at suggestions that the president made. At this point Murray was extremely unhappy with Steve and wasn't about to join in on his silent character assassination of Sculley. Then, as they were finally reaching agreement, Sculley excused himself to go back into the house and attend to some business. As soon as he had walked away, Steve changed gears and Murray recalls Steve telling him that "John's a complete bozo and we're going to have to do something about him."

A few minutes later, when Sculley returned, the conversation started up right where they had left off, as if all the bitter talk about Sculley as a "bozo" had never happened. Murray felt chills go down his spine. For the first time in three years, Murray, Steve's most loyal lieutenant, was thinking of deserting him.

On Monday the news of Gassée's new job swept through Apple like wildfire. Murray expected a personal memo from Steve on his new job appointment to counter rumors of his demise, but nothing was forthcoming. He was depressed and felt yet again that he had been used by Steve. He had discovered, as had so many others, that a relationship with Steve was a one-way street.

Steve had more important matters on his mind—at least, they were more important to him. He was pursuing the creation of AppleLabs in Palo Alto. That week Steve and Sculley brought a team of high-level Sony engineers to see the flat-panel display, and a few days later Kitchen showed him another remarkable prototype they had created, this one having to do with voice recognition. Steve was energized again about AppleLabs. As far as the top management of

Apple was concerned, the company's product visionary could live out his fantasies there.

But at the same time that he was letting Sculley think he had every intention of stepping out of the day-to-day affairs of the company, Steve was looking into other options. Although Sculley was the president of Apple, Steve was both the chairman of the board and the chief executive officer, a role that he had never relinquished. This meant that with some fancy procedural footwork he could conceivably remove Sculley without the other man's knowledge. Legally, Steve had the power to get rid of him in his absence, something Sculley couldn't in turn do to him.

As Steve contemplated ever more byzantine strategies, he broached the subject of a coup with a few of the members of the executive staff, chiefly Jay Elliott. "John Sculley was going to China later in the month as part of Apple's signing an agreement to sell computers to the Chinese," he says. "Steve thought that would be a perfect time to stage a coup. The trip was scheduled for the Memorial Day weekend, and Steve decided that with a quorum of board members and key executives planning to attend a celebration at Mike Markkula's Carmel ranch that weekend, he would oust Sculley there."

Elliott repeatedly told him that he didn't think it would work. The board was still behind Sculley, and the other members of the executive staff were even less likely to go for the Machiavellian plot than he. "I thought they were both being incredibly childish," contends Elliott. "Steve was trying to pull off a palace coup, and John was acting like a spoiled child by refusing to make any decisions until he knew that he had Steve out of his hair. We had serious business to worry about. The two of them were going to take Apple under."

Steve was struggling to find a way to get rid of Sculley. Sculley was hearing reports from his executive staff that Steve was itching to bring the whole affair to a final firefight. By now the friendship had eroded, and Sculley was fighting to save the company. And he was coming to the unhappy conclusion that the only way of doing so was by removing Steve. Some of Sculley's strongest supporters on the board were growing increasingly annoyed with his cautious handling of the cofounder. One was upset that Steve was still even on the premises of Apple—he suggested that if Steve refused to step down voluntarily Apple should have him physically ejected from the premises. In the infighting and politics of the boardroom, Steve was no match for the experienced and diplomatic Sculley. Once he was finally roused to take his gloves off, Sculley was the master. In his two years with Apple he had carefully tended his fences and consolidated all the essential power relationships. In eight years at the company, Steve never had.

On Tuesday, May 14, two days after the meeting with Murray at Steve's house, an all-day Macintosh division review was scheduled. This one was attended by Gassée as well as all the key Macintosh managers. From the first minutes of the meeting, it was clear that chaos reigned. Immediately Steve and Sculley clashed, and the first hour of the day-long review was spent with the two of them arguing over the fundamental charter for the Macintosh division. Steve wanted it to be to sell more machines; Sculley wanted the division to fit better into Apple as a whole. That altercation set the tenor for the day.

As one after another of the group leaders gave their presentations, the newcomer Gassée watched, listened, and absorbed. A few days later he wrote out his first observations in a memo to Sculley, Elliott, and Steve. For the first time, an intelligent, dispassionate criticism of the division emerged. The memo had to be troubling to all who read it. Finally someone was willing to call a spade a spade, to tell the Macintosh emperor that he had no clothes on. And while the memo was gentle and clearly aimed at finding solutions to the internal chaos of the division, between the lines the message was apparent. The following are some sentences from the document:

- While I have no problem with the diversity of formats in the presentations, I am inclined towards a more organized approach.
- The interplay between the members of the group was . . . frank, that's okay with me, the less the agendas are hidden the better.
- The ROM upgrade and New Filer/File system are still up in the air. To my knowledge, the code is not written, therefore far from debugged. And we are less than 4.5 months away from the dealer shelves date.
- Little Big Mac is another problem. What we saw was not a prototype. The bus and slots are far from ironed out, there very well might be other open issues. In any case, the product definition does not exist yet. How can we believe we will ship in a year?

- Why did we design a 20-megabyte disk that the Apple II division cannot use? Why is our 800K external drive different from the one the Apple II division is preparing?
- File Server—A lot has been said. What remains is that we made commitments, slipped several times, had unclear product definition(s) and finally gave up.[10]

Gassée made Belleville and Steve admit that the FileServer was dead in the water. One of the cornerstones of The Macintosh Office was canceled, but it would be six more months before the world was told. Then Gassée added the kicker that infuriated Steve and set the stage for the final act:

- As we do not seem to know who and where the Macintosh users are, we will find out so that we can validate our strategies. So far we are blind.[11]

By the time Steve saw Gassée's ideas about the division on paper, he had changed his mind about relinquishing control of the Macintosh or anything else. Gassée was right, but Steve didn't want to hear it. The division review had been a harrowing experience and put Steve up against a wall. It was do or die now. He finally decided to remove Sculley while the president was in China and thus out of communication. He arranged with Markkula to spend the weekend at his ranch, where most of the executive staff and board of directors had been invited for the Memorial Day weekend, and started to formulate his plans to regain control of the company he had founded.

Steve's plotting became all the more urgent when he saw the reorganization plan that Sculley was toying with at a high-level strategy meeting on Monday, May 20, the beginning of the week when Sculley would leave on his trip. The proposed reorganization consolidated the company under two executive vice-presidents: Del Yocam to head operations and Bill Campbell for marketing and sales. Under each would be a tier of four directors taken from both the Apple II and Macintosh product divisions. Steve was offered a position as vice-president of new product development. He had been given the same role by Scotty in the late 1970s. He was not thrilled.

As the week proceeded, Steve talked individually with each executive staff member. He told them that he was unhappy with the direction in which Sculley was taking the company and was thinking of calling an emergency executive session over the upcoming Memorial Day weekend. Campbell and Yocam were torn. They knew how powerful Steve was, but both also recognized the importance of not alienating Sculley in what was shaping up as a major league battle of wills.

On Thursday, May 23, Steve held his regularly scheduled Macintosh division staff meeting. He told them that Sculley wanted him out of Apple and that one of them would have to go. The band of four Macintosh managers—Belleville, Coleman, Murray, and Barnes—told him that he should fight back and offered to call board members themselves to help. Then, halfway through the meeting Steve abruptly asked Murray to take a walk with him, and the two headed out along Bandley Drive.

According to Murray, this was when Steve revealed his true plans for the first time to the former director of Macintosh marketing. "I'm going to launch a coup while John is in China," Steve told him conspiratorially. "Bandley 4 is going to be my headquarters. I want you to know, but let's not tell the others." Although Murray was amazed, it was too late to back out. Even though Steve had shafted him a few weeks earlier in replacing him with Gassée, Murray reluctantly offered whatever help he could give.

Unfortunately for Steve, he had told one person too many. He liked Gassée and mistakenly trusted him. That morning he had told Gassée, vaguely, about his plans and asked for support. The Frenchman said he would think it over. That evening Gassée went to a barbecue at Al Eisenstadt's house for some of the senior staff, including Sculley. He and Eisenstadt were friends, and apparently Gassée told the company's chief lawyer about what seemed to be a coup afoot. Thoroughly alarmed, Eisenstadt called Sculley into the living room and had Gassée tell the president what Steve had told him. It only confirmed what Sculley had feared.

In that same period Steve had called the investment house of Morgan Stanley and asked about the possibility of using his position in Apple stock as the basis for a leveraged buyout. Steve was desperate. Making the call was an incredibly naïve move—after all Sculley was one of the good old boys of the financial establishment who had Wall Street's trust. Within minutes of the call, Sculley heard about it. The talk of a coup was only too credible.

The next morning, at 8 A.M., Sculley convened an emergency executive staff meeting and accused Steve of working behind his back to topple him in front of the entire senior staff. "I'm running this company, Steve," the president screamed at the chairman of the board, according to one of the attendees, "and I want you out for good. Now!"

Steve was silent for once in his life. Then he slowly let go with what had been building in him for months. Sculley recalls the words he used. "I think you're bad for Apple, and I think you're the wrong person to run this company," he carefully explained, atypically staying under tight control, keeping his composure icily impassive, and not blowing up once during the ordeal. "You really should leave this company. I'm more worried about Apple than I ever have been. I'm afraid of you. You don't know how to operate and never have.

"John, you manage by monologue. You have no understanding of the product development process. You don't know how manufacturing works. You're not close to the company. The middle managers don't respect you. In the first year you helped build the company, but in the second you hurt the company."[11]

From there all semblance of friendship evaporated. It was an intense three hours. Steve told Sculley that he thought he knew how Apple needed to be run. Sculley grew furious. Behind closed doors the president polled the executive staff, forcing each to pledge allegiance publicly either to himself or to Steve. Elliott was disgusted by the whole thing. "I told John that I thought he was being an ass," he says, "and I refused to do it. Right then I thought they both should get out." When he had the votes he needed, Sculley told Steve that he was fired as general manager of the Macintosh division. Finally Steve responded, telling Sculley that on the contrary, as chairman of the board, he was firing Sculley. But he didn't have the votes to back up his attempted coup. The prince was all alone on a mountaintop of his own making. He had burned all his bridges.

Meanwhile, the rest of the company's senior managers were waiting in an auditorium, wondering what was going on. That Friday was the date of Sculley's long-scheduled senior strategy meeting, and rumors quickly went around the 25 key people gathered in wait. An emergency closed-door executive staff meeting was not something that could easily be hidden in gossip-filled Apple Computer. Murray guessed that something had gone very wrong with Steve's revolutionary plans. The senior executives filed into the auditorium at 11 A.M.

Campbell and Yocam looked disgusted, according to Murray, and Steve spent the entire meeting, which consisted of a brief speech by Sculley, glowering at Elliott, who he was sure had betrayed him.

Sculley's speech was disconnected, and his body language mirrored the content of his speech. Murray recalls that Sculley stood behind a pillar in front of the room, as though he were hiding from the assembled managers as he delivered the speech. The president articulated his points without impact or emotion, as if he were simply reading from a prepared list. Apple had to become one unified company, a major expense reduction was necessary across the board, and the company had to make an investment in education and business through its dealers, he told them. He also placed an emphasis on new products, accountability, and on top management communicating better with the troops. It was time to get through the bad times of the summer selling season and go for the Christmas quarter.

Sculley didn't mention the foiled plot that Steve had hatched. He told them that he was forming study teams to help them through the crisis. Murray was disappointed with Sculley's crisis management style: "He needed to dictate. He needed to come in and tell us what he was going to do. He was losing all of us with his low-key messages about studying things. You can't declare war and then wait 30 days for your tactical plan to arrive."

The meeting broke up with Sculley leaving the room without taking any questions and returning to his office. He called Al Eisenstadt into his office and told him that he was resigning. Then he called his wife to tell her that their trip to China was off and that he had quit. She came roaring down to the office from their Woodside home. When she arrived, she went looking for Steve, and finally found him outside a little health food restaurant in a nearby shopping center. "You've got the devil in you, Steve Jobs," she screamed at him in the parking lot, according to an Apple employee who witnessed the event. "You'll pay for this."

Steve was upset by the day's events, and the scene in the crowded parking lot didn't help. A few minutes past 1 P.M. he walked into the office he kept in the Macintosh building where he found the loyal Macintosh team waiting for him. He looked around at his four key colleagues, and with tears in his eyes told them he was resigning. Immediately, Bob Belleville said that he would do the same. "I won't work for Gassée," he vowed, according to Murray, and walked out. With that Steve stood up and tried to leave. Debi Coleman and Susan Barnes hugged him and were crying as well. Then, as he headed for the door, Mike Murray said, "You had better make sure you know what you're doing. The minute you walk out that door your world will change."

In mid-stride, Steve stopped and came back. His loyal team then spent an hour reviewing the options. They decided that instead of acting hastily, it would be better to give everything a few days to calm down. It was the Memorial Day weekend anyway; why not think it over? Steve eventually agreed. The final act was averted for a few more days. Meanwhile, in the executive suite, Sculley was being counseled by his trusted lieutenants to stay on. That afternoon he thought better of his hasty resignation and rescinded it.

The battle with Sculley had consumed all of Steve's energy. He was drained. The next day, Saturday, May 25, Murray had an all-day management seminar scheduled for his staff with Oswald Swallow, a charismatic South African. Swallow, known by the ironically appropriate moniker Oz, was a management consultant who specialized in teaching groups how to handle decision-making and interpersonal relations.

On this crisis Saturday, Murray canceled the class and instead ferried the South African up to Steve's mansion in the Woodside hills, where they spent the better part of the day trying to devise a strategy that would allow the chairman to stay on at Apple without relinquishing all his power. It was a long and desultory meeting. Steve was extremely unhappy, and Murray kept trying to cheer him up, to make him see the advantages of the impending reorganization. It was his chance to return to what he did best, new product development. Murray was convinced it was the right step for both Steve and Apple.

Forever obstinate, Steve still couldn't see it. He wanted to run Apple and felt that this demotion meant he would never get there. And since Sculley's last words to him had been, "There is no place for you in my Apple," he was not exactly optimistic. Oz and Murray tried to convince him to have one last talk with Sculley, to see if they couldn't patch up at least some of their differences and work out a role for Steve in the reorganization. But Steve was never very good at contrition, and this was a meeting where, to be successful, he would have to hang his head and hold his hat in his hand, asking for forgiveness.

For most of the afternoon he resisted. He came up with all kinds of excuses but finally agreed to try one last time. With Murray and Swallow listening, he called Sculley. He asked if they could get together the following day to discuss matters and see if they could come to some amicable agreement. Sculley agreed to meet him at 3 P.M. the next day, Sunday afternoon. Their rendezvous would be in the hills above Stanford University, unspoiled parklands where they had often met in happier times to walk and talk. Steve was shaking as he hung up the phone.[1]

Murray didn't want to leave him alone that evening. They decided that after taking Oz back to his hotel, they would watch a film together. Steve suddenly developed a passion to watch *Patton*, an epic about the individualistic World War II general who was able to weather numerous adversities in his long career. Steve had refused to buy a VCR—only a laserdisc player would do for him. He always had to have the latest high-tech gadgets. They went searching for the film on laserdisc but couldn't find it. Instead, they rented *Betrayal*, which was based on a Harold Pinter play. It is the story of an adulterous triangle between three close friends: a married couple and the wife's lover, the best friend of the husband. Steve was still trying to seduce Apple away from Sculley, although he thought his intentions were honorable and motivated solely by his love for the company. The film is about the inexorable pull of dangerous emotions, even in basically moral people. It was a foreshadowing of the final act that was about to be played out. That night, at Murray's Los Altos house, Steve, Murray, and Murray's wife Joyce watched the movie and tried not to talk about the meeting scheduled for the next day. Before midnight, Steve left to return home. Murray wished him good luck.

The following afternoon Steve met Sculley to try to convince the president that he had only been trying to do the right thing for Apple and that his machinations weren't meant to be a reflection on Sculley's performance. Steve was at his most charming, and by then he had simply forgotten the tense confrontation in front of the executive staff the previous Friday. He really did want only what was best for Apple, and, he explained, if that meant he had to leave the company, then so be it. He would abide by whatever decision Sculley ultimately made, but he wanted one more chance to stay with the company that he had founded. Wasn't there some way that they could split up the company? he asked. He could run product operations and Sculley could handle marketing. The two men started walking in the hills above Stanford.

Sculley knew that a messy divorce would only strain his chances of bringing Apple out of its current tailspin, but he wasn't about to let Steve meddle in the operations of the company any longer. He had to be the clear leader of the company, but nonetheless there was a role for Steve to play in his vision of the future Apple. He allowed himself to be persuaded by the young prince one last time.

"When we were walking through the Stanford hills talking about it," Sculley recalls, "Steve said 'I feel like somebody just punched me in the stomach and knocked all my wind out.' He went on, 'I'm only 30 years old and I want to have a chance to continue creating things. I know I've got at least one more great computer in me. And Apple is not going to give me a chance to do that.'

"I said, 'We'll give you a chance to create the next great computer, but you're not going to run the operation. The company is in a precarious position, and right now, all our energies have to be focused on getting the company turned around.'"[12]

As they passed horses grazing in pastures amid the mansions and stables, Sculley told him that he was willing to let the past be water under the bridge if Steve would agree to work for the good of the company. No problem, Steve said, that was what he wanted anyway. Sculley offered to let him run new product development at AppleLabs, and reluctantly Steve agreed to it. Finally, several hours later, the two shook hands and parted. As far as Sculley was concerned, he had agreed only to consider the role that Steve should play in the new Apple he was carving out, but he had done so in good faith.

On the other hand, before his Mercedes had pulled out of the parking lot, Steve was already plotting a final attempt at a coup. He knew he had to act fast, so he stopped on the way home to see Markkula. He needed to present his case to the vice-chairman of the company, who still controlled 9 percent of the stock. Markkula wasn't in—he was at his ranch in Carmel for the three-day weekend—but Steve left an urgent message inviting him over for dinner the following night. Then he called Murray, Belleville, Coleman, and Barnes and asked them to attend the dinner as well. The scheme he was hatching would give them a chance to show Markkula how good they really were, to explain their plans for the Macintosh division, and to convince him that Steve should stay on as head of the division, if not take over the company.

It was Memorial Day of 1985, a beautiful, stunning day along the coastal mountains above Silicon Valley. In the afternoon, as the fog started to drift in over the ridge, Steve's lieutenants started to gather.

They discussed how to bring Markkula around to their point of view. Murray and Steve pushed for the Phoenix Project, which they had formulated a few weeks before, while Debi Coleman thought that Sculley's reorganization plan was basically correct. She thought that Steve should be given a new product division to create the next "insanely great" product—AppleLabs.

After whole-wheat pizzas had been served, Markkula showed up and nibbled on a bowl of cherries. A quiet, thoughtful man, he was at his quietest that evening. As the sun set out over the trees, the group sat on the back patio. Steve explained that he wanted his team to have a chance to tell Markkula what their vision was for the future, away from all the high-strung emotions and chaos of the events at Apple. Markkula was visibly uncomfortable and agreed to listen, but only as long as Steve didn't say anything. He wanted to hear what the people working for Steve thought, without his interference. He had enough experience with his glib cofounder to know that he could twist any conversation to his advantage.

One after another they described the situation as they saw it and expressed their visions of how the company could be reorganized without losing the unique spirit of the Macintosh division. Markkula listened impassively and finally, when they had all had a turn, told them that the board was indeed going to approve a reorganization but that it wasn't clear what form it would take. He thanked them for their input and left. None of them was sure what the result of the meeting would be, but Steve was optimistic and thought that he had persuaded Markkula to his point of view.

Early the next morning as he arrived at work, Sculley met Steve in his office. The president told him that he had heard from Markkula that Steve was once again plotting behind his back, even after his assurances of the previous Sunday. Sculley's cool and calculating personality started to assert itself. He had lined up the support he needed at the top of the company, he explained, and now Steve would have to leave. That day Sculley met with Markkula, outlined his plan for the reorganization, and told him that he wanted Steve out. Markkula told him that he had the support of the board and to do what he needed to implement his strategy. Steve's cofounder had not been influenced by the previous night's cozy dinner.

That evening, after waiting until Steve had left the premises to drive home, Sculley convened an emergency board meeting by teleconference. He polled each member on the issue of removing Steve from office. One by one they gave Sculley leave to remove Steve from an operating position at the company and to proceed with his own reorganization plans.

As soon as Steve reached his house, just after seven that evening, Sculley called to tell him that it was all over. He was going ahead with the reorganization and had the votes of the board to strip him of any operating role at Apple. He was welcome to stay on as a product visionary, but he would not be in charge of a division any longer.

Shortly thereafter, in tears, Steve called Bill Campbell, Jay Elliott, and then Mike Murray to tell them the news. It was Tuesday evening, May 28, 1985. Murray's wife was on a long-distance call when an emergency interrupt came through. She told the operator that it had better be important, and then heard Steve's voice saying, with almost no emotion, "It is." She called her husband to the phone, and Steve told him, "It's all over. John and the board have voted me out of Apple. Goodbye Mike." Before the former marketing director could say anything Steve hung up.

Murray was frightened, especially when he called back and there was no answer. Although it was 10:30 at night, he decided to drive to Steve's house and make sure that he was all right and didn't do something foolish.

When he arrived on the moonless night, the Woodside house was completely dark. There was no answer at the front door. He walked around to the back of the house and climbed up an outside staircase that led to Steve's bedroom. As he pushed open the door, he could see Steve lying on his mattress on the floor of the room, alone in his ascetic surroundings. The only other furniture in the room was a bread rack with shirts neatly stacked on it. For several hours Murray sat with him and they talked. Finally, in the wee hours of the morning, convinced that Steve wasn't going to end it all that night, Murray slipped out of the house and drove home.

The next day Steve didn't show up at Apple, although rumors were already swirling about what had happened. Sculley finally convened his reorganization meetings and in two days of sessions restructured the company. Steve took a ride on his motorcycle and then a long walk through the hills above his house. He was down, but still hadn't quite given up. When he came back down the hill, he finally found a copy of *Patton* on a laserdisc and retreated to his house to watch it. That evening Murray came back to check on him and stayed to see it. Steve was still talking about coming back, making a last stand. Murray tried to argue him out of it, but then gave up.

Steve didn't show up at Apple the next morning either, finally appearing that afternoon. He immediately came to see Murray. They had a long talk about how he should handle himself. Should he take a leave of absence? Should he fight? Should he roll over and die? Murray told him that he had two options: He could take the low road, getting out now and giving the press all the comments they would be looking for; or he could take the high road, be a statesman, rising above it all and refraining from backbiting or bitterness. It was up to him, but Murray recommended the latter course. He also suggested that Steve come to the company-wide announcement meeting that Sculley had scheduled for the next day to lend his support to the reorganization. He could show that he was bigger than the petty power squabbles. Steve said he would sleep on it.

The next morning was Friday, May 31. At the communications meeting Steve slipped into the back row of the auditorium. He had decided, no matter how painful, to lend his public support to Sculley. Steve Jobs was growing up.

Taking the podium, the president explained that owing to a worsening slump, Apple was going to have to lay off between 1,200 and 1,500 employees and reorganize the company to better manage its affairs. As the meeting proceeded, Sculley explained his new organization but refused to acknowledge Steve. He introduced all the key members of his new team, which included both Gassée and Coleman but no other members of the Macintosh division. When he displayed the organization chart of his new Apple, one name was conspicuously missing. No mention was made of the company's former Macintosh division leader, cofounder, product visionary, front man, and evangelist. For John Sculley and the new Apple Computer, Steve Jobs didn't exist.

Fifteen minutes after the meeting ended, in his corner office at Bandley 3, the building he had built to house his superstars on the elite Macintosh team, Steve and Mike Murray shook hands. A few minutes later, Steve walked out to his Mercedes and drove away. For one of the first times in his life, Steve Jobs had lost. And this time it wasn't just one battle—he had lost the war.

VI

The Journey Continues . . .

20
NeXT

On Saturday morning, June 1, the *San Jose Mercury News* led its front page with the banner headline: "Apple Co-Founder Jobs Demoted." The story also made the front pages of the *San Francisco Chronicle* and *Examiner*. In the rest of the United States the tale of his fall from grace merited coverage, but only on the inside pages or the business section.

Steve switched his answering machine on and spent the day listening to callers' voices as the phone rang continuously. He avoided reporters and editors and talked only to a few friends and family members. Fiona came over to keep him company. With the shades down and the house dark, he listened to Bob Dylan.

> *The line it is drawn*
> *The curse it is cast*
> *The slow one now will*
> *Later be fast*
> *As the present now*
> *Will later be past*
> *The order is rapidly fadin'*
> *And the first one now*
> *Will later be last*
> *For the times they are a-changin'[1]*

Steve was shell-shocked. He understood the angst that Dylan had sung about throughout his body of work. The chip on the shoulder and the outlaw's stance were only the visible trappings of dissatisfaction that ran deep in the poet's heart. You had to have pain to be a real artist, and Steve was having tortuous pain. Not the kind of self-imposed suburban pain of the upper middle-class, but the raw and naked hurt of losing a loved one. Steve had been orphaned again, this time by his company.

It was the end of the line. He had grabbed the trappings of Zen Buddhism—the asceticism and spartan environment—but he had missed the heart of the religion. He had looked for love in the machines he willed into existence. For all his money and power, for all his charisma and celebrity, he was alone. There weren't any brothers in arms to commiserate with here.

Like many of his generation, Steve was spoiled by his era and had the luxury to search for meaning in his life rather than struggle for survival. His particular path had started as the orphan's search for parents, moved through the mysteries of electronics and electronics pranks, to drugs, diets, and Eastern philosophies. He had slipped easily into and out of psychological fads such as primal therapy and entertainment fads such as video games. Finally, the search for a guiding force in his life had led him to personal computers. But it could just as well have been something else. Steve had a deep well of passion that found its match in the birth of the personal computer industry. The same drive that sends people to the moon or deep into the intricacies of genetic code drove Steve along his journey. He wanted to find the latest, the "whizziest" of new technologies, grab hold of it, and make it seductively attractive and affordable to the public. He was the populist of computing at a time when the magic of electronics finally produced something extraordinary that could capture the imagination of the world.

His goal would always be around the next corner, in the next discovery, in the next product. Through his machines, Steve was trying to find himself, to uncover the answers to the illusory questions about life that had plagued him since his adolescence.

"My philosophy is that everything starts with a great product," he says. "I obviously believed in listening to customers, but customers can't tell you about the great breakthrough that's going to happen next year that's going to change the whole industry. So you have to listen very carefully. But then you have to go and sort of stow away, you have to go hide away with people who really understand the technology, but also really care about the customers, and dream up this next breakthrough."[2]

By chance he happened upon the personal computer at a remarkable time, and the serendipity of the meeting belied the explosion that resulted. Steve dreamed of changing history, of having an impact, and he did. He wanted to be like Patton, who won a war, or Bob Dylan, who changed a generation with his music. What drove him was the chance to do something great. The Macintosh was his chance to make a dent in the universe. And it did.

But Steve was never the inventor; he was the packager. He sucked up the best ideas he could find and transformed them into real products that combined aesthetics and engineering that could pass for art. Like an artist, Steve's reward came from seeing the product out in the world and then going on to the next canvas where he would really get it right.

By 1985 he had given everything to Apple and the computers they had produced, and he wasn't about to fade quietly into the background. Steve was a fighter, a competitor who believed that he knew better than anyone what was right. For a week he brooded and considered his options. Then he packed his suitcases and caught a flight to Paris to begin a long-scheduled business and pleasure trip. He was stumping throughout Europe for The Macintosh Office and planned to go on to Russia to promote Apple IIs, which had recently been approved for sale behind the Iron Curtain. Perhaps in action he might find some solace.

From Paris, after doing his corporate bit, he headed for the Tuscan hills outside Florence in central Italy, bought a sleeping bag and a bicycle, and camped out under the stars in an orchard in San Gimignano, a medieval village. No one recognized him as he bicycled through the little hill towns of Italy. As he pondered his fate, instead of coming to grips with it, he grew more depressed.

By late June he was in Sweden, still trying to do the right thing for the company. His attitude had mellowed a little. "Things don't always happen the way I want them," he said to a Swedish journalist. "Just like Mick Jagger said, 'You can't always get what you want; sometimes you get what you need.'

"Five years ago this would have bothered me. Now I'm sitting back and thinking that maybe there is some wisdom in this. Henry Ford had a couple of difficult quarters, too, in the 1920s.

"I'm not a power-oriented person. I care about Apple a great deal. I put pretty much my entire adult life into building great products and building a great company. So I'm going to give what I can to further Apple. If that means sweeping the floors, I'll sweep the floors. If that means cleaning the toilet, I'll clean the toilet."[3]

But he was hardly chastened. "Woz hasn't done much in many years," he answered, in response to a question about the recent departures of several key Apple people. "Andy Hertzfeld is always complaining. He'll come back anyway. What I did with the Macintosh team was to give them recognition for their work: I'm not so sure it was good. I may have made a mistake. It was a good concept, but it went a little too far."[4]

Steve Jobs was down but not out. He continued talking about his team, but his words could just as easily have described himself: "A lot of it went to their heads. For a few people, it is very difficult when things happen. You have to think very strongly about your inner values—what really is important for you. When things happen very fast, you don't have the time. It can scramble your brain."[5]

By July 4, he was in Russia, but he was ready to return to Cupertino. He was ready to patch up his differences with Sculley and get on with his new job, whatever that was. However, when he arrived back at Apple in the middle of July, he found that the corporation didn't want him.

"I was asked to move out of my office," he explained. "They leased a little building across the street from most of the other Apple buildings. I nicknamed it Siberia.

"So I moved across the street, and I made sure that all of the executive staff had my home phone number. I knew that John had it, and I called the rest of them personally and made sure they had it, and told them I wanted to be useful in anyway I could, and to please call me if I could help on anything.

"They all had a cordial phrase, but none of them ever called. So I used to go to work. I'd get there, and I would have one or two phone calls to perform, a little bit of mail to look at. But most of the corporate management reports stopped flowing by my desk. A few people might see my car in the parking lot and come over and commiserate. And I would get depressed and go home in two or three or four hours, really depressed.

"I did that a few times, and I decided that it was mentally

unhealthy. So I just stopped going in. You know, there was nobody really there to miss me."[6]

Murray did. He moved into the office next to Steve's. One day Murray had gathered his things and joined Steve in the empty building. No one missed him for a week. In the reorganization, the job that the loyal lieutenant had been promised only weeks earlier suddenly evaporated. He couldn't be trusted—he was too close to Steve. Nonetheless, ever the sloganeer, Murray had coined the phrase "One Apple" as his last effort to influence the new management. The phrase became Sculley's rallying cry that summer and fall as the company president tried to win back the Apple II corps and win over the remaining Macintosh partisans.

Still chairman of the board, Steve avoided corporate duties and focused on supervising repairs being made to his house. Then he decided that he wanted to conquer a new dimension—space—and asked NASA if he could ride the Space Shuttle. He found that being a "global visionary" didn't cut the mustard with the government. He was turned down. Christa McAuliffe, an elementary schoolteacher, was selected instead.

Apple's stock continued to drop, eventually falling as low as $15 a share. Then, for the quarter ending June 28, the company announced its first loss ever: $17.2 million, with a drop in sales of 11 percent from the corresponding quarter a year earlier. It hurt, and Steve began to blame himself for the troubles the company was experiencing. However, a few days later, he was even more stunned by a comment that Sculley made to securities analysts at the company's quarterly meeting to describe Apple's most recent results and future plans.

"There is no role for Steve Jobs in the operations of this company," Sculley told the closed meeting, "either now or in the future." The comment instantly leaked to the press, and a couple of days later the president reconfirmed it to a collection of reporters trying to interview him as he slipped into his limousine. Steve was staggered.

"You've probably had somebody punch you in the stomach," Steve explains, trying to describe how he felt. "It knocks the wind out of you and you can't breathe. If you relax you can start breathing again. That's how I felt. The thing I had to do was try to relax. It was hard. But I went for a lot of long walks in the woods and didn't really talk to a lot of people."[7]

A few days later, he decided to sell a little more than 10 percent of his Apple shares—850,000—which was the maximum quarterly sale allowed under SEC regulations. The sale netted him around $11 million and squelched rumors of a leveraged buy-out that had been circulating since he had made his call to Morgan Stanley in late May. He just wanted to get out, and the rules of selling founder's shares were such that he had to sell off his stake piecemeal—he still had 6 million shares, which were worth about $90 million, even at the depressed price. Nonetheless, the sale started a flurry of rumors about his plans. Few expected the 30-year-old to quietly accept being put out to pasture. Speculation centered on either an investment group or a new company. He was known to have been pursuing the computer graphics division of George Lucas' empire, Pixar, in the months before the final reorganization. He now had the beginnings of a war chest, but what would he use it for?

The answer wouldn't be long in coming. With time on his hands, he hired a political consulting firm to help him find a way into politics. It was the same group that had worked with his sometime role model and fellow Zen Buddhist disciple, former California governor Jerry Brown. But Steve had never voted or belonged to a political party. The group apparently told him that gaining a constituency would be difficult.[8] He started looking in other directions.

"I think what I'm best at is creating new, innovative products. That's what I enjoy doing," he said later that summer, finally starting to understand what those around him had been saying for years. "I enjoy, and I'm best working with, a small team of talented people. That's what I did with the Apple II, and that's what I did with the Macintosh.

"I had a piece of paper one day, and I was writing down the things that I cared the most about, that I was most proud of personally in my ten years at Apple. There's obviously the creation of the Apple II and the Macintosh. But other than that, the thing that I really cared about was helping to set up the Apple Education Foundation. I came up with this crazy idea that turned into a program called 'The Kids Can't Wait,' in which we tried to give a computer to every school in America and ended up giving one to every school in California, about 10,000 computers.

"I put those two together, working with small teams of talented people to create breakthrough products and education."[9]

He spent a lot of time wandering around the semideserted Stanford campus and the rolling hills that framed it. He had always felt at home there, starting as a high school junior hanging out in the cafeteria, then auditing physics classes, and later preaching to small groups of interested MBA students. Apple photographed many of its Macintosh advertising shots among the eucalyptus trees and along the covered walkways and bicycle paths of the campus. Steve and Sculley had even posed there during happier times. Stanford meant something special to the college dropout and high-tech preacher.

In the Stanford libraries he began to delve into the world of biochemistry and recombinant DNA research, trying to understand the Bay area's other rapidly growing industry. He had met Paul Berg, one of Stanford's Nobel Prize-winning biochemists, at a dinner for France's president, François Mitterand, a year earlier. He called him up and invited him to lunch to ask a few questions. Over a meal in a coffeeshop near the Stanford campus, he and Berg talked.

"He was showing me how they were doing gene repairing," Steve says. "Actually it's straightforward. It's kind of neat. It smells a lot like some of the concepts you find in computer science.

"He was explaining how he does experiments in a wet laboratory, and they take a week or two to run. I asked him, 'Why don't you simulate them on a computer? Not only will it allow you to run your experiments faster, but someday every freshman microbiology student in the country can play with Paul Berg recombinant software.' His eyes lit up."[10]

Berg remembers the conversation a little differently. According to him, it was Steve whose eyes lit up. The scientist explained to the young entrepreneur that the computers used to run such simulations were presently too expensive and the software primitive. "Suddenly he was excited by the possibilities," recalls Berg. "He had it in mind to start a new company. He was young and rich, and had to find something to do with the rest of his life. This sounded like it."[11]

It had been a long time since Steve felt the surge of energy that he had experienced with the blue boxes, the Apple I, II, early Lisa, and the Macintosh. With the possibilities of something on the horizon, the inspiration started coming through again. It was a new product, a new machine. A fresh love affair. A new trail to blaze.

Just as Steve was getting excited by this idea of creating a new computer for the university market, in late August something happened at Apple that crystallized what would be the formation of his next project. Gassée canceled the Big Mac project in favor of the less ambitious Little Big Mac. When he took over the Macintosh division that summer, Gassée expanded the development program for an advanced interim version of the Mac, based loosely on the FileServer that had been abandoned and centered in the same engineering group. Codenamed Little Big Mac, it kept the basic design of the Macintosh and substituted a more powerful chip, the 68020. This contrasted sharply with the Big Mac, which was an extremely powerful machine built around a custom chip set, codenamed the Jonathon, created by Rich Page, who was one of the key designers of the Lisa. When Gassée canceled the Big Mac, Page was miffed. He talked about leaving Apple with his close friend Bud Tribble, the original Macintosh software project leader who had returned after medical school and was again in charge of software development for the Macintosh.

Tribble was one of the first people Steve thought of as he formulated his new venture. Over the Labor Day weekend, Steve broached the subject of a new company to the softspoken manager and was encouraged that Tribble found his ideas intriguing. They discussed the "3M" machines that universities were settling on as the computers of the future: advanced workstations with 1 million pixels of resolution on screen, 1 million bytes of main memory, and the ability to process up to 1 million instructions per second. Although machines of this caliber were available from workstation companies and IBM, they cost over $10,000 apiece, much more than the target $3,000 universities were willing to pay.

Tribble knew just who could build such a machine. He suggested a couple of people at Apple who might be willing to help get it off the ground, including Page and George Crow, the analog engineer who had been a member of the original Macintosh team. Steve also suggested Susan Barnes, the Macintosh controller, for the financial side of things, and Dan'l Lewin, architect of the successful Apple University Consortium, who had been promoted to marketing manager for all higher education applications during the recent reorganization. When Steve asked each of them, sub rosa, they all agreed to join him. He was at his most inspired and persuasive as he wove the dream of his new enterprise. He was talking to a group of people who had never been at the heart of the Macintosh project—essential, yes, but not the key superstars. They were all individualists who, like Steve, were searching for another chance to create something great, and Apple no longer seemed like the place to do it.

As Tribble said, "Everyone wants to be involved in a start-up."[12] This would be a start-up with a bang that would return them to the roots of Apple. The way Steve described it, how could it fail? Overnight, he had the kernel of a company.

"We have no business plan. We haven't done anything," Steve would say a few days later, when their plans went public. "Now, you might say we're all crazy. But we've all known each other for four years. And we have an immense amount of confidence in each other's abilities and genuinely like each other. We all have a desire to have a small company where we can influence its destiny and have a really fun place to work."[13]

With that Steve realized that he had better tell Apple about the new venture. A board meeting was scheduled for September 12, and though he hadn't attended them for the last several months, as chairman he was still entitled to. As the meeting was called to order, he briefly explained that he had done a lot of thinking about things over the summer and had come to a few conclusions. Although no one recorded the speech, when Steve described his motivations to *Newsweek* a few days later, it sounded like a speech he might have given before:

> I personally, man, want to build things. I'm 30. I'm not ready to be an industry pundit. I got three offers to be a professor during the summer, and I told all of the universities that I thought I would be an awful professor.
>
> What I'm best at doing is finding a group of talented people and making things with them. I respect the direction that Apple is going in. But for me personally, you know, I want to make things. And if there's no place for me to make things there, then I'll do what I did twice before. I'll make my own place. You know I did it in the garage when Apple started, and I did it in the metaphorical garage when the Mac started.
>
> I helped shepherd Apple from a garage to a billion-and-a-half dollar company. It took a bunch of rambunctious upstarts, working with very little resources but a certain vision and commitment, to do it. I'm probably not the best person in the world to shepherd it to a five or ten billion dollar company, which I think is probably its destiny. And so I haven't got any sort of odd chip on my shoulder about

proving anything to myself or anybody else. I had 10 of the best years of my life, you know, and I don't regret much of anything. I want to get on with my life.[14]

Phil Schlein recalls that it was one of Steve's finest moments, and he had seen the charismatic young man sway some mighty skeptical board members before. If the board were inclined to tears, there wouldn't have been a dry eye in the place. Steve was giving a farewell speech, and it was a great performance. He then went on to describe his still embryonic plans for a new firm and assured them that he had no intention of taking any technology or proprietary ideas out of Apple. He mentioned that he would be taking a few people from the company, but by no means enough to disrupt operations or the products they were working on, and they would be those who were already leaving. He offered his resignation as chairman if the board thought that the new company would compete with Apple.

The board asked Steve to step outside while they discussed it. They were sold on his candor and were favorably disposed to letting him take on the building of a quasi-Apple workstation computer. It could be the high-end Macintosh workstation for the educational market, a project that seemed perfectly suited to him and definitely in Apple's best interests. A few minutes later he was invited back in, and Sculley, very friendly, told him that Apple thought it sounded like a marvelous project. They were interested in buying 10 percent of his new venture while keeping him on the board, although not as chairman. Mike Markkula joined in and suggested that Steve and Sculley should discuss it further during the coming week. They made a date for Sculley and Apple's counsel, Al Eisenstadt, to meet with Steve. With good cheer all around, the meeting adjourned.

That night, at Steve's house, the new group met for the first time as a team. Steve told them what had transpired in the boardroom. The group decided that they didn't feel comfortable drawing things out. They wanted to tell Sculley their names right away and make a clean break. "We decided to cut the umbilical cord and go as a group so there wouldn't be one hit after another," said Susan Barnes.[15] Furthermore, they wanted to sever ties completely with Apple. They didn't want any investment from the company.

Steve was up at dawn. He got into his car and headed for Cupertino. Sculley appeared at 7:25 that morning, Friday, September

13, and immediately encountered the chairman of the board. Steve told him that the group had decided it was best to leave en masse and handed him a handwritten list of the names. Sculley scanned it, said nothing for a moment, and then asked about the other two issues about which the board had inquired: an investment in the venture and Steve's staying on the board of directors. Steve told him that they felt uncomfortable about committing 10 percent of the company to Apple and that he had no intention of staying on the board. They shook hands, and Sculley said he really hoped they could work together. Steve was heartened and felt that they really could split up on a friendly basis.

Although Sculley didn't appear upset to Steve, he claims that he was "absolutely taken aback when Steve walked in and handed me the list."[16] He felt that "the board had been deceived. He said he was going to take a few low-level people not involved in anything Apple considered important."[17] Instead the list named two senior engineers: Page, an Apple Fellow, which was the company's highest honor for scientists; and Crow, the top engineer for power circuitry. There were two key managers on the list as well: Tribble was manager of software development for the Macintosh computers, and Lewin headed marketing to all schools and colleges, the only bright spot in Apple's woeful financial picture during that quarter. By the time Sculley came out of his executive staff meeting that morning, Apple's attitude had changed.

"The executive staff has been stunned and shocked that this has happened. I had no idea Steve was forming a company," said Bill Campbell, executive vice-president in charge of marketing and sales. "Losing those people was a shock. But losing the chairman of the board was even more shocking. We've had a good quarter; the organization has come together after the reorganization. This seems to highlight turmoil at Apple and nothing could be further from the truth."[18]

Campbell's counterpart in operations, Del Yocam, was incensed and hinted at legal action. "I'm quite surprised that all this was being done while he was chairman, and furthermore, it would concern me if he gets into a business that's competitive with Apple."[19] Jean Louis Gassée was even more furious. Later in the afternoon he blasted Steve and his group of conspirators in front of 200 people in the Macintosh new product development group.

An aroused Sculley informed the board of Steve's plans and had the five "traitors," as they were referred to at Apple, escorted unceremoniously off the property. At the board meeting Steve had indicated that it was still a nebulous venture, but by presenting names the next morning he had demonstrated otherwise. The attempt to home in on the company's strongest market, education, with the defection of Lewin, caused considerable grumbling. The company's position was that the appearance of unseemly plotting while Steve was still chairman of the board gave Apple strong legal grounds to use against him and the new business.

That day the company was in an uproar. The news of Steve's new venture spread like wildfire around Cupertino, and Apple was stunned. Group meetings were held throughout the company, and the news was passed along to employees. Black Friday quickly joined Black Wednesday—the day of Scotty's mass firings four and a half years earlier—in the company's folklore. There was shock and dismay that the company's visionary could have abandoned them. And in the Macintosh group, some of the team were disappointed that Steve had passed them over when selecting his new group.

Emergency meetings of the board were held by telephone over the weekend, and the company was uncertain how to proceed. The news hit the front page of the Sunday *San Jose Mercury News*, was carried on all the major wire services, and this time the story was also front-page news across the country.

Mike Markkula, the largest shareholder other than Steve, released a statement after a Monday board meeting: "The board interpreted this action to be in direct contradiction to his statements of the previous day and began the evaluation which is currently underway." The reticent vice-chairman still refused to meet the press in person. "We are evaluating what possible actions should be taken to assure protection of Apple's technology and assets."[20]

Steve was silent throughout the weekend. He didn't respond to reporters' phone calls until he heard about the statement Markkula had made. It was time to take control of the publicity apparatus he had learned to play so well over the years. On Tuesday he delivered his resignation letter to a spate of newspapers and magazines before he drove to Mike Markkula's nearby house and hand delivered it. Then, in front of the press gathered at his house, he burned all the bridges. The love affair was over. He faced the future with a kind of tough and brutal honesty that was immensely compelling.

He described the end in romantic, almost melodramatic terms that painted him as the aggrieved party. "My heart will always be there," he said, referring to Apple. "My relationship with the company is like a first love. I'll always remember Apple in the same way any man remembers the first woman he's fallen in love with.

"To me Apple exists in the spirit of the people who work there and the philosophies and purpose by which they go about their business. If Apple becomes a place where computers are a commodity item, where the romance is gone, and where people forget that computers are the most incredible invention that man has ever invented, I'll feel I have lost Apple.

"But if I'm a million miles away, and all those people still feel those things and they're still working to make the next great personal computer, then I will feel that my genes are still there."[21]

A few days later Steve announced that he had settled on a name for the new venture. He named it NeXT, and set about doing the paperwork to incorporate it. All week long Apple and Steve's attorneys tried to come to some agreement to allow them all to part on, if not amicable, at least amenable terms. While Steve was willing to agree to a hiring freeze on Apple employees for a period of six months and not to use any proprietary Apple technology, he was unwilling to specify that his new products would not compete with Apple's present or future machines.

At the beginning of the following week, it looked as if the company had done a little gene splicing of its own. On that day, September 23, 1985, Apple Computer filed suit in the Santa Clara County courts against Steve and Rich Page, contending that they had launched a "nefarious scheme" to use company research for a new venture, research that as chairman of the board Steve was privy to, and then deceived the company's board as to their intentions. Steve was incensed by the accusation and went back to the press, where once again he was treated royally.

"When somebody calls you a thief in public, you have to respond. I'm very surprised that Apple is suing me. We have spent an entire week talking with Apple lawyers, showing them that we have no intention of taking or using any Apple confidential information or proprietary technology in our new company.

"This sort of thing sure is hell and doesn't help Apple or its employees. We don't want to get involved with an unjustified lawsuit. We just want to build our company and invent something new. It has gotten to the point where I can't listen to this stuff anymore, and it is time to tell the real story. I guess the fact that I'm not coming back to Apple is finally sinking in, and people are scared. I thought Apple was big enough to find a place for me.

"I wasn't aware that Apple owned me, you know. I don't think they do. I think that I own me. And for me not to be able to practice my craft ever again in my life seems odd.

"We're not going to take any technology, any proprietary ideas out of Apple. We're willing to put that in writing. It is the law anyway. There is nothing, by the way, that says Apple can't compete with us if they think what we're doing is such a great idea. It's hard to think that a $2 billion company with 4300 plus people couldn't compete with six people in blue jeans."[22]

And with that as his parting shot, the new team headed across the country to visit universities, trying to find out what they should build into their new machine. The lawsuit degenerated into legal squabbles and one-upmanship over deposition scheduling, and finally, in the wake of a record profit posted for the company during the final quarter of 1985, the suit was quietly dropped. By then Steve had sold most of his stock, and early in 1986 he completed the divestiture—all but one share, so that he could get the annual report, he claims.

A few weeks later he bought controlling interest in Pixar, the Lucasfilm computer graphics division, for several million dollars. Speculation centered on the high-quality graphics technology the company owned as the basis for the new workstation computer being developed by NeXT, but it wasn't true. NeXT was building a new machine from the ground up. The Pixar computer was a $100,000 machine for very specialized applications, while the NeXT academic workstation was a $3,000 machine designed for college students, professors, and researchers.

The market is a tough one, however, and profits in the education sector are generally slim. Competition for NeXT came from a number of established workstation vendors, all fighting to lower their prices, and from Apple, with its more advanced versions of the Macintosh. Apple's new machines—the Macintosh SE and the Mac II—reflected the needs of the marketplace and in many ways could only have gone ahead with Steve out of the way. They had fans for hard disks, cursor keys for professional typists, and most important of all, expansion slots for adding functionality.

John Sculley found himself at the head of a company perfectly poised to take advantage of a groundswell of profits from the advent of desktop publishing. Ironically, desktop publishing was ushered in by the marriage of Macintosh and the laser printer, a combination that Steve had foreseen and championed in 1983. By the time revenues from it started to turn the company around late in 1985, he was gone. Sculley was given credit for turning Apple around. His reorganization, streamlining, and appearance of stability all contributed, but the financial basis for it was in the Macintosh and LaserWriter that Steve alone had championed and then brought to market.

There's a hint of sadness in Sculley's description of the ending now. "Apple was Steve's whole life," he explains. "It was almost impossible to separate the two personalities. Macintosh was like a son to Steve. And then to have the person he had brought in—I wouldn't have come here without Steve's persuasion—be the one who finally pushed him out was an incredibly difficult thing to handle . . . to this day Steve and I still haven't spoken."[23]

At NeXT, as usual, Steve set exacting deadlines for the machine. It was originally due to be completed in early 1986 but slipped to mid-1987 and eventually to 1988. The software that he wanted to create was, as always, more complex and took longer than he had originally predicted. It wasn't courseware that he was after (courseware refers to programs designed for classroom use), since by early 1987 the Macintosh had pretty much sewn up that end of the educational market. NeXT was trying to build "academic software" aimed at the researcher, a limited market at best. Others at NeXT felt that the proliferation of medium-cost workstations by many other manufacturers made it important that any NeXT software run on a variety of work-station machines. Steve resisted this idea. He still wanted to do it his way or no way at all.

They discovered that their ideas for an educational computer workstation had some serious conceptual problems. Steve had decided that he wanted to make the machine before he really knew if there was a market for it. He believed that NeXT would be able to sell its high-powered, low-cost workstation initially to professors and staff, but that it would be so neat that soon students would buy the machines, too. But why would students buy a specialized machine, even with lots of graphics and power, when they could buy a Macintosh that would do coursework and had several thousand application programs available? The Macintosh, unlike NeXT's workstation, would also be useful when they left the university. To prepare students for success in the real world, the universities wanted students using the same machine as businesses and consumers. A specialized machine aimed only at the academic market had little appeal. They didn't want to get caught in an isolated and unsupported blind alley. The success of the Macintosh continued to haunt Steve and NeXT.

In 1987 there were basically three standard operating systems to choose from in the workstation marketplace: MS-DOS, Macintosh, and UNIX. Two were unacceptable or unavailable to Steve. (Ironically, Apple's board had been willing to license the Macintosh operating system and ROM to NeXT before he was labeled a traitor.) By default he settled on the UNIX environment, which is a powerful but memory-intensive system developed at Bell Labs for mainframe use more than 20 years ago. His idea was to redesign the operating system so that it was easy to use and graphically attractive, not unlike the Macintosh interface. The announcement of an Apple version of UNIX running on the Macintosh before NeXT had been able to start shipping early versions of their machine was a serious blow, especially since Apple's Macintosh machines could now run all three operating systems. (Sculley had finally had his way with an MS-DOS expansion card for the new Macintoshes.) And as a price war on other more advanced workstations caused prices to drop within $1,000 of the proposed NeXT machine, it was not at all clear that NeXT would be able to compete effectively.

But then Steve didn't have dreams of a billion-dollar company any longer, or so he claimed. He just wanted to work in a nice "niche" market with maybe $50 million a year in revenues. As deadlines invariably slipped and the company was without a product but supporting 40 employees, NeXT found itself running out of cash. Early in 1986, Steve acquired the rights to the word processing program that he had originally commissioned as a second source for *MacWrite* (originally called *MacAuthor*) and renamed it *WriteNow*. He vacillated about whether NeXT should market it or not. Since he didn't really want to be associated with a Macintosh product, he eventually licensed it to another firm to market and distribute. He was still driven by his passions rather than by any kind of coherent, unified business plan. He was still driving NeXT.

When Apple dropped Chiat/Day as their advertising agency in the spring of 1986, Steve took out a full-page ad in the *Wall Street Journal* and the *New York Times* that showed he still controlled the purse strings. It echoes another ad that the now-fallen agency had created when Steve was riding on top of the world in 1981:

<blockquote>
Congratulations,
Chiat/Day.
Seriously.

Congratulations on seven years of consistently outstanding work.

You helped build Apple and were an integral part of the marketing team.

You took risks, sometimes failed, never compromised.

The personal computer industry is now being handed over from the "builders" to the "caretakers"; that is, from the individuals who created and grew a multi-billion-dollar American industry to those who will maintain the industry as it is and work to achieve marginal future growth.

It is inevitable that in this turbulent transition many faces will change.

You created some truly great work—the kind that gives advertising a good name.

The kind people will remember for years. The kind people remain proud to have been associated with.

I'm expecting some new, "insanely great" advertising from you soon.

Because I can guarantee you: there is life after Apple.

Thanks for the memories.[24]
</blockquote>

He signed it in his distinctive handwriting (all lowercase, no capitals): steven p. jobs. It was the kind of public display that he was so good at.

Style was always more important than almost anything else for Steve, and when it came to designing the logo for NeXT, he enlisted the help of a world-famous designer, Paul Rand. Rand was most famous for his work with IBM; it was he who convinced the giant company during the mid-sixties to drop their full name and use only initials. For Steve the designer created a variation on a child's wooden block, with the distinctive lowercase *e* framed by the capitals *N*, *X*, and *T*. The logo cost $100,000. To Steve, the right design and aesthetics were priceless.

During the second half of 1986, NeXT ran through money like water but was still without any products to create a flow of income. To start the company, he had invested nearly $10 million as seed money in return for 70 percent of the stock. By the fall of 1986 that investment was running low. He started circulating an investment prospectus to the venture capital community. According to those who have seen the document, he was looking for another $10 million and was offering 20 percent of the company's equity for it. But there were no takers. The Silicon Valley financial community had seen how he worked, and they wanted nothing to do with him. As the months passed, the amount of investment required reportedly dropped as low as $3 million for the same equity, but still there were no serious offers.

Nonetheless, Steve was still a celebrity, and a fascinating one at that. He was approached by a public television station producer, who was doing a special on entrepreneurs and wanted to focus on NeXT. The company decided to allow the cameras into one of their retreats, and late in 1986 the special aired. It was a remarkable déjà vu for anyone who had been to the old retreats of the Mac group, and a few of the same faces were there. He had assembled a new team of young people and led them with the same charismatic, aggressive style he had cultivated over the years. In a couple of biting moments, it was clear that he had lost none of his sharp edges.

What was remarkable in the videotape was how he ignored the protests of his own staff as they warned him that the dates of delivery for products and software were unrealistic. Joanna Hoffmann, who had been head of international marketing for the Macintosh, was adamant about the unreality in the projected dates. Steve overpowered her reservations and went ahead with an agenda that he had already decided was correct.

He had come so far, yet he had gone nowhere. A few months later she left the firm. "I was burned out by it. I could not do that again," she explained. Her early warnings were correct. The deadline that he was setting on the video came and went, without the software anywhere near completion.

However, in Boulder, Colorado, the PBS show was seen by a man who had been fascinated by Steve before and who similarly found himself cut adrift from the company he had founded. Ross Perot, the button-down Texan data processing multimillionaire, had been bounced by General Motors in a highly acrimonious parting of the ways. The outspoken Perot had publicly criticized the management of G.M. and found himself bought out for more than $700 million. He no longer owned EDS, the firm he had founded, and when he saw Steve on television, he decided he might like to invest. Although the pair were as different as could be—the countercultural vegetarian and former acid-head on the one hand, and a flag-waving patriot and private financier to hostage-release missions in Iran on the other—they had in common a bond of entrepreneurship and a willingness to chase their dreams.

Perot flew out to California and in the course of a few days decided to invest $20 million in NeXT in return for a 16 percent equity position. It was a better deal than Steve had been reportedly offering to the venture capital community, so he had reason to celebrate. Now he had a partner with deep pockets who had long been interested in the possibilities of workstations, as well as a strong, business-savvy investor who provided a new level of credibility to his company. It was a shrewd move and perhaps signaled a future direction beyond the educational marketplace. It is hard to imagine either of these men aiming for small mountains, when there are the huge ones of the home and business computing markets out there as well. Only time will tell.

Steve has changed, at least a little. He sees his daughter, Lisa, with more regularity and has started to remember her birthday. He reportedly subsidizes Colleen's rent so they can live in a nicer home and has offered to help her buy a house. His adoptive mother, Clara, passed away in late 1986, after a long and debilitating bout with cancer. And the sales projections for the first year of NeXT's machines are realistically in the hundreds, not the hundreds of thousands.

In some ways, however, Steve hasn't changed at all. He split up with Fiona, who was his girlfriend for two years. As the time for finally turning NeXT's dreams into a working machine arrived, he had to choose between a woman and the product. He made the same choice he always has. At an industry seminar on desktop publishing he gave a speech with some of the old fire and brimstone. He called Hewlett-Packard, the company that he credits with starting it all for Apple by providing them with inspiration, "brain dead" for its choice of a page-description language. Then he went on to tell all the participants, who had paid hundreds of dollars to learn all about the field, that desktop publishing was an "interim market" that would disappear in a year. The same old Steve.

On the outskirts of Palo Alto, NeXT's new offices are filled with Macintoshes—not the newer models, but the older ones he was responsible for—along with black-and-white photographs, modern sculpture, and large cacti artfully arranged in ascetic offices with bleached hardwood floors. The receptionist answers the phone with his own name, not the company's. It is all terribly democratic. Dozens of young programmers and marketing associates toil long hours to bring their leader's vision of the computer workstation for the educational marketplace to fruition.

The top floor, where Steve's egalitarian cubicle is located, looks west over the undulating hills above Stanford. Surrounding the modern building on the nearby hillsides are dozens of grazing ponies and an advanced H-P research facility. NeXT's building faces the same Santa Cruz Mountains that frame the Silicon Valley, and every night he can watch the fading sun and the mist paintings of fog and cloud as they inch over from the Pacific. A quarter of a mile away, on a rise above him, stands a giant radio telescope antenna commanding the territory. It sits just inside the border of the Santa Clara County line, the county that is Silicon Valley. At its peak is a small red navigational light that burns constantly in the night. On a dark night, it's the only light he can see in the distance from NeXT's windows.

Steve is building a new product now and is trying to find his answers in a machine again. He will keep looking and the journey will continue. Because after all, it's the journey that is the reward. And the answers must be around the next bend in the path . . . .

Author's Note on Sources

I first met Steve Jobs during late summer of 1983 in my role as one of the founding editors of the magazine *Macworld*. My role was to provide nontechnical, journalistic coverage for the unveiling and introduction of the Macintosh and as a consequence I was given carte blanche to interview all the Mac team members. One evening, as I stood inside the Bandley 3 fishbowl where the Mac programmers lived, Steve appeared. He stopped dead in his tracks, looked me up and down, and yelled "Who the hell are you?"

I happened to have a few of my published articles with me—I had given them to a programmer as credentials—and by waving them was able to mollify him. Since I didn't back down I gained a certain respect from the project leader. In the months to come, with Steve's tacit approval, I became a silent member of the team and was welcome in meetings, discussions, parties, and the group's endless informal pizza and falafel feasts. I had a unique ringside seat to the last six months of frenetic activity as the Macintosh was prepared and released.

Over the next few years I ran into Steve on numerous occasions—the lobby of Bandley 3, Friday afternoon beer "busts" in the Mac building, big events at Apple and elsewhere, private dinner parties, industry forums and seminars, annual meetings—and we would discuss whatever was on his mind. After the release of the Macintosh he grew much more guarded and calculating, and as a member of the press I had a hard time getting through the charming mask he wore in public to reach the off-the-cuff and unpredictable personality that made him so interesting. From mid-1983 through 1985 I witnessed close-up his ascent to enormous fame and worldwide celebrity, and then his swift

429

fall from grace. And on Black Friday—September 13, 1985—the day he left the company to found NeXT, I happened to be in Cupertino interviewing original Mac team members for a story about the history of the making of the Macintosh.

Steve was given a number of chances to comment on the contents of this book. I last saw him in person at a small Christmas party in December of 1986 given by one of the key Macintosh creators. Surrounded by Woz and many of his former employees, he was nervous and skittish. I told him about this project and asked for an interview. He agreed. Several letters were sent to him both at his home and his office with no reply. Phone messages were left on his answering machine, with no reply. Finally I reached him one Saturday morning, and this time he initially turned me down. But it was a couple of days after the millionth Macintosh had come off the factory assembly line. In celebration there had been an informal party and regrouping of the gang at ViVi's, the Cupertino falafel place. Steve was angry and a little bitter that the machine had been given to Jef Raskin, not to him, and he wanted to talk. So we did, and eventually he warmed to the idea and agreed to be interviewed. A week later an employee of NeXT called and abruptly canceled the interview. It was the last time I tried.

By far the bulk of the book, and many of Steve's quotes, come from more than 200 hours of taped interviews done specifically for this book between September of 1986 and June of 1987. These were conducted with more than 50 key characters who played important roles on Steve's journey. These tapes were supplemented by dozens of interviews with people, both inside and outside Apple, conducted over the past few years in the course of covering the personal computer industry for a variety of publications.

Everyone who is mentioned in the book, and can be located, was contacted and asked for an interview to present his or her point-of-view on the events described. Certain key participants, such as John Sculley, refused, and their roles have been recreated from the first-hand accounts of others as well as public documents and news reports. A few others have requested anonymity, and I've kept their identities confidential. And furthermore, a very few names and facts have been changed to protect the privacy of certain participants. None of this in any way affects the overall accuracy of the book.

Those who granted interviews, both in the current sessions and the recent past, include: Stewart Brand, Phil Roybal, Larry Tessler, Andy Hertzfeld, Mike Boich, John McCollum, Jay Elliott, Rich Melman, Chris Espinosa, Jerome Coonen, Phil Schlein, Bana Whitt, Carl Ho, Mike Murray, Lee Felsenstein, Douglas Englebart, Mike Kane, Jim Hennefer, Bruce Tognazzini, John Warnock, Alfred Mandel, Brian Fitzgerald, Dick Olson, Al Alcorn, Paul Terrell, Jef Raskin, Joanna Hoffmann, Donn Denman, Steve Capps, Margie Boots, Bill Atkinson, Regis McKenna, Nolan Bushnell, Adam Osborne, Daniel Kottke, Hildy Licht, Jeff Harbers, Bruce Horn, Larry Kenyon, Patti King, Wendell Sander, Cliff Huston, Peter Quinn, Dave Larson, Barbara Koalkin, Bill Fernandez, Elizabeth Holmes, Ed Riddle, Martin Haeberli, Randy Wigginton, Fred Hoar, Don Breuner, Ed Ruder, Alex Kamradt, Owen Densmore, Carol Kaehler, Bruce Courture, Terri Anzur, Jean Louis Gassée, Joe Shelton, Jeff Eastwood, Bud Colligan, and Bob Albrecht. To all of them I owe a deep debt of gratitude.

In reconstructing the internal events inside Apple and within the Macintosh division, I was greatly aided by a vast collection of memos provided by various former Apple employees. These were supplemented by numerous documents provided by others and allowed the course of certain sequences of events to be recreated in exhaustive detail. Several of these memos have been quoted in their entirety and, other than a few typographical corrections, are reproduced verbatim.

There have also been several books published concerning the history of Apple, and three in particular are worth noting. *The Little Kingdom*, by Michael Moritz, is an anecdotal history of the company that ends with the introduction of the Macintosh, and provides much information about the first five years of Apple's existence. *Fire in the Valley*, by Paul Freiberger and Michael Swaine, is a history of the personal computer industry as a whole, with some information about Apple's roots and a great deal of useful background to the beginnings of the grass-roots movement. *Hackers*, by Steven Levy, is an irreverent and charming history of the spirit of exuberant computing that the Macintosh team exemplified, even though the book does not deal with that computer per se.

Because Steve is a public figure, and has been for several years, there are a number of published interviews, as well as hundreds of newspaper and magazine articles, available to the careful researcher. Apple Computer maintains an extensive library of these clips, and the company was kind enough to allow me access to them. Many of his quotes in the book come from these sources. Two published interviews were particularly valuable and deserve note: the February 1985 *Playboy* magazine interview; and a September 30, 1985, *Newsweek* interview. All key reference sources are specifically listed in the footnotes and a wide spectrum of supplementary materials are covered in the bibliography.

Notes

Chapter 1

1. *San Jose Mercury News*, 17 September 1985; *San Francisco Examiner*, 17 September 1985; *San Francisco Chronicle*, 18 September 1985; *Los Angeles Times*, 18 September 1985; et al.
2. Steven Jobs, *Computers and People*, July–August 1981, p. 8.

Chapter 2

1. Michael Moritz, *The Little Kingdom* (William Morrow, 1984), p. 99.
2. David Sheff, "Playboy Interview: Steven Jobs," *Playboy*, February 1985, p. 176.
3. Moritz, *Little Kingdom*, p. 37.
4. *Ibid.*, p. 38.
5. *Ibid.*, p. 39.
6. Sheff, "Interview," p. 176.
7. *Ibid.*
8. *Ibid.*
9. Moritz, *Little Kingdom*, p. 39.
10. *Ibid.*, p. 40.
11. Sheff, "Interview," p. 176.
12. *Ibid.*

Chapter 3

1. Michael Moritz, *The Little Kingdom* (William Morrow, 1984), p. 45.
2. *Ibid.*, p. 50.
3. *Ibid.*, p. 55.
4. David Sheff, "Playboy Interview: Steven Jobs," *Playboy*, February 1985, p. 176.
5. Moritz, *Little Kingdom*, p. 72.
6. *Ibid.*, p. 73.
7. *Ibid.*, p. 74.
8. *Ibid.*
9. *Ibid.*
10. Sheff, "Interview," p. 176.
11. Moritz, *Little Kingdom*, p. 68.
12. Sheff, "Interview," p. 176.
13. Moritz, *Little Kingdom*, p. 77.
14. *Ibid.*, p. 78.
15. *Ibid.*, p. 68.

Chapter 4

1. Michael Moritz, *The Little Kingdom* (William Morrow, 1984), p. 86.
2. *Ibid.*, p. 87.
3. David Sheff, "Playboy Interview: Steven Jobs," *Playboy*, February 1985, p. 178.
4. Moritz, *Little Kingdom*, p. 89.
5. *Ibid.*, p. 90.
6. *Ibid.*, p. 88.
7. *Ibid.*, p. 89.
8. *Ibid.*
9. *Ibid.*, p. 90
10. *Ibid.*, p. 92.

Chapter 5

1. David Sheff, "Playboy Interview: Steven Jobs," *Playboy*, February 1985, p. 178.
2. Michael Moritz, *The Little Kingdom* (William Morrow, 1984), p. 97.
3. *Ibid.*, p. 98.
4. *Ibid.*, p. 99.
5. *Ibid.*, p. 95.
6. *Ibid.*, p. 95.
7. *Ibid.*, p. 91.
8. *Ibid.*, p. 99.
9. Sheff, "Interview," p. 178.

Chapter 6

1. Michael Moritz, *The Little Kingdom* (William Morrow, 1984), p. 135.
2. *Ibid.*, p. 122.
3. *Ibid.*, p. 101.
4. *Ibid.*, p. 140.
5. David Sheff, "Playboy Interview: Steven Jobs," *Playboy*, February 1985, p. 178.
6. Moritz, *The Little Kingdom* p. 142.
7. *Ibid.*, p. 143.
8. *Ibid.*
9. *Ibid.*, p. 144.
10. *Ibid.*, p. 148.
11. *Ibid.*, p. 151.
12. *Ibid.*, p. 150.
13. *Ibid.*

Chapter 7

1. Michael Moritz, *The Little Kingdom* (William Morrow, 1984), p. 157.
2. Moritz, *Little Kingdom*, p. 154.
3. *Ibid.*, p. 161.
4. *Ibid.*, p. 186.
5. *Ibid.*, p. 163.
6. *Ibid.*
7. *Ibid.*, p. 164.
8. Steven Levy, *Hackers* (Doubleday, 1984), p. 260.
9. Moritz, *Little Kingdom*, p. 172.
10. Memo in the Apple Museum, Cupertino, CA.
11. Moritz, *Little Kingdom*, p. 174.
12. *Ibid.*, p. 188.

Chapter 8

1. Michael Moritz, *The Little Kingdom* (William Morrow, 1984), p. 175.
2. Steve Ditlea, *Digital Deli* (Workman, 1984), p. 75.
3. Moritz, *Little Kingdom*, p. 178.
4. *Ibid.*, p. 180.
5. *Ibid.*, p. 181.
6. *Ibid.*, p. 189.
7. *Ibid.*, p. 151.
8. *Ibid.*, p. 198.
9. Flyer distributed at the West Coast Computer Faire.
10. Moritz, *Little Kingdom*, p. 203.

Chapter 9

1. Michael Moritz, *The Little Kingdom* (William Morrow, 1984), p. 223.
2. Apple internal memo.
3. Moritz, *Little Kingdom*, p. 277.
4. David Sheff, "Playboy Interview: Steven Jobs," *Playboy*, February 1985, p. 179.

Chapter 10

1. Michael Moritz, *The Little Kingdom* (William Morrow, 1984), p. 277.
2. *Ibid.*, p. 301.
3. Apple memo quoted in Moritz, *Little Kingdom*, p. 260.
4. Apple internal "Quality of Life" memo.

5. *Wall Street Journal*, August 1980; and Steven Jobs, *Computers and People*, July–August 1981, p. 7.
6. Paul Freiberger and Michael Swaine, *Fire in the Valley* (Osborne/ McGraw Hill, 1984), p. 219.
7. David Sheff, "Playboy Interview: Steven Jobs," *Playboy*, February 1985, p. 58.

Chapter 11

1. David Sheff, "Playboy Interview: Steven Jobs," *Playboy*, February 1985, p. 184.
2. Michael Moritz, *The Little Kingdom* (William Morrow, 1984), p. 271.
3. *Ibid.*, p. 276.
4. Sheff, "Interview," p. 184.
5. Mortiz, *Little Kingdom*, p. 270.
6. Internal Apple memo dated 12 December 1980.
7. Sheff, "Interview," p. 58.
8. Jay Cocks, "The Updated Book of Jobs," *Time*, 3 January 1983, p. 25.
9. B. Uttal, "Behind the Fall of Steve Jobs," *Fortune*, 5 August 1985, p. 22.
10. Internal Apple memo dated 19 February 1981.
11. Copy of document in author's possession.

Chapter 12

1. Michael Moritz, *The Little Kingdom* (William Morrow, 1984), p. 264.
2. *Ibid.*, p. 291.
3. David Sheff, "Playboy Interview: Steven Jobs," *Playboy*, February 1985, p. 58.
4. Macintosh Marketing Plan, dated 12 July 1981.
5. Steven Levy, "Interview with Steve Jobs," *Rolling Stone*, 1 March 1984, p. 41.
6. Sheff, "Interview," p. 70.
7. Apple advertisement from *Wall Street Journal* and *New York Times*, August 1981.
8. Macintosh Business Plan, November 1981.
9. *San Jose Mercury News*, 16 December 1981.
10. *Ibid.*

Chapter 13

1. *Business Week*, 8 February 1982.
2. Lemmons, "Interview," *Byte*, February 1984, p. 61.
3. David Sheff, "Playboy Interview: Steven Jobs," *Playboy*, February 1985, p. 50.
4. Daniel Farber, unpublished interview with Matt Carter.

Chapter 14

1. Preliminary Macintosh Business Plan, 12 July 1981.
2. Danny Goodman, "Playboy Interview: John Sculley," *Playboy*, September 1987, p. 54.
3. Letter to Gordon Gow from Steve Jobs, 16 November 1982.
4. Jay Cocks, "The Updated Book of Jobs," *Time*, 3 January 1982, p. 25.
5. *Ibid.*
6. *Ibid.*
7. *Ibid.*
8. *Ibid.*

Chapter 15

1. Steven Levy, "Interview with Steve Jobs," *Rolling Stone*, 1 March 1984, p. 39.
2. *Business Week*, 31 January 1983, p. 70.
3. David Sheff, "Playboy Interview: Steven Jobs," *Playboy*, February 1985, p. 58.
4. *Ibid.*, p. 180.
5. Daniel Farber, unpublished interview with Matt Carter.
6. *Business Week*, 26 November 1984, p. 149.
7. *Harvard Business School Case*, #9-486-002.
8. *Stanford Business School Case*, S-BP-235.
9. Daniel Farber, unpublished interview with Matt Carter.
10. *Ibid.*
11. *Ibid.*
12. *Adweek*, 31 January 1984, p. 7.
13. Apple internal memos, various dates in August 1983.
14. Levy, "Interview," p. 41.
15. *Ibid.*

Chapter 16

1. Apple internal memo.
2. David Sheff, "Playboy Interview: Steven Jobs," *Playboy*, February 1985, p. 58.
3. Bob Dylan, "The Times They Are A-Changin'," Warner Brothers Music. Used by Permission.
4. Author's recording.
5. *Ibid.*
6. *Ibid.*
7. *Ibid.*
8. *Ibid.*
9. Sheff, "Interview," p. 58.

Chapter 17

1. Apple internal memo dated 5 February 1984.
2. Zito, "Interview with Steve Jobs," *Newsweek Access*, Fall 1984, p. 44.
3. Danny Goodman, "Playboy Interview: John Sculley," *Playboy*, September 1987, p. 52.
4. Zito, "Interview," p. 44.
5. *Business Week*, 26 November 1984.
6. Apple Annual Report, 1984.
7. *Ibid.*

Chapter 18

1. Letters to Apple, 1984–1985.
2. *Kitchen et al. v. Apple, Jobs et al.*, San Mateo County, filed 29 May 1985.
3. Author's recording.
4. Letter to Jobs from Murray, dated 11 January 1985.
5. *San Jose Mercury News*, 7 February 1985.
6. Michael Moritz, *The Little Kingdom* (William Morrow, 1984), p. 312.
7. *Wall Street Journal*, 25 February 1985.
8. *Kitchen et al. v. Apple.*
9. David Sheff, "Playboy Interview: Steven Jobs," *Playboy*, February 1985, p. 58.
10. *Ibid.*, p. 184.
11. Apple memo dated 25 February 1985.
12. Apple memo dated 17 March 1985.
13. Apple memo dated 7 March 1985.
14. Danny Goodman, "Playboy Interview: John Sculley," *Playboy*, September 1987, p. 52.
15. *Wall Street Journal*, 25 March 1985.
16. *Ibid.*
17. *Ibid.*

Chapter 19

1. Danny Goodman, "Playboy Interview: John Sculley," *Playboy*, September 1987, p. 53.
2. *Kitchen et al. v. Apple, Jobs et al.*, San Mateo County, filed 29 May 1985.
3. *Ibid.*
4. B. Uttal, "Behind the Fall of Steve Jobs," *Fortune*, 5 August 1985.
5. Goodman, "Interview," p. 53.
6. *Ibid.*
7. Apple memo dated 8 May 1985.
8. *Ibid.*

9. *Ibid.*

10. Apple memo dated 20 May 1985.

11. John Scully, *Odyssey: Pepsi to Apple* (Harper & Row, 1987).

12. Goodman, "Interview," p. 53.

Chapter 20

1. Bob Dylan, "The Times They Are A-Changin'," Warner Brothers Music. Used by Permission.

2. G. C. Lubenow and M. Rogers, "Jobs Talks About His Rise and Fall," *Newsweek*, 30 September 1985.

3. "Interview," *San Francisco Examiner*, 27 June 1985.

4. *Ibid.*

5. *Ibid.*

6. Lubenow and Rogers, "Jobs Talks."

7. *Ibid.*

8. B. Uttal, "Behind the Fall of Steve Jobs," *Fortune*, 5 August 1985.

9. Lubenow and Rogers, "Jobs Talks."

10. *Ibid.*

11. B. Uttal, "The Adventures of Steve Jobs," *Fortune*, 14 October 1985.

12. Lubenow and Rogers, "Jobs Talks."

13. *Ibid.*

14. *Ibid.*

15. *Ibid.*

16. *Ibid.*

17. *Ibid.*

18. *Wall Street Journal*, 17 September 1985.

19. Lubenow and Rogers, "Jobs Talks."

20. Apple press release dated 16 September 1985.

21. Lubenow and Rogers, "Jobs Talks."

22. *Ibid.*

23. Danny Goodman, "Playboy Interview: John Sculley," *Playboy*, September 1987, p. 53.

24. Ad in *Wall Street Journal*, 27 May 1986.

Bibliography

Books

Dass, Baba Ram. *Be Here Now*. Lama Foundation, 1971.

Davies, Owen, ed. *The Omni Book of Computers & Robots*. Kensington, 1978.

Ditlea, Steve. *Digital Deli*. Workman Publishing, 1984.

Enrico, Roger. *The Other Guy Blinked*. Bantam, 1986.

Fishman, Katharine. *The Computer Establishment*. Harper & Row, 1981.

Fitzgerald, F. Scott. *The Great Gatsby*. Scribner's, 1925.

Freiberger, Paul, and Michael Swaine, *Fire in the Valley*. Osborne/McGraw Hill, 1984.

Govinda, Lama. *The Way of the White Clouds*. Shambhala Publications, 1966.

Kidder, Tracy. *The Soul of a New Machine*. Atlantic-Little Brown, 1981.

Levy, Steven. *Hackers*. Doubleday, 1984.

Mahon, Thomas. *Charged Bodies*. New American Library, 1985.

McKenna, Regis. *The Regis Touch*. Addison-Wesley, 1985.

Moritz, Michael. *The Little Kingdom*. William Morrow, 1984.

Rogers, Everett, and Judith Larson. *Silicon Valley Fever*. Basic Books, 1984.

Suzuki, Shunryu. *Zen Mind, Beginner's Mind*. Weatherhill, 1970.

Published Interviews

Goodman, Danny. "Playboy Interview: John Sculley." *Playboy*, September 1987.

Levy, Steven. "Interview with Steve Jobs." *Rolling Stone*, 1 March 1984.

Lubenow, G. C., and M. Rogers. "Jobs Talks About His Rise and Fall." *Newsweek*, 30 September 1985.

Sheff, David. "Playboy Interview: Steven Jobs." *Playboy*, February 1985.

Zito. "Interview with Steve Jobs." *Newsweek Access*, Fall 1984.

Unpublished Materials

Harvard Business School. *John Sculley at Apple Computer*. Two-part business case.

Stanford Business School. *Apple Computer Inc.—Macintosh*. Business case.